Spanish

for the
Construction
Trade

For all builders, developers, general contractors,
subcontractors, superintendents, journeymen,
laborers, and trade professionals working in
construction, as well as all manufacturers,
inspectors, and on-site personnel

by
William C. Harvey, M.S.

BARRON'S

Acknowledgment

With thanks to my brother Roger, a contractor,
and everyone else in the construction field who gave me a hand.

All inquiries should be addressed to:
Barron's Educational Series, Inc.
250 Wireless Boulevard
Hauppauge, NY 11788
www.barronseduc.com

Library of Congress Catalog Card Number: 2007006964

ISBN-13: 978-0-7641-3588-0 (book only)
ISBN-10: 0-7641-3588-0 (book only)
ISBN-13: 978-0-7641-7986-0 (book & CD package)
ISBN-10: 0-7641-7986-1 (book & CD package)

Library of Congress Cataloging-in-Publication Data
Harvey, William C.
   Spanish for the construction trade / by William C. Harvey.
      p. cm.
   "For all builders, developers, general contractors, subcontractors,
superintendents, journeymen, laborers, and trade professionals
working in construction, as well as all manufacturers, inspectors,
and on-site personnel."
   ISBN-13: 978-0-7641-3588-0 (alk. paper)
   ISBN-10: 0-7641-3588-0 (alk. paper)
   ISBN-13: 978-0-7641-7986-0
   ISBN-10: 0-7641-7986-1
   1. Spanish language—Conversation and phrase books (for
construction industry employees) I. Title.

PC4120.C64H37 2007
468.3′421′024624—dc22   2007006964

Contents

Before You Begin

A NOTE FROM THE AUTHOR

All across our country, the scene is pretty much the same. Trucks full of workers, equipment, and tools show up on a construction site, and the job-specific chatter begins as everyone springs into action. What is interesting is that not everyone you hear is speaking English.

I found this out personally a few years ago, when my wife and I decided it was time for some remodeling at our home. As the construction project got under way, some of the crew began asking for specific information in their native language—Spanish. All I can say is, I'm sure glad we knew what they were talking about!

Spanish for the Construction Trade is designed for anyone who works in the field of construction and communicates regularly with those who speak only Spanish. Necessary words and phrases are divided into easy-to-follow chapters, which can be accessed on the job simply by finding a particular topic. The first two chapters provide fundamental instruction in Spanish, whereas the remaining chapters focus on specific fields in the world of home building and construction. Pronunciation in English follows every Spanish word, and the most frequently used terminology is strategically placed for quick reference and review. At the end of the book, readers will find a variety of useful support material along with an English-to-Spanish glossary.

Please note that this book focuses on formal ways of communication (the **usted** form). Although the familiar way of addressing anyone with the Spanish **tú** may at times seem friendly and informal, all too often it can be interpreted as overbearing.

TEACHING SEGMENTS

This book provides readers with the following teaching segments, which are scattered throughout the text:

WORKING WORDS
This segment includes construction-site terminology, questions, descriptions, and commands that relate to the chapter's theme.

ONE-LINERS
This segment lists a specialized group of words and phrases, that can communicate complete messages all by themselves.

GRAMMAR TIME

This segment presents shortcuts and tips on how to put several Spanish words together using the appropriate verb forms.

CULTURE ISSUES

This segment offers practical insights into the Latino culture, with details related to traditions, beliefs, and general way of life.

JUST A SUGGESTION

This segment includes additional information, tips, and suggestions about learning Spanish on your own.

TRY SOME

This segment closes each section with various self-grading practice activities and exercises, so that you won't forget what you're trying to learn.

Basic Skills
Las habilidades básicas
(lahs ah-bee-lee-'dah-dehs 'bah-see-kahs)

Pronunciation
La pronunciación *(lah proh-noon-see-ah-see-'ohn)*

Here's the only thing you need to know about Spanish pronunciation: ALMOST ALL SPANISH LETTERS HAVE ONLY <u>ONE</u> SOUND. Start by repeating the five Spanish vowels:

a *(ah)*	(like *yacht*)	**cha-cha-cha**
e *(eh)*	(like *met*)	**excelente**
i *(ee)*	(like *keep*)	**dividir**
o *(oh)*	(like *open*)	**solo**
u *(oo)*	(like *spoon*)	**mula**

These are the consonant sounds you'll need to know. Don't forget—Spanish sounds are pronounced the way they're written:

Grammar Time

Spanish letter	*English sound*
c (after an **e** or **i**)	S as in *Sam* (**cigarro**)
g (after an **e** or **i**)	*h* as in *Harry* (**general**)
h	silent, like the *k* in *knife* (**hola**)
j	*h* as in *hot* (**Juan**)
ll	*y* as in *yes* (**llama**)
qu	*k* as in *kit* (**tequila**)
rr	the rolled *r* sound (**carro**)
z	*s* as in *sun* (**cabeza**)

The rest of the letters in Spanish are very similar to their equivalents in English, so reviewing them isn't really necessary.

— Remember that your poor pronunciation won't really hurt communication. Not only are people generally forgiving, but in reality, the differences between the two sound systems are not that significant.
— Just tell yourself: Spanish is pronounced the way it's spelled, and vice versa. So pronounce each sound the same way every time the corresponding letter appears.
— Spanish sounds are usually made toward the front of the mouth instead of back—with little or no air coming out. And, short, choppy sounds are better than long stretched-out ones.
— Accented (´) parts of words should always be pronounced LOUDER and with more emphasis (**olé**—*oh-'leh*). If there's no accent mark, say the last part of the word LOUDER and with more emphasis (**español**—*ehs-pahn-'yohl*). For words ending in a vowel, or in **n** or **s**, the next to the last part of the word is stressed (**impor-tante**—*eem-pohr-'tahn-teh*). In some cases, the letter **u** doesn't make the *oo* sound (**guitarra**—*hee-'tah-rrah*, **quema**—*'keh-mah*).

The Spanish Alphabet
El abecedario
(ehl ah-beh-seh-'dah-ree-oh)

Take a few moments to review the alphabet. It can be helpful either when you're on the phone or when you haven't a clue what someone is saying. The key question to ask is: How do you spell it? **¿Cómo se deletrea?** *('koh-moh seh deh-leh-'treh-ah)*. To practice, say each letter aloud:

a *(ah)*	**j** *('hoh-tah)*	**r** *('eh-reh)*
b *(beh)*	**k** *(kah)*	**rr** *('eh-rreh)*
c *(seh)*	**l** *('eh-leh)*	**s** *('eh-seh)*
ch *(cheh)**	**ll** *('eh-yeh)**	**t** *(teh)*
d *(deh)*	**m** *('eh-meh)*	**u** *(oo)*
e *(eh)*	**n** *('eh-neh)*	**v** *(veh)*
f *('eh-feh)*	**ñ** *('ehn-yeh)**	**w** *('doh-bleh veh)*
g *(heh)*	**o** *(oh)*	**x** *('eh-kees)*
h *('ah-cheh)*	**p** *(peh)*	**y** *(ee-gree-'eh-gah)*
i *(ee)*	**q** *(koo)*	**z** *('seh-tah)*

* These letters have been removed from the official Spanish alphabet. However, people still refer to them when spelling out a word.

Try Some

Pronounce these common words on your own, and then check their spelling to see how close you were.

amigo *(ah-'mee-goh)*
amor *(ah-'mohr)*
carro *('kah-rroh)*
español *(ehs-pahn-'yohl)*
excelente *(ex-eh-'lehn-teh)*
dinero *(dee-'neh-roh)*
grande *('grahn-deh)*
hombre *('ohm-breh)*

macho *('mah-choh)*
enchilada *(ehn-chee-'lah-dah)*
pollo *('poh-yoh)*
chiquita *(chee-'kee-tah)*
trabajo *(trah-'bah-hoh)*
nada *('nah-dah)*
señor *(sehn-'yohr)*
vino *('vee-noh)*

Greetings and Expressions
Los saludos y las expresiones
(lohs sah-'loo-dohs ee lahs ehks-preh-see-'oh-nehs)

Look over these popular exchanges, and highlight the ones you'll need right away. And check the upside down marks—that's just how they write it in Spanish:

Hi!	**¡Hola!** *('oh-lah)*
How are you?	**¿Cómo está?** *('koh-moh ehs-'tah)*
How's it going?	**¡Qué tal!** *(keh tahl)*
Real well.	**Muy bien.** *('moo-ee bee-'ehn)*
And you?	**¿Y usted?** *(ee oos-'tehd)*
Not bad.	**Más o menos.** *(mahs oh 'meh-nohs)*
What's happening?	**¿Qué pasa?** *(keh 'pah-sah)*
Nothing much!	**¡Sin novedad!** *(seen noh-veh-'dahd)*
Good morning.	**Buenos días.** *('bweh-nohs 'dee-ahs)*
Good afternoon.	**Buenas tardes.** *('bweh-nahs 'tahr-dehs)*
Good evening, good night.	**Buenas noches.** *('bweh-nahs 'noh-chehs)*
Good-bye.	**Adiós.** *(ah-dee-'ohs)*
Take it easy.	**Cúidese bien.** *('koo-ee-deh-seh bee-'ehn)*
See you tomorrow.	**Hasta mañana.** *('ahs-tah mahn-'yah-nah)*

Here are some more.

Ready?	**¿Listo?** *('lees-toh)*
Any trouble?	**¿Algún problema?** *(ahl-'goon proh-'bleh-mah)*
Finished?	**¿Terminó?** *(tehr-mee-'noh)*

Wait a moment.	**Espere un momento.** *(ehs-'peh-reh oon moh-'mehn-toh)*
Pay attention.	**Preste atención.** *('prehs-teh ah-tehn-see-'ohn)*
Be careful.	**Tenga cuidado.** *('tehn-gah kwee-'dah-doh)*
Let's go!	**¡Vamos!** *('vah-mohs)*
Move it!	**¡Muévanlo!** *('mweh-vahn-loh)*
Quickly!	**¡Rápido!** *('rah-pee-doh)*

Try Some

Read these conversations without looking up the translations. Do you understand?

¡Qué tal! *(keh tahl)*
Muy bien, gracias. ¿Y usted? *('moo-ee bee-'ehn 'grah-see-ahs ee oos-'tehd)*
Más o menos. *(mahs oh 'meh-nohs)*

¡Achú! Perdón. *(ah-'choo! Pehr-'dohn)*
¡Salud! *(sah-'lood)*
Muchas gracias. *('moo-chahs 'grah-see-ahs)*

¿Cómo se llama? *('koh-moh seh 'yah-mah)*
Me llamo Felipe. ¿Y usted? *(meh 'yah-moh feh-'lee-peh ee oos-'tehd)*
Me llamo Clayton. *(meh 'yah-moh 'kleh-ee-tohn)*
Mucho gusto. *('moo-choh 'goos-toh)*
Igualmente. *(ee-gwahl-'mehn-teh)*

Grammar Time

The names for people, places, and things are either masculine or feminine, and *the* is either **el** *(ehl)* or **la** *(lah)* when the word is singular. Generally, if the word ends in the letter **o**, there's an **el** in front (**el carro**—*ehl 'kah-rroh*, **el niño**—*(ehl 'neen-yoh*). If the word ends in **a**, there's a **la** in front (**la tortilla**—*(lah tohr-'tee-yah*, **la persona**—*lah pehr-'soh-nah*). There are very few exceptions, for example, **el agua**—*ehl 'ah-gwah*, **la mano**—*lah 'mah-noh*, **el sofá**—*ehl soh-'fah*.

Words not ending in either **o** or **a** need to be memorized, for example, **el amor** *(ehl ah-'mohr*—*love*), **la luz** *(lah loos*—*light*). In the case of single objects, use **el** and **la** exactly as you would use *the* in English: *The house is big:* **La casa es grande** *(lah 'kah-sah ehs 'grahn-deh*).

Since **el** and **la** are used to indicate a person's sex, **el supervisor** *(ehl soo-per-vee-'sohr)* is a male, while **la supervisora** *(lah soo-pehr-vee-'soh-rah)* is a female. Here's how we change words to refer to the female gender:

doctor	**el doctor** *(ehl dohk-'tohr)*
	la doctora *(lah dohk-'toh-rah)*
child	**el niño** *(ehl 'neen-yoh)*
	la niña *(lah 'neen-yah)*
teenager	**el muchacho** *(ehl moo-'chah-choh)*
	la muchacha *(lah moo-'chah-chah)*

To form the plural, words ending in a vowel end in -**s**, whereas words ending in a consonant end in -**es**. Notice how **el** becomes **los** *(lohs)* and **la** becomes **las** *(lahs)*:

man	**el hombre** *(ehl 'ohm-breh)*
woman	**la mujer** *(lah moo-'hehr)*
men	**los hombres** *(lohs 'ohm-brehs)*
women	**las mujeres** *(lahs moo-'heh-rehs)*

Pronouns
Los pronombres
(lohs pro-'nohm-brehs)

This group of words is used to identify everyone:

I	**Yo** *(yoh)*
You (informal)	**Tú** *(too)*
You (formal)	**Usted** *(oos-'tehd)*
He	**Él** *(ehl)*
She	**Ella** *('eh-yah)*
We	**Nosotros** *(noh-'soh-trohs)*
You (plural)	**Ustedes** *(oos-'teh-dehs)*
They	**Ellos/Ellas** *('eh-yohs 'eh-yahs)*

And the following words indicate possession.

my	**mi** *(mee)*
your, his, her, their	**su** *(soo)*
our	**nuestro** *('nwehs-troh)*

Examples: **mi amigo** *(mee ah-'mee-goh)*, **su casa** *(soo 'kah-sah)*, **nuestro carro** *('nwehs-troh 'kah-rroh)*.

Try Some

Practice by inserting your name and the name of a friend, and reading aloud:

¿Yo? Mi nombre es <u>Roberto</u>. *(yoh? mee 'nohm-breh ehs ...)*
¿Él? Su nombre es <u>Francisco</u>. *(ehl? soo 'nohm-breh ehs ...)*
¿Nosotros? Nuestros nombres son <u>Roberto</u> y <u>Francisco.</u>
(noh-'soh-trohs? 'nwehs-trohs 'nohm-brehs sohn ... ee ...)

Everyday Questions
Preguntas diarias
(preh-'goon-tahs dee-'ah-ree-ahs)

Look at the ten most common question words in Spanish:

What?	**¿Qué?** *(keh)*
How?	**¿Cómo?** *('koh-moh)*
Where?	**¿Dónde?** *('dohn-deh)*
When?	**¿Cuándo?** *('kwahn-doh)*
Which?	**¿Cuál?** *(kwahl)*
Who?	**¿Quién?** *(kee-'ehn)*
Whose?	**¿De quién?** *(deh kee-'ehn)*
How much?	**¿Cuánto?** *('kwahn-toh)*
How many?	**¿Cuántos?** *('kwahn-tohs)*
Why?	**¿Por qué?** *(pohr keh)*

Here's how they work in everyday conversations:

What?	**¿Qué?** *(keh)*
What's happening?	**¿Qué pasa?** *(keh 'pah-sah)*
How?	**¿Cómo?** *('koh-moh)*
How are you?	**¿Cómo está?** *('koh-moh ehs-'tah)*
Where?	**¿Dónde?** *('dohn-deh)*
Where is it?	**¿Dónde está?** *('dohn-deh ehs-'tah)*
When?	**¿Cuándo?** *('kwahn-doh)*
When is it?	**¿Cuándo es?** *('kwahn-doh ehs)*
Which?	**¿Cuál?** *(kwahl)*
Which is it?	**¿Cuál es?** *(kwahl ehs)*
Who?	**¿Quién?** *(kee-'ehn)*
Who is it?	**¿Quién es?** *(kee-'ehn ehs)*

Whose?	**¿De quién?** *(deh kee-'ehn)*
Whose is it?	**¿De quién es?** *(deh kee-'ehn ehs)*

How much?	**¿Cuánto?** *('kwahn-toh)*
How much does it cost?	**¿Cuánto cuesta?** *('kwahn-toh 'kwehs-tah)*

How many?	**¿Cuántos?** *('kwahn-tohs)*
How old are you?	**¿Cuántos años tiene?** *('kwahn-tohs 'ahn-yohs tee-'eh-neh)*

Why?	**¿Por qué?** *(pohr keh)*
Why not?	**¿Por qué no?** *(pohr keh noh)*

By the way, the word **porque** *('pohr-keh)* means *because*, and it sounds a lot like **¿Por qué?** *(pohr-'keh)(Why?)* except that the stress is on the last syllable.

Why doesn't he have a car?	**¿Por qué no tiene carro?** *(pohr-'keh noh tee-'eh-neh 'kah-rroh)*
Because he doesn't have a license.	**Porque no tiene licencia.** *('pohr-keh noh tee-'eh-neh lee-'sehn-see-ah)*

Obviously, not all questions can be translated literally, so use them as one-liners whenever you can. For example, notice how *you* and *your* are implied, but not included:

What's your name?	**¿Cómo se llama?** *('koh-moh seh 'yah-mah)*
How old are you?	**¿Cuántos años tiene?** *('kwahn-tohs 'ahn-yohs tee-'eh-neh)*
What's your address?	**¿Cuál es su dirección?** *(kwahl ehs soo dee-rehk-see-'ohn)*

Here are some of the most common phrases that include question words:

How can I help you?	**¿Cómo puedo ayudarle?** *('koh-moh 'pweh-doh ah-yoo-'dahr-leh)*
What's the matter?	**¿Qué pasa?** *(keh 'pah-sah)*
Who's calling?	**¿Quién llama?** *(kee-'ehn 'yah-mah)*

This popular series of questions can be used with the phrase **¿Cuál es su...?** *(kwahl ehs soo...)*

What's your...?	**¿Cuál es su...?** *(kwahl ehs soo)*
full name	**nombre completo** *('nohm-breh kohm-'pleh-toh)*
address	**dirección** *(dee-rehk-see-'ohn)*
phone number	**número de teléfono** *('noo-meh-roh deh teh-'leh-foh-noh)*
age	**edad** *(eh-'dahd)*
social security number	**número de seguro social** *('noo-meh-roh deh seh-'goo-roh soh-see-'ahl)*
driver's license number	**número de licencia de manejar** *('noo-meh-roh del lee-'sehn-see-ah deh mah-neh-'hahr)*
date of birth	**fecha de nacimiento** *('feh-chah deh nah-see-mee-'ehn-toh)*
place of birth	**lugar de nacimiento** *(loo-'gahr deh nah-see-mee-'ehn-toh)*

Culture Issues

When referring to others by name, it really helps if you're able to pronounce the names correctly, as it makes people feel much more at ease. Also remember that it's not uncommon for someone in Latin America to have no middle name and two last names. Don't get confused. Here's the order for males:

José Antonio García Sánchez

First name
primer nombre *(pree-'mehr 'nohm-breh)*
JOSÉ ANTONIO *(hoh-'seh ahn-'toh-nee-oh)*

Father's last name
apellido paterno *(ah-peh-'yee-doh pah-'tehr-noh)*
GARCÍA *(gahr-'see-ah)*

Mother's last name
apellido materno *(ah-peh-'yee-doh mah-'tehr-noh)*
SÁNCHEZ *('sahn-chehs)*

Try Some

When referring to others, utilize these new words:

Mr. or a man	**Señor** *(sehn-'yohr)* **(Sr.)**
Mrs. or a lady	**Señora** *(sehn-'yoh-rah)* **(Sra.)**
Miss or a young lady	**Señorita** *(sehn-yoh-'ree-tah)* **(Srta.)**

Now try naming these common objects if they're somewhere within view:

It's the...	**Es...** *(ehs)*
armchair	**el sillón** *(ehl see-'yohn)*
book	**el libro** *(ehl 'lee-broh)*
car	**el carro** *(ehl 'kah-rroh)*
chair	**la silla** *(lah 'see-yah)*
clothing	**la ropa** *(lah 'roh-pah)*
couch	**el sofá** *(ehl soh-'fah)*
desk	**el escritorio** *(ehl ehs-kree-'toh-ree-oh)*
door	**la puerta** *(lah 'pwehr-tah)*
equipment	**el equipo** *(ehl eh-'kee-poh)*
floor	**el piso** *(ehl 'pee-soh)*
food	**la comida** *(lah koh-'mee-dah)*
furniture	**el mueble** *(ehl 'mweh-bleh)*
house	**la casa** *(lah 'kah-sah)*
job	**el trabajo** *(ehl trah-'bah-hoh)*
lamp	**la lámpara** *(lah 'lahm-pah-rah)*
light	**la luz** *(lah loos)*
machine	**la máquina** *(lah 'mah-kee-nah)*
money	**el dinero** *(ehl dee-'neh-roh)*
paper	**el papel** *(ehl pah-'pehl)*

pen	**el lapicero** *(ehl lah-pee-'seh-roh)*
pencil	**el lápiz** *(ehl 'lah-pees)*
room	**el cuarto** *(ehl 'kwahr-toh)*
table	**la mesa** *(lah 'meh-sah)*
telephone	**el teléfono** *(ehl teh-'leh-foh-noh)*
tool	**la herramienta** *(lah eh-rrah-mee-'ehn-tah)*
truck	**el camión** *(ehl kah-mee-'ohn)*
water	**el agua** *(ehl 'ah-gwah)*
window	**la ventana** *(lah vehn-'tah-nah)*

Key Commands
Los mandatos principales
(lohs mahn-'dah-tohs preen-see-'pah-lehs)

Another powerful way to plant Spanish into the memory is through the use of commands. The imperative form of verbs can be practiced all day, since all you're doing is telling others what to do. Be sure to add the word *please:*

Por favor... *(pohr fah-'vohr)*

Call!	**¡Llame!** *('yah-meh)*
Check!	**¡Revise!** *(reh-'vee-seh)*
Come!	**¡Venga!** *('vehn-gah)*
Continue!	**¡Siga!** *('see-gah)*
Drive!	**¡Maneje!** *(mah-'neh-heh)*
Finish!	**¡Termine!** *(tehr-'mee-neh)*
Go up!	**¡Suba!** *('soo-bah)*
Go!	**¡Vaya!** *('vah-yah)*
Help!	**¡Ayude!** *(ah-'yoo-deh)*
Listen!	**¡Escuche!** *(ehs-'koo-cheh)*
Look!	**¡Mire!** *('mee-reh)*
Read!	**¡Lea!** *('leh-ah)*
Rest!	**¡Descanse!** *(dehs-'kahn-seh)*
Run!	**¡Corra!** *('koh-rrah)*
Sign!	**¡Firme!** *('feer-meh)*
Speak!	**¡Hable!** *('ah-bleh)*
Start!	**¡Comience!** *(koh-mee-'ehn-seh)*
Walk!	**¡Camine!** *(kah-'mee-neh)*
Work!	**¡Trabaje!** *(trah-'bah-heh)*

These commands are expressions and a little harder to pronounce:

Hurry up!	**¡Apúrese!** *(ah-'poo-reh-seh)*
Sit down!	**¡Siéntese!** *(see-'ehn-teh-seh)*
Stand up!	**¡Levántese!** *(leh-'vahn-teh-seh)*
Stay!	**¡Quédese!** *('keh-deh-seh)*
Wait!	**¡Espere!** *(ehs-'peh-reh)*

Most commands can be used with an object. For example, *Bring the wood* is **Traiga la madera** *('trah-ee-gah lah mah-'deh-rah)*.

Bring...	**Traiga...** *('trah-ee-gah)*
Buy...	**Compre...** *('kohm-preh)*
Carry...	**Lleve...** *('yeh-veh)*
Change...	**Cambie...** *('kahm-bee-eh)*
Clean...	**Limpie...** *('leem-pee-eh)*
Close...	**Cierre...** *(see-'eh-rreh)*
Connect...	**Conecte...** *(koh-'nehk-teh)*
Empty...	**Vacíe...** *(vah-'see-eh)*
Fill...	**Llene...** *('yeh-neh)*
Fix...	**Arregle...** *(ah-'rreh-gleh)*
Give...	**Dé...** *(deh)*
Load...	**Cargue...** *('kahr-geh)*
Look for...	**Busque...** *('boos-keh)*
Lower...	**Baje...** *('bah-heh)*
Move...	**Mueva...** *('mweh-vah)*
Open...	**Abra...** *('ah-brah)*
Park...	**Estacione...** *(ehs-tah-see-'oh-neh)*
Pick up...	**Recoja...** *(reh-'koh-hah)*
Put inside...	**Meta...** *('meh-tah)*
Put...	**Ponga...** *('pohn-gah)*
Raise...	**Levante...** *(leh-'vahn-teh)*
Remove...	**Saque...** *('sah-keh)*
Set up...	**Prepare...** *(preh-'pah-reh)*
Take...	**Tome...** *('toh-meh)*
Throw out...	**Tire...** *('tee-reh)*
Unload...	**Descargue...** *(dehs-'kahr-geh)*
Use...	**Use...** *('oo-seh)*

Colors
Los colores
(lohs koh-'loh-rehs)

The best way to practice these words is to call out the colors of things around you when you're out on the job:

It's...   **Es...** *(ehs)*

black	**negro** *('neh-groh)*
blue	**azul** *(ah-'sool)*
brown	**café** *(kah-'feh)*
gray	**gris** *(grees)*
green	**verde** *('vehr-deh)*
orange	**anaranjado** *(ah-nah-rahn-'hah-doh)*
purple	**morado** *(moh-'rah-doh)*
red	**rojo** *('roh-hoh)*
white	**blanco** *('blahn-koh)*
yellow	**amarillo** *(ah-mah-'ree-yoh)*
pink	**rosado** *(roh-'sah-doh)*

Just a Suggestion

Two words that simplify things are *light* (**claro**—*'klah-roh*) and *dark* (**oscuro**—*ohs-'koo-roh*).

Notice how the word order is reversed in Spanish:

<u>light</u> brown	**café <u>claro</u>** *(kah-'feh 'klah-roh)*
<u>dark</u> brown	**café <u>oscuro</u>** *(kah-'feh ohs-'koo-roh)*
<u>light</u> blue	**azul <u>claro</u>** *(ah-'sool 'klah-roh)*
<u>dark</u> blue	**azul <u>oscuro</u>** *(ah-'sool ohs-'koo-roh)*
<u>light</u> green	**verde <u>claro</u>** *('vehr-deh 'klah-roh)*
<u>dark</u> green	**verde <u>oscuro</u>** *('vehr-deh ohs-'koo-roh)*

Grammar Time

A reversal rule is applied when you give a description in Spanish. The descriptive word generally goes <u>after</u> the word being described. Study these examples:

The big house	**La casa grande** *(lah 'kah-sah 'grahn-deh)*
The green car	**El carro verde** *(ehl 'kah-rroh 'vehr-deh)*
The important man	**El hombre importante** *(ehl 'ohm-breh eem-pohr-'tahn-teh)*

To make a description plural, not only do all the nouns and adjectives need to end in -**s** or -**es**, but when they are used together, the genders (the **os** and **as**) must match as well:

Two white doors	**Dos puertas blancas** *(dohs 'pwehr-tahs 'blahn-kahs)*
Many red trucks	**Muchos camiones rojos** *('moo-chohs kah-mee-'oh-nehs 'roh-hohs)*
Three big jobs	**Tres trabajos grandes** *(trehs trah-'bah-hohs 'grahn-dehs)*

Try Some

Change these sentences to plural:

el carro rojo   los _____

la casa grande   las _____

la mesa negra   las _____

Numbers
Los números
(lohs 'noo-meh-rohs)

You can't say much in Spanish without knowing your numbers:

0 **cero** *('seh-roh)*	14 **catorce** *(kah-'tohr-seh)*
1 **uno** *('oo-noh)*	15 **quince** *('keen-seh)*
2 **dos** *(dohs)*	16 **dieciséis** *(dee-eh-see-'seh-ees)*
3 **tres** *(trehs)*	17 **diecisiete** *(dee-eh-see-see-'eh-teh)*
4 **cuatro** *('kwah-troh)*	18 **dieciocho** *(dee-eh-see-'oh-choh)*
5 **cinco** *('seen-koh)*	19 **diecinueve** *(dee-eh-see-'nweh-veh)*
6 **seis** *('seh-ees)*	20 **veinte** *('veh-een-teh)*
7 **siete** *(see-'eh-teh)*	30 **treinta** *('treh-een-tah)*
8 **ocho** *('oh-choh)*	40 **cuarenta** *(kwah-'rehn-tah)*
9 **nueve** *('nweh-veh)*	50 **cincuenta** *(seen-'kwehn-tah)*
10 **diez** *(dee-'ehs)*	60 **sesenta** *(seh-'sehn-tah)*
11 **once** *('ohn-seh)*	70 **setenta** *(seh-'tehn-tah)*
12 **doce** *('doh-seh)*	80 **ochenta** *(oh-'chehn-tah)*
13 **trece** *('treh-seh)*	90 **noventa** *(noh-'vehn-tah)*

For all the numbers in-between, just add **y** *(ee)*, which means *and*:

21 **veinte y uno**	34	_____
22 **veinte y dos**	55	_____
23 **veinte** _____	87	_____

Sooner or later, you'll need to know how to say the larger numbers. It is best if you practice aloud:

100	**cien** *(see-'ehn)*
200	**doscientos** *(doh-see-'ehn-tohs)*
300	**trescientos** *(treh-see-'ehn-tohs)*
400	**cuatrocientos** *(kwah-troh-see-'ehn-tohs)*
500	**quinientos** *(kee-nee-'ehn-tohs)*
600	**seiscientos** *(seh-ee-see-'ehn-tohs)*
700	**setecientos** *(seh-teh-see-'ehn-tohs)*
800	**ochocientos** *(oh-choh-see-'ehn-tohs)*
900	**novecientos** *(noh-veh-see-'ehn-tohs)*
1000	**mil** *(meel)*
million	**millón** *(mee-'yohn)*

Everyone on the job needs the ordinal numbers as well:

first	**primero** *(pree-'meh-roh)*
second	**segundo** *(seh-'goon-doh)*
third	**tercero** *(tehr-'seh-roh)*
fourth	**cuarto** *('kwahr-toh)*
fifth	**quinto** *('keen-toh)*
sixth	**sexto** *('sehks-toh)*
seventh	**séptimo** *('sehp-tee-moh)*
eighth	**octavo** *(ohk-'tah-voh)*
ninth	**noveno** *(noh-'veh-noh)*
tenth	**décimo** *('deh-see-moh)*
eleventh	**undécimo** *(oon-'deh-see-moh)*
twelfth	**duodécimo** *(doo-oh-'deh-see-moh)*

Try Some

Change these ordinal numbers to cardinals:

quinto _____

octavo _____

primero _____

Say these numbers aloud in Spanish:

5,000   **300**   **67**

Time and Place
El tiempo y el lugar
(ehl tee-'ehm-poh ee ehl loo-'gahr)

You'll eventually need to include some time-referenced and place-referenced vocabulary. These will do for now:

after	**después** *(dehs-'pwehs)*
already	**ya** *(yah)*
always	**siempre** *(see-'ehm-preh)*
before	**antes** *('ahn-tehs)*
during	**durante** *(doo-'rahn-teh)*
early	**temprano** *(tehm-'prah-noh)*
late	**tarde** *('tahr-deh)*
later	**luego** *(loo-'eh-goh)*
never	**nunca** *('noon-kah)*
now	**ahora** *(ah-'oh-rah)*
since	**desde** *('dehs-deh)*
sometimes	**a veces** *(ah 'veh-sehs)*
soon	**pronto** *('prohn-toh)*
then	**entonces** *(ehn-'tohn-sehs)*
today	**hoy** *('oh-ee)*
tomorrow	**mañana** *(mah-'nyah-nah)*
until	**hasta** *('ahs-tah)*
while	**mientras** *(mee-'ehn-trahs)*
yesterday	**ayer** *(ah-'yehr)*

When it comes to locating people or things, always respond as briefly as possible, and don't be afraid to point:

Where is it?	**¿Dónde está?** *('dohn-deh ehs-'tah)*
above	**encima** *(ehn-'see-mah)*
along	**a lo largo** *(ah loh 'lahr-goh)*
around	**alrededor** *(ahl-reh-deh-'dohr)*
at the bottom	**en el fondo** *(ehn ehl 'fohn-doh)*
back	**atrás** *(ah-'trahs)*
behind	**detrás** *(deh-'trahs)*

between	**entre** *('ehn-treh)*
down	**abajo** *(ah-'bah-hoh)*
far	**lejos** *('leh-hohs)*
forward	**adelante** *(ah-deh-'lahn-teh)*
here	**aquí** *(ah-'kee)*
in front	**enfrente** *(ehn-'frehn-teh)*
in the middle	**en medio** *(ehn 'meh-dee-oh)*
inside	**adentro** *(ah-'dehn-troh)*
near	**cerca** *('sehr-kah)*
next to	**al lado** *(ahl 'lah-doh)*
outside	**afuera** *(ah-'fweh-rah)*
over	**sobre** *('soh-breh)*
straight ahead	**adelante** *(ah-deh-'lahn-teh)*
there	**allí** *(ah-'yee)*
to the left	**a la izquierda** *(ah lah ees-kee-'ehr-dah)*
to the right	**a la derecha** *(ah lah deh-'reh-chah)*
toward	**hacia** *('ah-see-ah)*
under	**debajo** *(deh-'bah-hoh)*
up	**arriba** *(ah-'rree-bah)*
way over there	**allá** *(ah-'yah)*

To Tell Time
Decir la hora
(deh-seer lah 'oh-rah)

In Spanish, *time* in general is **el tiempo** *(ehl tee-'ehm-poh)*. The specific time is **la hora** *(lah 'oh-rah)*. Time in reference to an occurrence is **la vez** *(lah vehs)*.

Here's a common question in any language:

What time is it?   **¿Qué hora es?** *(keh 'oh-rah ehs)*

To answer in Spanish, simply give the hour, followed by the word **y** *(and)*, and the minutes. For example, 6:15 is **seis y quince** *('seh-ees ee 'keen-seh)*. To give a specific hour, there is no need for *o'clock*:

It's...	**Son las...** *(sohn lahs)*
8:00	**ocho** *('oh-choh)*
3:40	**tres y cuarenta** *(trehs ee kwah-'rehn-tah)*
10:30	**diez y treinta** *(dee-'ehs ee 'treh-een-tah)*
5:00	**cinco** *('seen-koh)*
12:05	**doce y cinco** *('doh-seh ee 'seen-koh)*

To express *at* a certain time, use this phrase:

At...	**A las...** *(ah lahs)*
2:35	**dos y treinta y cinco** *(dohs ee 'treh-een-tah ee 'seen-koh)*
11:00	**once** *('ohn-seh)*
7:10	**siete y diez** *(see-'eh-teh ee dee-'ehs)*

A.M. is **de la mañana** *(deh lah mah-'nyah-nah)* and P.M. is **de la tarde** *(deh lah 'tahr-deh)* or **de la noche** *(deh lah 'noh-cheh)*:

It's 6:20 A.M.	**Son las seis de la mañana.** *(sohn lahs 'seh-ees deh lah mah-'nyah-nah)*
At 9:00 P.M.	**A las nueve de la tarde.** *(ah lahs 'nweh-veh deh lah 'tahr-deh)*

For 1:00–1:59, use **Es la ...** *(ehs lah)* instead of **Son las...** *(sohn lahs)*.

It's one o'clock.	**Es la una.** *(ehs lah 'oo-nah)*
It's one-thirty.	**Es la una y treinta.** *(ehs lah 'oo-nah ee 'treh-een-tah)*

Try Some

Translate into Spanish:	
What time is it?	_____
At 8:45 A.M.	_____
It's five o'clock.	_____

Days and Months
Los días y los meses
(lohs 'dee-ahs ee lohs 'meh-sehs)

Check out the basic questions and answers related to the date (**la fecha**—*lah 'feh-chah*):

What's the date?	**¿Cuál es la fecha?** *(kwahl ehs lah 'feh-chah)*
On what date?	**¿En qué fecha?** *(ehn keh 'feh-chah)*

Days of the Week
Los días de la semana *(lohs 'dee-ahs deh lah seh-'mah-nah)*

Monday	**lunes** *('loo-nehs)*
Tuesday	**martes** *('mahr-tehs)*
Wednesday	**miércoles** *(mee-'ehr-koh-lehs)*
Thursday	**jueves** *(hoo-'eh-vehs)*
Friday	**viernes** *(vee-'ehr-nehs)*
Saturday	**sábado** *('sah-bah-doh)*
Sunday	**domingo** *(doh-'meen-goh)*

Months of the Year
Los meses del año *(lohs 'meh-sehs dehl 'ahn-yoh)*

January	**enero** *(eh-'neh-roh)*
February	**febrero** *(feh-'breh-roh)*
March	**marzo** *('mahr-soh)*
April	**abril** *(ah-'breel)*
May	**mayo** *('mah-yoh)*
June	**junio** *('hoo-nee-oh)*
July	**julio** *('hoo-lee-oh)*
August	**agosto** *(ah-'gohs-toh)*
September	**septiembre** *(seh-tee-'ehm-breh)*
October	**octubre** *(ohk-'too-breh)*
November	**noviembre** *(noh-vee-'ehm-breh)*
December	**diciembre** *(dee-see-'ehm-breh)*

To give the date in Spanish, just reverse the word order:

May 5th	**el cinco de mayo** *(ehl 'seen-koh deh 'mah-yoh)*
June 3rd	**el tres de junio** *(ehl trehs deh 'hoo-nee-oh)*
February 15th	**el quince de febrero** *(ehl 'keen-seh deh feh-'breh-roh)*

The word *year* is **el año** *(ehl 'ahn-yoh)*. Just read it as one large number:

2009	**dos mil nueve** *(dohs meel 'nweh-veh)*

One-Liners

Memorize these other timely one-liners:

last night	**anoche** *(ah-'noh-cheh)*
the next day	**el día siguiente** *(ehl 'dee-ah see-gee-'ehn-teh)*
next month	**el próximo mes** *(ehl 'prohk-see-moh mehs)*
last week	**la semana pasada** *(lah seh-'mah-nah pah-'sah-dah)*
the weekend	**el fin de semana** *(ehl feen deh seh-'mah-nah)*
the day after tomorrow	**pasado mañana** *(pah-'sah-doh mah-'nyah-nah)*
the day before yesterday	**anteayer** *(ahn-teh-ah-'yehr)*

Try Some

Fill in the blanks with the missing words:

lunes, _____, miércoles, jueves, _____, sábado, _____

_____, febrero, marzo, _____, mayo, _____,

julio, agosto, septiembre, _____, _____, diciembre

The Weather
El tiempo
(ehl tee-'ehm-poh)

Did you notice? *Weather* in Spanish is the same as *time*. In the world of construction, business is often controlled by weather conditions. Here's the simple question and answer:

How's the weather?	**¿Qué tiempo hace?** *(keh tee-'ehm-poh 'ah-seh)*
It's going to...	**Va a...** *(vah ah)*
rain	**llover** *(yoh-'vehr)*
snow	**nevar** *(neh-'vahr)*
It's...	**Hace...** *('ah-seh)*

cold	**frío** *('free-oh)*
hot	**calor** *(kah-'lohr)*
nice weather	**buen tiempo** *('bwehn tee-'ehm-poh)*
sunny	**sol** *(sohl)*
windy	**viento** *(vee-'ehn-toh)*

It's...	**Está...** *(ehs-'tah)*

clear	**despejado** *(dehs-peh-'hah-doh)*
cloudy	**nublado** *(noo-'blah-doh)*
drizzling	**lloviznando** *(yoh-vees-'nahn-doh)*
raining	**lloviendo** *(yoh-vee-'ehn-doh)*
snowing	**nevando** *(neh-'vahn-doh)*

There's...	**Hay...** *('ah-ee)*

ice	**hielo** *(ee-'eh-loh)*
frost	**escarcha** *(ehs-'kahr-chah)*
fog	**neblina** *(neh-'blee-nah)*
a storm	**una tormenta** *('oo-nah tohr-'mehn-tah)*
a tornado	**un tornado** *(oon tohr-'nah-doh)*
a hurricane	**un huracán** *(oon oo-rah-'kahn)*

Working Words: DESCRIBING THE JOB

Construction is seasonal, isn't it?

It's...   **Es...** *(ehs)*

spring   **la primavera** *(lah pree-mah-'veh-rah)*
summer   **el verano** *(ehl veh-'rah-noh)*
fall   **el otoño** *(ehl oh-'tohn-yoh)*
winter   **el invierno** *(ehl een-vee-'ehr-noh)*

Try Some

Translate these phrases about the weather:

It's cold.   _____

It's summer.   _____

There's a storm.   _____

How's the weather?   _____

It's hot and windy.   _____

Descriptions
Las descripciones
(lahs dehs-kreep-see-'oh-nehs)

Descriptive words for construction will fill each of the following chapters, but for now, use these words to describe people and things:

bad   **malo** *('mah-loh)*
big   **grande** *('grahn-deh)*
good   **bueno** *('bweh-noh)*
handsome   **guapo** *('gwah-poh)*
long   **largo** *('lahr-goh)*
new   **nuevo** *(noo-'eh-voh)*
old   **viejo** *(vee-'eh-hoh)*

pretty	**bonito** *(boh-'nee-toh)*
short (in height)	**bajo** *('bah-hoh)*
short (in length)	**corto** *('kohr-toh)*
small	**chico** *('chee-koh)*
tall	**alto** *('ahl-toh)*
ugly	**feo** *('feh-oh)*
young	**joven** *('hoh-vehn)*

Here are more descriptions everyone should know. Let's break them into pairs of opposites:

fat	**gordo** *('gohr-doh)*
thin	**delgado** *(dehl-'gah-doh)*
strong	**fuerte** *('fwehr-teh)*
weak	**débil** *('deh-beel)*
dirty	**sucio** *('soo-see-oh)*
clean	**limpio** *('leem-pee-oh)*
slow	**lento** *('lehn-toh)*
fast	**rápido** *('rah-pee-doh)*
easy	**fácil** *('fah-seel)*
difficult	**difícil** *(dee-'fee-seel)*
cold	**frío** *('free-oh)*
hot	**caliente** *(kah-lee-'ehn-teh)*
rich	**rico** *('ree-koh)*
poor	**pobre** *('poh-breh)*
inexpensive	**barato** *(bah-'rah-toh)*
expensive	**caro** *('kah-roh)*

Just a Suggestion

Add these words to elaborate:

más grande *(mahs 'grahn-deh)*	bigger
lo más grande *(loh mahs 'grahn-deh)*	biggest
tan grande como *(tahn 'grahn-deh 'koh-moh)*	as big as
un poco grande *(oon 'poh-koh 'grahn-deh)*	rather big
muy grande *(mwee 'grahn-deh)*	very big
demasiado grande *(deh-mah-see-'ah-doh 'grahn-deh)*	too big
tan grande *(tahn 'grahn-deh)*	so big

Grammar Time

To say *a* or *an* in Spanish, use **un** *(oon)* for masculine words or **una** *('oo-nah)* for feminine words:

A truck	**Un camión** *(oon kah-mee-'ohn)*
A big truck	**Un camión grande** *(oon kah-mee-'ohn 'grahn-deh)*
A machine	**Una máquina** *('oo-nah 'mah-kee-nah)*
A red machine	**Una máquina roja** *('oo-nah 'mah-kee-nah 'roh-hah)*

And to say *some*, use **unos** *('oo-nohs)* or **unas** *('oo-nahs)*, and don't forget the rule about plurals:

Some floors	**Unos pisos** *('oo-nohs 'pee-sohs)*
Some dirty floors	**Unos pisos sucios** *('oo-nohs 'pee-sohs 'soo-see-ohs)*
Some tables	**Unas mesas** *('oo-nahs 'meh-sahs)*
Some new tables	**Unas mesas nuevas** *('oo-nahs 'meh-sahs 'nweh-vahs)*

Try Some

Match these opposites:

viejo	fácil
limpio	chico
malo	sucio
gordo	joven
difícil	pobre
rico	delgado
grande	bueno

To Be
Ser *(sehr)* or Estar *(ehs-'tahr)*

There are two ways to say *to be* in Spanish: **Estar** *(ehs-'tahr)* and **Ser** *(sehr)*.

To Be	Estar *(ehs-'tahr)*	Ser *(sehr)*
I'm	estoy *(ehs-'toh-ee)*	soy *('soh-ee)*
You're (sing.), he's, she's, it's	está *(ehs-'tah)*	es *(ehs)*
We're	estamos *(ehs-'tah-mohs)*	somos *('soh-mohs)*
You're (pl.), they're	están *(ehs-'tahn)*	son *(sohn)*

Both **estar** and **ser** mean *to be* in Spanish, but are used differently. For example, the word **está** *(ehs-'tah)* expresses a temporary state, condition, or location, while **es** *(ehs)* expresses an inherent characteristic or quality, including origin and ownership:

The man is fine.	**El hombre está bien.** *(ehl 'ohm-breh ehs-'tah bee-'ehn)*
The man is in the room.	**El hombre está en el cuarto.** *(ehl 'ohm-breh ehs-'tah ehn ehl 'kwahr-toh)*
The man is big.	**El hombre es grande.** *(ehl 'ohm-breh ehs 'grahn-deh)*
The man is American.	**El hombre es americano.** *(ehl 'ohm-breh ehs ah-meh-ree-'kah-noh)*

Now, to talk about more than one person, place, or thing, replace **está** *(ehs-'tah)* with **están** *(ehs-'tahn)*, and **es** *(ehs)* with **son** *(sohn)*. Don't forget that all words must *agree* when you change to plurals:

The paper is on the table.	**El papel está en la mesa.** *(ehl pah-'pehl ehs-'tah ehn lah 'meh-sah)*
The papers are on the table.	**Los papeles están en la mesa.** *(lohs pah-'peh-lehs ehs-'tahn ehn lah 'meh-sah)*
It's a neighbor.	**Es un vecino.** *(ehs oon veh-'see-noh)*
They are neighbors.	**Son vecinos.** *(sohn veh-'see-nohs)*

Check out these other examples and read them aloud as you focus on their structure and meaning:

Are the doors black?	**¿Son negras las puertas?** *(sohn 'neh-grahs lahs 'pwehr-tahs)*
The tools are in the house.	**Las herramientas están en la casa.** *(lahs eh-rrah-mee-'ehn-tahs ehs-'tahn ehn lah 'kah-sah)*
They are not important.	**No son importantes.** *(noh sohn eem-pohr-'tahn-tehs)*
Are they clean?	**¿Están limpios?** *(ehs-'tahn 'leem-pee-ohs)*

To say *I am* and *we are* in Spanish, you must also learn the different forms. As with **está** *(ehs-'tah)* and **están** *(ehs-'tahn)*, the words **estoy** *(ehs-'toh-ee)* and **estamos** *(ehs-'tah-mohs)* refer to the location or condition of a person, place, or thing. And, just like **es** *(ehs)* and **son** *(sohn)*, the words **soy** *('soh-ee)* and **somos** *('soh-mohs)* are used with everything else:

I am fine.	**Estoy bien.** *(ehs-'toh-ee bee-'ehn)*
We are in the truck.	**Estamos en el camión.** *(ehs-'tah-mohs ehn ehl kah-mee-'ohn)*
I am Lupe.	**Soy Lupe.** *('soh-ee 'loo-peh)*
We are Cuban.	**Somos cubanos.** *('soh-mohs koo-'bah-nohs)*

Two other words, **estás** *(ehs-'tahs)* and **eres** *('eh-rehs)* (from the informal **tú** *(too)* form), may also be used to mean *you are* among friends, family, and small children:

How are you, Mary? You are very pretty.
¿Cómo estás, María? Tú eres muy bonita.
('koh-moh ehs-'tahs mah-'ree-ah? too 'eh-rehs 'moo-ee boh-'nee-tah)

Try Some

Fill in the blanks with correct form of **estar**:

Yo _____ bien.

Ella no _____ en su casa.

Ellas _____ en la mesa.

Fill in the blanks with correct form of **ser**:

Nosotros _____ americanos.

Yo _____ hombre.

Juan _____ doctor.

Grammar Time

You may have noticed that sometimes it's OK to drop the subject pronoun since it's usually understood who is involved:

I am fine.   **Estoy bien. (Yo)**
                               (ehs-'toh-ee bee-'ehn. yoh)
They are not at home.   **No están en casa. (Ellos)**
                               (noh ehs-'tahn ehn 'kah-sah. 'eh-yohs)

To Have
Tener
(teh-'nehr)

Tener—*teh-nehr* (*to have*) is another very basic verb. Practice:

To Have	Tener *(teh-'nehr)*
I have	**tengo** *('tehn-goh)*
You have (sing.), he has, she has, it has	**tiene** *(tee-'eh-neh)*
We have	**tenemos** *(teh-'neh-mohs)*
You (pl.), they have	**tienen** *(tee-'eh-nen)*

Read these sample sentences aloud:

I have a problem.	**Tengo un problema.** *('tehn-goh oon proh-'bleh- mah)*
He has a white car.	**Tiene un carro blanco.** *(tee-'eh-neh oon 'kah-rroh 'blahn-koh)*
They have four children.	**Tienen cuatro niños.** *(tee-'eh-nehn 'kwah-troh 'neen-yohs)*
We have a big house.	**Tenemos una casa grande.** *(teh-'neh-mohs 'oo-nah 'kah-sah 'grahn-deh)*

Even though **tener** *(teh-'nehr)* literally means *to have*, sometimes it's used instead to mean *to be* in order to express the following:

(I am) afraid.	**(Tengo) miedo.** *('tehn-goh mee-'eh-doh)*
(We are) at fault.	**(Tenemos) la culpa.** *(teh-'neh-mohs lah 'kool-pah)*
(They are) cold.	**(Tienen) frío.** *(tee-'eh-nehn 'free-oh)*
(She is) 15 years old.	**(Tiene) quince años.** *(tee-'eh-neh 'keen-seh 'ahn-yohs)*
(I am) hot.	**(Tengo) calor.** *('tehn-goh kah-'lohr)*
(They are) hungry.	**(Tienen) hambre.** *(tee-'eh-nehn 'ahm-breh)*
(He is) sleepy.	**(Tiene) sueño.** *(tee-'eh-neh 'swehn-yoh)*
(We are) thirsty.	**(Tenemos) sed.** *(teh-'neh-mohs sehd)*
(You are) right.	**(Tiene) razón.** *(tee-'eh-neh rah-'sohn)*
(I am) lucky.	**(Tengo) suerte.** *(tehn-goh 'swehr-teh)*
(You guys are) careful.	**(Tienen) cuidado.** *(tee-'eh-nehn kwee-'dah-doh)*

Try Some

Use **tengo** *('tehn-goh)* to answer these questions:

¿Tiene usted un carro blanco?
(tee-'eh-neh oos-'tehd oon 'kah-rroh 'blahn-koh)

¿Cuántos amigos tiene usted?
('kwahn-tohs ah-'mee-gohs tee-'eh-neh oos-'tehd)

¿Tiene mucha hambre?
(tee-'eh-neh 'moo-chah 'ahm-breh)

There Is and There Are
Hay
('ah-ee)

There is and *there are* are very common expressions in Spanish. In both cases, use the little word, **hay** *('ah-ee)*:

There's one bathroom.	**Hay un baño.** *('ah-ee oon 'bahn-yoh)*
There are two bathrooms.	**Hay dos baños.** *('ah-ee dohs 'bahn-yohs)*

Try Some

Translate these:

Hay dos hombres en la casa. *('ah-ee dohs 'ohm-brehs ehn lah 'kah-sah)*

No hay agua. *(noh 'ah-ee 'ah-gwah)*

¿Hay problema? *('ah-ee proh-'bleh-mah)*

Grammar Time

To express the negative in Spanish, put the word **no** *(noh)* in front of the verb.

There are no more.	**No hay más.** *(noh 'ah-ee mahs)*
José is not my friend.	**José no es mi amigo.** *(hoh-'seh ehs mee ah-'mee-goh)*
I do not have the job.	**No tengo el trabajo.** *(noh 'tehn-goh ehl trah-'bah-hoh)*

Spanish also uses the double negative, so when you respond, say **no** twice in your sentences. To ask a question, simply raise your voice at the end:

¿Hay problemas? *('ah-ee proh-'bleh-mahs)*
No, no hay problemas. *(noh noh 'ah-ee proh-'bleh-mahs)*

Chapter Two

More Vocabulary
Más vocabulario
(mahs voh-kah-boo-'lah-ree-oh)

General Health
La salud en general *(lah sah-'lood ehn heh-neh-'rahl)*

Begin this chapter on Spanish vocabulary with one-word responses about your health. Notice that all the words ending in **o** refer to males; to make them female, just change the **o** to **a**:

How are you?	**¿Cómo está?** *('koh-moh ehs-'tah)*
I'm…	**Estoy…** *(ehs-'toh-ee)*

angry	**enojado** *(eh-noh-'hah-doh)*
bored	**aburrido** *(ah-boo-'rree-doh)*
fine	**bien** *(bee-'ehn)*
happy	**feliz** *(feh-'lees)*
not bad	**así – así** *(ah-'see ah-'see)*
not well	**mal** *(mahl)*
OK	**regular** *(reh-goo-lahr)*
sad	**triste** *('trees-teh)*
sick	**enfermo** *(ehn-'fehr-moh)*
tired	**cansado** *(kahn-'sah-doh)*
worried	**preocupado** *(preh-oh-koo-'pah-doh)*

The Body
El cuerpo
(ehl 'kwehr-poh)

Here's an overview of body parts in Spanish, in addition to a command phrase, so that you can practice while you follow along:

Point to (the)...   **Señale...** *(seh-'nyah-leh)*

arm	**el brazo** *(ehl 'brah-soh)*
back	**la espalda** *(lah ehs-'pahl-dah)*
chest	**el pecho** *(ehl 'peh-choh)*
ear	**la oreja** *(lah oh-'reh-hah)*
eye	**el ojo** *(ehl 'oh-hoh)*
face	**la cara** *(lah 'kah-rah)*
finger	**el dedo** *(ehl 'deh-doh)*
foot	**el pie** *(ehl pee-'eh)*
hair	**el pelo** *(ehl 'peh-loh)*
hand	**la mano** *(lah 'mah-noh)*
head	**la cabeza** *(lah kah-'beh-sah)*
hip	**la cadera** *(lah kah-'deh-rah)*
knee	**la rodilla** *(lah roh-'dee-yah)*
leg	**la pierna** *(lah pee-'ehr-nah)*
mouth	**la boca** *(lah 'boh-kah)*
neck	**el cuello** *(ehl 'kweh-yoh)*
nose	**la nariz** *(lah nah-'rees)*
rib	**la costilla** *(lah kohs-'tee-yah)*
shoulder	**el hombro** *(ehl 'ohm-broh)*
stomach	**el estómago** *(ehl ehs-'toh-mah-goh)*
throat	**la garganta** *(lah gahr-'gahn-tah)*
tooth	**el diente** *(ehl dee-'ehn-teh)*

When there is pain involved, try these:

My_____ hurts.   **Me duele** _____. *(meh 'dweh-leh)*
Me duele el cuello. *(meh 'dweh-leh ehl 'kweh-yoh)*

My_____hurt.   **Me duelen** _____. *(meh 'dweh-lehn)*
Me duelen los hombros. *(meh 'dweh-lehn lohs 'ohm-brohs)*

Family
La familia
(lah fah-'mee-lee-ah)

Here are the basic family members in Spanish:

brother	**el hermano** *(ehl ehr-'mah-noh)*
daughter	**la hija** *(lah 'ee-hah)*
father	**el padre** *(ehl 'pah-dreh)*
husband	**el esposo** *(ehl ehs-'poh-soh)*
mother	**la madre** *(lah 'mah-dreh)*
sister	**la hija** *(lah 'ee-hah)*
son	**el hijo** *(ehl 'ee-hoh)*
wife	**la esposa** *(lah ehs-'poh-sah)*

Occupations
Las profesiones
(lahs proh-feh-see-'oh-nehs)

Do you know what your job title is **en español**? These common professions in construction refer to males (**el**), while for females (**la**), the **o** endings simply change to **a**:

I'm (the)…	**Soy…** *('soh-ee)*
architect	**el arquitecto** *(ehl ahr-kee-'tehk-toh)*
builder	**el constructor** *(ehl kohns-trook-'tohr)*
carpenter	**el carpintero** *(ehl kahr-peen-'teh-roh)*
contractor	**el contratista** *(ehl kohn-trah-'tees-tah)*
designer	**el diseñador** *(ehl dee-seh-nyah-'dohr)*
dry waller	**el yesero** *(ehl yeh-'seh-roh)*
electrician	**el electricista** *(ehl eh-lehk-tree-'sees-tah)*
engineer	**el ingeniero** *(ehl een-heh-nee-'eh-roh)*
inspector	**el inspector** *(ehl eens-pehk-'tohr)*
installer	**el instalador** *(ehl eens-tah-lah-'dohr)*
laborer	**el obrero** *(ehl oh-'breh-roh)*
landscaper	**el diseñador de jardines** *(ehl dee-seh-nyah-'dohr deh hahr-'dee-nehs)*
painter	**el pintor** *(ehl peen-'tohr)*
plumber	**el plomero** *(ehl plo-'meh-roh)*

stonemason	**el albañil** *(ehl ahl-bah-'neel)*
subcontractor	**el subcontratista** *(ehl soob-kohn-trah-'tees-tah)*
truck driver	**el camionero** *(ehl kah-mee-oh-'neh-roh)*

He's (the)…	**Es…** *(ehs)*

apprentice	**el aprendiz** *(ehl ah-prehn-'dees)*
boss	**el jefe** *(ehl 'heh-feh)*
client	**el cliente** *(ehl klee-'ehn-teh)*
employee	**el empleado** *(ehl ehm-pleh-'ah-doh)*
employer	**el empresario** *(ehl ehm-preh-'sah-ree-oh)*
foreman	**el capataz** *(ehl kah-pah-'tahs)*
general	**el contratista principal** *(ehl kohn-trah-'tees-tah preen-see-'pahl)*
helper	**el ayudante** *(ehl ah-yoo-'dahn-teh)*
lead man	**el líder** *(ehl 'lee-dehr)*
manager	**el gerente** *(ehl heh-'rehn-teh)*
owner	**el dueño** *(ehl 'dweh-nyoh)*
supervisor	**el supervisor** *(ehl soo-pehr-vee-'sohr)*

 ## Grammar Time

Jot down the forms of this popular verb. It's ideal for work-related communication:

To Need	**Necesitar** *(neh-seh-see-tahr)*
I need	**Necesito** *(neh-seh-'see-toh)*
You (sing.) need, he, she, it needs	**Necesita** *(neh-seh-'see-tah)*
We need	**Necesitamos** *(neh-seh-see-'tah-mohs)*
You (pl.), they need	**Necesitan** *(neh-seh-'see-tahn)*

You can translate these with no problem at all:

Necesito un carro. *(neh-seh-'see-toh oon 'kah-rroh)*
No necesita el plomero. *(noh neh-seh-'see-tah ehl ploh-'meh-roh)*
Necesitamos más trabajo. *(neh-seh-see-'tah-mohs mahs trah-'bah-hoh)*
¿Necesitan usar el baño? *(neh-seh-'see-tahn oo-'sahr ehl 'bah-nyoh)*

Try Some

Translate these:

Mi hermano es carpintero. _____

Mi tío es contratista. _____

Mis primas son pintoras. _____

Food and Drink
La comida y la bebida
(lah koh-'mee-dah ee lah beh-'bee-dah)

Listen for these Spanish words around mealtime.

Working Words: BREAKAFAST

bread	**el pan** *(ehl pahn)*
breakfast	**el desayuno** *(ehl deh-sah-'yoo-noh)*
cheese	**el queso** *(ehl 'keh-soh)*
ham	**el jamón** *(ehl hah-'mohn)*
butter	**la mantequilla** *(lah mahn-teh-'kee-yah)*
egg	**el huevo** *(ehl 'hweh-voh)*
coffee	**el café** *(ehl kah-'feh)*
tea	**el té** *(ehl teh)*
sugar	**el azúcar** *(ehl ah-'soo-kahr)*
salt	**la sal** *(lah sahl)*
cereal	**el cereal** *(ehl seh-reh-'ahl)*
juice	**el jugo** *(ehl 'hoo-goh)*
milk	**la leche** *(lah 'leh-cheh)*
water	**el agua** *(ehl 'ah-gwah)*

Working Words: LUNCH and DINNER

lunch	**el almuerzo** *(ehl ahl-'mwehr-soh)*
dinner	**la cena** *(lah 'seh-nah)*
soup	**la sopa** *(lah 'soh-pah)*
meat	**la carne** *(lah 'kahr-neh)*
fish	**el pescado** *(ehl pehs-'kah-doh)*
chicken	**el pollo** *(ehl 'poh-yoh)*
steak	**el bistec** *(ehl bees-'tehk)*
salad	**la ensalada** *(lah ehn-sah-'lah-dah)*
turkey	**el pavo** *(ehl 'pah-voh)*
rice	**el arroz** *(ehl ah-'rrohs)*
pork	**el cerdo** *(ehl 'sehr-doh)*
roast beef	**el rosbíf** *(ehl rohs-'beef)*

Working Words: DRINKS

drink	**la bebida** *(lah beh-'bee-dah)*
beer	**la cerveza** *(lah sehr-'veh-sah)*
soda	**la soda** *(lah 'soh-dah*
iced tea	**el té helado** *(ehl teh eh-'lah-doh)*
lemonade	**la limonada** *(lah lee-moh-'nah-dah)*
shake	**el batido** *(ehl bah-'tee-doh)*
soft drink	**el refresco** *(ehl reh-'frehs-koh)*
wine	**el vino** *(ehl 'vee-noh)*

Clothing
La ropa
(lah 'roh-pah)

To identify people on the job site, you may need the names for clothing:

Working Words: CLOTHING

belt	**el cinturón** *(ehl seen-too-'rohn)*
boots	**las botas** *(lahs 'boh-tahs)*
cap	**la gorra** *(lah 'goh-rrah)*
gloves	**los guantes** *(lohs 'gwahn-tehs)*
jacket	**la chaqueta** *(lah chah-'keh-tah)*
hat	**el sombrero** *(ehl sohm-'breh-roh)*
overcoat	**el abrigo** *(ehl ah-'bree-goh)*
pants	**los pantalones** *(lohs pahn-tah-'loh-nehs)*
raincoat	**el impermeable** *(ehl eem-pehr-meh-'ah-bleh)*
sandals	**las sandalias** *(lahs sahn-'dah-lee-ahs)*
shirt	**la camisa** *(lah kah-'mee-sah)*
shoes	**los zapatos** *(lohs sah-'pah-tohs)*
shorts	**los calzoncillos** *(lohs kahl-sohn-'see-yohs)*
socks	**los calcetines** *(lohs kahl-seh-'tee-nehs)*
sweater	**el suéter** *(ehl 'sweh-tehr)*
sweatsuit	**la sudadera** *(lah soo-dah-'deh-rah)*
T-shirt	**la camiseta** *(lah kah-mee-'seh-tah)*
sneakers	**los tenis** *(lohs 'teh-nees)*
uniform	**el uniforme** *(ehl oo-nee-'fohr-meh)*

Transportation
El transporte
(ehl trahns-'pohr-teh)

There are vehicles all over the job site. Although more will be mentioned ahead, try these phrases with the common transportation words:

We need (the)...	**Necesitamos...** *(neh-seh-see-'tah-mohs)*
car	**el carro** *(ehl 'kah-rroh)*
truck	**el camión** *(ehl kah-mee-'ohn)*
pickup	**la camioneta** *(lah kah-mee-oh-'neh-tah)*

semitrailer	**el semi-remolque** *(ehl seh-mee-reh-'mohl-keh)*
tractor trailer	**el camión tractor** *(ehl kah-mee-'ohn trahk-'tohr)*
dump truck	**el camión volquete** *(ehl kah-mee-'ohn vohl-'keh-teh)*
flatbed truck	**el camión de plataforma** *(ehl kah-mee-'ohn deh plah-tah-'fohr-mah)*
van	**la vagoneta** *(lah vah-goh-'neh-tah)*, **la furgoneta** *(lah foor-goh-'neh-tah)*

Now name all the vehicles on the street:

delivery truck	**el camión de reparto** *(ehl kah-mee-'ohn deh reh-'pahr-toh)*
garbage truck	**el camión para basura** *(ehl kah-mee-'ohn 'pah-rah bah-'soo-rah)*
street sweeper	**la barredora** *(lah bah-rreh-'doh-rah)*
tank truck	**el camión cisterna** *(ehl kah-mee-'ohn sees-'tehr-nah)*
tow truck	**la grúa** *(lah 'groo-ah)*

These words are used in conversations about vehicles:

It needs…	**Necesita…** *(neh-seh-'see-tah)*
gas	**la gasolina** *(lah gah-soh-'lee-nah)*
oil	**el aceite** *(ehl ah-'seh-ee-teh)*
lubrication	**el lubricante** *(ehl loo-bree-'kahn-teh)*
maintenance	**el mantenimiento/la mantención** *(ehl mahn-teh-nee-mee-'ehn-toh/lah mahn-tehn-see-'ohn)*
diesel	**diésel** *(dee-'eh-sel)*
regular	**regular** *(reh-goo-'lahr)*
super	**súper** *('soo-pehr)*
unleaded	**sin plomo** *(seen 'ploh-moh)*
Go to (the)…	**Vaya a…** *('vah-yah ah)*
loading zone	**la zona de carga** *(lah 'soh-nah deh 'kahr-gah)*
unloading zone	**la zona de descarga** *(lah 'soh-nah deh dehs-'kahr-gah)*
parking area	**el estacionamiento** *(ehl ehs-tah-see-oh-nah-mee-'ehn-toh)*
lot	**el lote** *(ehl 'loh-teh)*
site	**el sitio** *(ehl 'see-tee-oh)*
road	**el camino** *(ehl kah-'mee-noh)*

Culture Issues

Car in Spanish can be **carro** *('kah-rroh)*, **coche** *('koh-cheh)*, **auto** *('ah-oo-toh)*, or **automóvil** *(ah-oo-toh-'moh-veel)*, depending upon where a person is from. Look at these other means of transport:

It's (the)...	**Es...** *(ehs)*
bus	**el autobús** *(ehl ah-oo-toh-'boos)*
train	**el tren** *(ehl trehn)*
subway	**el metro** *(ehl 'meh-troh)*
bike	**la bicicleta** *(lah bee-see-'kleh-tah)*
motorcycle	**la motocicleta** *(la moh-toh-see-'kleh-tah)*
plane	**el avión** *(ehl ah-vee-'ohn)*
helicopter	**el helicóptero** *(ehl eh-lee-'kohp-teh-roh)*
boat	**el bote** *(ehl 'boh-teh)*

...and *to go on foot* is **ir a pie** *(eer ah pee-'eh)*.

The City
La ciudad
(lah see-oo-'dahd)

If your job is in town, learn words related to a city.

Where's (the)...	**¿Dónde está...?** *('dohn-deh ehs-'tah)*
airport	**el aeropuerto** *(ehl ah-eh-roh-'pwehr-toh)*
bank	**el banco** *(ehl 'bahn-koh)*
bus station	**la estación de autobús** *(lah ehs-tah-see-'ohn deh ah-oo-toh-'boos)*
church	**la iglesia** *(lah ee-'gleh-see-ah)*
college	**el colegio** *(ehl koh-'leh-ee-oh)*
factory	**la fábrica** *(lah 'fah-bree-kah)*
fire department	**el departamento de bomberos** *(ehl deh-pahr-tah-'mehn-toh deh bohm-'beh-rohs)*
gas station	**la gasolinera** *(lah gah-soh-lee-'neh-rah)*

hospital	**el hospital** *(ehl ohs-pee-'tahl)*
library	**la biblioteca** *(lah bee-blee-oh-'teh-kah)*
supermarket	**el supermercado** *(ehl soo-pehr-mehr-'kah-doh)*
movie theater	**el cine** *(ehl 'see-neh)*
park	**el parque** *(ehl 'pahr-keh)*
police station	**la estación de policía** *(lah ehs-tah-see-'ohn deh poh-lee-'see-ah)*
post office	**el correo** *(ehl koh-'rreh-oh)*
school	**la escuela** *(lah ehs-'kweh-lah)*
store	**la tienda** *(lah tee-'ehn-dah)*
shopping center	**el centro commercial** *(ehl 'sehn-troh koh-mehr-see-'ahl)*
city hall	**el municipio** *(ehl moo-nee-'see-pee-oh)*
warehouse	**el almacén** *(ehl ahl-mah-'sehn)*

Now give directions:

It's near (the) ...	**Está cerca de ...** *(ehs-'tah 'sehr-kah deh)*
building	**el edificio** *(ehl eh-dee-'fee-see-oh)*
city block	**la cuadra** *(lah 'kwah-drah)*
corner	**la esquina** *(lah ehs-'kee-nah)*
highway	**la carretera** *(lah kah-rreh-'teh-rah)*
sidewalk	**la acera** *(lah ah-'seh-rah)*
street	**la calle** *(lah 'kah-yeh)*
traffic light	**el semáforo** *(ehl seh-'mah-foh-roh)*

Go to (the)...	**Vaya a...** *('vah-yah ah)*
neighborhood	**el vecindario** *(ehl veh-seen-'dah-ree-oh)*
outskirts	**las afueras** *(lahs ah-'fweh-rahs)*
downtown	**el centro** *(ehl 'sehn-troh)*

These are the four basic directions:

east	**el este** *(ehl 'ehs-teh)*
north	**el norte** *(ehl 'nohr-teh)*
south	**el sur** *(ehl soor)*
west	**el oeste** *(ehl oh-'ehs-teh)*

Tools and Materials
Las herramientas y los materiales
(lahs eh-rrah-mee-'ehn-tahs ee lohs mah-teh-ree-'ah-lehs)

Build up your skills with some basic tools and equipment. Pound away at these items using a few command words:

Unload (the)...	**Descargue...** *(dehs-'kahr-geh)*
Bring (the)...	**Traiga...** *('trah-ee-gah)*
Use (the)...	**Use...** *('oo-seh)*

compressor	**el compresor de aire** *(ehl kohm-preh-'sohr deh 'ah-ee-reh)*
generator	**el generador** *(ehl heh-neh-rah-'dohr)*
sawhorse	**el caballete** *(ehl kah-bah-'yeh-teh)*
scaffold	**el andamio** *(ehl ahn-'dah-mee-oh)*
toolbox	**la caja de herramientas** *(lah 'kah-hah deh eh-rrah-mee-'ehn-tahs)*
trash can	**el bote de basura** *(ehl 'boh-teh deh bah-'soo-rah)*
worktable	**el tablero de trabajo** *(ehl tah-'bleh-roh deh trah-'bah-hoh)*
wheelbarrow	**la carretilla** *(lah kah-rreh-'tee-yah)*

☞ Working Words: TOOLS

ax	**el hacha** *(ehl 'ah-chah)*
caulking gun	**la pistola de sellador** *(lah pees-'toh-lah deh seh-yah-'dohr)*
chain	**la cadena** *(lah kah-'deh-nah)*
chisel	**el cincel** *(ehl seen-'sehl)*
circular saw	**el serrucho circular** *(ehl seh-'rroo-choh seer-koo-'lahr)*
clamp	**la abrazadera** *(lah ah-brah-sah-'deh-rah)*
cordless drill	**el taladro a pilas** *(ehl tah-'lah-droh ah 'pee-lahs)*
extension cord	**el cordón eléctrico** *(ehl kohr-'dohn eh-'lehk-tree-koh)*
glue	**el pegamento/la cola** *(ehl peh-gah-'mehn-toh/lah 'koh-lah)*
hacksaw	**la sierra para metales** *(lah see-'eh-rrah 'pah-rah meh-'tah-lehs)*
hammer	**el martillo** *(ehl mahr-'tee-yoh)*
hose	**la manguera** *(lah mahn-'geh-rah)*
ladder	**la escalera** *(lah ehs-kah-'leh-rah)*

level	el **nivel** *(ehl nee-'vehl)*
measuring tape	la **cinta de medir** *(lah 'seen-tah deh meh-'deer)*
nail gun	la **pistola clavadora** *(lah pees-'toh-lah klah-vah-'doh-rah)*
nail	el **clavo** *(ehl 'klah-voh)*
paint brush	la **brocha** *(lah 'broh-chah)*
paint	la **pintura** *(lah peen-'too-rah)*
Phillips head	el **destornillador de cruz** *(ehl dehs-tohr-nee-yah-'dohr deh kroos)*
pliers	los **alicates** *(lohs ah-lee-'kah-tehs)*
rope	la **soga/la cuerda/el cordel** *(lah 'soh-gah/lah 'kwehr-dah/ehl kohr-'dehl)*
sandpaper	el **papel de lija** *(ehl pah-'pehl deh 'lee-hah)*
saw	el **serrucho/la sierra** *(ehl seh-'rroo-choh/lah see-'eh-rrah)*
scraper	el **raspador** *(ehl rahs-pah-'dohr)*
screw	el **tornillo** *(ehl tohr-'nee-yoh)*
screwdriver	el **destornillador** *(ehl dehs-tohr-nee-yah-'dohr)*
shovel	la **pala** *(lah 'pah-lah)*
staple	la **grapa** *(lah 'grah-pah)*
tape	la **cinta** *(lah 'seen-tah)*
utility knife	la **cuchilla** *(lah koo-'chee-yah)*
vise	la **prensa de tornillo** *(lah 'prehn-sah deh tohr-'nee-yoh)*
wire	el **alambre** *(ehl ah-'lahm-breh)*
wrench	la **llave inglesa** *(lah 'yah-veh een-'gleh-sah)*

Working Words: MATERIALS

alloy	la **aleación** *(lah ah-leh-ah-see-'ohn)*
aluminum	el **aluminio** *(ehl ah-loo-'mee-nee-oh)*
bronze	el **bronce** *(ehl 'brohn-seh)*
cardboard	el **cartón** *(ehl kahr-'tohn)*
copper	el **cobre** *(ehl 'koh-breh)*
fabric	la **tela** *(lah 'teh-lah)*
fiberglass	la **fibra de vidrio** *(lah 'fee-brah deh 'vee-dree-oh)*
foam	la **espuma** *(lah ehs-'poo-mah)*
glass	el **vidrio** *(ehl 'vee-dree-oh)*
iron	el **hierro** *(ehl ee-'eh-rroh)*
liquid	el **líquido** *(ehl 'lee-kee-doh)*
lumber	el **madero** *(ehl mah-'deh-roh)*

mesh	**la malla** *(lah 'mah-yah)*
metal	**el metal** *(ehl meh-'tahl)*
plaster	**el yeso** *(ehl 'yeh-soh)*
plastic	**el plástico** *(ehl 'plahs-tee-koh)*
plywood	**la madera contrachapada** *(lah mah-'deh-rah kohn-trah-chah-'pah-dah)*
powder	**el polvo** *(ehl 'pohl-voh)*
rubber	**la goma** *(lah 'goh-mah)*
steel	**el acero** *(ehl ah-'seh-roh)*
stone	**la piedra** *(lah pee-'eh-drah)*
wall tile	**el azulejo** *(ehl ah-soo-'leh-hoh)*
floor tile	**la baldosa** *(lah bahl-'doh-sah)*
roof tile	**la teja** *(lah 'teh-hah)*
tin	**el estaño** *(ehl ehs-'tah-nyoh)*
wood	**la madera** *(lah mah-'deh-rah)*

You messed up the place—don't forget your cleaning tools:

broom	**la escoba** *(lah ehs-'koh-bah)*
brush	**el cepillo** *(ehl seh-'pee-yoh)*
bucket	**el balde** *(ehl 'bahl-deh)*
dustpan	**la pala de recoger basura** *(lah 'pah-lah deh reh-koh-'hehr bah-'soo-rah)*
mop	**el trapeador** *(ehl trah-peh-ah-'dohr)*
rag	**el trapo** *(ehl 'trah-poh)*
sponge	**la esponja** *(lah ehs-'pohn-hah)*
towel	**la toalla** *(lah toh-'ah-yah)*
trashbag	**la bolsa para basura** *(lah 'bohl-sah 'pah-rah bah-'soo-rah)*

At Work
En el trabajo
(ehn ehl trah-'bah-hoh)

We need more…	**Necesitamos más…** *(neh-seh-see-'tah-mohs mahs)*
materials	**materiales** *(mah-teh-ree-'ah-lehs)*
machines	**máquinas** *('mah-kee-nahs)*
workers	**obreros** *(oh-'breh-rohs)*

Pick up (the)…	**Recoja…** *(reh-'koh-hah)*
debris	**los escombros** *(lohs ehs-'kohm-brohs)*
spillage	**el derrame** *(ehl deh-'rrah-meh)*
trash	**la basura** *(lah bah-'soo-rah)*
It doesn't have…	**No tiene…** *(noh tee-'eh-neh)*
air	**el aire** *(ehl 'ah-ee-reh)*
fuel	**el combustible** *(ehl kohm-boos-'tee-bleh)*
gas	**el gas** *(ehl gahs)*
gas(oline)	**la bencina** *(lah behn-'see-nah)*
kerosene	**la parafina** *(lah pah-rah-'fee-nah)*
light	**la luz** *(lah loos)*
power (electric)	**la electricidad** *(lah eh-lehk-tree-see-'dahd)*
power (potency)	**la potencia** *(lah poh-'tehn-see-ah)*
water	**el agua** *(ehl 'ah-gwah)*
Where's (the)…?	**¿Dónde está…?** *('dohn-deh ehs-'tah)*
dumpster	**el basurero grande** *(ehl bah-soo-'reh-roh 'grahn-deh)*
fence	**la cerca** *(lah 'sehr-kah)*
office	**la oficina** *(lah oh-fee-'see-nah)*
Porta-potty	**el retrete portátil** *(ehl reh-'treh-teh pohr-'tah-teel)*
shack	**la chabola** *(lah chah-'boh-lah)*
shed	**el cobertizo** *(ehl koh-behr-'tee-soh)*

Just a Suggestion

Interject these questions to get more detail about the project:

What_____?	**¿Qué_____?** *(keh)*
kind	**clase** *('klah-seh)*
type	**tipo** *('tee-poh)*
brand	**marca** *('mahr-kah)*

Grammar Time

The magic word *me* (**me**—*meh*) can be added to the end of a simple command to indicate *to me*:

Listen to me	**Escúcheme** *(ehs-'koo-cheh-meh)*
Explain to me	**Explíqueme** *(ehks-'plee-keh-meh)*
Tell me	**Dígame** *('dee-gah-meh)*
Call me	**Llámeme** *('yah-meh-meh)*
Give me	**Deme** *('deh-meh)*
Send me	**Mándeme** *('mahn-deh-meh)*
Answer me	**Contésteme** *(kohn-'tehs-teh-meh)*
Bring me	**Tráigame** *('tra-ee-gah-meh)*

Measurements
Las medidas
(lahs meh-'dee-dahs)

All workers require this vocabulary. Focus on the questions first:

How much?	**¿Cuánto?** *('kwahn-toh)*
How many?	**¿Cuántos?** *('kwahn-tohs)*
What's it measure?	**¿Cuánto mide?** *('kwahn-toh 'mee-deh)*
What's it weigh?	**¿Cuánto pesa?** *('kwahn-toh 'peh-sah)*
How...?	**¿Cuánto mide de...?** *('kwahn-toh 'mee-deh deh)*
long	**largo** *('lahr-goh)*
high	**alto** *('ahl-toh)*
deep	**profundidad** *(proh-foon-dee-'dahd)*

When you respond, remember to drop the **el** or **la** if you add a number: inch **la pulgada**
(lah pool-'gah-dah) ➤ two inches **dos pulgadas** *(dohs pool-'gah-dahs)*

cent	**el centavo** *(ehl sehn-'tah-voh)*
cup	**la taza** *(lah 'tah-sah)*
feet	**el pie** *(ehl pee-'eh)*
gallon	**el galón** *(ehl gah-'lohn)*
inch	**la pulgada** *(lah pool-'gah-dah)*
mile	**la milla** *(lah 'mee-yah)*
ounce	**la onza** *(lah 'ohn-sah)*
pint	**la pinta** *(lah 'peen-tah)*
pound	**la libra** *(lah 'lee-brah)*
quart	**el cuarto** *(el 'kwahr-toh)*
ton	**la tonelada** *(lah toh-neh-'lah-dah)*
yard	**la yarda** *(lah 'yahr-dah)*

What's (the)...?	**¿Cuál es...?** *('kwahl ehs)*

amount	**la cantidad** *(lah kahn-tee-'dahd)*
count	**la cuenta** *(lah 'kwehn-tah)*
depth	**la profundidad** *(lah proh-foon-dee-'dahd)*
distance	**la distance** *(lah dees-'tahn-see-ah)*
height	**la altura** *(lah ahl-'too-rah)*
length	**el largo** *(ehl 'lahr-goh)*
size	**el tamaño** *(ehl tah-'mahn-yoh)*
speed	**la velocidad** *(lah veh-loh-see-'dahd)*
temperature	**la temperatura** *(lah tehm-peh-rah-'too-rah)*
width	**el ancho** *(ehl 'ahn-choh)*

Just a Suggestion

Feet: the word **pies** *(pee-'ehs)* is used all the time in construction:

linear feet	**pies lineales** *(pee-'ehs lee-neh-'ah-lehs)*
square feet	**pies cuadrados** *(pee-'ehs kwah-'drah-dohs)*
cubic feet	**pies cúbicos** *(pee-'ehs 'koo-bee-kohs)*

Try Some

Go ahead and translate:

dos galones _____

cinco pulgadas _____

tres toneladas _____

eight ounces _____

twelve feet _____

fifty pints _____

Spanish Verbs
Los verbos en español
(lohs 'vehr-bohs ehn ehs-pahn-'yohl)

Although the verbs **estar** *(ehs-'tahr)*, **ser** *(sehr)*, and **tener** *(teh-'nehr)* are extremely useful, they do not express action. Learning how to use Spanish verbs will allow you to talk about anything. Spend a few moments memorizing this brief list of helpful beginning verbs. Notice that Spanish action words end in the letters **-ar**, **-er**, or **-ir**, and they aren't to be confused with the command forms you learned earlier:

-AR verbs

to answer	**contestar** *(kohn-tehs-'tahr)*
to arrive	**llegar** *(yeh-'gahr)*
to ask	**preguntar** *(pre-goon-'tahr)*
to begin	**empezar** *(ehm-peh-'sahr)*
to buy	**comprar** *(kohm-'prahr)*
to call	**llamar** *(yah-'mahr)*
to carry	**llevar** *(yeh-'vahr)*
to change	**cambiar** *(kahm-bee-'ahr)*
to clean	**limpiar** *(leem-pee-'ahr)*
to close	**cerrar** *(seh-'rrahr)*

to drive	**manejar** *(mah-neh-'hahr)*
to end	**terminar** *(tehr-mee-'nahr)*
to give	**dar** *(dahr)*
to help	**ayudar** *(ah-yoo-'dahr)*
to lift	**levantar** *(leh-vahn-'tahr)*
to listen	**escuchar** *(ehs-koo-'chahr)*
to load	**cargar** *(kahr-'gahr)*
to look	**mirar** *(mee-'rahr)*
to pay	**pagar** *(pah-'gahr)*
to rest	**descansar** *(dehs-kahn-'sahr)*
to speak	**hablar** *(ah-'blahr)*
to stop	**parar** *(pah-'rahr)*
to take	**tomar** *(toh-'mahr)*
to throw away	**tirar** *(tee-'rahr)*
to turn off	**apagar** *(ah-pah-'gahr)*
to unload	**descargar** *(dehs-kahr-'gahr)*
to use	**usar** *(oo-'sahr)*
to walk	**caminar** *(kah-mee-'nahr)*
to wash	**lavar** *(lah-'vahr)*
to work	**trabajar** *(trah-bah-'hahr)*

-ER verbs

to bring	**traer** *(trah-'ehr)*
to do	**hacer** *(ah-'sehr)*
to drink	**beber** *(beh-'behr)*
to eat	**comer** *(koh-'mehr)*
to learn	**aprender** *(ah-prehn-'dehr)*
to move	**mover** *(moh-'vehr)*
to put	**poner** *(poh-'nehr)*
to read	**leer** *(leh-'ehr)*
to return	**volver** *(vohl-'vehr)*
to run	**correr** *(koh-'rrehr)*
to see	**ver** *(vehr)*
to sell	**vender** *(vehn-'dehr)*
to turn on	**prender** *(prehn-'dehr)*
to understand	**entender** *(ehn-tehn-'dehr)*

-IR verbs

to allow	**permitir** *(pehr-mee-'teer)*
to come	**venir** *(veh-'neer)*
to go	**ir** *(eer)*
to leave	**salir** *(sah-'leer)*
to live	**vivir** *(vee-'veer)*
to measure	**medir** *(meh-'deer)*
to open	**abrir** *(ah-'breer)*
to receive	**recibir** *(reh-see-'beer)*
to say	**decir** *(deh-'seer)*
to sleep	**dormir** *(dohr-'meer)*
to write	**escribir** *(ehs-kree-'beer)*

As you might have guessed, many Spanish verbs resemble their English equivalent:

to connect	**conectar** *(koh-nehk-'tahr)*
to control	**controlar** *(kohn-troh-'lahr)*
to install	**instalar** *(eens-tah-'lahr)*
to organize	**organizar** *(ohr-gah-nee-'sahr)*
to refer	**referir** *(reh-feh-'reer)*

Try Some

Write a Spanish verb with an opposite meaning:

escuchar _____

venir _____

sentarse _____

correr _____

vender _____

Careful! False look-alikes are everywhere!

contestar *(kohn-tehs-'tahr)*	=	to answer, not *to contest*
embarazar *(ehm-bah-rah-'sahr)*	=	to get somebody pregnant, not *to embarrass*
asistir *(ah-sees-'teer)*	=	to attend, not *to assist*

You can never learn enough action words in Spanish. Over five hundred verbs are listed in this book. So, whenever you hear a verb you don't know, look up its base form and meaning.

One of the most effective ways to put your verbs into action is to combine them with simple phrases that create complete commands. For example, look what happens when you add these verb infinitives to **Favor de...** *(fah-'vohr deh)*, which implies *Would you please...*:

Would you please...	**Favor de...** *(fah-'vohr deh)*
write the number	**escribir el número** *(ehs-kree-'beer ehl 'noo-meh-roh)*
drive the truck	**manejar el camión** *(mah-neh-'hahr ehl kah-mee-'ohn)*
speak more slowly	**hablar más despacio** *(ah-'blahr mahs dehs-'pah-see-oh)*

Try Some

Practice these short questions and answers aloud:

¿Quién? *(kee-'ehn)*	**Nadie.** *('nah-dee-eh)*
¿Cuántos? *('kwahn-tohs)*	**Ninguno.** *(neen-'goo-noh)*
¿Dónde? *('dohn-deh)*	**Por todas partes.** *(pohr 'toh-dahs 'pahr-tehs)*

One-Liners

As a beginning Spanish student involved in training, you are going to need practical one-word responses to communicate with people who work for you. Scan this list, and choose those that suit you best.

alone	**solo** *('soh-loh)*
also	**también** *(tahm-bee-'ehn)*
anyone	**cualquier persona** *(kwahl-kee-'ehr pehr-'soh-nah)*
anything	**cualquier cosa** *(kwahl-kee-'ehr 'koh-sah)*
anywhere	**en cualquier sitio** *(ehn kwahl-kee-'ehr 'see-tee-oh)*
enough	**bastante** *(bahs-'tahn-teh)*
everybody	**todos** *('toh-dohs)*
everything	**todo** *('toh-doh)*
everywhere	**por todas partes** *(pohr 'toh-dahs 'pahr-tehs)*
no one	**nadie** *('nah-dee-eh)*
no where	**en ningún sitio** *(ehn neen-'goon 'see-tee-oh)*
none	**ninguno** *(neen-'goo-noh)*
nothing	**nada** *('nah-dah)*
only	**solamente** *(soh-lah-'mehn-teh)*
same	**mismo** *('mees-moh)*
someone	**alguien** *('ahl-gee-ehn)*
something	**algo** *('ahl-goh)*
somewhere	**en algún sitio** *(ehn ahl-'goon 'see-tee-oh)*
too much	**demasiado** *(deh-mah-see-'ah-doh)*
most	**la mayor parte** *(lah mah-'yohr 'pahr-teh)*
the rest	**los demás** *(lohs deh-'mahs)*

INTRODUCTION TO CHAPTERS THREE TO NINE

Chapters Three to Nine address seven different trades in the field of construction. Please take note of the following tips as you read through the entire text:

- Several words are repeated in each chapter, because not all vocabulary or activities in construction are entirely trade-specific.
- You may find more than one Spanish translation for an English word, since the meaning of one word may change slightly when used in a different setting or context. The same holds true for some of the Spanish words.
- Simply for convenience, everything presented in this book is in the masculine form. Changes should be made when referring to a female.
- Commands, questions, and statements are primarily addressed to an individual. Changes should be made when addressing more than one person.
- Although each chapter is filled with the names for items in Spanish, many Spanish-speaking construction workers will attempt to use English or a mixture of the two languages (*Spanglish*) in order to communicate. In fact, if the item you are looking for is not mentioned in the book, there's a good chance it is generally referred to in English.

Chapter Three

Grading and Foundation
La nivelación y los cimientos

(lah nee-veh-lah-see-'ohn ee lohs see-mee-'ehn-tohs)

 Working Words: GRADING AND FOUNDATION

Everyone involved in this phase of the project should know the following vocabulary words:

ground	**el suelo** *(ehl 'sweh-loh)*
soil	**la tierra** *(lah tee-'eh-rrah)*
trench	**la zanja** *(lah 'sahn-hah)*
concrete	**el concreto** *(ehl kohn-'kreh-toh)*
slab	**la losa** *(lah 'loh-sah)*
form	**el molde** *(ehl 'mohl-deh)*
footing	**la zapata** *(lah sah-'pah-tah)*
rebar	**la varilla** *(lah vah-'ree-yah)*
brace	**la riostra/la abrazadera** *(lah ree-'ohs-trah/lah ah-brah-sah-'deh-rah)*

Now create a few simple phrases:

Look at (the)…	**Mire…** *('mee-reh)*
boundary	**el límite** *(ehl 'lee-mee-teh)*
land	**el terreno** *(ehl teh-'rreh-noh)*
layout	**el diseño** *(ehl dee-'seh-nyoh)*
lot	**el lote** *(ehl 'loh-teh)*
plot	**la parcela** *(lah pahr-'seh-lah)*
property	**la propiedad** *(lah proh-pee-eh-'dahd)*
surface	**la superficie** *(lah soo-pehr-'fee-see-eh)*

Where's the…?	**¿Dónde está…?** *('dohn-deh ehs-'tah)*
area	**la área** *(lah 'ah-reh-ah)*
line	**la linea** *(lah 'lee-neh-ah)*
place	**el lugar** *(ehl loo-'gahr)*
site	**el sitio** *(ehl 'see-tee-oh)*
space	**el espacio** *(ehl ehs-'pah-see-oh)*
spot	**el punto** *(ehl 'poon-toh)*
zone	**la zona** *(lah 'soh-nah)*

Now tell the crew what kind of ground they are standing on:

It is …	**Es…** *(ehs)*
bedrock	**el lecho de roca** *(ehl 'leh-choh deh 'roh-kah)*
clay	**la arcilla/la greda** *(lah ahr-'see-yah/lah 'greh-dah)*
dirt	**la tierra** *(lah tee-'eh-rrah)*
gravel	**la grava** *(lah 'grah-vah)*
landfill	**el terreno suelto** *(ehl teh-'rreh-noh 'swehl-toh)*
limestone	**la piedra caliza** *(lah pee-'eh-drah kah-'lee-sah)*
mud	**el lodo** *(ehl 'loh-doh)*
rock	**la roca** *(lah 'roh-kah)*
rubble	**la rocalia** *(lah roh-'kah-lee-ah)*
sand	**la arena** *(lah ah-'reh-nah)*
sandstone	**la arenisca** *(ah-ree-'nees-kah)*
sediment	**el sedimento** *(ehl seh-dee-'mehn-toh)*

Try Some

Translate these sentences into Spanish:

Where is the place? _____

Look at the surface. _____

It has rocks. _____

Working Words: GRADING EQUIPMENT

Open up with common hand tools:

Give me (the)…	**Deme…** *('deh-meh)*
pick	**el pico** *(ehl 'pee-koh)*
shovel	**la pala** *(lah 'pah-lah)*
wheelbarrow	**la carretilla** *(lah kah-rreh-'tee-yah)*

The word for truck is **el camión** *(ehl kah-mee-'ohn)*:

Where's (the)…?	**¿Dónde está…?** *('dohn-deh ehs-'tah)*
cement truck	**el camión hormigonero** *(ehl kah-mee-'ohn ohr-mee-goh-'neh-roh)*
crane truck	**el camión grúa** *(ehl kah-mee-'ohn 'groo-ah)*
dump truck	**el camión volquete** *(ehl kah-mee-'ohn vohl-'keh-teh)*
flatbed truck	**el camión plataforma** *(ehl kah-mee-'ohn plah-tah-'fohr-mah)*
pick-up truck	**la camioneta** *(lah kah-mee-oh-'neh-tah)*
water tank truck	**el camión cisterna** *(ehl kah-mee-'ohn sees-'tehr-nah)*

Now identify some heavy equipment. Notice how many words that refer to machinery end in the letters **-adora**:

Bring (the)…	**Traiga…** *('trah-ee-gah)*
loader	**la cargadora** *(lah kahr-gah-'doh-rah)*
grader	**la niveladora** *(lah nee-veh-lah-'doh-rah)*
roller	**la aplanadora** *(lah ah-plah-nah-'doh-rah)*
scraper	**la rastreadora** *(lah rahs-treh-ah-'doh-rah)*
trencher	**la excavadora** *(lah ex-kah-vah-'doh-rah)*
compactor	**la compactadora** *(lah kohm-pahk-tah-'doh-rah)*
driller	**la perforadora** *(lah pehr-foh-rah-'doh-rah)*
backhoe	**la retroexcavadora** *(reh-troh-ex-kah-vah-'doh-rah)*

The actual word for bulldozer is **el bulldozer** *(bool-'doh-sehr)* or **el tractor oruga** *(ehl trahk-'tohr oh-'roo-gah)*, but sometimes workers simply refer to machines in English by their make, brand, or function:

el Bobcat	**el SuperPac**
el DynaPac	**los earthmovers**
los eighteen-wheelers	**el Caterpillar**
el Deere	**el Padfoot**

Keep talking about your grading equipment:

Move (the)...	**Mueva...** *('mweh-vah)*
jackhammer	**el martillo neumático** *(ehl mahr-'tee-yoh neh-oo-'mah-tee-koh)*
electric trowel	**la paleta eléctrica** *(lah pah-'leh-tah eh-'lehk-tree-kah)*
power shovel	**la pala motorizada** *(lah 'pah-lah moh-toh-ree-'sah-dah)*
hand compactor	**la compactadora manual** *(lah kohm-pak-tah-'doh-rah mah-'nwahl)*
hydraulic pile driver	**el vibrador hidráulico** *(ehl vee-brah-'dohr ee-'drah-oo-lee-koh)*

And, be specific when it comes to equipment parts:

Fix (the)...	**Arregle...** *(ah-'rreh-gleh)*
bit	**la broca** *(lah 'broh-kah)*
blade	**la hoja** *(lah 'oh-hah)*
bucket	**el cucharón** *(ehl koo-chah-'rohn)*
cab	**la cabina** *(lah kah-'bee-nah)*
cable	**el cable** *(ehl 'kah-bleh)*
drum	**el rulo/el tambor** *(ehl 'roo-loh/ehl tahm-'bohr)*
engine	**el motor** *(ehl moh-'tohr)*
gear	**el engranaje** *(ehl ehn-grah-'nah-heh)*
handle	**el mango** *(ehl 'mahn-goh)*
hose	**la manguera** *(lah mahn-'geh-rah)*
lever	**la palanca** *(lah pah-'lahn-kah)*
lid	**la tapa** *(lah 'tah-pah)*
nozzle	**la boquilla** *(lah boh-'kee-yah)*

panel	**el panel** *(ehl pah-'nehl)*
screen	**el mosquitero/la malla** *(ehl mohs-kee-'teh-roh/lah 'mah-yah)*
shaft	**el eje** *(ehl 'eh-heh)*
valve	**la válvula** *(lah 'vahl-voo-lah)*
wheel	**la rueda** *(lah 'rweh-dah)*

Among construction tools, these are basic:

The pneumatic …	… **neumático** *(neh-oo-'mah-tee-koh)*

drill	**el taladro** *(ehl tah-'lah-droh)*
hammer	**el martillo** *(ehl mahr-'tee-yoh)*
nailer	**la clavadora** *(lah klah-vah-'doh-rah)*
screwdriver	**el destornillador** *(ehl dehs-tohr-nee-yah-'dohr)*
wrench	**la llave** *(lah 'yah-veh)*

Just a Suggestion

You may be sending crew members to the truck to get something, so these words will be needed, too:

It's in, on, or at (the)…	**Está en…** *(ehs-'tah ehn)*

dashboard	**el tablero** *(ehl tah-'bleh-roh)*
glove compartment	**la guantera** *(lah gwahn-'teh-rah)*
steering wheel	**el volante** *(ehl voh-'lahn-teh)*
seat	**el asiento** *(ehl ah-see-'ehn-toh)*
visor	**la visera** *(lah vee-'seh-rah)*
truckbed	**el trasero** *(ehl trah-'seh-roh)*

Now, put words together to give detail:

front seat	**el asiento delantero** *(ehl ah-see-'ehn-toh deh-lahn-'teh-roh)*
passenger side	**el lado del pasajero** *(ehl 'lah-doh dehl pah-sah-'heh-roh)*
rear seat	**el asiento trasero** *(ehl ah-see-'ehn-toh trah-'seh-roh)*

Try Some

Name three pieces of grading equipment that end with the letters **-adora.**

_____

_____

_____

Quick! Translate the following:

la manguera _____

la rueda _____

el volante _____

Working Words: LAYING THE FOUNDATION

Begin this section by mentioning what is being built:

It's (the)...	**Es...** *(ehs)*
basement	**el sótano** *(ehl 'soh-tah-noh)*
building	**el edificio** *(ehl eh-dee-'fee-see-oh)*
garage	**el garaje** *(ehl gah-'rah-heh)*
house	**la casa** *(lah 'kah-sah)*
room	**el cuarto** *(ehl 'kwahr-toh)*

Now see the words for other dwellings:

apartment	**el apartamento** *(ehl ah-pahr-tah-'mehn-toh)*
cabin	**la cabaña** *(lah kah-'bahn-yah)*
complex	**el complejo** *(ehl kohm-'pleh-hoh)*
condominium	**el condominio** *(ehl kohn-doh-'mee-nee-oh)*
farm house	**la granja** *(lah 'grahn-hah)*
high-rise	**el edificio de muchos pisos** *(ehl eh-dee-'fee-see-oh deh 'moo-chohs 'pee-sohs)*
townhouse	**la casa de ciudad** *(lah 'kah-sah deh see-oo-'dahd)*

Now mention other features that require cement work:

Work on (the)...	**Trabaje en...** *(trah-'bah-heh ehn)*
curb	**el bordillo** *(ehl bohr-'dee-yoh)*
deck	**el piso exterior** *(ehl 'pee-soh ex-'teh-ree-ohr)*
driveway	**el camino de entrada** *(ehl kah-'mee-noh deh ehn-'trah-dah)*
fence	**la cerca** *(lah 'sehr-kah)*
floor	**el piso** *(ehl 'pee-soh)*
ground floor	**el primer piso** *(ehl pree-'mehr 'pee-soh)*
patio	**el patio** *(ehl 'pah-tee-oh)*
porch	**el pórtico** *(ehl 'pohr-tee-koh)*
sidewalk	**la acera** *(lah ah-'seh-rah)*
stairs	**las escaleras** *(lahs ehs-kah-'leh-rahs)*
steps	**los escalones** *(los ehs-kah-'loh-nehs)*
stoop	**el umbral** *(ehl oom-'brahl)*
subfloor	**el subpiso** *(ehl soob-'pee-soh)*
wall	**el muro/la pared** *(ehl 'moo-roh/lah pah-'rehd)*

Foundation work has begun, so make your statements clear:

(The) _____ goes here. _____ **va aquí.** *(vah ah-'kee)*

base	**la base** *(la 'bah-seh)*
form	**el molde** *(ehl 'mohl-deh)*
joint	**la junta** *(lah 'hoon-tah)*
pad	**la plataforma** *(lah plah-tah-'fohr-mah)*
slab	**la losa** *(lah 'loh-sah)*
template	**la plancha** *(lah 'plahn-chah)*

It needs (the)...	**Necesita...** *(neh-seh-'see-tah)*
anchor	**el anclaje** *(ehl ahn-'klah-heh)*
bar	**la barra** *(lah 'bah-rrah)*
barrier	**la barrera** *(lah bah-'rreh-rah)*
block	**el bloque** *(ehl 'bloh-keh)*
brace	**la riostra** *(lah ree-'ohs-trah)*
brick	**el ladrillo** *(ehl lah-'dree-yoh)*
buttress	**el contrafrente** *(ehl kohn-trah-'frehn-teh)*
caisson	**el cajón** *(ehl kah-'hohn)*
chicken wire	**el alambre de gallinero** *(ehl ah-'lahm-breh deh gah-yee-'neh-roh)*

drainpipe	**el tubo de drenaje** *(ehl 'too-boh deh dreh-'nah-heh)*
fitting	**el acoplamiento** *(ehl ah-koh-plah-mee-'ehn-toh)*
footing	**la zapata/el cimiento** *(lah sah-'pah-tah/ehl see-mee-'ehn-toh)*
girder	**la viga maestra** *(lah 'vee-gah mah-'ehs-trah)*
hook	**el gancho** *(ehl 'gahn-choh)*
insulation	**el aislamiento** *(ehl ah-ees-lah-mee-'ehn-toh)*
pilaster	**la pilastra** *(lah pee-'lahs-trah)*
pilon	**la columna** *(lah koh-'loom-nah)*
rebar	**la varilla** *(lah vah-'ree-yah)*
retaining wall	**el muro de apoyo** *(ehl 'moo-roh deh ah-'poh-yoh)*
sandbag	**el saco de arena** *(ehl 'sah-koh deh ah-'reh-nah)*
shoring	**el apuntamiento** *(ehl ah-poon-tah-mee-'ehn-toh)*
sill plate	**la placa de solera** *(lah 'plah-kah deh soh-'leh-rah)*
stud	**el montante/el barrote** *(ehl mohn-'tahn-teh/ehl bah-'rroh-teh)*
tie	**el amarre** *(ehl ah-'mah-rreh)*
weep hole	**el hueco para drenaje** *(ehl 'hweh-koh 'pah-rah dreh-'nah-heh)*
wire mesh	**la malla de alambre** *(lah 'mah-yah deh ah-'lahm-breh)*

When working on the foundation, use the appropriate equipment and materials:

Unload (the)…	**Descargue…** *(dehs-'kahr-geh)*
chipper	**la melladora/la cinceladora** *(lah meh-yah-'doh-rah/lah seen-seh-lah-'doh-rah))*
crusher	**la trituradora** *(lah tree-too-rah-'doh-rah)*
cutter	**la cortadora** *(lah kohr-tah-'doh-rah)*
driller	**la perforadora** *(lah pehr-foh-rah-'doh-rah)*
grinder	**la moledora** *(lah moh-leh-'doh-rah)*
spreader	**la esparcidora** *(lah ehs-pahr-see-'doh-rah)*

Carry (the)…	**Lleve …** *('yeh-veh)*

cement	**el cemento** *(seh-'mehn-toh)*
mixture	**la mezcla** *(lah 'mehs-klah)*
mortar	**la argamasa** *(lah ahr-gah-'mah-sah)*
sand	**la arena** *(lah ah-'reh-nah)*
water	**el agua** *(ehl 'ah-gwah)*

Do you have (the)...?	¿Tiene...? *(tee-'eh-neh)*
mallet	**el mazo** *(ehl 'mah-soh)*
mixer	**la mezcladora** *(lah mehs-klah-'doh-rah)*
pick	**el pico** *(ehl 'pee-koh)*
pump	**la bomba** *(lah 'bohm-bah)*
rake	**el rastrillo** *(ehl rahs-'tree-yoh)*
shovel	**la pala** *(lah 'pah-lah)*
sledge	**la almádena** *(lah ahl-'mah-deh-nah)*
wheelbarrow	**la carretilla** *(lah kah-rreh-'tee-yah)*

Give me (the)...	Deme... *('deh-meh)*
brick-cutting saw	**la sierra para cortar ladrillos** *(lah see-'eh-rrah 'pah-rah kohr-'tahr lah-'dree-yos)*
bush hammer	**el martillo para texturizar** *(ehl mahr-'tee-yoh 'pah-rah tehks-too-ree-'sahr)*
cement saw	**la sierra para cortar cemento** *(lah see-'eh-rrah 'pah-rah kohr-'tahr seh-'mehn-toh)*
chisel	**el cincel** *(ehl seen-'sehl)*
darby	**la paleta de madera** *(lah pah-'leh-tah deh mah-'deh-rah)*
edger	**la llana para bordes** *(lah 'yah-nah 'pah-rah 'bohr-dehs)*
finishing broom	**el cepillo de acabado** *(ehl seh-'pee-yoh deh ah-kah-'bah-doh)*
finishing trowel	**la llana para acabado** *(lah 'yah-nah 'pah-rah ah-kah-'bah-do)*
groover	**la ranuradora** *(lah rah-noo-rah-'doh-rah)*
hawk	**el esparavel** *(ehl ehs-pah-rah-'vehl)*
joint compound	**la pasta para las uniones** *(lah 'pahs-tah 'pah-rah lahs oo-nee-'oh-nehs)*
jointer	**el marcador de juntas** *(ehl mahr-kah-'dohr deh 'hoon-tahs)*
mason's trowel	**la llana de madera** *(lah 'yah-nah deh mah-'deh-rah)*
masonry hammer	**la maceta** *(lah mah-'seh-tah)*
steel trowel	**la paleta de acero** *(lah pah-'leh-tah deh ah-'seh-roh)*
stretcher	**el tensor** *(ehl 'tehn-sohr)*
tamper	**el pisón** *(ehl pee-'sohn)*
tie	**el sujetador** *(ehl soo-heh-tah-'dohr)*
tongs	**las tenazas** *(lahs teh-'nah-sahs)*

I have (the)...	**Tengo...** *('tehn-goh)*
_____ float	**la llana** _____ *(lah 'yah-nah)*

rubber	**de goma** *(deh 'goh-mah)*
magnesium	**metálica** *(meh-'tah-lee-kah)*
bull	**mecánica** *(meh-'kah-nee-kah)*

It has a _____ finish.	**Tiene acabado de** _____. *(tee-'eh-neh ah-kah-'bah-doh deh)*

trowel	**paleta** *(pah-'leh-tah)*
broom	**escoba** *(ehs-'koh-bah)*
salt	**sal** *(sahl)*

And the names for minerals and chemicals?

Use...	**Use...** *('oo-seh)*

alkaline	**el alcalino** *(ehl ahl-kah-'lee-noh)*
gypsum	**el yeso** *(ehl 'yeh-soh)*
lime	**la cal** *(lah kahl)*
salt	**la sal** *(lah sahl)*
sulfate	**el sulfato** *(ehl sool-'fah-toh)*

Just a Suggestion

As always, listen for words that are similar to English:

concrete	**el concreto** *(ehl kohn-'kreh-toh)*
pavement	**el pavimento** *(ehl pah-vee-'mehn-toh)*
cement	**el cemento** *(ehl seh-'mehn-toh)*

It's _____ cement.	**Es el cemento** _____. *(ehs ehl seh-'mehn-toh)*

structural	**estructural** *(ehs-trook-too-'rahl)*
reinforced	**reforzado** *(reh-fohr-'sah-doh)*
sulphate resistant	**resistente al sulfato** *(reh-sees-'tehn-teh ahl sool-'fah-toh)*

Try Some

Circle the one word that doesn't belong with the others:

el cincel, el martillo, el sótano
el taladro, la argamasa, el cemento
el piso, el pico, la pared

Now translate these new words into English (it's easy).

el experto	**el condominio**
la mansión	**el especialista**
el dúplex	**el profesional**

Working Words: ON THE JOB SITE

As you break ground, identify everyone who's been working on the project. Begin with those words you already know:

He's (the)...   **Es...** *(ehs)*

builder	el **constructor** *(ehl kohns-trook-'tohr)*
contractor	el **contratista** *(ehl kohn-trah-'tees-tah)*
inspector	el **inspector** *(ehl eens-pehk-'tohr)*
general contractor	el **contratista principal** *(ehl kohn-trah-'tees-tah preen-see-'pahl)*
owner	el **dueño** *(ehl 'dweh-nyoh)*
project manager	el **gerente del proyecto** *(ehl heh-'rehn-teh dehl proh-'yehk-toh)*
sub-contractor	el **subcontratista** *(ehl soob-kohn-trah-'tees-tah)*
supervisor	el **supervisor** *(ehl soo-pehr-vee-'sohr)*
worker, laborer	el **obrero** *(ehl oh-'breh-roh)*

Now name the land, grading, or foundation experts:

architect	el **arquitecto** *(ehl ahr-kee-'tehk-toh)*
designer	el **diseñador** *(ehl dee-seh-nyah-'dohr)*
electrician	el **electricista** *(ehl eh-lehk-tree-'sees-tah)*
engineer	el **ingeniero** *(ehl een-heh-nee-'eh-roh)*

geologist	**el geólogo** *(ehl heh-'oh-loh-goh)*
plumber	**el fontanero/el plomero** *(ehl fohn-tah-'neh-roh/ehl ploh-'meh-roh)*
surveyor	**el agrimensor** *(ehl ah-gree-mehn-'sohr)*
technician	**el técnico** *(ehl 'tehk-nee-koh)*

You'll need plenty of words as the grading project gets under way. Some were presented earlier:

The _____ goes there.   _____ **va allí.** *(vah ah-'yee)*

canal	**el canal** *(ehl kah-'nahl)*
drainage	**el drenaje** *(ehl dreh-'nah-heh)*
hole	**el hoyo** *(ehl 'oh-yoh)*
load	**la carga** *(lah 'kahr-gah)*
marker	**el marcador** *(ehl mahr-kah-'dohr)*
post	**el poste** *(ehl 'pohs-teh)*
slope	**la cuesta** *(lah 'kwehs-tah)*
stake	**la estaca** *(lah ehs-'tah-kah)*
string	**la cuerda** *(lah 'kwehr-dah)*
trench	**la zanja** *(lah 'sahn-hah)*
walk board	**la tabla para caminar** *(lah 'tah-blah 'pah-rah kah-mee-'nahr)*

Where's the...   **¿Dónde está...?** *('dohn-deh ehs-'tah)*

gas line	**la línea de gas** *(lah 'lee-neh-ah deh gahs)*
power cable	**el cable eléctrico** *(ehl 'kah-bleh eh-'lehk-tree-koh)*
sewage system	**el alcantarillado** *(ehl ahl-kahn-tah-ree-'yah-doh)*
sewer	**la alcantarilla** *(lah ahl-kahn-tah-'ree-yah)*
water main	**la cañería matriz** *(lah kah-nyeh-'ree-ah mah-'trees)*
water pipe	**la tubería de agua** *(lah too-beh-'ree-ah deh 'ah-gwah)*

The word **nivel**—*nee-'vehl* (*level*) is also used a lot in grading and foundation work:

at sea level	**a nivel del mar** *(ah nee-'vehl dehl mahr)*
on grade	**a nivel** *(ah nee-'vehl)*
water table	**el nivel de agua** *(ehl nee-'vehl deh 'ah-gwah)*

And if problems with the project arise, look at these:

There's trouble with (the)…	**Hay problemas con…** *('ah-ee proh-'bleh-mahs kohn)*
age	**la edad** *(lah eh-'dahd)*
condition	**la condición/el estado** *(lah kohn-dee-see-'ohn/ehl ehs-'tah-doh)*
movement	**el movimiento** *(ehl moh-vee-mee-'ehn-toh)*
shape	**la forma** *(lah 'fohr-mah)*
strength	**la resistencia** *(lah reh-sees-'tehn-see-ah)*
support	**el apoyo** *(ehl ah-'poh-yoh)*

There are…	**Hay…** *('ah-ee)*

bubbles	**burbujas** *(boor-'boo-hahs)*
bumps	**bultos** *('bool-tohs)*
cracks	**grietas** *(gree-'eh-tahs)*
holes	**hoyos/huecos** *('oh-yohs/'hweh-kohs)*
leaks	**fugas** *('foo-gahs)*

It's…	**Está…** *(ehs-'tah)*

bent	**doblado** *(doh-'blah-doh)*
broken	**quebrado** *(keh-'brah-doh)*
cracked	**agrietado** *(ah-gree-eh-'tah-doh)*
damaged	**dañado** *(dah-'nyah-doh)*
defective	**defectuoso** *(deh-fehk-too-'oh-soh)*
eroded	**erosionado** *(eh-roh-see-oh-'nah-doh)*
ruined	**arruinado** *(ah-roo-ee-'nah-doh)*
stained	**manchado** *(mahn-'chah-doh)*

Just a Suggestion

When you're hauling or towing, use the word **remolque** *(reh-'mohl-keh)*:

towing	**el remolque** *(ehl reh-'mohl-keh)*
tow hook	**el gancho de remolque** *(ehl 'gahn-choh deh reh-'mohl-keh)*
tow line	**la cuerda de remolque** *(lah 'kwehr-dah deh reh-'mohl-keh)*

Try Some

Translate these sentences into English:

La zanja va allí. _____

Hable con la dueña. _____

¿Dónde está el arquitecto? _____

Connect the words that go together best:

húmedo	**agujero**
sal	**quebrado**
hueco	**mojado**
dañado	**piedra**
roca	**sulfato**

 ## Working Words: DESCRIBING THE JOB

Look! It'll be easier if you learn descriptions as opposites:

hard	**duro** *('doo-roh)*	↔ soft	**blando** *('blahn-doh)*
open	**abierto** *(ah-bee-'ehr-toh)*	↔ closed	**cerrado** *(seh-'rrah-doh)*
thick	**grueso** *(groo-'eh-soh)*	↔ narrow	**estrecho** *(ehs-'treh-choh)*
straight	**recto** *('rehk-toh)*	↔ crooked	**torcido** *(tohr-'see-doh)*
better	**mejor** *(meh-'hohr)*	↔ worse	**peor** *(peh-'ohr)*
deep	**profundo** *(proh-'foon-doh)*	↔ shallow	**bajo** *('bah-hoh)*
wet	**mojado** *(moh-'hah-doh)*	↔ dry	**seco** *('seh-koh)*
dull	**romo** *('roh-moh)*	↔ sharp	**afilado** *(ah-fee-'lah-doh)*
empty	**vacío** *(vah-'see-oh)*	↔ full	**lleno** *('yeh-noh)*
rough	**áspero** *('ahs-peh-roh)*	↔ smooth	**liso** *('lee-soh)*
tight	**apretado** *(ah-preh-'tah-doh)*	↔ loose	**flojo** *('floh-hoh)*
wide	**ancho** *('ahn-choh)*	↔ narrow	**estrecho** *(ehs-'treh-choh)*
heavy	**pesado** *(peh-'sah-doh)*	↔ light	**ligero** *(lee-'heh-roh)*
clear	**claro** *('klah-roh)*	↔ dark	**oscuro** *(ohs-'koo-roh)*
real	**verdadero** *(vehr-dah-'deh-roh)*	↔ fake	**falso** *('fahl-soh)*

| loud | **ruidoso** *(rwee-'doh-soh)* | ↔ | quiet | **quieto** *(kee-'eh-toh)* |
| sloppy | **chapucero** *(chah-poo-'seh-roh)* | ↔ | neat | **ordenado** *(ohr-deh-'nah-doh)* |

Where something is will be determined by these words:

high	**alto** *('ahl-toh)*	↔	low	**bajo** *('bah-hoh)*
above	**encima** *(ehn-'see-mah)*	↔	under	**debajo** *(deh-'bah-hoh)*
up	**arriba** *(ah-'rre-bah)*	↔	down	**abajo** *(ah-'bah-hoh)*
near	**cerca** *('sehr-kah)*	↔	far	**lejos** *('leh-hohs)*
backward	**hacia atrás** *('ah-see-ah ah-'trahs)*	↔	forward	**hacia adelante** *('ah-see-ah ah-deh-'lahn-teh)*

Grading and foundation projects will also need specialized descriptions:

level	**a nivel** *(ah nee-'vehl)*	↔	sloped	**inclinado** *(een-klee-'nah-doh)*
partial	**parcial** *(pahr-see-'ahl)*	↔	complete	**completo** *(kohm-'pleh-toh)*
solid	**sólido** *('soh-lee-doh)*	↔	hollow	**hueco** *('hweh-koh)*
even	**igual** *(ee-'gwahl)*	↔	uneven	**desigual** *(deh-see-'gwahl)*
flat	**llano** *('yah-noh)*	↔	steep	**empinado** *(ehm-pee-'nah-doh)*
temporary	**provisional** *(proh-vee-see-oh-'nahl)*	↔	permanent	**permanente** *(pehr-mah-'nehn-teh)*

Keep looking for patterns. For example, the prefixes **in-** *(een)* and **des-** *(dehs)* in Spanish imply *not*:

correct	**correcto** *(koh-'rrehk-toh)*
incorrect	**incorrecto** *(een-koh-'rrehk-toh)*
stable	**estable** *(ehs-'tah-bleh)*
unstable	**inestable** *(een-ehs-'tah-bleh)*
comfortable	**cómodo** *('koh-moh-doh)*
uncomfortable	**incómodo** *(een-'koh-moh-doh)*
covered	**tapado** *(tah-'pah-doh)*
uncovered	**destapado** *(dehs-tah-'pah-doh)*
stuck	**pegado** *(peh-gah-doh)*
unstuck	**despegado** *(dehs-peh-'gah-doh)*
loaded	**cargado** *(kahr-'gah-doh)*
unloaded	**descargado** *(dehs-kahr-'gah-doh)*

Now be a bit more detailed as you describe everything:

It's...	**Es.../Está...** *(ehs/ehs-'tah)*
adjustable	**ajustable** *(ah-hoos-'tah-bleh)*
continuous	**continuo** *(kohn-'tee-noo-oh)*
embedded	**incrustado** *(een-kroos-'tah-doh)*
enclosed	**encerrado** *(ehn-seh-'rrah-doh)*
expansive	**expansivo** *(ex-pahn-'see-voh)*
exposed	**expuesto** *(ex-'pwehs-toh)*
muddy	**lodoso** *(loh-'doh-soh)*
organized	**organizado** *(ohr-gah-nee-'sah-doh)*
perforated	**perforado** *(pehr-foh-'rah-doh)*
prefabricated	**prefabricado** *(preh-fah-bree-'kah-doh)*
protected	**protegido** *(proh-teh-'hee-doh)*
removable	**desmontable** *(dehs-mohn-'tah-bleh)*
rocky	**rocoso** *(roh-'koh-soh)*
symmetrical	**simétrico** *(see-'meh-tree-koh)*
underground	**subterráneo** *(soob-teh-'rrah-neh-oh)*

If water is a concern, use these descriptive words:

Is it...?	**¿Es/Está...?** *(ehs/ehs-'tah)*
dry	**seco** *('seh-koh)*
frozen	**congelado** *(kohn-heh-'lah-doh)*
moist	**húmedo** *('oo-meh-doh)*
rustproof	**inoxidable** *(ee-noh-ksee-'dah-bleh)*
soaked	**empapado** *(ehm-pah-'pah-doh)*
waterproof	**impermeable** *(eem-pehr-meh-'ah-bleh)*
watertight	**hermético** *(ehr-'meh-tee-koh)*
wet	**mojado** *(moh-'hah-doh)*

Just a Suggestion

Practice putting descriptive words AFTER the objects, instead of before:

fine	**fino** *('fee-noh)*	➤	<u>fine</u> material	**material <u>fino</u>** *(mah-teh-ree-'ahl 'fee-noh)*
used	**usado** *(oo-'sah-doh)*	➤	<u>used</u> car	**carro <u>usado</u>** *('kah-rroh oo-'sah-doh)*
lost	**perdido** *(pehr-'dee-doh)*	➤	<u>lost</u> money	**dinero <u>perdido</u>** *(dee-'neh-roh pehr-'dee-doh)*

Try Some

What's the opposite?

ancho   _____

correcto   _____

ruidoso   _____

seco   _____

alto   _____

vacío   _____

Tricks ahead: the following words are identical to English in spelling, but their stresses and pronunciations are different:

natural *('nah-too-rahl)*
interior *(een-teh-ree-'ohr)*
total *(toh-'tahl)*
irregular *(ee-rreh-goo-'lahr)*
exterior *(ex-teh-ree-'ohr)*
simple *('seem-pleh)*
normal *(nohr-'mahl)*

regular *(reh-goo-'lahr)*
terrible *(teh-'rree-bleh)*
artificial *(ahr-tee-fee-see-'ahl)*
rural *(roo-'rahl)*
original *(oh-ree-hee-'nahl)*
lateral *(lah-teh-'rahl)*
probable *(proh-'bah-bleh)*

Working Words: TECHNICAL DETAIL

Here are some technical words that are needed during grading or foundation work. Some you learned earlier:

What's (the)…?   **¿Cuál es…?** *('kwahl ehs)*

measurement   **la medida** *(lah meh-'dee-dah)*
height   **la altura** *(lah ahl-'too-rah)*
depth   **la profundidad** *(lah proh-foon-dee-'dahd)*
length   **el largo** *(ehl 'lahr-goh)*
distance   **la distancia** *(lah dees-'tahn-see-ah)*
width   **el ancho** *(ehl 'ahn-choh)*
temperature   **la temperatura** *(lah tehm-peh-rah-'too-rah)*
size   **el tamaño** *(ehl tah-'mahn-yoh)*

grade	el **grado** *(ehl 'grah-doh)*
angle	el **ángulo** *(ehl 'ahn-goo-loh)*
volume	el **volumen** *(ehl voh-'loo-mehn)*
percent	el **porcentaje** *(ehl pohr-sehn-'tah-heh)*
load	la **carga** *(lah 'kahr-gah)*
flow	el **flujo** *(ehl 'floo-hoh)*
force	la **fuerza** *(lah 'fwehr-sah)*
pressure	la **presión** *(lah preh-see-'ohn)*
thickness	el **grueso** *(ehl groo-'eh-soh)*
amount	la **cantidad** *(lah kahn-tee-'dahd)*
count	la **cuenta** *(lah 'kwehn-tah)*
ratio	la **proporción** *(lah proh-pohr-see-'ohn)*
speed	la **velocidad** *(lah veh-loh-see-'dahd)*
circumference	la **circunferencia** *(lah seer-koon-feh-'rehn-see-ah)*
time	la **hora** *(lah 'oh-rah)*

Use these phrases to cover shapes:

| It's… | **Es/está…** *(ehs/ehs-'tah)* |

U-shaped	**en forma de U** *(ehn 'fohr-mah deh oo)*
L-shaped	**en forma de L** *(ehn 'fohr-mah deh 'eh-leh)*
oval	**oval** *(oh-'vahl)*
round	**redondo** *(reh-'dohn-doh)*
square	**cuadrado** *(kwah-'drah-doh)*
circular	**circular** *(seer-koo-'lahr)*
conical	**cónico** *('koh-nee-koh)*
curved	**curvo** *('koor-voh)*
cylindrical	**cilíndrico** *(see-'leen-dree-koh)*
straight	**recto** *('rehk-toh)*

Use these examples to create your own set of measurements:

2 inches above	**dos pulgadas por encima** *(dohs pool-'gah-dahs pohr ehn-'see-mah)*
2 inches below	**dos pulgadas por debajo** *(dohs pool-'gah-dahs pohr deh-'bah-hoh)*
2 inches thick	**dos pulgadas de grosor** *(dohs pool-'gah-dahs deh groh-'sohr)*
2 inches high	**dos pulgadas de alto** *(dohs pool-'gah-dahs deh 'ahl-toh)*
2 inches by 4 inches	**dos por cuatro pulgadas** *(dohs pohr 'kwah-troh pool-'gah-dahs)*

twice	**dos veces** *(dohs 'veh-sehs)*
one at a time	**una a la vez** *('oo-nah ah lah vehs)*
once again	**una vez más** *('oo-nah vehs mahs)*
a half	**una mitad** *('oo-nah mee-'tahd)*
a quarter	**un cuarto** *(oon 'kwahr-toh)*
a third	**un tercio** *(oon 'tehr-see-oh)*

How technical do you want to get?

HP	**caballos de fuerza** *(kah-'bah-yohs deh 'fwehr-sah)*
PSI	**libras por pulgada cuadrada** *('lee-brahs pohr pool-'gah-dah kwah-'drah-dah)*
MPH	**millas por hora** *('mee-yahs pohr 'oh-rah)*

Just a Suggestion

Don't forget the metric system:

5/8 mi.	=	**el kilómetro** *(ehl kee-'loh-meh-troh)*
2.2 lbs.	=	**el kilógramo** *(ehl kee-'loh-grah-moh)*
32° F	=	0° C *('seh-roh 'grah-doh 'sehl-see-oos)*

Try Some

Write these out in Spanish:

ht.   _____

½   _____

lb.   _____

psi   _____

2 × 6   _____

Working Words: ON-SITE ACTIONS

The following are Spanish verbs that help to put all of this vocabulary into action. To practice, use this expression:

We're going...   **Vamos a...** *('vah-mohs ah)*

to build	**construir** *(kohns-troo-'eer)*
to bury	**enterrar** *(ehn-teh-'rrahr)*
to channel	**canalizar** *(kah-nah-lee-'sahr)*
to compact	**compactar** *(kohm-pahk-'tahr)*
to cover	**cubrir** *(koo-'breer)*
to crush	**triturar** *(tree-too-'rahr)*
to cut	**cortar** *(kohr-'tahr)*
to dig	**excavar** *(ex-kah-'vahr)*
to dump	**botar** *(boh-'tahr)*
to filter	**filtrar** *(feel-'trahr)*
to float	**flotar** *(floh-'tahr)*
to grade	**nivelar** *(nee-veh-'lahr)*
to grind	**moler** *(moh-'lehr)*
to haul	**transportar** *(trahns-pohr-'tahr)*
to hold	**sostener** *(sohs-teh-'nehr)*
to join	**juntar** *(hoon-'tahr)*
to lay foundation	**cementar** *(seh-mehn-'tahr)*
to level	**nivelar** *(nee-veh-'lahr)*
to mark	**marcar** *(mahr-'kahr)*
to measure	**medir** *(meh-'deer)*
to mix	**mezclar** *(mehs-'klahr)*
to mount	**montar** *(mohn-'tahr)*
to plane	**enrasar** *(ehn-rah-'sahr)*
to pour	**verter/echar** *(vehr-'tehr/eh-'chahr)*
to prep	**dejar listo** *(deh-'hahr 'lees-toh)*
to pump	**bombear** *(bohm-beh-'ahr)*
to reinforce	**reforzar** *(reh-fohr-'sahr)*
to set up	**erigir** *(eh-ree-'heer)*
to shore up	**apuntalar** *(ah-poon-tah-'lahr)*
to smooth out	**alisar** *(ah-lee-'sahr)*
to soak	**empapar** *(ehm-pah-'pahr)*
to spread	**esparcir** *(ehs-pahr-'seer)*
to sprinkle	**rociar** *(roh-see-'ahr)*

to stamp (crush)	**triturar** *(tree-too-'rahr)*
to stamp (cut out)	**troquelar** *(troh-keh-'lahr)*
to stamp (pound)	**hollar** *(oh-'yahr)*
to step	**pisar** *(pee-'sahr)*
to support	**apoyar** *(ah-poh-'yahr)*
to surround	**rodear** *(roh-deh-'ahr)*
to survey	**medir** *(meh-'deer)*
to tape	**encintar** *(ehn-seen-'tahr)*
to tie	**atar** *(ah-'tahr)*
to trench	**atrincherar** *(ah-treen-cheh-'rahr)*
to trowel	**paletear** *(pah-leh-teh-'ahr)*
to ventilate	**ventilar** *(vehn-tee-'lahr)*
to vibrate	**vibrar** *(vee-'brahr)*
to water down	**regar** *(reh-'gahr)*
to waterproof	**impermeabilizar** *(eem-pehr-meh-ah-bee-lee-'sahr)*
to wrap	**forrar** *(foh-'rrahr)*

Work on those other actions that you'll need right away:

I want…	**Quiero…** *(kee-'eh-roh)*
to calculate	**calcular** *(kahl-koo-'lahr)*
to design	**diseñar** *(dee-seh-'nyahr)*
to draw	**dibujar** *(dee-boo-'hahr)*
to examine	**examinar** *(ehk-sah-mee-'nahr)*
to guess	**suponer** *(soo-poh-'nehr)*
to plan	**planear** *(plah-neh-'ahr)*
to test	**probar** *(proh-'bahr)*

Remember the verbs with **-se** *(seh)* at the end? **-Se** indicates self-action.

It's going…	**Va a…** *(vah ah)*
to crack	**agrietarse** *(ah-gree-eh-'tahr-seh)*
to overlap	**superponerse** *(soo-pehr-poh-'nehr-seh)*
to settle	**depositarse** *(deh-poh-see-'tahr-seh)*
to shift	**desplazarse** *(dehs-plah-'sahr-seh)*
to sink	**hundirse** *(oon-'deer-seh)*

Notice how similar are the English and the Spanish in these:

to absorb	**absorber** *(ahb-sohr-'behr)*
to adjust	**ajustar** *(ah-hoos-'tahr)*
to indicate	**indicar** *(een-dee-'kahr)*
to insist	**insistir** *(een-sees-'teer)*
to inspect	**inspeccionar** *(eens-pehk-see-oh-'nahr)*
to install	**instalar** *(eens-tah-'lahr)*
to permit	**permitir** *(pehr-mee-'teer)*
to prohibit	**prohibir** *(proh-ee-'beer)*
to recommend	**recomendar** *(reh-koh-mehn-'dahr)*
to reduce	**reducir** *(reh-doo-'seer)*

Add your own words to this model:

It needs ...	**Necesita...** *(neh-seh-'see-tah)*
to withstand	**aguantar** *(ah-gwahn-'tahr)*
to harden	**endurecer** *(ehn-doo-reh-sehr)*
to flow	**fluir** *(floo-'eer)*

And keep memorizing words in pairs with opposite meanings:

to break	↓	**romper** *(rohm-'pehr)*
to repair	↑	**reparar** *(reh-pah-'rahr)*
to pull out	↓	**sacar** *(sah-'kahr)*
to insert	↑	**meter** *(meh-'tehr)*
to begin	↓	**comenzar** *(koh-mehn-'sahr)*
to finish	↑	**acabar** *(ah-kah-'bahr)*
to add	↓	**añadir** *(ah-nyah-'deer)*
to remove	↑	**quitar** *(kee-'tahr)*
to fill	↓	**llenar** *(yeh-'nahr)*
to empty	↑	**vaciar** *(vah-see-'ahr)*

And here's another pattern in Spanish verbs:

to cover	↓	**tapar** *(tah-'pahr)*
to uncover	↑	**destapar** *(dehs-tah-'pahr)*

| to fold | ↓ | **doblar** *(doh-'blahr)* |
| to unfold | ↑ | **desdoblar** *(dehs-doh-'blahr)* |

| to plug in | ↓ | **enchufar** *(ehn-choo-'fahr)* |
| to unplug | ↑ | **desenchufar** *(deh-sehn-choo-'fahr)* |

| to hook | ↓ | **enganchar** *(ehn-gahn-'chahr)* |
| to unhook | ↑ | **desenganchar** *(deh-sehn-gahn-'chahr)* |

Try Some

Fill in a Spanish verb with an opposite meaning:

enterrar _____

reducir _____

permitir _____

desdoblar _____

comenzar _____

Grammar Time

To express your thoughts in Spanish, you'll need to learn as many verbal tenses as possible. We'll start with the present progressive tense because it refers to what's happening <u>right now</u>. The present progressive is similar to our *-ing* form in English. You will have to change the base verb ending slightly, and then combine the new form with the four forms of the verb **estar** *(ehs-'tahr)*: **estoy** *(ehs-'toh-ee)*, **está** *(ehs-'tah)*, **están** *(ehs-'tahn)*, **estamos** *(ehs-'tah-mohs)*. The **-ar** verbs change to **-ando**, while the **-er** and **-ir** verbs become **-iendo**. Study these examples:

to walk	**caminar** *(kah-mee-'nahr)*
walking	**caminando** *(kah-mee-'nahn-doh)*
We're walking to work.	**Estamos caminando al trabajo.** *(ehs-'tah-mohs kah-mee-'nahn-doh ahl trah-'bah-hoh)*

to eat	**com<u>er</u>** *(koh-'mehr)*
eating	**com<u>iendo</u>** *(koh-mee-'ehn-doh)*
The boss is eating.	**El jefe está comiendo.** *(ehl 'heh-feh ehs-'tah koh-mee-'ehn-doh)*

to write	**escrib<u>ir</u>** *(ehs-kree-'beer)*
writing	**escrib<u>iendo</u>** *(ehs-kree-bee-'ehn-doh)*
I'm writing the number.	**Estoy escribiendo el número.** *(ehs-'toh-ee ehs-kree-bee-'ehn-doh ehl 'noo-meh-roh)*

Grammar Time

Learn the differences between the <u>affirmative</u>, <u>negative</u>, and <u>interrogative</u> forms in Spanish. Notice the word order in each one:

Affirmative

| The boss is eating. | **El jefe está comiendo.** *(ehl 'heh-feh ehs-'tah koh-mee-'ehn-doh)* |

Negative

| The boss isn't eating. | **El jefe no está comiendo.** *(ehl 'heh-feh noh ehs-'tah koh-mee-'ehn-doh)* |

Interrogative

| Is the boss eating? | **¿Está comiendo el jefe?** *(ehs-'tah koh-mee-'ehn-doh ehl 'heh-feh)* |

Try Some

Now change these base verbs to the present progressive tense:

caminar	<u>caminando</u>
manejar	_____
vender	_____
recibir	_____
seguir	_____

One-Liners

If you usually get lost when someone is speaking Spanish to you, just try to relax and do the best you can with the phrases below. They really help!

Do you understand?	**¿Entiende usted?** *(ehn-tee-'ehn-deh oos-'tehd)*
I don't understand.	**No entiendo.** *(noh ehn-tee-'ehn-doh)*
I understand.	**Yo comprendo.** *(yoh kohm-'prehn-doh)*
I don't know.	**No sé.** *(noh seh)*
I speak a little Spanish.	**Hablo poquito español.** *('ah-bloh poh-'kee-toh ehs-pah-'nyohl)*
I'm learning Spanish.	**Estoy aprendiendo español.** *(ehs-'toh-ee ah-prehn-dee-'ehn-doh ehs-pah-'nyohl)*

Culture Issues

As with every language, Spanish is full of informal idiomatic expressions. You'll probably hear the word **chingadera** *(cheen-gah-'deh-rah)* used a lot on construction sites throughout the Southwest. It is basically equivalent to *whatchamacallit*. The difference is that **chingadera** is a derivative of a dirty word, so be careful.

Structural Work
El trabajo estructural

(ehl trah-'bah-hoh ehs-trook-too-'rahl)

 Working Words: STRUCTURAL WORK

Interject these words related to structural projects whenever they are useful:

framework	**la armazón** *(lah ahr-mah-'sohn)*
flooring	**la instalación del piso** *(lah eens-tah-lah-see-'ohn dehl 'pee-soh)*
roofing	**la instalación del tejado** *(lah eens-tah-lah-see-'ohn dehl teh-'hah-doh)*
carpentry	**la carpintería** *(lah kahr-peen-teh-'ree-ah)*
welding	**la soldadura** *(lah sohl-dah-'doo-rah)*
masonry	**la mampostería** *(lah mahm-pohs-teh-'ree-ah)*
mounting	**el montaje** *(ehl mohn-'tah-heh)*
reinforcement	**el refuerzo** *(ehl reh-foo-'ehr-soh)*
support	**el soporte** *(ehl soh-'pohr-teh)*

Now be a bit more specific:

Look at (the)...	**Mira...** *('mee-rah)*
anchoring	**el anclaje** *(ehl ahn-'klah-heh)*
backing	**el respaldo** *(ehl rehs-'pahl-doh)*
barrier	**la barrera** *(lah bah-'rreh-rah)*
base	**la base** *(lah 'bah-seh)*
blocking	**el bloqueo** *(ehl bloh-'keh-oh)*
brace	**la abrazadera/la riostra** *(lah ah-brah-sah-'deh-rah/lah ree-'ohs-trah)*
buttress	**el contrafuerte** *(ehl kohn-trah-'fwehr-teh)*

cap	**la corona** *(lah koh-'roh-nah)*
clip	**la sujetadora** *(lah soo-heh-tah-'doh-rah)*
column	**la columna** *(lah koh-'loom-nah)*
connector	**el conector/la conexión** *(ehl koh-nehk-'tohr/lah koh-nehk-see-'ohn)*
crossbar	**el travesaño** *(ehl trah-veh-'sah-nyoh)*
fascia	**la fachada** *(lah fah-'chah-dah)*
footing	**la zapata** *(lah sah-'pah-tah)*
girder	**la viga** *(lah 'vee-gah)*
hanger	**el gancho** *(ehl 'gahn-choh)*
header	**la cabecera** *(lah kah-beh-'seh-rah)*
iron fitting	**el herraje** *(ehl eh-'rrah-heh)*
joint	**la unión** *(lah oo-nee-'ohn)*
joist	**la vigueta** *(lah vee-'geh-tah)*
lining	**el forro** *(ehl 'foh-rroh)*
molding	**el encofrado** *(ehl ehn-koh-'frah-doh)*
main beam	**la viga maestra** *(lah 'vee-gah mah-'ehs-trah)*
partition	**el tabique** *(ehl tah-'bee-keh)*
pillar	**el pilar** *(ehl pee-'lahr)*
pipe	**el tubo** *(ehl 'too-boh)*
plate	**la placa** *(lah 'plah-kah)*
post	**el poste** *(ehl 'pohs-teh)*
rail	**el riel** *(ehl ree-'ehl)*
rebar	**la varilla** *(lah vah-'ree-yah)*
retaining wall	**el muro de contención** *(ehl 'moo-roh deh kohn-tehn-see-'ohn)*
saddle	**el asiento** *(ehl ah-see-'ehn-toh)*
sheer panel	**la cabria** *(lah 'kah-bree-ah)*
shim	**la calza** *(lah 'kahl-sah)*
sill	**el antepecho** *(ehl ahn-teh-'peh-choh)*
stirrup	**el estribo** *(ehl ehs-'tree-boh)*
strap	**la cubrejunta** *(lah koo-breh-'hoon-tah)*
strong wall	**el muro fuerte** *(ehl 'moo-roh 'fwehr-teh)*
strut	**el puntal** *(ehl poon-'tahl)*
stud	**el barrote** *(ehl bah-'rroh-teh)*
tie	**la traviesa** *(lah trah-vee-'eh-sah)*
truss	**el armazón** *(ehl ahr-mah-'sohn)*
wedge	**la cuña** *(lah 'koo-nyah)*

The words **la viga** *(lah 'vee-gah)* and **la vigueta** *(lah vee-'geh-tah)* can refer to beams, girders, rafters, or joists, depending on where the speaker is from. Like all technical vocabulary, they are often used with other words to provide more descriptive detail:

load-bearing girder   **la viga de carga** *(lah 'vee-gah deh 'kahr-gah)*
reinforcement beam   **la vigueta de refuerzo** *(lah vee-'geh-tah deh reh-'fwehr-soh)*
temporary support joist   **la viga de soporte provisional** *(lah 'vee-gah deh soh-'pohr-teh proh-vee-see-oh-'nahl)*

Just a Suggestion

Don't forget those words that were used to lay the foundation:

foundation   **el cimiento** *(ehl see-mee-'ehn-toh)*
slab   **la losa** *(lah 'loh-sah)*
reinforced concrete   **el hormigón armado** *(ehl ohr-mee-'gohn ahr-'mah-doh)*

Try Some

Draw a picture of the following:

el tubo
la columna
el muro

Working Words: MORE STRUCTURAL MATERIALS

Move (the)...   **Mueva...** *('mweh-vah)*

raw lumber   **la madera en bruto** *(lah mah-'deh-rah ehn 'broo-toh)*
iron rebar   **la varilla de hierro** *(lah vah-'ree-yah deh ee-'eh-rroh)*
steel mesh   **la malla de acero** *(lah 'mah-yah deh ah-'seh-roh)*
cement block   **el bloque de hormigón** *(ehl 'bloh-keh deh ohr-mee-'gohn)*
sheet metal   **la plancha de metal** *(lah 'plahn-chah deh meh-'tahl)*

Structural work often includes the use of steel, or **el acero** *(ehl ah-'seh-roh)*:

corrugated steel	**el acero corrugado** *(ehl ah-'seh-roh koh-rroo-'gah-doh)*
steel beam	**la viga de acero** *(lah 'vee-gah deh ah-'seh-roh)*
steel plate	**la plancha de acero** *(lah 'plahn-chah deh ah-'seh-roh)*
steel tube	**el tubo de acero** *(ehl 'too-boh deh ah-'seh-roh)*
structural steel	**el acero estructural** *(ehl ah-'seh-roh ehs-trook-too-'rahl)*

Describe the shape of each steel beam required:

angle beam	**la viga angular** *(lah 'vee-gah ahn-goo-'lahr)*
channel beam	**la viga de canal** *(lah 'vee-gah deh kah-'nahl)*
I-beam	**la viga en I** *(lah 'vee-gah ehn ee)*
T-beam	**la viga en T** *(lah 'vee-gah ehn teh)*

As always, use English to name specialized materials. Note the word order:

ABS stabilizers	**los soportes ABS** *(lohs soh-'pohr-tehs ah-beh-eh-seh)*
Glue-lam beams	**las vigas Glue-lam** *(lahs 'vee-gahs gloo-lahm)*
Hardy walls	**los muros Hardy** *(lohs 'moo-rohs 'har-dee)*
OSB boards	**las tablas OSB** *(lahs 'tah-blahs oh-eh-seh-beh)*
PSL beams	**las vigas PSL** *(lahs 'vee-gahs peh-eh-seh-eh-leh)*
SDS screws	**los tornillos SDS** *(lohs tohr-'nee-yohs eh-'seh-deh-eh-seh)*
Simpson strong walls	**los muros Simpson** *(lohs 'moo-rohs 'seem-psohn)*
ST straps	**las cubrejuntas ST** *(lahs koo-breh-'hoon-tahs eh-seh-teh)*
UBC caps	**las coronas UBC** *(lahs koh-'roh-nahs oo-beh-seh)*

And memorize these words related to structures:

I have (the)…	**Tengo…** *('tehn-goh)*
bar	**la barra** *(lah 'bah-rrah)*
bundle	**el bulto** *(ehl 'bool-toh)*
coil	**el rollo** *(ehl 'roh-yoh)*
course	**la hilera** *(lah ee-'leh-rah)*
panel	**el panel** *(ehl pah-'nehl)*
piece	**la pieza** *(lah pee-'eh-sah)*
section	**la sección** *(lah sehk-see-'ohn)*
sheeting	**la lámina** *(lah 'lah-mee-nah)*
strip	**la tira** *(lah 'tee-rah)*

Just a Suggestion

There's a good chance these other metals will be needed:

alloy	**la aleación** *(lah ah-leh-ah-see-'ohn)*
aluminum	**el aluminio** *(ehl ah-loo-'mee-nee-oh)*
brass	**el latón** *(ehl lah-'tohn)*
bronze	**el bronce** *('brohn-seh)*
copper	**el cobre** *(ehl 'koh-breh)*
manganese	**el manganeso** *(ehl mahn-gah-'neh-soh)*
nickel	**el níquel** *(ehl 'nee-kehl)*
tin	**el estaño** *(ehl ehs-'tahn-yoh)*
zinc	**el cinc** *(ehl seenk)*

Try Some

Name three different types of metal in Spanish.

What is the difference between **una barra** and **una lámina**?

Name two different types of steel beams in Spanish.

Working Words: MORE EQUIPMENT

Get busy unloading everything you need for your structural project:

We need (the)...	**Necesitamos...** *(neh-seh-see-'tah-mohs)*
bar bender	**la dobladora** *(lah doh-blah-'doh-rah)*
boom	**el aguilón** *(ehl ah-ghee-'lohn)*
conveyor	**la cinta transportadora** *(lah 'seen-tah trahns-pohr-tah-'doh-rah)*
crane	**la grúa** *(lah 'groo-ah)*
cutter	**la cortadora** *(lah kohr-tah-'doh-rah)*
driller	**el taladrador** *(ehl tah-lah-drah-'dohr)*
forklift	**la carretilla elevadora** *(lah kah-rreh-'tee-yah eh-leh-vah-'doh-rah)*

hoist	el **montacargas** *(ehl mohn-tah-'kahr-gahs)*
impact wrench	la **llave eléctrica** *(lah 'yah-veh eh-'lehk-tree-kah)*
jackhammer	el **martillo neumático** *(ehl mahr-'tee-yoh neh-oo-'mah-tee-koh)*
loader	la **cargadora** *(lah kahr-gah-'doh-rah)*
mixer	la **mezcladora** *(lah mehs-klah-'doh-rah)*
pulley	la **polea** *(lah poh-'leh-ah)*
screw gun	la **pistola de tornillos** *(lah pees-'toh-lah deh tohr-'nee-yohs)*
track	el **carril** *(ehl kah-'rreel)*
wheelbarrow	la **carretilla** *(lah kah-rreh-'tee-yah)*
winch	el **torno** *(ehl 'tohr-noh)*
Where's (the)…	¿**Dónde está**…? *('dohn-deh ehs-'tah)*

chisel	el **cincel** *(ehl seen-'sehl)*
hammer	el **martillo** *(ehl mahr-'tee-yoh)*
mallet	el **mazo** *(ehl 'mah-soh)*
pick	el **pico** *(ehl 'pee-koh)*
saw	la **sierra** *(lah see-'eh-rrah)*
shovel	la **pala** *(lah 'pah-lah)*
sledge	la **almádena** *(lah ahl-'mah-deh-nah)*

Bring (the)…	**Traiga**… *('trah-ee-gah)*
bolt	el **perno** *(ehl 'pehr-noh)*
bracket	la **ménsula** *(lah 'mehn-soo-lah)*
clamp	la **abrazadora** *(lah ah-brah-sah-'deh-rah)*
clip	la **sujetadora** *(lah soo-heh-tah-'doh-rah)*
connector	la **conexión** *(lah koh-nehk-see-'ohn)*
coupling	el **enganche** *(ehl ehn-'gahn-cheh)*
dowel	la **espiga** *(lah ehs-'pee-gah)*
fastener	el **trabe** *(ehl 'trah-beh)*
fitting	el **acoplamiento** *(ehl ah-koh-plah-mee-'ehn-toh)*
lag bolt	el **perno grande** *(ehl 'pehr-noh 'grahn-deh)*
nail	el **clavo** *(ehl 'klah-voh)*
nut	la **tuerca** *(lah 'twehr-kah)*
pin	la **clavija** *(lah klah-'vee-hah)*
rivet	el **remache** *(ehl reh-'mah-cheh)*

screw	**el tornillo** *(ehl tohr-'nee-yoh)*
staple	**la grapa** *(lah 'grah-pah)*
washer	**la arandela** *(lah ah-rahn-'deh-lah)*

When welding is involved, these will be handy:

welding	**la soldadura** *(lah sohl-dah-'doo-rah)*

Trabaja en soldadura. *(trah-'bah-hah ehn sohl-dah-'doo-rah)*

arc welder	**el soldador eléctrico** *(ehl sohl-dah-'dohr eh-'lehk-tree-koh)*

¿Tiene el soldador eléctrico? *(tee-'eh-neh ehl sohl-dah-'dohr eh-'lehk-tree-koh)*

spot welding	**la soldadura en puntos** *(lah sohl-dah-'doh-rah ehn 'poon-tohs)*

¿Dónde está la soldadura en puntos?
('dohn-deh ehs-'tah lah sohl-dah-'doh-rah ehn 'poon-tohs)

As the metal framework is being set in place, listen for the following:

bar	**la barra** *(lah 'bah-rrah)*
gas	**el gas** *(ehl gahs)*
grating	**el enrejado** *(ehl ehn-reh-'hah-doh)*
lead	**el plomo** *(ehl 'ploh-moh)*
mesh	**la malla** *(lah 'mah-yah)*
paste	**la pasta** *(lah 'pahs-tah)*
sheet	**la plancha** *(lah 'plahn-chah)*
wire	**el alambre** *(ehl ah-'lahm-breh)*

He needs (the)	**Necesita...** *(neh-seh-'see-tah)*

arm	**el brazo** *(ehl 'brah-soh)*
cable	**el cable** *(ehl 'kah-bleh)*
clamp	**las pinzas** *(lahs 'peen-sahs)*
electrode holder	**el portaelectrodos** *(ehl pohr-tah-eh-lehk-'troh-dohs)*
file	**la lima** *(lah 'lee-mah)*
hacksaw	**la sierra de arco** *(lah see-'eh-rrah deh 'ahr-koh)*
hammer	**el martillo** *(ehl mahr-'tee-yoh)*
hose	**la manguera** *(lah mahn-'geh-rah)*
lead line	**el cable de conexión** *(ehl 'kah-bleh deh koh-nehk-see-'ohn)*
mallet	**el mazo** *(ehl 'mah-soh)*

measuring tape	la **cinta métrica** *(lah 'seen-tah 'meh-tree-kah)*
mold	el **molde** *(ehl 'mohl-deh)*
nozzle	la **boquilla** *(lah boh-'kee-yah)*
rod	la **varilla** *(lah vah-'ree-yah)*
spacer	el **separador** *(ehl seh-pah-rah-'dohr)*
tank	el **tanque** *(ehl 'tahn-keh)*
tongs	las **tenazas** *(lahs teh-'nah-sahs)*
torch	la **antorcha** *(lah ahn-'tohr-chah)*
transformer	el **transformador** *(ehl trahns-fohr-mah-'dohr)*
valve	la **válvula** *(lah 'vahl-voo-lah)*
vice	el **torno** *(ehl 'tohr-noh)*
wire brush	el **cepillo de alambre** *(ehl seh-'pee-yoh deh ah-'lahm-breh)*
How's (the)…	**¿Cómo está…?** *('koh-moh ehs-'tah)*
acetylene	el **acetileno** *(ehl ah-seh-tee-'leh-noh)*
alloy	la **aleación** *(lah ah-leh-ah-see-'ohn)*
amperage	el **amperaje** *(ehl ahm-peh-'rah-heh)*
arc	el **arco** *(ehl 'ahr-koh)*
CO_2	el **anhídrido carbónico** *(ehl ah-'nee-dree-doh kahr-'boh-nee-koh)*
oxygen	el **oxígeno** *(ehl ohk-'see-heh-noh)*
voltage	el **voltaje** *(ehl vohl-'tah-heh)*
Look at (the)…	**Mire…** *('mee-reh)*
angle	el **ángulo** *(ehl 'ahn-goo-loh)*
edge	el **borde** *(ehl 'bohr-deh)*
middle	el **centro** *(ehl 'sehn-troh)*
position	la **posición** *(lah poh-see-see-'ohn)*
side	el **lado** *(ehl 'lah-doh)*
tip	la **punta** *(lah 'poon-tah)*
Check (the)…	**Revise…** *(reh-'vee-seh)*
control	el **control** *(ehl kohn-'trohl)*
current	la **corriente** *(lah koh-rree-'ehn-teh)*
dripping	el **goteo** *(ehl goh-'teh-oh)*
flame	la **llama** *(lah 'yah-mah)*
heat	el **calor** *(ehl kah-'lohr)*
pressure	la **presión** *(lah preh-see-'ohn)*

scrap	**el desecho** *(ehl deh-'seh-choh)*
sparks	**las chispas** *(lahs 'chees-pahs)*

Study (the)...	**Estudie...** *(ehs-'too-dee-eh)*
blueprint	**el cianotipo** *(ehl see-ah-noh-'tee-poh)*
drawing	**el dibujo** *(ehl dee-'boo-hoh)*
layout	**el diseño** *(ehl dee-'seh-nyoh)*
plan	**el plano** *(ehl 'plah-noh)*
specs	**las especificaciones** *(lahs ehs-peh-see-fee-kah-see-'oh-nehs)*

Just a Suggestion

When it comes to welding, it's safety first:

Put on (the)...	**Póngase...** *('pohn-gah-seh)*
helmet	**la capucha protectora** *(lah kah-'poo-chah proh-tehk-'toh-rah)*
apron	**el mandil** *(ehl mahn-'deel)*
gloves	**los guantes** *(lohs 'gwahn-tehs)*
shin guard	**la espinillera** *(lah ehs-pee-nee-'yeh-rah)*
safety glasses	**las gafas de seguridad** *(lahs 'gah-fahs deh seh-goo-ree-'dahd)*

Try Some

Translate into Spanish:

Bring the tongs and the mallet.

_____

Bring the lumber and the rebar.

_____

Bring the bolt and the washer.

_____

Working Words: ON THE JOB SITE

As you walk around, identify everyone who's been working on the project. Begin with those you already know:

Ask (the)...	**Pregunte a...** *(preh-'goon-teh ah)*
contractor	**el contratista** *(ehl kohn-trah-'tees-tah)*
laborer	**el obrero** *(ehl oh-'breh-roh)*
truck driver	**el camionero** *(ehl kah-mee-oh-'neh-roh)*
designer	**el diseñador** *(ehl dee-seh-nyah-'dohr)*
technician	**el técnico** *(ehl 'tehk-nee-koh)*
architect	**el arquitecto** *(ehl ahr-kee-'tehk-toh)*
engineer	**el ingeniero** *(ehl een-heh-nee-'eh-roh)*
plumber	**el fontanero** *(ehl fohn-tah-'neh-roh)*
electrician	**el electricista** *(ehl eh-lehk-tree-'sees-tah)*
mason	**el albañil** *(ehl ahl-bah-'neel)*
welder	**el soldador** *(ehl sohl-dah-'dohr)*
machine operator	**el maquinista** *(ehl mah-kee-'nees-tah)*

As the job moves forward, discuss details with your crew:

Where's (the)...?	**¿Dónde está...?** *('dohn-deh ehs-'tah)*
duct	**el conducto** *(ehl kohn-'dook-toh)*
hole	**el hoyo/el hueco** *(ehl 'oh-yoh/ehl 'hweh-koh)*
opening	**la abertura** *(lah ah-behr-'too-rah)*
pit	**el foso/el pozo** *(ehl 'foh-soh/ehl 'poh-soh)*
slot	**la ranura** *(lah rah-'noo-rah)*

The hole is for the...	**El hueco es para...** *(ehl 'hweh-koh ehs 'pah-rah)*
door	**la puerta** *(lah 'pwehr-tah)*
window	**la ventana** *(lah vehn-'tah-nah)*
stairs	**las escaleras** *(lahs ehs-kah-'leh-rahs)*

It's for (the)...	**Es para...** *(ehs 'pah-rah)*
air conditioning	**el aire acondicionado** *(ehl 'ah-ee-reh ah-kohn-dee-see-oh-'nah-doh)*
cabling	**el cableado** *(ehl kah-bleh-'ah-doh)*
drainage tank	**el tanque de drenaje** *(ehl 'tahn-keh deh dreh-'nah-heh)*

electrical wiring	**la instalación eléctrica** *(lah eens-tah-lah-see-'ohn eh-'lehk-tree-kah)*
gas line	**la línea de gas** *(lah 'lee-neh-ah deh gahs)*
heating	**la calefacción** *(lah kah-leh-fahk-see-'ohn)*
insulation	**el aislamiento** *(ehl ah-ees-lah-mee-'ehn-toh)*
lighting	**la iluminación** *(lah ee-loo-mee-nah-see-'ohn)*
plumbing	**la tubería** *(lah too-beh-'ree-ah)*
septic system	**el sistema séptico** *(ehl sees-'teh-mah 'sehp-tee-koh)*
ventilation	**la ventilación** *(lah vehn-tee-lah-see-'ohn)*
waste pipe	**el desagüe** *(ehl deh-'sah-gweh)*

Structures are built upon flooring, so practice these key words:

subfloor	**el subpiso** *(ehl soob-'pee-soh)*
ground floor	**el primer piso** *(ehl pree-'mehr 'pee-soh)*
second floor	**el segundo piso** *(ehl seh-'goon-doh 'pee-soh)*

Getting the correct measurement is the key to success:

What's the…?	**¿Cuál es…?** *(kwahl ehs)*
cutting	**el corte** *(ehl 'kohr-teh)*
elevation	**la altura** *(lah ahl-'too-rah)*
flexibility	**la flexibilidad** *(lah flehk-see-bee-lee-'dahd)*
gauge	**el calibrador** *(ehl kah-lee-brah-'dohr)*
load	**la carga** *(lah 'kahr-gah)*
measurement	**la medida** *(lah meh-'dee-dah)*
position	**la posición** *(lah poh-see-see-'ohn)*
shape	**la forma** *(lah 'fohr-mah)*
size	**el tamaño** *(ehl tah-'mahn-yoh)*
strength	**la resistencia** *(lah reh-sees-'tehn-see-ah)*
weight	**el peso** *(ehl 'peh-soh)*

The measurement…	**La medida…** *(lah meh-'dee-dah)*
…isn't exact.	**…no es exacta.** *(noh ehs ex-'ahk-tah)*
…must be this high.	**…tiene que ser de esta altura.** *(tee-'eh-neh keh sehr deh 'ehs-tah ahl-'too-rah)*
…is off by…	**…le falta …** *(leh 'fahl-tah)*

Precautions must be taken to protect any structure:

It's protected from... **Está protegido de...** *(ehs-'tah proh-teh-'hee-doh deh)*

corrosion	**la corrosión** *(lah koh-rroh-see-'ohn)*
dry rot	**la podredumbre seca** *(lah poh-dreh-'doom-breh 'seh-kah)*
fire	**el incendio** *(ehl een-'sehn-dee-oh)*
hurricane	**el huracán** *(ehl oo-rah-'kahn)*
ice	**el hielo** *(ehl ee-'eh-loh)*
rain	**la lluvia** *(lah 'yoo-vee-ah)*
rust	**el óxido** *(ehl 'ohk-see-doh)*
snow	**la nieve** *(lah nee-'eh-veh)*
storm	**la tormenta** *(lah tohr-'mehn-tah)*
wind	**el viento** *(ehl vee-'ehn-toh)*

One-Liners

Continue to combine words to create key command phrases:

Build the forms.	**Construya los moldes.** *(kohns-'troo-yah lohs 'mohl-dehs)*
Install the steel.	**Instale el acero.** *(eens-'tah-leh ehl ah-'seh-roh)*
Dig the trench.	**Excave la zanja.** *(ex-'kah-veh lah 'sahn-hah)*
Use the stakes.	**Use las estacas.** *('oo-seh lahs ehs-'tah-kahs)*
Cut the braces.	**Corte las riostras.** *('kohr-teh lahs ree-'ohs-trahs)*

Try Some

What do you think these words mean?

zonas sísmicas
condiciones geológicas
diferencias climáticas

Working Words: DESCRIBING THE JOB

It's time to describe what you need done. Warm up with words that are the same in English:

interior	**exterior**	**lateral**
frontal	**diagonal**	**rectangular**
triangular	**hexagonal**	**perpendicular**

Now describe everything in front of you by using words you learned before:

small   **chico** *('chee-koh)*
                  La viga chica *(lah 'vee-gah 'chee-kah)*

medium   **mediano** *(meh-dee-'ah-noh)*
                  El poste mediano *(ehl 'pohs-teh meh-dee-'ah-noh)*

large   **grande** *('grahn-deh)*
                  La vigueta grande *(lah vee-'geh-tah 'grahn-deh)*

Group them in sets of opposites:

It's...   **Es/Está** *(ehs/ehs-'tah)*

long	**largo** *('lahr-goh)*	↔ short	**corto** *('kohr-toh)*
thick	**grueso** *(groo-'eh-soh)*	↔ thin	**delgado** *(dehl-'gah-doh)*
smooth	**liso** *('lee-soh)*	↔ rough	**áspero** *('ahs-peh-roh)*
loose	**flojo** *('floh-hoh)*	↔ tight	**apretado** *(ah-preh-'tah-doh)*
light	**ligero** *(lee-'heh-roh)*	↔ heavy	**pesado** *(peh-'sah-doh)*
partial	**parcial** *(pahr-see-'ahl)*	↔ complete	**completo** *(kohm-'pleh-toh)*
solid	**sólido** *('soh-lee-doh)*	↔ hollow	**hueco** *('hweh-koh)*
even	**igual** *(ee-'gwahl)*	↔ uneven	**desigual** *(deh-see-'gwahl)*
level	**nivel** *(nee-'vehl)*	↔ pitched	**inclinado** *(een-klee-'nah-doh)*
temporary	**provisional** *(proh-vee-see-oh-'nahl)*	↔ permanent	**permanente** *(pehr-mah-'nehn-teh)*

Structures may be...

sealed	**sellado** *(seh-'yah-doh)*
secure	**seguro** *(seh-'goo-roh)*
pointed	**en punta** *(ehn 'poon-tah)*
reinforced	**reforzado** *(reh-fohr-'sah-doh)*

adjustable	**ajustable** *(ah-hoos-'tah-bleh)*
straight	**recto** *('rehk-toh)*
durable	**duradero** *(doo-rah-'deh-roh)*
galvanized	**galvanizado** *(gahl-vah-nee-'sah-doh)*
rolled	**enrollado** *(ehn-roh-'yah-doh)*
cut	**cortado** *(kohr-'tah-doh)*
pre-cut	**precortado** *(preh-kohr-'tah-doh)*
hardened	**endurecido** *(ehn-doo-reh-'see-doh)*
finished	**acabado** *(ah-kah-'bah-doh)*
semi-finished	**semiacabado** *(seh-mee-ah-kah-'bah-doh)*
fabricated	**fabricado** *(fah-bree-'kah-doh)*
laminated	**laminado** *(lah-mee-'nah-doh)*
forged	**fundido** *(foon-'dee-doh)*
perforated	**perforado** *(pehr-foh-'rah-doh)*
threaded	**roscado** *(rohs-'kah-doh)*
protected	**protegido** *(proh-teh-'hee-doh)*
embedded	**incrustado** *(een-kroos-'tah-doh)*
spaced	**espaciado** *(ehs-pah-see-'ah-doh)*
attached	**conectado** *(koh-nehk-'tah-doh)*
rust-proof	**inoxidable** *(ee-nohk-see-'dah-bleh)*
coated	**bañado** *(bahn-'yah-doh)*
uniform	**uniforme** *(oo-nee-'fohr-meh)*
balanced	**balanceado** *(bah-lahn-seh-'ah-doh)*
stable	**estable** *(ehs-'tah-bleh)*
flat	**llano** *('yah-noh)*
round	**redondo** *(reh-'dohn-doh)*
squared	**cuadrado** *(kwah-'drah-doh)*
shaped	**formado** *(fohr-'mah-doh)*
welded	**soldado** *(sohl-'dah-doh)*
butted	**a tope** *(ah 'toh-peh)*
symmetrical	**simétrico** *(see-'meh-tree-koh)*

Notice how all the vocabulary fits together:

side beam support	**el soporte de la viga lateral** *(ehl soh-'pohr-teh deh lah 'vee-gah lah-teh-'rahl)*
welded metal post	**el poste de metal fundido** *(ehl 'pohs-teh deh meh-'tahl foon-'dee-doh)*
reinforced wood stud	**el barrote de madera reforzado** *(ehl bah-'rroh-teh deh mah-'deh-rah reh-fohr-'sah-doh)*

Just a Suggestion

Many expressions in construction include descriptive words. Practice each as one long phrase:

maximum strength | **la fuerza máxima** *(lah 'fwehr-sah 'mahk-see-mah)*
double plate | **la placa doble** *(lah 'plah-kah 'doh-bleh)*
steel pipe column | **la columna tubular de acero** *(lah koh-'loom-nah too-boo-lahr deh ah-'seh-roh)*

Try Some

Find the opposite:

llano _____

parcial _____

áspero _____

igual _____

chico _____

Working Words: ON-SITE ACTIONS

The following are verbs related to the structural phase of construction. To practice, insert the words that are most useful to you:

It needs... | **Necesita...** *(neh-seh-'see-tah)*

to interlace | **entrelazar** *(ehn-treh-lah-'sahr)*
to withstand | **resistir** *(reh-sees-'teer)*
to cross | **cruzar** *(kroo-'sahr)*
to attach | **conectar** *(koh-nehk-'tahr)*

to support	**soportar** *(soh-pohr-'tahr)*
to shape	**formar** *(fohr-'mahr)*
to overlap	**superponerse** *(soo-pehr-poh-'nehr-seh)*

You need...	**Usted necesita...** *(oos-'tehd neh-seh-'see-tah)*

to adjust	**ajustar** *(ah-hoos-'tahr)*
to insert	**meter** *(meh-'tehr)*
to mount	**montar** *(mohn-'tahr)*
to weld	**soldar** *(sohl-'dahr)*
to build	**construir** *(kohns-troo-'eer)*
to erect	**erigir** *(eh-ree-'heer)*
to raise	**levantar** *(leh-vahn-'tahr)*
to lower	**bajar** *(bah-'hahr)*
to add	**añadir** *(ahn-yah-'deer)*
to remove	**quitar** *(kee-'tahr)*
to bend	**doblar** *(doh-'blahr)*
to support	**soportar** *(soh-pohr-'tahr)*
to hold	**sostener** *(sohs-teh-'nehr)*
to lean	**inclinar** *(een-klee-'nahr)*

We need...	**Necesitamos...** *(neh-seh-see-'tah-mohs)*

to allow	**dejar** *(deh-'hahr)*
to block	**bloquear** *(bloh-keh-'ahr)*
to bore	**taladrar** *(tah-lah-'drahr)*
to crown	**coronar** *(koh-roh-'nahr)*
to cut	**cortar** *(kohr-'tahr)*
to enclose	**encerrar** *(ehn-seh-'rrahr)*
to glue	**adherir** *(ahd-eh-'reer)*
to line up	**alinear** *(ah-lee-neh-'ahr)*
to nail	**clavar** *(klah-'vahr)*
to plate	**poner placas** *(poh-'nehr 'plah-kahs)*
to plumb	**aplomar** *(ah-ploh-'mahr)*
to screw	**atornillar** *(ah-tohr-nee-'yahr)*
to snap-line	**marcar con tiza** *(mahr-'kahr kohn 'tee-sah)*
to spread	**esparcir** *(ehs-pahr-'seer)*
to stagger	**espaciar** *(ehs-pah-see-'ahr)*
to tie	**amarrar** *(ah-mah-'rrahr)*

| to tighten | **apretar** *(ah-preh-'tahr)* |
| to toenail | **clavar en ángulo** *(klah-'vahr ehn 'ahn-goo-loh)* |

And notice the difference between these two phrases:

| to straighten vertically | **enderezar** *(ehn-deh-reh-'sahr)* |
| to straighten horizontally | **poner recto** *(poh-nehr 'rehk-toh)* |

One-Liners

This expression is used with verbs to comment on future activity:

It's going...	**Va a...** *(vah ah)*
to twist	**torcer** *(tohr-'sehr)*
to fall	**caer** *(kah-'ehr)*
to move	**mover** *(moh-'vehr)*
to break	**romper** *(rohm-'pehr)*
to sag	**hundirse** *(oon-'deer-seh)*

Try Some

Follow the pattern with these action words:

levantar postes	**Estamos levantando postes.**	We're raising posts.
mover bloques	_____	_____
cortar varilla	_____	_____
soldar acero	_____	_____
espaciar estacas	_____	_____

Grammar Time

In Chapter Three, we learned the present progressive tense, which refers to what's happening right now. Now we will look at the simple present tense, which refers to what happens every day. Remember that verbs end in **-ar**, **-er**, or **–ir**, which alters their conjugation:

To Speak	Hablar *(ah-'blahr)*
I speak	**hablo** *('ah-bloh)*
You (sing.) speak; he, she speaks	**habla** *('ah-blah)*
We speak	**hablamos** *(ah-'blah-mohs)*
You (pl.), they speak	**hablan** *('ah-blahn)*

To Eat	Comer *(koh-'mehr)*
I eat	**como** *('koh-moh)*
You (sing.) eat; he, she eats	**come** *('koh-meh)*
We eat	**comemos** *(koh-'meh-mohs)*
You (pl.), they eat	**comen** *('koh-mehn)*

To Write	Escribir *(ehs-kree-'beer)*
I write	**escribo** *(ehs-'kree-boh)*
You (sing.) write; he, she writes	**escribe** *(ehs-'kree-beh)*
We write	**escribimos** *(ehs-kree-'bee-mohs)*
You (pl.), they write	**escriben** *(ehs-'kree-behn)*

Notice how the **-ar** verb, **hablar**, doesn't change the same as the **-er** and **-ir** verbs. This tip will be helpful as you pick up more verbs later on. By the way, here are two important irregular verbs in Spanish, and they need to be memorized:

To Want	Querer *(keh-'rehr)*
I want	**quiero** *(kee-'eh-roh)*
You (sing.) want; he, she wants	**quiere** *(kee-'eh-reh)*
We want	**queremos** *(keh-'reh-mohs)*
You (pl.); they want	**quieren** *(kee-'eh-rehn)*

I want the nails.   **Quiero los clavos.** *(kee-'eh-roh lohs 'klah-vohs)*

To Be Able to (can)	Poder *(poh-'dehr)*
I can	**pu_e_do** *('pweh-doh)*
You (sing.) can; he, she can	**pu_e_de** *('pweh-deh)*
We can	**podemos** *(poh-'deh-mohs)*
You (pl.), they can	**pu_e_den** *('pweh-dehn)*

I can understand.   **Puedo entender.** *('pweh-doh ehn-tehn-'dehr)*

Some irregular verbs are extremely useful in construction work. Notice how the present tense of *to go* in Spanish can also be used to refer to future time:

To Go	Ir *(eer)*
I go	**voy** *('voh-ee)*
You (sing.) go; he, she goes	**va** *(vah)*
We go	**vamos** *('vah-mohs)*
You (pl.); they go	**van** *(vahn)*

I go home.   **Voy a mi casa.** *('voh-ee ah mee 'kah-sah)*

To talk about the future, all you add is a basic verb:

I'm going to finish.   **Voy a terminar.** *('voh-ee ah tehr-mee-'nahr)*
He's going to unload.   **Va a descargar.** *(vah ah dehs-kahr-'gahr)*
We're going to weld.   **Vamos a soldar.** *('vah-mohs ah sohl-'dahr)*

Try Some

Change these sentences from the present progressive tense to the simple present tense. Look at the example:

I'm working.	**Estoy trabajando.**	I work.	**Trabajo.**
I'm driving.	**Estoy manejando.**	I drive.	_____
I'm cutting.	**Estoy cortando.**	I cut.	_____
I'm speaking.	**Estoy hablando.**	I speak.	_____

One-Liners

Some of the most useful construction phrases in any language are those that direct others to a specific location. Think of all the ways these one-liners will come in handy:

It's...	**Está...** *(ehs-'tah)*
back to back	**espalda con espalda** *(ehs-'pahl-dah kohn ehs-'pahl-dah)*
downhill	**cuesta abajo** *('kwehs-tah ah-'bah-hoh)*
from the ground up	**del suelo hacia arriba** *(dehl soo-'eh-loh 'ah-see-ah ah-'rree-bah)*
inside out	**al revés** *(ahl reh-'vehs)*
right side up	**boca arriba** *('boh-kah ah-'rree-bah)*
side by side	**lado a lado** *('lah-doh ah 'lah-doh)*
uphill	**cuesta arriba** *('kwehs-tah ah-'rree-bah)*
upside down	**boca abajo** *('boh-kah ah-'bah-hoh)*

In, on, or *at* (the)...	**En...** *(ehn)*
back part	**la parte trasera** *(lah 'pahr-teh trah-'seh-rah)*
bottom part	**la parte abajo** *(lah 'pahr-teh ah-'bah-hoh)*
corner	**la esquina** *(lah ehs-'kee-nah)*
edge	**el borde** *(ehl 'bohr-deh)*
end	**el final** *(ehl fee-'nahl)*
front part	**la parte delantera** *(lah 'pahr-teh deh-lahn-'teh-rah)*
middle	**el medio** *(ehl 'meh-dee-oh)*
side	**el lado** *(ehl 'lah-doh)*
tip	**la punta** *(lah 'poon-tah)*
top part	**la parte de arriba** *(lah 'pahr-teh deh ah-'rree-bah)*

Try Some

Translate into Spanish:

It's upside down. _____

Where is the place? _____

Look at the edge. _____

Culture Issues

If you get stuck in the middle of a phrase or sentence, don't be afraid to send messages using hand gestures or facial expressions. Body signals are very common in the Spanish-speaking world. And remember, there's nothing wrong with repeating your message several times until you're understood!

Chapter Five

Framing
El armazón

(ehl ahr-mah-'sohn)

 Working Words: WOOD FRAMING

Here are some common words in the world of wood framing:

lumber	**la madera** *(lah mah-'deh-rah)*
carpenter	**el carpintero** *(ehl kahr-peen-'teh-roh)*
plans	**los planos** *(lohs 'plah-nohs)*
structure	**la construcción** *(lah kohns-trook-see-'ohn)*
frame	**el marco** *(ehl 'mahr-koh)*
support	**el apoyo** *(ehl ah-'poh-yoh)*
floor	**el piso** *(ehl 'pee-soh)*
wall	**la pared** *(lah pah-'rehd)*
roof	**el tejado** *(ehl teh-'hah-doh)*
hammer	**el martillo** *(ehl mahr-'tee-yoh)*
nails	**los clavos** *(lohs 'klah-vohs)*
saw	**la sierra** *(lah see-'eh-rrah)*

Keep going:

We use (the)…	**Usamos…** *(oo-'sah-mohs)*
backing	**el respaldo** *(ehl rehs-'pahl-doh)*
beam	**la viga** *(lah 'vee-gah)*
board	**la tabla** *(lah 'tah-blah)*
brace	**la abrazadera/la riostra** *(lah ah-brah-sah-'deh-rah/lah ree-'ohs-trah)*

cap	**la corona** *(lah koh-'roh-nah)*
crossbar	**el travesaño** *(ehl trah-veh-'sahn-yoh)*
cripple	**el refuerzo** *(ehl reh-foo-'ehr-soh)*
expansion bolt	**el perno de expansión** *(ehl 'pehr-noh deh ex-pahn-see-'ohn)*
fire block	**el cortafuego** *(ehl kohr-tah-'fweh-goh)*
hanger	**el gancho** *(ehl 'gahn-choh)*
header	**la cabecera** *(lah kah-beh-'seh-rah)*
jack	**el cabrio corto** *(ehl 'kah-bree-oh 'kohr-toh)*
joint	**la unión** *(lah oo-nee-'ohn)*
joist	**la vigueta** *(lah vee-'geh-tah)*
lag bolt	**el tirafondo** *(ehl tee-rah-'fohn-doh)*
lap block	**el bloque de revestimiento** *(ehl 'bloh-keh deh reh-vehs-tee-mee-'ehn-toh)*
ledger	**el larguero** *(ehl lahr-'geh-roh)*
panel	**el panel** *(ehl pah-'nehl)*
post	**el poste** *(ehl 'pohs-teh)*
rafter	**el cabrio** *(ehl 'kah-bree-oh)*
ridge	**el caballete** *(ehl kah-bah-'yeh-teh)*
sill	**el antepecho** *(ehl ahn-teh-'peh-choh)*
sole plate	**la placa de solera** *(lah 'plah-kah deh soh-'leh-rah)*
strap	**la cubrejunta** *(lah koo-breh-'hoon-tah)*
stud	**el montante** *(ehl mohn-'tahn-teh)*
tie	**la traviesa** *(lah trah-vee-'eh-sah)*
trimmer	**la cortadora/la cepilladora** *(lah kohr-tah-'doh-rah/lah seh-pee-yah-'doh-rah)*
truss	**la armadura** *(lah ahr-mah-'doo-rah)*

Add words to provide better detail:

hip post	**el poste de la lima** *(ehl 'pohs-teh deh lah 'lee-mah)*
top plate	**la placa superior** *(lah 'plah-kah soo-peh-ree-'ohr)*
floor joist	**la vigueta del piso** *(lah vee-'geh-tah dehl 'pee-soh)*

Many of the words used in framing are also used in structural work:

bearing wall	**el muro de carga** *(ehl 'moo-roh deh 'kahr-gah)*
rake wall	**el muro de tope inclinado** *(ehl 'moo-roh deh 'toh-peh een-klee-'nah-doh)*
shear wall	**el muro sismorresistente** *(ehl 'moo-roh sees-moh-rreh-sees-'tehn-teh)*

The word *board* in Spanish has a variety of translations, but is often simply identified by its size:

Bring me a 2 by 6.	**Tráigame una dos por seis.** *('trah-ee-gah-meh 'oo-nah dohs pohr 'seh-ees)*
Where are the 16-footers?	**¿Dónde están las de dieciséis?** *('dohn-deh ehs-'tahn lahs deh dee-eh-see-'seh-ees)*
I need more 4 by 4s.	**Necesito más cuatro por cuatros.** *(neh-seh-'see-toh mahs 'kwah-troh pohr 'kwah-trohs)*

Here are other words that refer to wood:

large board	**el tablón** *(ehl tah-'blohn)*
long beam	**el larguero** *(ehl lahr-'geh-roh)*
rail	**el riel** *(ehl ree-'ehl)*
raw timber	**la madera en bruto** *(lah mah-'deh-rah ehn 'broo-toh)*
round timber	**el rollizo** *(ehl roh-'yee-soh)*
wood block	**el bloque** *(ehl 'bloh-keh)*

There are several types of wood used in construction. These are from nature:

birch	**el abedul** *(ehl ah-beh-'dool)*
cedar	**el cedro** *(ehl 'seh-droh)*
cherry	**el cerezo** *(ehl seh-'reh-soh)*
fir	**el abeto** *(ehl ah-'beh-toh)*
mahogany	**la caoba** *(lah kah-'oh-bah)*
maple	**el arce** *(ehl 'ahr-seh)*
oak	**el roble** *(ehl 'roh-bleh)*
pine	**el pino** *(ehl 'pee-noh)*
redwood	**la secoya** *(lah seh-'koh-yah)*
teak	**la teca** *(lah 'teh-kah)*

It's…	**Es…** *(ehs)*
hard wood	**la madera brava** *(lah mah-'deh-rah 'brah-vah)*
soft wood	**la madera blanda** *(lah mah-'deh-rah 'blahn-dah)*

These are man-made:

plywood	**la madera contrachapada** *(lah mah-'deh-rah kohn-trah-chah-'pah-dah)*
pressed wood	**la madera prensada** *(lah mah-'deh-rah prehn-'sah-dah)*
wood composite	**la madera compuesta** *(lah mah-'deh-rah kohm-'pwehs-tah)*

What about buildings constructed of something else?

It's made of...	**Está hecho de...** *(ehs-'tah 'eh-choh deh)*

block	**el bloque** *(ehl 'bloh-keh)*
brick	**el ladrillo** *(ehl lah-'dree-yoh)*
cement	**el cemento** *(ehl seh-'mehn-toh)*
iron	**el hierro** *(ehl ee-'eh-rroh)*
aluminum	**el aluminio** *(ehl ah-loo-'mee-nee-oh)*
steel	**el acero** *(ehl ah-'seh-roh)*
stone	**la piedra** *(lah pee-'eh-drah)*

Try Some

Which word would be the best match?

el acero y _____   la piedra

el tablón y _____   el clavo

el ladrillo y _____   el respaldo

el refuerzo y _____   el hierro

el martillo y _____   el pino

Working Words: FRAMER'S TOOLS

Framers use a variety of tools, so spend some time with the list below:

Where's (the)...?	**¿Dónde está...?** *('dohn-deh ehs-'tah)*

air compressor	**el compresor de aire** *(ehl kohm-preh-'sohr deh 'ah-ee-reh)*
carpenter's glue	**el adhesivo** *(ehl ah-deh-'see-voh)*
caulking	**el sellador** *(ehl seh-yah-'dohr)*
chalk	**la tiza** *(lah 'tee-sah)*
chisel	**el cincel** *(ehl seen-'sehl)*
drill	**el taladro** *(ehl tah-'lah-droh)*
extension cord	**la extensión eléctrica** *(lah ex-tehn-see-'ohn eh-'lehk-tree-kah)*

framing square	**la escuadra** *(lah ehs-'kwah-drah)*
hammer	**el martillo** *(ehl mahr-'tee-yoh)*
hand saw	**el serrucho** *(ehl seh-'rroo-choh)*
ladder	**la escalera** *(lah ehs-kah-'leh-rah)*
level	**el nivel** *(ehl nee-'vehl)*
mallet	**el mazo** *(ehl 'mah-soh)*
marker	**el marcador** *(ehl mahr-kah-'dohr)*
measuring tape	**la cinta métrica** *(lah 'seen-tah 'meh-tree-kah)*
pencil	**el lápiz** *(ehl 'lah-pees)*
pliers	**los alicates** *(lohs ah-lee-'kah-tehs)*
plumb bob	**la plomada** *(lah ploh-'mah-dah)*
plumb line	**el hilo de plomada** *(ehl 'ee-loh deh ploh-'mah-dah)*
ratchet	**el trinquete** *(ehl treen-'keh-teh)*
router	**la ranuradora** *(lah rah-noo-rah-'doh-rah)*
sander	**la lijadora** *(lah lee-hah-'doh-rah)*
screwdriver	**el destornillador** *(ehl dehs-tohr-nee-yah-'dohr)*
shears	**las tijeras** *(lahs tee-'heh-rahs)*
transit	**la niveladora electrónica** *(lah nee-veh-lah-'doh-rah eh-lehk-'troh-nee-kah)*
utility knife	**la navaja** *(lah nah-'vah-hah)*
vice	**la prensa** *(lah 'prehn-sah)*
wrench	**la llave inglesa** *(lah 'yah-veh een-'gleh-sah)*

These three tools are also in high demand in carpentry:

nail puller	**el sacaclavos** *(ehl sah-kah-'kla-vohs)*
pry bar	**la pata de cabra** *(lah 'pah-tah deh 'kah-brah)*
flat bar	**la palanca** *(lah pah-'lahn-kah)*

Now just focus on the different kinds of saws:

handsaw	**el serrucho** *(ehl seh-'rroo-choh)*
hacksaw	**el serrucho para metales** *(ehl seh-'rroo-choh 'pah-rah meh-'tah-lehs)*
band saw	**la sierra cinta/la sierra sinfín** *(lah see-'eh-rrah 'seen-tah/lah see-'eh-rrah seen-'feen)*
skill saw	**la sierra circular** *(lah see-'eh-rrah seer-koo-'lahr)*
jigsaw	**la sierra de vaivén** *(lah see-'eh-rrah deh vah-ee-'vehn)*
reciprocating saw (sawzall)	**la sierra alternativa** *(lah see-'eh-rrah ahl-tehr-nah-'tee-vah)*

miter saw	**la sierra de corte angular** *(lah see-'eh-rrah deh 'kohr-teh ahn-goo-'lahr)*
scroll saw	**la sierra caladora** *(lah see-'eh-rrah kah-lah-'doh-rah)*
table saw	**la sierra de banco** *(lah see-'eh-rrah deh 'bahn-koh)*

Just a Suggestion

Continue to build phrases around a single word:

chalk box	**la cajita de tiza** *(lah kah-'hee-tah deh 'tee-sah)*
chalk line	**la cuerda de tiza** *(lah 'kwehr-dah deh 'tee-sah)*
chalk powder	**el polvo de tiza** *(ehl 'pohl-voh deh 'tee-sah)*

Try Some

¿Cuál es la diferencia entre…?
(kwahl ehs lah dee-feh-'rehn-see-ah 'ehn-treh)

la tiza y el lápiz
el destornillador y la llave inglesa
la sierra circular y la sierra alternativa

 ## Working Words: MORE TOOLS AND EQUIPMENT

Some Spanish workers will say **pistola** *(pees-'toh-lah)* when referring to a power tool, while others might call it a **neumática** *(neh-oo-'mah-tee-kah)*. Notice these examples:

nail gun	**la pistola de clavos** *(lah pees-'toh-lah deh 'klah-vohs)* or **la clavadora neumática** *(lah klah-vah-'doh-rah neh-oo-'mah-tee-kah)*
screw gun	**la pistola de tornillos** *(lah pees-'toh-lah deh tohr-'nee-yohs)* or **la atornilladora neumática** *(lah ah-tohr-nee-yah-'doh-rah neh-oo-'mah-tee-kah)*
staple gun	**la pistola de grapas** *(lah pees-'toh-lah deh 'grah-pahs)* or **la engrapadora neumática** *(lah ehn-grah-pah-'doh-rah neh-oo-'mah-tee-kah)*

We need (the)…	**Necesitamos…** *(neh-seh-see-'tah-mohs)*
workbench	**el tablero de trabajo** *(ehl tah-'bleh-roh deh trah-'bah-hoh)*
scaffolding	**el andamio** *(ehl ahn-'dah-mee-oh)*
sawhorses	**los caballetes** *(lohs kah-bah-'yeh-tehs)*
crane	**la grúa** *(lah 'groo-ah)*
conveyor	**la cinta transportadora** *(lah 'seen-tah trahns-pohr-tah-'doh-rah)*
forklift	**la carretilla elevadora** *(lah kah-rreh-'tee-yah eh-leh-vah-'doh-rah)*
flatbed	**el camión plataforma** *(ehl kah-mee-'ohn plah-tah-'fohr-mah)*
impact wrench	**la llave eléctrica** *(lah 'yah-veh eh-'lehk-tree-kah)*

These smaller items are important, too:

Look for (the)…	**Busque…** *('boos-keh)*
bit	**la broca** *(lah 'broh-kah)*
blade	**la hoja** *(lah 'oh-hah)*
bolt	**el perno** *(ehl 'pehr-noh)*
bracket	**la ménsula** *(lah 'mehn-soo-lah)*
clamp	**la abrazadera** *(lah ah-brah-sah-'deh-rah)*
clip	**la sujetadora** *(lah soo-heh-tah-'doh-rah)*
nail	**el clavo** *(ehl 'klah-voh)*
nut	**la tuerca** *(lah 'twehr-kah)*
pin	**la clavija** *(lah klah-'vee-hah)*
screw	**el tornillo** *(ehl tohr-'nee-yoh)*
staple	**la grapa** *(lah 'grah-pah)*
washer	**la arandela** *(lah ah-rahn-'deh-lah)*

There are several kinds of nails. Check these out:

I want (the)…	**Quiero…** *(kee-'eh-roh)*
barbed nail	**el clavo afilado** *(ehl 'klah-voh ah-fee-lah-doh)*
box nail	**el clavo para madera** *(ehl 'klah-voh 'pah-rah mah-'deh-rah)*
casing nail	**el clavo de cabeza perdida** *(ehl 'klah-voh deh kah-'beh-sah pehr-'dee-dah)*
finishing nail	**el clavo sin cabeza** *(ehl 'klah-voh seen kah-'beh-sah)*
masonary nail	**el clavo de mampostería** *(ehl 'klah-voh deh mahm-pohs-teh-'ree-ah)*

roofing nail	**el clavo para tejado** *(ehl 'klah-voh 'pah-rah teh-'hah-doh)*
siding nail	**el clavo para revestimiento** *(ehl 'klah-voh 'pah-rah reh-vehs-tee-mee-'ehn-toh)*
spiral nail	**el clavo espiral** *(ehl 'klah-voh ehs-pee-'rahl)*

One-Liners

See how numbers are combined with fasteners:

I need more sixteens.
Necesito más clavos de dieciséis.
(neh-seh-'see-toh mahs 'klah-vohs deh dee-eh-see-'seh-ees)

Look for the three-eighths.
Busque los tornillos de tres octavos.
('boos-keh lohs tohr-'nee-yohs deh trehs ohk-'tah-vohs)

The bolts are four inches long.
Los pernos son cuatro pulgadas de largo.
(lohs 'pehr-nohs sohn 'kwah-troh pool-'gah-dahs deh 'lahr-goh)

Working Words: ON THE JOB SITE

These are the basic areas of your job site:

cut yard	**la área para cortar** *(lah 'ah-reh-ah 'pah-rah kohr-'tahr)*
entrance	**la entrada** *(lah ehn-'trah-dah)*
exit	**la salida** *(lah sah-'lee-dah)*

And these are the basic parts:

ceiling	**el techo** *(ehl 'teh-choh)*
door	**la puerta** *(lah 'pwehr-tah)*
floor	**el piso** *(ehl 'pee-soh)*
roof	**el tejado** *(ehl teh-'hah-doh)*
room	**el cuarto** *(ehl 'kwahr-toh)*
wall	**la pared** *(lah pah-'rehd)*
window	**la ventana** *(lah vehn-'tah-nah)*

Now, be a bit more specific:

The _____ goes here.   _____ **va aquí.** *(vah ah-'kee)*

deck	**el piso exterior** *(ehl 'pee-soh ex-teh-ree-'ohr)*
doorway	**el portal** *(ehl pohr-'tahl)*
flooring	**el solado** *(ehl soh-'lah-doh)*
stairway	**la escalera** *(lah ehs-kah-'leh-rah)*
window frame	**el marco de la ventana** *(ehl 'mahr-koh deh lah vehn-'tah-nah)*

As the job moves forward, so do details to be discussed with the crew:

This space is for (the)...	**Este espacio es para...** *('ehs-teh ehs-'pah-see-oh ehs 'pah-rah)*
air conditioning	**el aire acondicionado** *(ehl 'ah-ee-reh ah-kohn-dee-see-oh-'nah-doh)*
bay	**la ventana saliente** *(lah vehn-'tah-nah sah-lee-'ehn-teh)*
chimney	**la chimenea** *(lah chee-meh-'neh-ah)*
drain	**el drenaje** *(ehl dreh-'nah-heh)*
duct	**el conducto** *(ehl kohn-'dook-toh)*
electrical wiring	**la instalación eléctrica** *(lah eens-tah-lah-see-'ohn eh-'lehk-tree-kah)*
elevator	**el ascensor** *(ehl ah-sehn-'sohr)*
gas line	**la línea de gas** *(lah 'lee-neh-ah deh gahs)*
heating	**la calefacción** *(lah kah-leh-fahk-see-'ohn)*
insulation	**el aislamiento** *(ehl ah-ees-lah-mee-'ehn-toh)*
lighting	**la iluminación** *(lah ee-loo-mee-nah-see-'ohn)*
plumbing	**la tubería** *(lah too-beh-'ree-ah)*
skylight	**el tragaluz** *(ehl trah-gah-'loos)*
ventilation	**la ventilación** *(lah vehn-tee-lah-see-'ohn)*

These words focus on the stairs:

landing	**el descanso** *(ehl dehs-'kahn-soh)*
railing	**las barandas** *(lahs bah-'rahn-dahs)*
stairs	**las escaleras** *(lahs ehs-kah-'leh-rahs)*
stairwell	**la caja de la escalera** *(lah 'kah-hah deh lah ehs-kah-'leh-rah)*
step	**el escalón** *(ehl ehs-kah-'lohn)*

It's time to use commands with key vocabulary:

Build (the)...	**Construya...** *(kohns-'troo-yah)*
arch	**el arco** *(ehl 'ahr-koh)*
barrier	**la barrera** *(lah bah-'rreh-rah)*
base	**la base** *(lah 'bah-seh)*
bridging	**el puntal** *(ehl poon-'tahl)*
corbel	**el corbil** *(kohr-'beel)*
overhang	**el voladizo** *(ehl voh-lah-'dee-soh)*
partition	**el tabique** *(ehl tah-'bee-keh)*

When you give commands as a framer, add words to create new phrases:

Put (the)...	**Ponga...** *('pohn-gah)*
double	**doble** *('doh-bleh)*
double header	**la doble cabecera** *(lah 'doh-bleh kah-beh-'seh-rah)*
double beam	**la doble viga** *(lah 'doh-bleh 'vee-gah)*
upper	**superior** *(soo-peh-ree-'ohr)*
upper support	**el apoyo superior** *(ehl ah-'poh-yoh soo-peh-ree-'ohr)*
upper fire block	**el contrafuego superior** *(ehl kohn-trah-'fweh-goh soo-peh-ree-'ohr)*
underground	**subterráneo** *(soob-teh-'rrah-neh-oh)*
underground wall	**el muro subterráneo** *(ehl 'moo-roh soob-teh-'rrah-neh-oh)*
underground post	**el poste subterráneo** *(ehl 'pohs-teh soob-teh-'rrah-neh-oh)*

You should already know these:

Look at (the)...	**Mire...** *('mee-reh)*
back	**la parte de atrás** *(lah 'pahr-teh deh ah-'trahs)*
corner	**la esquina** *(lah ehs-'kee-nah)*
edge	**el borde** *(ehl 'bohr-deh)*
front	**la parte delantera** *(lah 'pahr-teh deh-lahn-'teh-rah)*
middle	**el centro** *(ehl 'sehn-troh)*
side	**el lado** *(ehl 'lah-doh)*

Just a Suggestion

If possible, learn one-liners in pairs, such as words with opposite meanings:

clockwise | **según las agujas del reloj** *(seh-'goon lahs ah-'goo-hahs dehl reh-'loh)*

counterclockwise | **en contra de las agujas del reloj** *(ehn 'kohn-trah deh lahs ah-'goo-hahs dehl reh-'loh)*

apart | **separados** *(seh-pah-'rah-dohs)*
together | **juntos** *('hoon-tohs)*

only one side | **solamente un lado** *(soh-lah-'mehn-teh oon 'lah-doh)*
both sides | **los dos lados** *(lohs dohs 'lah-dohs)*

Try Some

Find the opposites:

entrada _____

separado _____

adelante _____

Translate into Spanish:

This space is for the electrical wiring. _____

Pick up the scrap. _____

What's the back? _____

Working Words: DESCRIBING THE JOB

When referring to wood, most descriptions end in the letter **-a**:

It's very...   **Es muy...** *(ehs 'moo-ee)*
It's not...   **No es...** *(noh ehs)*

long	**larga** *('lahr-gah)*	short	**corta** *('kohr-tah)*
thick	**gruesa** *(groo-'eh-sah)*	thin	**delgada** *(dehl-'gah-dah)*
light	**ligera** *(lee-'heh-rah)*	heavy	**pesada** *(peh-'sah-dah)*

This time, use **Está** *(ehs-'tah)*, which indicates more of a temporary condition:

It's very...   **Está muy...**   *(ehs-'tah)*
It's not...   **No está...** *(noh ehs-'tah)*

loose	**floja** *('floh-hah)*	tight	**apretada** *(ah-preh-'tah-dah)*
smooth	**lisa** *('lee-sah)*	rough	**áspera** *('ahs-peh-rah)*
even	**igual** *(ee-'gwahl)*	uneven	**desigual** *(dehs-ee-'gwahl)*

It's...   **Es/Está...** *(ehs/ehs-'tah)*

attached	**conectado** *(koh-nehk-'tah-doh)*
balanced	**balanceado** *(bah-lahn-seh-'ah-doh)*
braced	**arriostrado** *(ah-rree-ohs-'trah-doh)*
cut	**cortado** *(kohr-'tah-doh)*
finished	**acabado** *(ah-kah-'bah-doh)*
fireproof	**incombustible** *(een-kohm-boos-'tee-bleh)*
flat	**llano** *('yah-noh)*
flush	**a ras de** *(ah rahs deh)*
framed	**enmarcado** *(ehn-mahr-'kah-doh)*
graded	**clasificado** *(klah-see-fee-'kah-doh)*
inverted	**volteado** *(vohl-teh-'ah-doh)*
laminated	**laminado** *(lah-mee-'nah-doh)*
overlapping	**sobrepuesto** *(soh-breh-'pwehs-toh)*
plumb	**a nivel** *(ah nee-'vehl)*
precut	**precortado** *(preh-kohr-'tah-doh)*
prefabricated	**prefabricado** *(preh-fah-bree-'kah-doh)*
reinforced	**reforzado** *(reh-fohr-'sah-doh)*
round	**redondo** *(reh-'dohn-doh)*

sealed	**sellado** *(seh-'yah-doh)*
secure	**seguro** *seh-'goo-roh)*
square	**cuadrado** *(kwah-'drah-doh)*
stable	**estable** *(ehs-'tah-bleh)*
straight	**recto** *('reh-ktoh)*
tongue & groove	**lengüeta y ranura** *(lehn-'gweh-tah ee rah-'noo-rah)*
treated	**tratado** *(trah-'tah-doh)*
uniform	**uniforme** *(oo-nee-'fohr-meh)*

Here's how you describe lumber in further detail:

There are...	**Hay...** *('ah-ee)*
bumps	**bultos** *('bool-tohs)*
cracks	**grietas** *(gree-'eh-tahs)*
gaps	**boquetes** *(boh-'keh-tehs)*
holes	**hoyos** *('oh-yohs)*
knots	**nudos** *('noo-dohs)*
marks	**marcas** *('mahr-kahs)*
splits	**rajas** *('rah-hahs)*
stains	**manchas** *('mahn-chahs)*
twists	**torceduras** *(tohr-seh-'doo-rahs)*

It's...	**Está...** *(ehs-'tah)*
broken	**rota** *('roh-tah)*
dirty	**sucia** *('soo-see-ah)*
rotten	**podrida** *(poh-'dree-dah)*
warped	**combada** *(kohm-'bah-dah)*
swollen	**hinchada** *(een-'chah-dah)*
wet	**mojada** *(moh-'hah-dah)*

Framers deal with words with very specific meanings:

It has (the)...	**Tiene...** *(tee-'eh-neh)*
ring	**el anillo** *(ehl ah-'nee-yoh)*
flange	**el ala** *(ehl 'ah-lah)*
loop	**el lazo** *(ehl 'lah-soh)*
bend	**el recodo** *(ehl reh-'koh-doh)*
slit	**la muesca** *(lah 'mwehs-kah)*
groove	**la ranura** *(lah rah-'noo-rah)*
hoop	**el zuncho** *(ehl 'soon-choh)*

Try Some

Underline one word in each group that doesn't belong with the others:

larga, delgada, grieta
torcido, redondo, cuadrado
combada, medida, hinchada

Working Words: ON-SITE ACTIONS

The following verbs are essential for on-site work. Picture a scenario as you practice aloud:

You have...	**Tiene que...** *(tee-'eh-neh keh)*
to cut	**cortar** *(kohr-'tahr)*
to glue	**encolar** *(ehn-koh-'lahr)*
to join	**unir** *(oo-'neer)*
to nail	**clavar** *(klah-'vahr)*
to remove	**sacar** *(sah-'kahr)*
to screw in	**atornillar** *(ah-tohr-nee-'yahr)*
to stabilize	**estabilizar** *(ehs-tah-bee-lee-'sahr)*
to support	**apoyar** *(ah-poh-'yahr)*
to tighten	**apretar** *(ah-preh-'tahr)*
to toenail	**clavar en ángulo** *(klah-'vahr ehn 'ahn-goo-loh)*
to pound	**golpear** *(gohl-peh-'ahr)*
to hold	**sostener** *(sohs-teh-'nehr)*
to tack	**fijar** *(fee-'hahr)*
to wrap	**forrar** *(foh-'rrahr)*
to add	**añadir** *(ah-'nyah-deer)*
to alter	**modificar** *(moh-dee-fee-'kahr)*
to attach	**conectar** *(koh-nehk-'tahr)*
to bypass	**evitar** *(eh-vee-tahr)*

Continue talking, but now add any vocabulary word you may consider logical and useful. Look at the examples:

We need…	**Necesitamos…** *(neh-seh-see-'tah-mohs)*	
to adjust	**ajustar** *(ah-hoos-'tahr)*	<u>el cabrio</u>
to insert	**meter** *(meh-'tehr)*	<u>el perno</u>
to mount	**montar** *(mohn-'tahr)*	<u>la pieza</u>
to stack	**apilar** *(ah-pee-'lahr)*	_____
to level	**nivelar** *(nee-veh-'lahr)*	_____
to build	**construir** *(kohn-stroo-'eer)*	_____
to erect	**erigir** *(eh-ree-'heer)*	_____
to raise	**levantar** *(leh-vahn-'tahr)*	_____
to lower	**bajar** *(bah-'hahr)*	_____
to line up	**alinear** *(ah-lee-neh-'ahr)*	_____
to enclose	**encerrar** *(ehn-seh-'rrahr)*	_____
to bore	**taladrar** *(tah-lah-'drahr)*	_____
to make	**hacer** *(ah-'sehr)*	_____
to sort	**clasificar** *(klah-see-fee-'kahr)*	_____
to snap a line	**marcar la línea** *(mahr-'kahr lah 'lee-neh-ah)*	_____
to clean	**limpiar** *(leem-pee-'ahr)*	_____
to redo	**volver a hacer** *(vohl-'vehr ah ah-'sehr)*	_____
to sharpen	**afilar** *(ah-fee-'lahr)*	_____

With the following, talk about things that go wrong:

It's going …	**Se va a…** *(seh vah ah)*
to twist	**torcer** *(tohr-'sehr)*
to fall over	**tumbar** *(toom-'bahr)*
to move	**mover** *(moh-'vehr)*
to slip	**resbalar** *(rehs-bah-'lahr)*
to break	**romper** *(rohm-'pehr)*
to sag	**hundir** *(oon-'deer)*
to fall	**caer** *(kah-'ehr)*
to spin	**girar** *(hee-'rahr)*
to overlap	**superponer** *(soo-pehr-poh-'nehr)*
to turn	**voltear** *(vohl-teh-'ahr)*

Try Some

Insert a verb from the lists above:

La viga se va a _____ .

El capintero tiene que _____ la tabla.

Usted no necesita _____ la vigueta.

Grammar Time

There are two ways to chat about future events in Spanish. One of them is the simple future tense, which requires the following conjugation. As you practice the following pattern, try to exaggerate the accented syllable:

To Speak	Hablar *(ah-'blahr)*
I will speak	**hablaré** *(ah-blah-'reh)*
You (sing.); he, she will speak	**hablará** *(ah-bla-'rah)*
We will speak	**hablaremos** *(ah-blah-'reh-mohs)*
You (pl.); they will speak	**hablarán** *(ah-blah-'rahn)*

To Eat	Comer *(koh-'mehr)*
I will eat	**comeré** *(koh-meh-'reh)*
You (sing.); he, she will eat	**comerá** *(koh-meh-'rah)*
We will eat	**comeremos** *(koh-meh-'reh-mohs)*
You (pl.); they will eat	**comerán** *(koh-meh-'rahn)*

To Write	Escribir *(ehs-kree-'beer)*
I will write	**escribiré** *(ehs-kree-bee-'reh)*
You (sing.), he, she will write	**escribirá** *(ehs-kree-bee-'rah)*
We will write	**escribiremos** *(ehs-kree-bee-'reh-mohs)*
You (pl.); they will write	**escribirán** *(ehs-kree-bee-'rahn)*

You'll need to learn irregular verbs on your own. Here are a few examples:

<u>To put</u>	**Poner** *(poh-'nehr)*
I'll put	**pondré** *(pohn-'dreh)*
<u>To come</u>	**Venir** *(veh-'neer)*
he'll come	**vendrá** *(vehn-'drah)*
<u>To say</u>	**Decir** *(deh-'seer)*
they'll say	**dirán** *(dee-'rahn)*

Try Some

Now, using the same formula, give these a try:

Trabajar	**Vender**	**Ir**
_____	_____	_____
_____	_____	_____
_____	_____	_____
_____	_____	_____

Chapter Six

Capítulo Seis
(kah-'pee-too-loh 'seh-ees)

Roofing
La techumbre
(lah teh-'choom-breh)

 Working Words: THE ROOF

In Spanish, *roof* is often called **el techo** *(ehl-'teh-choh)* or **el tejado** *(ehl teh-'hah-doh)*, although **el techo** may also refer to the ceiling. Regarding *roofer*, **el rufero** *(ehl roo-'feh-roh)* is used in Spanglish, but the best translation for roofer is **el instalador de tejados** *(ehl eens-tah-lah-'dohr deh teh-'hah-dohs)*. A roofer's vocabulary includes the following:

covering	**la cubierta** *(lah koo-bee-'ehr-tah)*
framing	**el armazón** *(ehl ahr-mah-'sohn)*
flashing	**el tapajuntas** *(ehl tah-pah-'hoon-tahs)*
coating	**la capa** *(lah 'kah-pah)*
slope	**la cuesta** *(lah 'kwehs-tah)*
edge	**el borde** *(ehl 'bohr-deh)*
deck	**el piso exterior** *(ehl 'pee-soh ehks-teh-ree-'ohr)*
overhang	**el voladizo** *(ehl voh-lah-'dee-soh)*
gable	**el aguilón** *(ehl ah-gee-'lohn)*
ridge	**el caballete** *(ehl kah-bah-'yeh-teh)*
valley	**la limahoya** *(lah lee-mah-'oh-yah)*
hip	**la limatesa** *(lah lee-mah-'teh-sah)*
shingle	**la teja de asfalto** *(lah 'teh-hah deh ahs-'fahl-toh)*
shake	**el listón** *(ehl lees-'tohn)*
slate	**la pizarra** *(lah pee-'sah-rrah)*
tile	**la teja** *(lah 'teh-hah)*

Roofing projects include the following:

It's...	Es... *(ehs)*
new roofing	**la techumbre nueva** *(lah teh-'choom-breh 'nweh-vah)*
re-roofing	**el reemplazo de la techumbre** *(ehl reh-ehm-'plah-soh deh lah teh-'choom-breh)*
built-up roofing	**la techumbre urbanizada** *(lah the-'choom-breh oor-bah-nee-'sah-dah)*
rolled roofing	**la techumbre del rodillo** *(lah teh-'choom-breh dehl roh-'dee-yoh)*

It has a _____ roof.	**Tiene un techo _____.** *(tee-'eh-neh oon 'teh-choh)*
flat	**plano** *('plah-noh)*
gabled	**de dos aguas** *(deh dohs 'ah-gwahs)*
gambrel	**granjero** *(grahn-'heh-roh)*
hipped	**de varias aguas** *(deh 'vah-ree-ahs 'ah-gwahs)*
mansard	**francés** *(frahn-'sehs)*
pyramidal	**pirámide** *(pee-'rah-mee-deh)*

Use this roofing vocabulary in a sentence:

It's for (the)...	Es para... *(ehs 'pah-rah)*
cornice	**la cornisa** *(lah kohr-'nee-sah)*
dormer	**la buhardilla** *(lah boo-ahr-'dee-yah)*
drip edge	**el borde de goteo** *(ehl 'bohr-deh deh goh-'teh-oh)*
eaves	**el alero** *(ehl ah-'leh-roh)*
fascia	**la fachada** *(lah fah-'chah-dah)*
rake board	**la moldura del techo** *(lah mohl-'doo-rah dehl 'teh-choh)*
ridge board	**la tabla del caballete** *(lah 'tah-blah dehl kah-bah-'yeh-teh)*
soffit	**la cubierta del alero** *(lah koo-bee-'ehr-tah dehl ah-'leh-roh)*

Work on (the)...	Trabaje con... *(trah-'bah-heh kohn)*
attic	**el ático** *(ehl 'ah-tee-koh)*
balcony	**el balcón** *(ehl bahl-'kohn)*
crawl space	**el entretecho** *(ehl ehn-treh-'teh-choh)*
roof top	**la azotea** *(lah ah-soh-'teh-ah)*
sub-roof	**el subtecho** *(ehl soob-'teh-choh)*

chimney	**la chimenea** *(lah chee-meh-'neh-ah)*
downspout	**el bajante de aguas** *(ehl bah-'hahn-teh deh 'ah-gwahs)*
drain	**el drenaje** *(ehl dreh-'nah-heh)*
gutter	**el canalón** *(ehl cah-nah-'lohn)*
skylight	**el tragaluz** *(ehl trah-gah-'loos)*

Now focus on the terminology related to ventilation:

Look at (the)…	**Mire…** *('mee-reh)*

hood	**la capota** *(lah kah-'poh-tah)*
jack	**la rejilla** *(lah reh-'hee-yah)*
duct	**el conducto** *(ehl kohn-'dook-toh)*
air filter	**el filtro de aire** *(ehl 'feel-troh deh 'ah-ee-reh)*
air intake vent	**el aspirador** *(ehl ahs-pee-rah-dohr)*
fan	**el ventilador** *(ehl vehn-tee-lah-'dohr)*
exhaust pipe	**el tubo de escape** *(ehl 'too-boh deh ehs-'kah-peh)*
louvers	**las persianas** *(lahs pehr-see-'ah-nahs)*
screen	**el mosquitero** *(ehl mohs-kee-'teh-roh)*
vent tube	**el tubo de ventilación** *(ehl 'too-boh deh vehn-tee-lah-see-'ohn)*

Don't forget the words used in framing that specifically relate to roofing:

Check the…	**Revise…** *(reh-'vee-seh)*

backing	**el respaldo** *(ehl rehs-'pahl-doh)*
beam	**la viga** *(lah 'vee-gah)*
brace	**el tirante** *(ehl tee-'rahn-teh)*
cross beam	**el travesaño** *(ehl trah-veh-'sah-nyoh)*
doubler	**el doble** *(ehl 'doh-bleh)*
header	**la cabecera** *(lah kah-beh-'seh-rah)*
joint	**la unión** *(lah oo-nee-'ohn)*
joist	**la vigueta** *(lah vee-'geh-tah)*
panel	**el panel** *(ehl pah-'nehl)*
plate	**la placa** *(lah 'plah-kah)*
post	**el poste** *(ehl 'pohs-teh)*
rafter	**el cabrio** *(ehl 'kah-bree-oh)*
sheathing	**el revestimiento** *(ehl reh-vehs-tee-mee-'ehn-toh)*
trimmer	**el moldeador** *(ehl mohl-deh-ah-'dohr)*
tripler	**el triple** *(ehl 'tree-pleh)*
truss	**la armadura** *(lah ahr-mah-'doo-rah)*

See how phrases can be developed from one single word:

collar	**el <u>amarre</u>** *(ehl ah-'mah-rreh)*
collar tie	**la vigueta de <u>amarre</u>** *(lah vee-'geh-tah deh ah-'mah-rreh)*
collar beam	**la viga de <u>amarre</u>** *(lah 'vee-gah deh ah-'mah-rreh)*

Roofing also requires a few location words:

Finish (the)...	**Termine con...** *(tehr-'mee-neh kohn)*
back	**la espalda** *(lah ehs-'pahl-dah)*
beginning	**el principio** *(ehl preen-'see-pee-oh)*
bottom	**el pie** *(ehl pee-'eh)*
cap	**la corona** *(lah koh-'roh-nah)*
center	**el centro** *(ehl 'sehn-troh)*
corner	**la esquina** *(lah ehs-'kee-nah)*
edge	**el borde** *(ehl 'bohr-deh)*
end	**el fin** *(ehl feen)*
face	**la cara** *(lah 'kah-rah)*
middle	**el medio** *(ehl 'meh-dee-oh)*
side	**el costado** *(ehl kohs-'tah-doh)*
top	**la cima** *(lah 'see-mah)*

To be specific, you usually need longer phrases:

ridge tile	**la teja del caballete** *(lah 'teh-hah dehl kah-bah-'yeh-teh)*
hip slate	**la pizarra de la limatesa** *(lah pee-'sah-rrah deh lah lee-mah-'teh-sah)*
eaves flashing	**el tapajuntas para el alero** *(ehl tah-pah-'hoon-tahs 'pah-rah ehl ah-'leh-roh)*

Try Some

Select the correct word to complete the series:

el drenaje, el canalón, _____   **el centro**

la teja, la pizarra, _____   **el bajante**

la cima, el pie, _____   **el listón**

Working Words: ROOFING MATERIALS

Check off all the roofing materials you'll need for your next job:

Unload (the)...   **Descargue...** *(dehs-'kahr-geh)*

asphalt   **el asfalto** *(ehl ahs-'fahl-toh)*
boards   **las tablas** *(lahs 'tah-blahs)*
bricks   **los ladrillos** *(lohs lah-'dree-yohs)*
caulking   **la masilla** *(lah mah-'see-yah)*
connectors   **las conexiones** *(lahs koh-nehk-see-'oh-nehs)*
felt   **el fieltro** *(ehl fee-'ehl-troh)*
gravel   **la grava** *(lah 'grah-vah)*
insulation   **el aislamiento** *(ehl ah-ees-lah-mee-'ehn-toh)*
membrane   **la membrana** *(lah mehm-'brah-nah)*
mortar   **la argamasa** *(lah ahr-gah-'mah-sah)*
paint   **la pintura** *(lah peen-'too-rah)*
roofing paper   **el papel protector** *(ehl pah-'pehl proh-tehk-'tohr)*
sealer   **el sellador** *(ehl seh-yah-'dohr)*
sheeting   **la lámina** *(lah 'lah-mee-nah)*
shims   **las calzas** *(lahs 'kahl-sahs)*
tape   **la cinta** *(lah 'seen-tah)*
tar   **la brea** *(lah 'breh-ah)*
waterproofing   **el material impermeable** *(ehl mah-teh-ree-'ahl eem-pehr-meh-'ah-ble)*

It's made of...   **Está hecho de...** *(ehs-'tah 'eh-choh deh)*

adobe   **el adobe** *(ehl ah-'doh-beh)*
aluminum   **el aluminio** *(ehl ah-loo-'mee-nee-oh)*
cedar   **el cedro** *(ehl 'seh-droh)*
cement   **el cemento** *(ehl seh-'mehn-toh)*
ceramic   **la cerámica** *(lah seh-'rah-mee-kah)*
clay   **la arcilla** *(lah ahr-'see-yah)*
composite   **el compuesto** *(ehl kohm-'pwehs-toh)*
copper   **el cobre** *(ehl 'koh-breh)*
enamel   **el esmalte** *(ehl ehs-'mahl-teh)*
fiber   **la fibra** *(lah 'fee-brah)*

fiberglass	**la fibra de vidrio** *(lah 'fee-brah deh 'vee-dree-oh)*
pine	**el pino** *(ehl 'pee-noh)*
plastic	**el plástico** *(ehl 'plahs-tee-koh)*
plywood	**el contrachapado** *(ehl kohn-trah-chah-'pah-doh)*
redwood	**la secoya** *(lah seh-'koh-yah)*
rubber	**la goma** *(lah 'goh-mah)*
steel	**el acero** *(ehl ah-'seh-roh)*
stone	**la piedra** *(lah pee-'eh-drah)*
tin	**el estaño** *(ehl ehs-'tahn-yoh)*
zinc	**el cinc** *(ehl seenk)*

Materials can also be described as parts of complete sets:

I need (the)...	**Necesito...** *(neh-seh-'see-toh)*
coarse of tiles	**la hilera de tejas** *(lah ee-'leh-rah deh 'teh-hahs)*
bundle of shake	**el paquete de listones** *(ehl pah-'keh-teh deh lees-'toh-nehs)*
box of slate	**la caja de pizarra** *(lah 'kah-hah deh pee-'sah-rrah)*
bag of cement	**el saco de cemento** *(ehl 'sah-koh deh seh-'mehn-toh)*
tube of caulking	**el tubo de masilla** *(ehl 'too-boh deh mah-'see-yah)*
pallet of plywood	**la plataforma de contrachapado** *(lah plah-tah-'fohr-mah deh kohn-trah-chah-'pah-doh)*
bucket of tar	**la cubeta de brea** *(lah koo-'beh-tah deh 'breh-ah)*
roll of paper	**el rollo de papel** *(ehl 'roh-yoh deh pah-'pehl)*
strip of adhesive	**la tira de adhesivo** *(lah 'tee-rah deh ah-deh-'see-voh)*

Try Some

Guess what these words mean in English:

plástico   adhesivo   concreto   aluminio   cerámica

Working Words: EQUIPMENT AND TOOLS

The larger pieces of equipment are often unloaded first:

We'll use (the)...	**Usaremos...** *(oo-sah-'reh-mohs)*
conveyor	**la cinta transportadora** *(lah 'seen-tah trahns-pohr-tah-'doh-rah)*
crane	**la grúa** *(lah 'groo-ah)*
forklift	**la carretilla elevadora** *(lah kah-rreh-'tee-yah eh-leh-vah-'doh-rah)*

Now break out the lighter stuff:

Where's (the)..?	**¿Dónde está...?** *('dohn-deh ehs-'tah)*
air compressor	**el compresor de aire** *(ehl kohm-preh-'sohr deh 'ah-ee-reh)*
caulking gun	**la pistola de masilla** *(lah pees-'toh-lah deh mah-'see-yah)*
chalk box	**la cajita de tiza** *(lah kah-'hee-tah deh 'tee-sah)*
extension cord	**la extensión eléctrica** *(lah ehks-tehn-see-'ohn eh-'lehk-tree-kah)*
hammer	**el martillo** *(ehl mahr-'tee-yoh)*
impact wrench	**la llave eléctrica** *(lah 'yah-veh eh-'lehk-tree-kah)*
ladder	**la escalera** *(lah ehs-kah-'leh-rah)*
level	**el nivelador** *(ehl nee-veh-lah-'dohr)*
measuring tape	**la cinta métrica** *(lah 'seen-tah 'meh-tree-kah)*
nail gun	**la pistola de clavos** *(lah pees-'toh-lah deh 'klah-vohs)*
pliers	**los alicates** *(lohs ah-lee-kah-tehs)*
pry bar	**la pata de cabra** *(lah 'pah-tah deh 'kah-brah)*
saw	**la sierra** *(lah see-'eh-rrah)*
scaffolding	**el andamio** *(ehl ahn-'dah-mee-oh)*
screw gun	**la pistola de tornillos** *(lah pees-'toh-lah deh tohr-'nee-yohs)*
screwdriver	**el destornillador** *(ehl dehs-tohr-nee-yah-'dohr)*
square	**la escuadra** *(lah ehs-'kwah-drah)*
tile cutters	**la cizalla de tejas** *(lah see-'sah-yah deh 'teh-hahs)*
utility knife	**la cuchilla** *(lah koo-'chee-yah)*

Some items are not only used by roofers, but throughout the building project:

I want (the)…	**Quiero…** *(kee-'eh-roh)*
bolt	**el perno** *(ehl 'pehr-noh)*
clip	**la sujetadora** *(lah soo-heh-tah-'doh-rah)*
fastener	**el sujetador** *(ehl soo-heh-tah-'dohr)*
nail	**el clavo** *(ehl 'klah-voh)*
nut	**la tuerca** *(lah too-'ehr-kah)*
pin	**la clavija** *(lah klah-'vee-hah)*
screw	**el tornillo** *(ehl tohr-'nee-yoh)*
staple	**la grapa** *(lah 'grah-pah)*
tack	**la tachuela** *(lah tah-choo-'eh-lah)*

Remember that descriptive words generally appear in reverse order in a Spanish phrase:

corrugated metal	**el metal corrugado** *(ehl meh-'tahl koh-rroo-'gah-doh)*
galvanized wire nail	**el clavo de alambre galvanizado** *(ehl 'klah-voh deh ah-'lahm-breh gahl-vah-nee-'sah-doh)*
plain tile	**la teja plana** *(lah 'teh-hah 'plah-nah)*
processed wood	**la madera procesada** *(lah mah-'deh-rah proh-seh-'sah-dah)*
wood screw	**el tornillo para madera** *(ehl tohr-'nee-yoh 'pah-rah mah-'deh-rah)*

Try Some

Translate these into Spanish:

I need the nail gun. _____

Unload the plain tiles. _____

We'll use the scaffolding. _____

Working Words: ON THE JOB SITE

Give a few tips for roofers:

Be careful with (the)... **Tenga cuidado con...** *('tehn-gah koo-ee-'dah-doh kohn)*

antenna	**la antena** *(lah ahn-'teh-nah)*
phone lines	**las líneas del teléfono** *(lahs 'lee-neh-ahs dehl teh-'leh-foh-noh)*
power lines	**los cables del tendido eléctrico** *(lohs 'kah-blehs dehl tehn-'dee-doh eh-'lehk-tree-koh)*
satellite dish	**el disco de satélite** *(ehl 'dees-koh deh sah-'teh-lee-teh)*
television cables	**los cables de televisión** *(lohs 'kah-blehs deh teh-leh-vee-see-'ohn)*
weathervane	**la veleta** *(lah veh-'leh-tah)*

Now use commands with more location words:

Move... **Mueva...** *('mweh-vah)*

above	**encima** *(ehn-'see-mah)*
across	**de un lado al otro** *(deh oon 'lah-doh ahl 'oh-troh)*
along	**a lo largo de** *(ah loh 'lahr-goh deh)*
around	**alrededor de** *(ahl-reh-deh-'dohr deh)*
backwards	**hacia atrás** *('ah-see-ah ah-'trahs)*
below	**debajo de** *(deh-'bah-hoh deh)*
down	**abajo** *(ah-'bah-hoh)*
forward	**adelante** *(ah-deh-'lahn-teh)*
inside	**adentro** *(ah-'dehn-troh)*
outside	**afuera** *(ah-'fweh-rah)*
through	**por** *(pohr)*
toward	**hacia** *('ah-see-ah)*
up	**arriba** *(ah-'rree-bah)*

Continue to give instructions:

Add... **Añada...** *(ahn-'yah-dah)*

another coat	**otra capa** *('oh-trah 'kah-pah)*
another layer	**otro nivel** *('oh-troh nee-'vehl)*
less	**menos** *('meh-nohs)*

more	**más** *(mahs)*
the same	**lo mismo** *(loh 'mees-moh)*
Check (the)...	**Revise...** *(reh-'vee-seh)*
angle	**el ángulo** *(ehl 'ahn-goo-loh)*
classification	**la clasificación** *(lah klah-see-fee-kah-see-'ohn)*
color	**el color** *(ehl koh-'lohr)*
design	**el diseño** *(ehl dee-'seh-nyoh)*
distance	**la distancia** *(lah dees-'tahn-see-ah)*
height	**la altura** *(lah ahl-'too-rah)*
length	**el largo** *(ehl 'lahr-goh)*
measurement	**la medida** *(lah meh-'dee-dah)*
pattern	**el patrón** *(ehl pah-'trohn)*
pitch	**la pendiente** *(lah pehn-dee-'ehn-teh)*
position	**la posición** *(lah poh-see-see-'ohn)*
rise	**la distancia vertical** *(lah dees-'tahn-see-ah vehr-tee-'kahl)*
size	**el tamaño** *(ehl tah-'mahn-yoh)*
space	**el espacio** *(ehl ehs-'pah-see-oh)*
span	**la distancia horizontal** *(lah dees-'tahn-see-ah oh-ree-sohn-'tahl)*
style	**el estilo** *(ehl ehs-'tee-loh)*
temperature	**la temperatura** *(lah tehm-peh-rah-'too-rah)*
texture	**la textura** *(lah tehks-'too-rah)*
width	**el ancho** *(ehl 'ahn-choh)*

Try Some

Find the opposites:

adentro _____

el largo _____

encima _____

☞ # Working Words: ROOF REPAIR

Discuss the repair work with a few simple statements:

It needs…	**Necesita…** *(neh-seh-'see-tah)*
changes	**cambios** *('kahm-bee-ohs)*
patching	**remiendo** *(reh-mee-'ehn-doh)*
reconstruction	**reconstrucción** *(reh-kohns-trook-see-'ohn)*
repair	**reparación** *(reh-pah-rah-see-'ohn)*
restoration	**restauración** *(rehs-tah-oo-rah-see-'ohn)*

There are…	**Hay…** *('ah-ee)*
bubbles	**burbujas** *(boor-'boo-hahs)*
bumps	**bultos** *('bool-tohs)*
corrosion	**corrosión** *(koh-rroh-see-'ohn)*
cracks	**grietas** *(gree-'eh-tahs)*
damage	**daño** *('dah-nyoh)*
decolorization	**descoloramiento** *(dehs-koh-loh-rah-mee-'ehn-toh)*
dripping	**goteo** *(goh-'teh-oh)*
exposure	**exposición** *(ehks-poh-see-see-'ohn)*
holes	**hoyos** *('oh-yohs)*
leaks	**goteras** *(goh-'teh-rahs)*
mold	**moho** *('moh-hoh)*
pieces	**pedazos** *(peh-'dah-sohs)*
scratches	**rajaduras** *(rah-hah-'doo-rahs)*
stains	**manchas** *('mahn-chahs)*
termites	**termitas** *(tehr-'mee-tahs)*

It's…	**Está…** *(ehs-'tah)*
broken	**rota** *('roh-tah)*
chipped	**mellada** *(meh-'yah-dah)*
dented	**abollada** *(ah-boh-'yah-dah)*
loose	**suelta** *('swehl-tah)*
missing	**perdida** *(pehr-'dee-dah)*
old	**vieja** *(vee-'eh-hah)*
rusty	**oxidada** *(ohk-see-'dah-dah)*
warped	**combada** *(kohm-'bah-dah)*
weak	**débil** *('deh-beel)*
worn	**gastada** *(gahs-'tah-dah)*

Continue to discuss the cause for alarm:

The _____ did it. _____ **lo hizo.** *(loh 'ee-soh)*

cold	**el frío** *(ehl 'free-oh)*
hail	**el granizo** *(ehl grah-'nee-soh)*
heat	**el calor** *(ehl kah-'lohr)*
hurricane	**el huracán** *(ehl oo-rah-'kahn)*
moisture	**la humedad** *(lah oo-meh-'dahd)*
pollution	**la contaminación** *(lah kohn-tah-mee-nah-see-'ohn)*
rain	**la lluvia** *(lah 'yoo-vee-ah)*
snow	**la nieve** *(lah nee-'eh-veh)*
storm	**la tormenta** *(lah tohr-'mehn-tah)*
sun	**el sol** *(ehl sohl)*
tree	**el árbol** *(ehl 'ahr-bohl)*
water	**el agua** *(ehl 'ah-gwah)*
weight	**el peso** *(ehl 'peh-soh)*
wind	**el viento** *(ehl vee-'ehn-toh)*

Just a Suggestion

Remember that the **-ción** ending in Spanish is a lot like *-tion* in English:

inspection	**la inspección** *(lah eens-pehk-see-'ohn)*
certification	**la certificación** *(lah sehr-tee-fee-kah-see-'ohn)*
classification A, B, C	**la clasificación A, B, C** *(lah klah-see-fee-kah-see-'ohn ah beh seh)*

Try Some

Say five words in Spanish that describe a damaged roof:

_____ _____ _____ _____ _____

Working Words: DESCRIBING THE JOB

Important! More words with opposite meanings:

apart	**separados** *(seh-pah-'rah-dohs)*	together	**juntos** *('hoon-tohs)*
lower	**inferior** *(een-feh-ree-'ohr)*	upper	**superior** *(soo-peh-ree-'ohr)*
first	**primero** *(pree-'meh-roh)*	last	**último** *('ool-tee-moh)*

Instead of **Es** *(ehs)*, use **Está** *(ehs-'tah)*, which indicates more of a temporary condition:

It's...   **Está...** *(ehs-'tah)* It's not...   **No está...** *(noh ehs-'tah)*

attached	**conectado** *(koh-nehk-'tah-doh)*
balanced	**balanceado** *(bah-lahn-seh-'ah-doh)*
braced	**arriostrado** *(ah-rree-ohs-'trah-doh)*
crossed	**cruzado** *(kroo-'sah-doh)*
curved	**curvado** *(koor-'vah-doh)*
decorative	**decorativo** *(deh-koh-rah-'tee-voh)*
durable	**duradero** *(doo-rah-'deh-roh)*
finished	**acabado** *(ah-kah-'bah-doh)*
fire resistant	**resistente al fuego** *(reh-sees-'tehn-teh ahl 'fweh-goh)*
fireproof	**incombustible** *(een-kohm-boos-'tee-bleh)*
framed	**enmarcado** *(ehn-mahr-'kah-doh)*
hollow	**hueco** *(oo-'eh-koh)*
laminated	**laminado** *(lah-mee-'nah-doh)*
rustproof	**inoxidable** *(ee-noh-ksee-'dah-bleh)*
sealed	**sellado** *(seh-'yah-doh)*
solid	**sólido** *('soh-lee-doh)*
square	**cuadrado** *(kwah-'drah-doh)*
steep	**empinado** *(ehm-pee-'nah-doh)*
sticky	**pegajoso** *(peh-gah-'hoh-soh)*
straight	**recto** *('rehk-toh)*
treated	**tratado** *(trah-'tah-doh)*
uniform	**uniforme** *(oo-nee-'fohr-meh)*
waterproof	**impermeable** *(eem-pehr-meh-'ah-bleh)*

Here's how you describe more than one thing:

They are…	**Están…** *(ehs-'tahn)*
flush	**a ras de** *(ah rahs deh)*
interwoven	**entretejidos** *(ehn-treh-teh-'hee-dohs)*
lined up	**en fila** *(ehn 'fee-lah)*
parallel	**paralelos** *(pah-rah-'leh-lohs)*
similar	**similares** *(see-mee-'lah-rehs)*

These should be easy:

diagonal	**diagonal** *(dee-ah-goh-'nahl)*
horizontal	**horizontal** *(oh-ree-sohn-'tahl)*
perpendicular	**perpendicular** *(pehr-pehn-dee-koo-'lahr)*
rectangular	**rectangular** *(rehk-tahn-goo-'lahr)*
vertical	**vertical** *(vehr-tee-'kahl)*

What do you know about architectural styles?

I like…	**Me gusta el estilo…** *(meh 'goos-tah ehl ehs-'tee-loh)*
classic	**clásico** *('klah-see-koh)*
colonial	**colonial** *(koh-loh-nee-'ahl)*
conventional	**convencional** *(kohn-vehn-see-oh-'nahl)*
Dutch	**holandés** *(oh-lahn-'dehs)*
Spanish	**español** *(ehs-pah-'nyohl)*

Just a Suggestion

Several roofing-specific terms have rather unusual translations and are generally expressed in English, but here you can see them as they should be:

rake	**el borde inclinado** *(ehl 'bohr-deh een-klee-'nah-doh)*
lap	**la solapa** *(lah soh-'lah-pah)*
tab	**la teja expuesta** *(lah 'teh-hah ex-'pwehs-tah)*
cricket	**el tapajuntas especial** *(ehl tah-pah-'hoon-tahs ehs-peh-see-'ahl)*
eyebrow	**el entretecho** *(ehl ehn-treh-'teh-choh)*

Try Some

Find the opposites in Spanish:

último   _____

vertical   _____

mojado   _____

curvado   _____

flojo   _____

hueco   _____

Working Words: ON-SITE ACTIONS

The following Spanish verbs work well as parts of action phrases in roofing:

It's going...	**Va a...** *(vah ah)*
to last	**durar** *(doo-'rahr)*
to line up	**alinearse** *(ah-lee-neh-'ahr-seh)*
to overhang	**sobresalir por encima** *(soh-breh-sah-'leer pohr ehn-'see-mah)*
to overlap	**superponerse** *(soo-pehr-poh-'nehr-seh)*
to overload	**sobrecargarse** *(soh-breh-kahr-'gahr-seh)*
to protect	**proteger** *(proh-teh-'hehr)*
to reach	**alcanzar** *(ahl-kahn-'sahr)*
to reinforce	**reforzar** *(reh-fohr-'sahr)*
to repel	**repeler** *(reh-peh-'lehr)*
to support	**apoyar** *(ah-poh-'yahr)*
It's not going...	**No se va a...** *(noh seh vah ah)*
to break	**romper** *(rohm-'pehr)*
to drip	**gotear** *(goh-teh-'ahr)*
to fade	**descolorar** *(dehs-koh-loh-'rahr)*
to fall over	**tumbar** *(toom-'bahr)*
to move	**mover** *(moh-'vehr)*

to penetrate	**penetrar** *(peh-neh-'trahr)*
to ruin	**arruinar** *(ah-rroo-ee-'nahr)*
to sag	**hundir** *(oon-'deer)*
to slip	**resbalar** *(rehs-bah-'lahr)*
to spill	**derramar** *(deh-rrah-'mahr)*
to splatter	**salpicar** *(sahl-pee-'kahr)*
to stain	**manchar** *(mahn-'chahr)*
to stick	**pegar** *(peh-'gahr)*
You need…	**Necesita…** *(neh-seh-'see-tah)*
to apply	**aplicar** *(ah-plee-'kahr)*
to attach	**conectar** *(koh-nehk-'tahr)*
to match	**armonizar** *(ahr-moh-nee-'sahr)*
to bore	**calar** *(kah-'lahr)*
to build	**construir** *(kohns-troo-'eer)*
to clean	**limpiar** *(leem-pee-'ahr)*
to climb	**subir** *(soo-'beer)*
to cover	**cubrir** *(koo-'breer)*
to cut	**cortar** *(kohr-'tahr)*
to enclose	**encerrar** *(ehn-seh-'rrahr)*
to fill	**llenar** *(yeh-'nahr)*
to glue	**encolar** *(ehn-koh-'lahr)*
to heat	**calentar** *(kah-lehn-'tahr)*
to hook	**enganchar** *(ehn-gahn-'chahr)*
to hot-mop	**poner brea** *(poh-'nehr 'bre-ah)*
to install	**instalar** *(eens-tah-'lahr)*
to join	**juntar** *(hoon-'tahr)*
to lean	**inclinar** *(een-klee-'nahr)*
to level	**nivelar** *(nee-veh-'lahr)*
to lift	**levantar** *(leh-vahn-'tahr)*
to loosen	**soltar** *(sohl-'tahr)*
to lower	**bajar** *(bah-'hahr)*
to measure	**medir** *(meh-'deer)*
to mount	**montar** *(mohn-'tahr)*
to nail	**clavar** *(klah-'vahr)*
to notch	**mellar** *(meh-'yahr)*
to overlay	**revestir** *(reh-vehs-'teer)*
to patch	**remendar** *(reh-mehn-'dahr)*
to place	**colocar** *(koh-loh-'kahr)*

to remove	**quitar** *(kee-'tahr)*
to repair	**reparar** *(reh-pah-'rahr)*
to screw in	**atornillar** *(ah-tohr-nee-'yahr)*
to seal	**sellar** *(seh-'yahr)*
to snap a line	**marcar una línea** *(mahr-'kahr 'oo-nah 'lee-neh-ah)*
to space	**espaciar** *(ehs-pah-see-'ahr)*
to spray	**rociar** *(roh-see-'ahr)*
to spread	**repartir** *(reh-pahr-'teer)*
to stack	**apilar** *(ah-pee-'lahr)*
to staple	**engrapar** *(ehn-grah-'pahr)*
to tape	**encintar** *(ehn-seen-'tahr)*
to toenail	**clavar en ángulo** *(klah-vahr ehn 'ahn-goo-loh)*
to ventilate	**ventilar** *(vehn-tee-'lahr)*
to waterproof	**impermeabilizar** *(eem-pehr-meh-ah-bee-lee-'sahr)*
to wrap	**forrar** *(foh-'rrahr)*

Grammar Time

To describe an action word in Spanish, try one of these. The secret is the **-mente** ending:

completely	**completamente** *(kohm-pleh-tah-'mehn-teh)*
quickly	**rápidamente** *('rah-pee-dah-mehn-teh)*
slowly	**lentamente** *(lehn-tah-'mehn-teh)*

You have to seal the pipes quickly.
Tiene que sellar la tubería rápidamente.
(tee-'eh-neh keh seh-'yahr lah too-beh-'ree-ah rah-pee-dah-'mehn-teh)

Try Some

Connect the verbs that belong together:

calar	**escurrir**
conectar	**cortar**
derramar	**juntar**

One-Liners

Here's a set of expressions that should be practiced regularly. They are used to motivate the folks around you:

How...!	**¡Qué...!** *(keh)*
great	**bueno** *('bweh-noh)*
excellent	**excelente** *(ex-seh-'lehn-teh)*
tremendous	**magnífico** *(mahg-'nee-fee-koh)*

Nothing works better than encouraging remarks!

What a great job!	**¡Qué buen trabajo!** *(keh boo-'ehn trah-'bah-hoh)*
Very good!	**¡Muy bien!** *('moo-ee bee-'ehn)*
Well done!	**¡Bien hecho!** *(bee-'ehn 'eh-choh)*

Grammar Time

One way for Spanish speakers to talk about activities that took place in the past is *to share what they were doing.* There are two steps to putting this together, so pay attention:

STEP ONE
Give your **-ar** verbs the **-ando** endings and the **-er** or **-ir** verbs the **-iendo** endings. You did this in a previous chapter:

hablar	hablando
comer	comiendo
escribir	escribiendo

STEP TWO
Now, change the verb **estar** to the following past tense forms:

Estar *(ehs-'tahr)*	
I, he, she was; you (sing.) were	**estaba** *(ehs-'tah-bah)*
We were	**estábamos** *(ehs-'tah-bah-mohs)*
They; you (pl.) were	**estaban** *(ehs-'tah-bahn)*

Now, put them together. Concentrate as you read each line below:

I was working.	**Estaba trabajando.** *(ehs-'tah-bah trah-bah-'hahn-doh)*
You (sing.) were; he, she was eating.	**Estaba comiendo.** *(ehs-'tah-bah koh-mee-'ehn-doh)*
We were nailing.	**Estábamos clavando.** *(ehs-'tah-bah-mohs klah-'vahn-doh)*
You (plur.), they were climbing.	**Estaban subiendo.** *(ehs-'tah-bahn soo-bee-'ehn-doh)*

Just a Suggestion

The negative and question forms are simple to create:

We weren't eating.	**No estábamos comiendo.** *(noh ehs-'tah-bah-mohs koh-mee-'ehn-doh)*
Were you guys leaving?	**¿Estaban saliendo?** *(ehs-'tah-bahn sah-lee-'ehn-doh)*

Try Some

Change these present progressive sentences to the past progressive:

Estoy trabajando.	<u>**Estaba trabajando.**</u>
Está resbalando.	_____
Estamos revisando.	_____
Están limpiando.	_____

Chapter Seven

Capítulo Siete
(kah-'pee-too-loh see-'eh-teh)

Mechanics in General
La mecánica en general
(lah meh-'kah-nee-kah ehn heh-neh-'rahl)

Begin by asking everyone about his profession:

Are you the…?	**¿Es usted…?** *(ehs oos-'tehd)*

electrician	**el electricista** *(ehl eh-lehk-tree-'sees-tah)*
plumber	**el fontanero** *(ehl fohn-tah-'neh-roh)*
installer	**el instalador** *(ehl eens-tah-lah-'dohr)*
technician	**el técnico** *(ehl 'tehk-nee-koh)*
mechanic	**el mecánico** *(ehl meh-'kah-nee-koh)*

Are you here for (the)…?	**¿Está aquí para…?** *(ehs-'tah ah-'kee 'pah-rah)*

installation	**la instalación** *(lah eens-tah-lah-see-'ohn)*
repair	**la reparación** *(lah reh-pah-rah-see-'ohn)*
service	**el servicio** *(ehl sehr-'vee-see-oh)*
plumbing	**la tubería** *(lah too-beh-'ree-ah)*
electricity	**la electricidad** *(lah eh-lehk-tree-see-'dahd)*
heating	**la calefacción** *(lah kah-leh-fahk-see-'ohn)*
air conditioning	**el aire condicionado** *(ehl 'ah-ee-reh ah-kohn-dee-see-oh-'nah-doh)*
insulation	**el aislamiento** *(ehl ah-ees-lah-mee-'ehn-toh)*

Where's (the)…?	**¿Dónde está…?** *('dohn-deh ehs-'tah)*

shut-off valve	**la válvula principal de corte** *(lah 'vahl-voo-lah preen-see-'pahl deh 'kohr-teh)*
shut-off switch	**el interruptor principal** *(ehl een-teh-rroop-'tohr preen-see-'pahl)*

power	**la fuente de energía** *(lah 'fwehn-teh deh eh-nehr-'hee-ah)*
supply	**el suministro** *(ehl soo-mee-'nees-troh)*
main line	**la línea principal** *(lah 'lee-neh-ah preen-see-'pahl)*
equipment	**el equipo** *(ehl eh-'kee-poh)*
appliance	**el electrodoméstico** *(ehl eh-lehk-troh-doh-'mehs-tee-koh)*
machinery	**la maquinaria** *(lah mah-kee-'nah-ree-ah)*
apparatus	**el aparato** *(ehl ah-pah-'rah-toh)*
device	**el mecanismo** *(ehl meh-kah-'nees-moh)*

Let's work on (the)…	**Trabajemos con…** *(trah-bah-'heh-mohs kohn)*

air conditioner	**el acondicionador de aire** *(ehl ah-kohn-dee-see-oh-nah-'dohr deh 'ah-ee-reh)*
bathtub	**la tina de baño** *(lah 'tee-nah deh 'bahn-yoh)*
dishwasher	**el lavaplatos** *(ehl lah-vah-'plah-tohs)*
dryer	**la secadora** *(lah seh-kah-'doh-rah)*
garbage disposal	**el desechador** *(ehl deh-seh-chah-'dohr)*
heater	**la calentadora** *(lah kah-lehn-tah-'doh-rah)*
hot water heater	**el calentador de agua** *(ehl kah-lehn-tah-'dohr deh 'ah-gwah)*
light	**la luz** *(lah loos)*
oven	**el horno** *(ehl 'ohr-noh)*
shower	**la ducha** *(lah 'doo-chah)*
sink	**el lavabo** *(ehl lah-'vah-boh)*
stove	**la estufa** *(lah ehs-'too-fah)*
toilet	**el excusado** *(ehl ex-koo-'sah-doh)*
washer	**la lavadora** *(lah lah-vah-'doh-rah)*

Include items that require specialized skills:

Install (the)…	**Instale…** *(eens-'tah-leh)*

fuse box	**la caja de fusibles** *(lah 'kah-hah deh foo-'see-blehs)*
gas meter	**el medidor de gas** *(ehl meh-'dee-dohr deh gahs)*
water valve	**la válvula de agua** *(lah 'vahl-voo-lah deh 'ah-gwah)*

security system	**el sistema de seguridad** *(ehl sees-'teh-mah deh seh-goo-ree-'dahd)*
sound system	**el sistema de sonido** *(ehl sees-'teh-mah deh soh-nee-doh)*
waste/vent system	**el sistema de drenaje y ventilación** *(ehl sees-'teh-mah deh dreh-'nah-heh ee vehn-tee-lah-see-'ohn)*

phone lines	**las líneas del teléfono** *(lahs 'lee-neh-ahs dehl teh-'leh-foh-noh)*
satellite dish	**el disco de satélite** *(ehl 'dees-koh deh sah-'teh-lee-teh)*
television cables	**los cables de televisión** *(lohs 'kah-blehs deh teh-leh-vee-see-'ohn)*

They want (the)...	**Quieren...** *(kee-'eh-rehn)*
blown insulation	**el aislamiento soplado** *(ehl ah-ees-lah-mee-'ehn toh soh-'plah-doh)*
central vacuuming	**el sistema de aspiradora central** *(ehl sees-'teh-mah deh ahs-pee-rah-'doh-rah sehn-'trahl)*
garage door opener	**el abridor de garajes** *(ehl ah-bree-'dohr deh gah-'rah-hehs)*
gas barbeque	**la parrilla de gas** *(lah pah-'rree-yah deh gahs)*
gas fireplace	**el fogón de gas** *(ehl foh-'gohn deh gahs)*
intercom system	**el sistema de intercomunicación** *(ehl sees-'teh-mah deh een-tehr-koh-moo-nee-kah-see-'ohn)*
outdoor lighting	**la iluminación al aire libre** *(lah ee-loo-mee-nah-see-'ohn ahl 'ah-ee-reh 'lee-breh)*
solar panels	**los paneles solares** *(lohs pah-'neh-lehs soh-'lah-rehs)*
sprinkler system	**el sistema de aspersores** *(ehl sees-'teh-mah deh ahs-pehr-'soh-rehs)*

Be sure everything is set up for installation:

Check (the)...	**Revise...** *(reh-'vee-seh)*
backing	**el respaldo** *(ehl rehs-'pahl-doh)*
brace	**la abrazadera** *(lah ah-brah-sah-'deh-rah)*
cabinet	**el gabinete** *(ehl gah-bee-'neh-teh)*
counter	**el mostrador** *(ehl mohs-trah-'dohr)*
floor	**el piso** *(ehl 'pee-soh)*
footing	**el cimiento** *(ehl see-mee-'ehn-toh)*
framing	**el armazón** *(ehl ahr-mah-'sohn)*
header	**el cabecero** *(ehl kah-beh-'seh-roh)*
stud	**el montante** *(ehl mohn-'tahn-teh)*
wall	**la pared** *(lah pah-'rehd)*

Just a Suggestion

Sometimes several words are required when installing a system:

integrated sound and video system
el sistema integral de sonido y video
(ehl sees-'teh-mah een-teh-'grahl deh soh-'nee-doh ee vee-'deh-oh)

closed circuit cable system
el sistema de cable de circuito cerrado
(ehl sees-'teh-mah deh 'kah-bleh deh seer-koo-'ee-toh seh-'rrah-doh)

heating and air conditioning system
el sistema de calefacción y aire acondicionado
(ehl sees-'teh-mah deh kah-leh-fahk-see-'ohn ee 'ah-ee-reh ah-kohn-dee-see-oh-'nah-doh)

Try Some

Connect the worker with the appropriate household item:

el instalador	**el excusado**
el plomero	**la luz**
el electricista	**el gabinete**

Working Words: MACHINE PARTS

Before installing anything, pick up the names for fixture, machine, and product parts in the worksite.

Give me (the)...	**Deme...** *('deh-meh)*
bar	**la barra** *(lah 'bah-'rrah)*
battery	**la batería** *(lah bah-teh-'ree-ah)*
bearing	**el cojinete** *(ehl koh-hee-'neh-teh)*
belt	**la banda** *(lah 'bahn-dah)*

board	el **tablero** *(ehl tah-'bleh-roh)*
bulb	el **foco** *(ehl 'foh-koh)*
button	el **botón** *(ehl boh-'tohn)*
cartridge	el **cartucho** *(ehl kahr-'too-choh)*
case	la **caja** *(lah 'kah-hah)*
cell	la **célula** *(lah 'seh-loo-lah)*
chamber	la **cámara** *(lah 'kah-mah-rah)*
chassis	el **bastidor** *(ehl bahs-tee-'dohr)*
coil	el **rollo** *(ehl 'roh-yoh)*
crank	la **manivela** *(lah mah-nee-'veh-lah)*
conduit	el **conducto** *(ehl kohn-'dook-toh)*
filter	el **filtro** *(ehl 'feel-troh)*
gauge	el **indicador** *(ehl een-dee-kah-'dohr)*
gear	el **engranaje** *(ehl ehn-grah-'nah-heh)*
handle	la **perilla** *(lah peh-'ree-yah)*
hinge	la **bisagra** *(lah bee-'sah-grah)*
hood	la **capota** *(lah kah-'poh-tah)*
knob	el **botón** *(ehl boh-'tohn)*
lid	la **tapa** *(lah 'tah-pah)*
lever	la **palanca** *(lah pah-'lahn-kah)*
motor	el **motor** *(ehl moh-'tohr)*
needle	la **aguja** *(lah ah-'goo-hah)*
nozzle	el **pitón** *(ehl pee-'tohn)*
panel	el **panel** *(ehl pah-'nehl)*
peg	la **clavija** *(lah klah-'vee-hah)*
pipe	el **tubo** *(ehl 'too-boh)*
piston	el **émbolo** *(ehl 'ehm-boh-loh)*
plate	la **placa** *(lah 'plah-kah)*
propeller	la **hélice** *(lah 'eh-lee-seh)*
pump	la **bomba** *(lah 'bohm-bah)*
rivet	el **remache** *(ehl reh-'mah-cheh)*
rod	la **varilla** *(lah vah-'ree-yah)*
roller	el **rodillo** *(ehl roh-'dee-yoh)*
rotor	la **rueda** *(lah 'rweh-dah)*
shaft	el **eje** *(ehl 'eh-heh)*
spool	el **carrete** *(ehl kah-'rreh-teh)*
spring	el **resorte** *(ehl reh-'sohr-teh)*
valve	la **válvula** *(lah 'vahl-voo-lah)*

When you can't recall the name for something, use one of these words:

Bring (the)...	**Traiga...** *('trah-ee-gah)*
component	**el componente** *(ehl kohm-poh-'nehn-teh)*
part	**la parte** *(lah 'pahr-teh)*
piece	**la pieza** *(lah pee-'eh-sah)*
section	**la sección** *(lah sehk-see-'ohn)*
thing	**la cosa** *(lah 'koh-sah)*

These concepts are tough to explain, but are needed to explain the machine's purpose or function:

the function is...	**la función es...** *(lah foon-see-'ohn ehs)*
the purpose is...	**el propósito es...** *(ehl proh-'poh-see-toh ehs)*
the use is...	**el uso es...** *(ehl 'oo-soh ehs)*
load	**la carga** *(lah 'kahr-gah)*
power	**la potencia** *(lah poh-'tehn-see-ah)*
pressure	**la presión** *(lah preh-see-'ohn)*
speed	**la velocidad** *(lah veh-loh-see-'dahd)*
temperature	**la temperatura** *(lah tehm-peh-rah-'too-rah)*
torque	**el esfuerzo de torsión** *(ehl ehs-foo-'ehr-soh deh tohr-see-'ohn)*

Just a Suggestion

Location words will be required for every mechanical installation.

Look at (the)...	**Mire...** *('mee-reh)*
back	**la parte trasera** *(lah 'pahr-teh trah-'seh-rah)*
bottom	**el fondo** *(ehl 'fohn-doh)*
front	**la parte delantera** *(lah 'pahr-teh deh-lahn-'teh-rah)*
side	**el lado** *(ehl 'lah-doh)*
top	**la tapa** *(lah 'tah-pah)*

Try Some

Translate the following words:

el resorte _____

la carga _____

el foco _____

la válvula _____

la cosa _____

Working Words: ELECTRICAL INSTALLATION

Here are a few of the most common words used on any project involving electrical work:

electricity	**la electricidad** _(lah eh-lehk-tree-see-'dahd)_
current	**la corriente** _(lah koh-rree-'ehn-teh)_
power	**la potencia** _(lah poh-'tehn-see-ah)_
cable	**el cable** _(ehl 'kah-bleh)_
electric cord	**el cable de extensión** _(ehl 'kah-bleh deh ex-tehn-see-'ohn)_
wire	**el alambre** _(ehl ah-'lahm-breh)_
switch	**el interruptor** _(ehl een-teh-rroop-'tohr)_
plug	**el enchufe** _(ehl ehn-'choo-feh)_
outlet	**la toma de corriente** _(lah 'toh-mah deh koh-rree-'ehn-teh)_
circuit board	**el tablero de circuitos** _(ehl tah-'bleh-roh deh seer-koo-'ee-tohs)_
fuse box	**la caja de fusibles** _(lah 'kah-hah deh foo-'see-blehs)_
control panel	**el panel de control** _(ehl pah-'nehl deh kohn-'trohl)_
light	**la luz** _(lah loos)_
bulb	**el foco** _(ehl 'foh-koh)_
appliance	**el electrodoméstico** _(ehl eh-lehk-troh-doh-'mehs-tee-koh)_

Install (the)...   **Instale...** *(eens-'tah-leh)*

main power switch   **el interruptor principal** *(ehl een-teh-rroop-'tohr preen-see-'pahl)*

contact plate   **la placa de contacto** *(lah 'plah-kah deh kohn-'tahk-toh)*

double wall socket   **la caja de dos enchufes** *(lah 'kah-hah deh dohs ehn-'choo-fehs)*

switch and socket   **la caja combinada** *(lah 'kah-hah kohm-bee-'nah-dah)*

four-way socket   **la caja de cuatro enchufes** *(lah 'kah-hah deh 'kwah-troh ehn-'choo-fehs)*

three-way plug   **el enchufe de tres puntas** *(ehl ehn-'choo-feh deh trehs 'poon-tahs)*

extension plug   **la clavija macho** *(lah klah-'vee-hah 'mah-choh)*

extension socket   **la clavija hembra** *(lah klah-'vee-hah 'ehm-brah)*

rotary switch   **el interruptor giratorio** *(ehl een-teh-rroop-'tohr hee-rah-'toh-ree-oh)*

circuit breaker   **el cortacircuitos** *(ehl kohr-tah-seer-koo-'ee-tohs)*

reset button   **el botón de reinicio** *(ehl boh-'tohn deh reh-ee-'nee-see-oh)*

dimmer switch   **el interruptor con regulador** *(ehl een-teh-rroop-'tohr kohn reh-goo-lah-'dohr)*

connection box   **la caja de empalmes** *(lah 'kah-hah deh ehm-'pahl-mehs)*

watt-hour meter   **el medidor de vatios por hora** *(ehl meh-dee-'dohr deh 'vah-tee-ohs pohr 'oh-rah)*

rocker switch   **el interruptor de balancín** *(ehl een-teh-rroop-'tohr deh bah-lahn-'seen)*

bypass switch   **el interruptor de derivación** *(ehl een-teh-rroop-'tohr deh deh-ree-vah-see-'ohn)*

splice plate   **la placa de empalme** *(lah 'plah-kah deh ehm-'pahl-meh)*

switch plate   **la placa del interruptor** *(lah 'plah-kah dehl een-teh-rroop-'tohr)*

distribution board   **el tablero auxiliar** *(ehl tah-'bleh-roh ah-oo-ksee-lee-'ahr)*

Electricians can't do much without saying the following:

watt	**el vatio** *(ehl 'vah-tee-oh)*
wattage	**la potencia en vatios** *(lah poh-'tehn-see-ah ehn 'vah-tee-ohs)*
volt	**el voltio** *(ehl 'vohl-tee-oh)*
voltage	**el voltaje** *(ehl vohl-'tah-heh)*
amp	**el amperio** *(ehl ahm-'peh-ree-oh)*
amperage	**el amperaje** *(ehl ahm-peh-'rah-heh)*

Is everything hooked up?

Connect (the)…	**Conecte…** *(koh-'nehk-teh)*
alarm	**la alarma** *(lah ah-'lahr-mah)*
doorbell	**el timbre** *(ehl 'teem-breh)*
fan	**el ventilador** *(ehl vehn-tee-lah-'dohr)*
microphone	**el micrófono** *(ehl mee-'kroh-foh-noh)*
speaker	**el altavoz** *(ehl ahl-tah-'vohs)*
thermostat	**el termostato** *(ehl tehr-mohs-'tah-toh)*

And don't forget your colors:

The cable/wire is…   **El cable/alambre es…** *(ehl 'kah-bleh/ah-'lahm-breh ehs)*

green	**verde** *('vehr-deh)*
white	**blanco** *('blahn-koh)*
black	**negro** *('neh-groh)*
red	**rojo** *('roh-hoh)*
yellow	**amarillo** *(ah-mah-'ree-yoh)*

Many words are identical in both languages, except for stress sometimes:

terminal *(tehr-mee-'nahl)*
sensor *(sehn-'sohr)*
control *(kohn-'trohl)*
detector *(deh-tehk-'tohr)*
conductor *(kohn-dook-'tohr)*

Try Some

Circle the word in each set that doesn't belong with the others:

ventilador, voltaje, voltio
altavoz, micrófono, corriente
timbre, enchufe, interruptor

Working Words: ELECTRICIAN'S TOOLS AND MATERIALS

Electricians will need the following tools, so use this simple command:

Unload (the)…	**Descargue…** *(dehs-'kahr-geh)*
caulking gun	**la pistola de masilla** *(lah pees-'toh-lah deh mah-'see-yah)*
charger	**la cargadora** *(lah kahr-gah-'doh-rah)*
circuit tester	**el probador de circuitos** *(ehl proh-bah-'dohr deh seer-koo-'ee-tohs)*
cutters	**la cizalla** *(lah see-'sah-yah)*
droplight	**el foco de extensión** *(ehl 'foh-koh deh ex-tehn-see-'ohn)*
electric drill	**el taladro eléctrico** *(ehl tah-'lah-droh eh-'lehk-tree-koh)*
electrician's tape	**la cinta aislante** *(lah 'seen-tah ah-ees-'lahn-teh)*
extension cord	**la extensión eléctrica** *(lah ex-tehn-see-'ohn eh-'lehk-tree-kah)*
hammer	**el martillo** *(ehl mahr-'tee-yoh)*
mallet	**el mazo** *(ehl 'mah-soh)*
measuring tape	**la cinta métrica** *(lah 'seen-tah 'meh-tree-kah)*
meter	**el medidor** *(ehl meh-dee-'dohr)*
pinchers	**las tenazas** *(lahs teh-'nah-sahs)*
pliers	**los alicates** *(lohs ah-lee-'kah-tehs)*
saw	**la sierra** *(lah see-'eh-rrah)*
screwdriver	**el destornillador** *(ehl dehs-tohr-nee-yah-'dohr)*
soldering iron	**la pistola de soldar** *(lah pees-'toh-lah deh sohl-'dahr)*
stepladder	**la escalera baja** *(lah ehs-kah-'leh-rah 'bah-hah)*
utility knife	**la cuchilla** *(lah koo-'chee-yah)*
wire brush	**el cepillo de alambre** *(ehl seh-'pee-yoh deh ah-'lahm-breh)*
wrench	**la llave inglesa** *(lah 'yah-veh een-'gleh-sah)*

Some tools come in a variety of forms:

SCREWDRIVERS

adjustable screwdriver	**el destornillador ajustable** *(ehl dehs-tohr-nee-yah-'dohr ah-hoos-'tah-bleh)*
cordless screwdriver	**el destornillador sin cable** *(ehl dehs-tohr-nee-yah-'dohr seen 'kah-bleh)*

expansive screwdriver	**el destornillador de expansión** *(ehl dehs-tohr-nee-yah-'dohr deh ex-pahn-see-'ohn)*
Phillips head screwdriver	**el destornillador en cruz** *(ehl dehs-tohr-nee-yah-'dohr ehn kroos)*
square shaft screwdriver	**el destornillador de mango cuadrado** *(ehl dehs-tohr-nee-yah-'dohr deh 'mahn-goh kwah-'drah-doh)*

PLIERS

channel-lock pliers	**los alicates ajustables** *(lohs ah-lee-'kah-tehs ah-hoos-'tah-blehs)*
needle-nose pliers	**los alicates de punta** *(lohs ah-lee-'kah-tehs deh 'poon-tah)*
Vise-grip® pliers	**los alicates de presión** *(lohs ah-lee-'kah-tehs deh preh-see-'ohn)*
wire cutters	**los alicates cortacables** *(lohs ah-lee-'kah-tehs kohr-tah-'kah-blehs)*
wire strippers	**los alicates para terminales** *(lohs ah-lee-'kah-tehs 'pah-rah tehr-mee-'nah-lehs)*

WRENCHES

box-ended wrench	**la llave fija** *(lah 'yah-veh 'fee-hah)*
combination wrench	**la llave combinada** *(lah 'yah-veh kohm-bee-'nah-dah)*
monkey wrench	**la llave de cremallera** *(lah 'yah-veh deh kre-mah-'yeh-rah)*
pipe wrench	**la llave para tubos** *(lah 'yah-veh 'pah-rah 'too-bohs)*
socket wrench	**la llave de cubo** *(lah 'yah-veh deh'koo-boh)*

Now grab some of these smaller things:

bolt	**el perno** *(ehl 'pehr-noh)*
bracket	**el soporte** *(ehl soh-'pohr-teh)*
clip	**la clavija** *(lah klah-'vee-hah)*
coupling	**el acoplamiento/el cople** *(ehl ah-koh-plah-mee-'ehn-toh/ehl 'koh-pleh)*
fastener	**el sujetador** *(ehl soo-heh-tah-'dohr)*
nail	**el clavo** *(ehl 'klah-voh)*
nut	**la tuerca** *(lah 'twehr-kah)*
screw	**el tornillo** *(ehl tohr-'nee-yoh)*
staple	**la grapa** *(lah 'grah-pah)*
washer	**la arandela** *(lah ah-rahn-'deh-lah)*

Of course, many tools are often named in English during communication in Spanish:

el hex driver   **el Allen wrench**   **el set screw**

Review more materials needed for electrical jobs:

I need (the)...   **Necesito...** *(neh-seh-'see-toh)*

cable	**el cable** *(ehl 'kah-bleh)*
caulking	**la masilla** *(lah mah-'see-yah)*
glue	**la cola** *(lah 'koh-lah)*
wire	**el alambre** *(ehl ah-'lahm-breh)*
adapter	**el adaptador** *(ehl ah-dahp-tah-'dohr)*
fitting	**la conexión** *(lah koh-nehk-see-'ohn)*
fuse	**el fusible** *(ehl foo-'see-bleh)*
insulation	**el aislamiento** *(ehl ah-ees-lah-mee-'ehn-toh)*
sealer	**el sellador** *(ehl seh-yah-'dohr)*

When the job is hi-tech, the materials are usually specialized:

They are...   **Son...** *(sohn)*

condensers	**los condensadores** *(lohs kohn-dehn-sah-'doh-rehs)*
detectors	**los detectores** *(lohs deh-tehk-'toh-rehs)*
diodes	**los diodos** *(lohs dee-'oh-dohs)*
insulators	**los aisladores** *(lohs ah-ees-lah-'doh-rehs)*
integrated circuits	**los circuitos integrados** *(los seer-koo-'ee-tohs een-teh-'grah-dohs)*
microprocessors	**los microprocesadores** *(los mee-kroh-proh-seh-sah-'doh-rehs)*
oscillators	**los osciladores** *(lohs oh-see-lah-'doh-rehs)*
processors	**los procesadores** *(lohs proh-seh-sah-'doh-rehs)*
resistors	**los resistores** *(lohs reh-sees-'toh-rehs)*
semiconductors	**los semiconductores** *(lohs seh-mee-kohn-dook-'toh-rehs)*
sensors	**los sensores** *(lohs sehn-'soh-rehs)*
transducers	**los transductores** *(lohs trahns-dook-'toh-rehs)*
transformers	**los transformadores** *(lohs trahns-fohr-mah-'doh-rehs)*
transistors	**los transistores** *(lohs trahn-sees-'toh-rehs)*

Look at (the)…	**Mire…** *('mee-reh)*
battery	**la batería** *(lah bah-teh-'ree-ah)*
channel	**el canal** *(ehl kah-'nahl)*
electrode	**el electrodo** *(ehl eh-lehk-'troh-doh)*
filament	**el filamento** *(ehl fee-lah-'mehn-toh)*
magnet	**el imán** *(ehl ee-'mahn)*
thread	**la rosca** *(lah 'rohs-kah)*

From objects let's shift to subjects:

What's (the)…?	**¿Cuál es…?** *(kwahl ehs)*
capacity	**la capacidad** *(lah kah-pah-see-'dahd)*
density	**la densidad** *(lah dehn-see-'dahd)*
frequency	**la frecuencia** *(lah freh-koo-'ehn-see-ah)*
intensity	**la intensidad** *(lah een-tehn-see-'dahd)*
memory	**la memoria** *(lah meh-'moh-ree-ah)*
polarity	**la polaridad** *(lah poh-lah-ree-'dahd)*
variation	**la variación** *(lah vah-ree-ah-see-'ohn)*

Check (the)…	**Revise…** *(reh-'vee-seh)*
contact	**el contacto** *(ehl kohn-'tahk-toh)*
energy	**la energía** *(lah eh-nehr-'hee-ah)*
flow	**el flujo** *(ehl 'floo-hoh)*
force	**la fuerza** *(lah 'fwehr-sah)*
friction	**el roce/la fricción** *(ehl 'roh-seh/lah freek-see-'ohn)*
movement	**el movimiento** *(ehl moh-vee-mee-'ehn-toh)*
power	**la potencia** *(lah poh-'tehn-see-ah)*
resistance	**la resistencia** *(lah reh-sees-'tehn-see-ah)*
static	**la estática** *(lah ehs-'tah-tee-kah)*

And don't forget the computer:

Fix (the)…	**Repare…** *(reh-'pah-reh)*
cable	**el cable** *(ehl 'kah-bleh)*
computer	**la computadora** *(lah kohm-poo-tah-'doh-rah)*
drive	**la disquetera** *(lah dees-keh-'teh-rah)*
hard drive	**el disco duro** *(ehl 'dees-koh 'doo-roh)*
keyboard	**el teclado** *(ehl tehk-'lah-doh)*

laptop	**la computadora portátil** *(lah kohm-poo-tah-'doh-rah pohr-'tah-teel)*
monitor	**el monitor** *(ehl moh-nee-'tohr)*
mouse	**el ratón** *(ehl rah-'tohn)*
screen	**la pantalla** *(lah pahn-'tah-yah)*

Try Some

List three common electrician's tools in Spanish.

_____   _____   _____

List three common parts of a computer in Spanish.

_____   _____   _____

List three materials that are used in most electrical projects.

_____   _____   _____

Working Words: PLUMBING INSTALLATION

A plumber is generally called **el plomero** *(ehl plo-'meh-roh)*, **el fontanero** *(ehl fohn-tah-'neh-roh)*, or **el gasfitero** *(ehl gahs-fee-'teh-roh)*. Regardless of which word you use, all plumbers are familiar with this word list below:

drinking water	**el agua potable** *(ehl 'ah-gwah poh-'tah-bleh)*
wastewater	**las aguas residuales** *(lahs 'ah-gwahs reh-see-doo-'ah-lehs)*
shutoff valve	**la válvula de cierre** *(lah 'vahl-voo-lah deh see-'eh-rreh)*
drain	**el desagüe** *(ehl deh-'sah-gweh)*
sewer	**la alcantarilla** *(lah ahl-kahn-tah-'ree-yah)*
pipe	**el tubo** *(ehl 'too-boh)*

Keep focusing on the key words:

Where's (the)…?	¿Dónde está…? *('dohn-deh ehs-'tah)*
hydrant	la boca de agua *(lah 'boh-kah deh 'ah-gwah)*
manhole	la boca de acceso *(lah 'boh-kah deh ahk-'seh-soh)*
meter box	la caja del medidor *(lah 'kah-hah dehl meh-dee-'dohr)*
water main	la cañería matriz *(lah kah-nyeh-'ree-ah mah-'trees)*
water meter	el medidor de agua *(ehl meh-dee-'dohr deh 'ah-gwah)*

Look at these common fixtures that use water:

Work on (the)…	Trabaje con… *(trah-'bah-heh kohn)*
bathtub	la tina de baño *(lah 'tee-nah deh 'bahn-yoh)*
shower stall	la ducha *(lah 'doo-chah)*
kitchen sink	el fregadero *(ehl freh-gah-'deh-roh)*
toilet	el excusado *(ehl ehks-koo-'sah-doh)*
bathroom sink	el lavabo *(ehl lah-'vah-boh)*
faucet	el grifo *(ehl 'gree-foh)*
water heater	el calentador de agua *(ehl kah-lehn-tah-'dohr deh 'ah-gwah)*
dishwasher	el lavaplatos *(ehl lah-vah-'plah-tohs)*
washing machine	la lavadora *(lah lah-vah-'doh-rah)*
urinal	el orinal *(ehl oh-ree-'nahl)*

Worksites may also include outdoor plumbing:

fountain	la fuente *(lah 'fwehn-teh)*
pool	la piscina *(lah pees-'see-nah)*
pool filter	el filtro de la piscina *(ehl 'feel-troh deh lah pees-'see-nah)*
pool cleaner	el limpiapiscina *(ehl leem-pee-ah-pees-'see-nah)*
sprinkler	el aspersor *(ehl ahs-pehr-'sohr)*

Check (the)…	Revise… *(reh-'vee-seh)*
water level	el nivel de agua *(ehl nee-'vehl deh 'ah-gwah)*
water tank	el depósito de agua *(ehl deh-'poh-see-toh deh 'ah-gwah)*
water inlet	la entrada del agua *(lah ehn-'trah-dah deh 'ah-gwah)*

Give me (the)…	**Deme…** *('deh-meh)*
fittings	**las conexiones** *(lahs koh-nehk-see-'oh-nehs)*
tools	**las herramientas** *(lahs eh-rrah-mee-'ehn-tahs)*
equipment	**el equipo** *(ehl eh-'kee-poh)*

Here's a common concern:

Look for (the)…	**Busque…** *('boos-keh)*
clog	**la obstrucción** *(lah ohbs-trook-see-'ohn)*
leak	**la fuga** *(lah 'foo-gah)*
break	**la rotura** *(lah roh-'too-rah)*

I need (the)…	**Necesito…** *(neh-seh-'see-toh)*
hose	**la manguera** *(lah mahn-'geh-rah)*
plunger	**el desatascador** *(ehl dehs-ah-tahs-kah-'dohr)*
snake	**la sonda motorizada** *(lah 'sohn-dah moh-toh-ree-'sah-dah)*

Try Some

Say in English where these are most likely found:

la ducha	**la piscina**	**la lavadora**
el excusado	**el aspersor**	

Working Words: PLUMBING TOOLS AND MATERIALS

Focus on those tools that every plumber needs:

Do you have…?	**¿Tiene…?** *(tee-'eh-neh)*
adhesive	**el adhesivo** *(ehl ah-deh-'see-voh)*
caulking gun	**la pistola de masilla** *(lah pees-'toh-lah deh mah-'see-yah)*
pipe joint compound	**el compuesto para juntar tubos** *(ehl kohm-'pwehs-toh 'pah-rah hoon-'tahr 'too-bohs)*

cordless drill	**el taladro neumático** *(ehl tah-'lah-droh neh-oo-'mah-tee-koh)*
dolly	**la carretilla** *(lah kah-rreh-'tee-yah)*
file	**la lima** *(lah 'lee-mah)*
flashlight	**la linterna** *(lah leen-'tehr-nah)*
glue	**el pegamento/la cola** *(ehl peh-gah-'mehn-toh/lah 'koh-lah)*
hacksaw	**la sierra de metales** *(lah see-'eh-rrah deh meh-'tah-lehs)*
heating gun	**la pistola térmica** *(lah pees-'toh-lah 'tehr-mee-kah)*
knife	**la cuchilla** *(lah koo-'chee-yah)*
level	**el nivel** *(ehl nee-'vehl)*
meter	**el medidor** *(ehl meh-dee-'dohr)*
miter saw	**la sierra de cortar en ángulos** *(lah see-'eh-rrah deh kohr-'tahr ehn 'ahn-goo-lohs)*
pipe cutter	**el cortatubos** *(ehl kohr-tah-'too-bohs)*
pipe vise	**el prensatubos** *(ehl prehn-sah-'too-bohs)*
pipe wrench	**la llave para tubos** *(lah 'yah-veh 'pah-rah 'too-bohs)*
pliers	**los alicates** *(lohs ah-lee-'kah-tehs)*
plumber's tape	**la cinta aislante** *(lah 'seen-tah ah-ees-'lahn-teh)*
probe	**la sonda** *(lah 'sohn-dah)*
pump	**la bomba** *(lah 'bohm-bah)*
putty	**la masilla** *(lah mah-'see-yah)*
stepladder	**la escalera baja** *(lah ehs-kah-'leh-rah 'bah-hah)*
tape measure	**la cinta métrica** *(lah 'seen-tah 'meh-tree-kah)*
tube bender	**la dobladora de tubos** *(lah doh-blah-'doh-rah deh 'too-bohs)*
wax	**la cera** *(lah 'seh-rah)*
wet-dry vac	**la aspiradora de agua** *(lah ahs-pee-rah-'doh-rah deh 'ah-gwah)*

You know that in plumbing wrenches are a dime a dozen:

chain wrench	**la llave de cadena** *(lah 'yah-veh deh kah-'deh-nah)*
disc wrench	**la llave de disco** *(lah 'yah-veh deh 'dees-koh)*
seat wrench	**la llave del grifo** *(lah 'yah-veh dehl 'gree-foh)*
strap wrench	**la llave de cincho** *(lah 'yah-veh deh 'seen-choh)*
tube wrench	**la llave tubular** *(lah 'yah-veh too-boo-'lahr)*

Install (the)...	**Instale...** *(eens-'tah-leh)*

drain	**el desagüe** *(ehl deh-'sah-gweh)*
faucet	**el grifo** *(ehl 'gree-foh)*
handle	**la manija** *(lah mah-'nee-hah)*
pipe	**el tubo** *(ehl 'too-boh)*
spigot	**la llave de paso** *(lah 'yah-veh deh 'pah-soh)*
valve	**la válvula** *(lah 'vahl-voo-lah)*

Now mention the plumbing pipe:

Carry (the)...	**Lleve...** *('yeh-veh)*
45° elbow pipe	**el codo de cuarenta y cinco grados** *(ehl 'koh-doh deh kwah-'rehn-tah ee 'seen-koh 'grah-dohs)*
ABS pipe	**la tubería negra** *(lah too-beh-'ree-ah 'neh-grah)*
cold water pipe	**el tubo para agua fría** *(ehl 'too-boh 'pah-rah 'ah-gwah 'free-ah)*
distribution pipe	**la tubería de derivación** *(lah too-beh-'ree-ah deh deh-ree-vah-see-'ohn)*
drain pipe	**el tubo de drenaje** *(ehl 'too-boh deh dreh-'nah-heh)*
end pipe	**el tubo de acabado** *(ehl 'too-boh deh ah-kah-'bah-doh)*
hot water pipe	**el tubo para agua caliente** *(ehl 'too-boh 'pah-rah 'ah-gwah kah-lee-'ehn-teh)*
PVC pipe	**la tubería de PVC** *(lah too-beh-'ree-ah deh peh veh seh)*
return pipe	**el tubo de retorno** *(ehl 'too-boh deh reh-'tohr-noh)*
riser pipe	**el tubo vertical** *(ehl 'too-boh vehr-tee-'kahl)*
T-pipe	**el tubo tipo T** *(ehl 'too-boh 'tee-poh teh)*

Group your plumbing vocabulary into related sets:

Where's (the)...?	**¿Dónde está...?** *('dohn-deh ehs-'tah)*
½-inch pipe	**el tubo de media pulgada** *(ehl 'too-boh deh 'meh-dee-ah pool-'gah-dah)*
¾-inch pipe	**el tubo de tres cuartos** *(ehl 'too-boh deh trehs 'kwahr-tohs)*
one-inch pipe	**el tubo de una pulgada** *(ehl 'too-boh deh 'oo-nah pool-'gah-dah)*

storm drain	**la tubería de desagüe** *(lah too-beh-'ree-ah deh deh-'sah-gweh)*
floor drain	**el desagüe del piso** *(ehl deh-'sah-gweh dehl 'pee-soh)*
shower drain	**el desagüe de la ducha** *(ehl deh-'sah-gweh deh lah 'doo-chah)*
C-clamp	**la abrazadera en C** *(lah ah-brah-sah-'deh-rah ehn seh)*
split ring clamp	**la abrazadera de anillo separado** *(lah ah-brah-sah-'deh-rah deh ah-'nee-yoh seh-pah-'rah-doh)*
extension clamp	**la abrazadera de extensión** *(lah ah-brah-sah-'deh-rah deh ex-tehn-see-'ohn)*

Keep going:

angle valve	**la válvula angular** *(lah 'vahl-voo-lah ahn-goo-'lahr)*
ball valve	**la válvula de bola** *(lah 'vahl-voo-lah deh 'boh-lah)*
butterfly valve	**la válvula de mariposa** *(lah 'vahl-voo-lah deh mah-ree-'poh-sah)*
check valve	**la válvula de antirretorno** *(lah 'vahl-voo-lah deh ahn-tee-reh-'tohr-noh)*
safety valve	**la válvula de seguridad** *(lah 'vahl-voo-lah deh seh-goo-ree-'dahd)*
waste valve	**la válvula de desagüe** *(lah 'vahl-voo-lah deh deh-'sah-gweh)*

To be specific, add the necessary descriptive words:

Do you have (the)…	**¿Tiene…?** *(tee-'eh-neh)*
clean-out stop	**el tapón de limpieza** *(ehl tah-'pohn deh leem-pee-'eh-sah)*
drain plug	**el tapón del desagüe** *(ehl tah-'pohn deh deh-'sah-gweh)*
drain-waste vent	**la chimenea de ventilación** *(lah chee-meh-'neh-ah deh vehn-tee-lah-see-'ohn)*
P-trap	**el sifón tipo P** *(ehl see-'fohn 'tee-poh peh)*
swivel tap	**el grifo giratorio** *(ehl 'gree-foh hee-rah-'toh-ree-oh)*

Bring (the)…	**Traiga…** *('trah-ee-gah)*
adapter	**el adaptador** *(ehl ah-dahp-tah-'dohr)*
ball	**la bola** *(lah 'boh-lah)*
bolt	**el perno** *(ehl 'pehr-noh)*
bracket	**el soporte** *(ehl soh-'pohr-teh)*
connector	**el conector** *(ehl koh-nehk-'tohr)*
coupler	**el acoplador** *(ehl ah-koh-plah-'dohr)*
duct	**el conducto** *(ehl kohn-'dook-toh)*
filter	**el filtro** *(ehl 'feel-troh)*
grating	**la rejilla** *(lah reh-'hee-yah)*
hanger rod	**la barra colgante** *(lah 'bah-rrah kohl-'gahn-teh)*
insert	**el anclaje** *(ehl ahn-'klah-heh)*
joint	**el codo** *(ehl 'koh-doh)*
nipple	**el niple** *(ehl 'nee-pleh)*
nut	**la tuerca** *(lah 'twehr-kah)*
plate	**la placa** *(lah 'plah-kah)*
ring	**el anillo** *(ehl ah-'nee-yoh)*
screw joint	**la junta roscada** *(lah 'hoon-tah rohs-'kah-dah)*
strap	**la tira** *(lah 'tee-rah)*
union	**la unión** *(lah oo-nee-'ohn)*
washer	**la arandela** *(lah ah-rahn-'deh-lah)*

These words target the work in the bathroom:

Repair (the)…	**Repare…** *(reh-'pah-reh)*
float	**el flotador** *(ehl floh-tah-'dohr)*
gasket	**el empaque** *(ehl ehm-'pah-keh)*
head	**la cabeza** *(lah kah-'beh-sah)*
nozzle	**la boquilla** *(lah boh-'kee-yah)*
overflow	**el rebosadero** *(ehl reh-boh-sah-'deh-roh)*
plug	**la espiga** *(lah ehs-'pee-gah)*
seal	**el sello** *(ehl 'seh-yoh)*
seat	**el asiento** *(ehl ah-see-'ehn-toh)*
tank	**el tanque** *(ehl 'tahn-keh)*
trap	**el sifón** *(ehl see-'fohn)*
tub	**la tina** *(lah 'tee-nah)*
washbasin	**el lavamanos** *(ehl lah-vah-'mah-nohs)*

Talk a bit more about your materials:

It's...	**Es...** *(ehs)*
ceramic	**de cerámica** *(deh seh-'rah-mee-kah)*
chrome	**cromado** *(kroh-'mah-doh)*
graphite	**de grafito** *(deh grah-'fee-toh)*
metallic	**metálico** *(meh-'tah-lee-koh)*
plastic	**plástico** *('plahs-tee-koh)*
porcelain	**de porcelana** *(deh pohr-seh-'lah-nah)*
flexible copper	**de cobre flexible** *(deh 'koh-breh fleh-'ksee-bleh)*
galvanized steel	**de hierro galvanizado** *(deh ee-'eh-rroh gahl-vah-nee-'sah-doh)*

Some soldering—**soldadura** *(sohl-dah-'doo-rah)* may be required:

We use (the)...	**Usamos...** *(oo-'sah-mohs)*
acetylene	**el acetileno** *(ehl ah-seh-tee-'leh-noh)*
brush	**la brocha** *(lah 'broh-chah)*
CO_2	**el anhídrido carbónico** *(ehl ahn-'ee-dree-doh kahr-'boh-nee-koh)*
emery cloth	**la tela de esmeril** *(lah 'teh-lah deh ehs-meh-'reel)*
oxygen	**el oxígeno** *(ehl oh-'ksee-heh-noh)*
paste	**la pasta** *(lah 'pahs-tah)*
propane	**el propano** *(ehl proh-'pah-noh)*
regulator	**el regulador** *(ehl reh-goo-lah-'dohr)*
soldering wire	**el alambre de soldadura** *(ehl ah-'lahm-breh deh sohl-dah-'doo-rah)*
gas tank	**el cilindro de gas** *(ehl see-'leen-droh deh gahs)*
torch lighter	**el encendedor** *(ehl ehn-sehn-deh-'dohr)*
torch	**el soplete** *(ehl soh-'pleh-teh)*

Just a Suggestion

Mechanical installation is full of simple sets of words with opposite meanings:

entrance	↓	**la entrada** *(lah ehn-'trah-dah)*
exit	↑	**la salida** *(lah sah-'lee-dah)*
positive	↓	**positivo** *(poh-see-'tee-voh)*
negative	↑	**negativo** *(neh-gah-'tee-voh)*
open	↓	**abierto** *(ah-bee-'ehr-toh)*
closed	↑	**cerrado** *(seh-'rrah-doh)*
male	↓	**macho** *('mah-choh)*
female	↑	**hembra** *('ehm-brah)*
inside	↓	**adentro** *(ah-'dehn-troh)*
outside	↑	**afuera** *(ah-'fweh-rah)*

Try Some

Connect the words that belong together:

el soplete	**la boquilla**
la manguera	**el perno**
la arandela	**el encededor**

👉 Working Words: HEATING AND AIR CONDITIONING

When it comes to installing heating or AC units, many of the same words used in plumbing and electrical work will be required.

Where's (the)…?	**¿Dónde está…?** *('dohn-deh ehs-'tah)*
main water line	**la tubería principal de agua** *(lah too-beh-'ree-ah preen-see-'pahl deh 'ah-gwah)*
main gas line	**la línea principal de gas** *(lah 'lee-neh-ah preen-see-'pahl deh gahs)*
main power line	**el cable principal de electricidad** *(ehl 'kah-bleh preen-see-'pahl deh eh-lehk-tree-see-'dahd)*
Check (the)…	**Revise…** *(reh-'vee-seh)*

air conditioner	**el acondicionador de aire** *(ehl ah-kohn-dee-see-oh-nah-'dohr deh 'ah-ee-reh)*
heater	**el calentador** *(ehl kah-lehn-tah-'dohr)*
heating system	**el sistema de calefacción** *(ehl sees-'teh-mah deh kah-leh-fahk-see-'ohn)*
radiator	**el radiador** *(ehl rah-dee-ah-'dohr)*
unit	**el aparato** *(ehl ah-pah-'rah-toh)*

What's (the)…?	**¿Cuál es…?** *(kwahl ehs)*
amount	**la cantidad** *(lah kahn-tee-'dahd)*
make	**la marca** *(lah 'mahr-kah)*
model	**el modelo** *(ehl moh-'deh-loh)*
number	**el número** *(ehl 'noo-meh-roh)*
quality	**la calidad** *(lah kah-lee-'dahd)*
shape	**la forma** *(lah 'fohr-mah)*
size	**el tamaño** *(ehl tah-'mahn-yoh)*
supply	**el suministro** *(ehl soo-mee-'nees-troh)*

It's not...   **No está...** *(noh ehs-'tah)*

cold	**frío** *('free-oh)*
cool	**fresco** *('frehs-koh)*
freezing	**helado** *(eh-'lah-doh)*
hot	**caliente** *(kah-lee-'ehn-teh)*
warm	**tibio** *('tee-bee-oh)*

Use (the)...   **Use...** *('oo-seh)*

cable	**el cable** *(ehl 'kah-bleh)*
hose	**la manguera** *(lah mahn-'geh-rah)*
pipe	**el tubo** *(ehl 'too-boh)*
plug	**el enchufe** *(ehl ehn-'choo-feh)*
switch	**el interruptor** *(ehl een-teh-rroop-'tohr)*
valve	**la válvula** *(lah 'vahl-voo-lah)*

Now focus on those AC and heating components that relate specifically to the job at hand:

Look at (the)...   **Mire...** *('mee-reh)*

air filter	**el filtro de aire** *(ehl 'feel-troh deh 'ah-ee-reh)*
air vent	**el respiradero** *(ehl rehs-pee-rah-'deh-roh)*
circuit board	**el tablero de circuitos** *(ehl tah-'bleh-roh deh seer-koo-'ee-tohs)*
compressor	**el compresor** *(ehl kohm-preh-'sohr)*
defroster	**el descongelador** *(ehl dehs-kohn-heh-lah-'dohr)*
fan	**el ventilador** *(ehl vehn-tee-lah-'dohr)*
flashing	**el tapajuntas** *(ehl tah-pah-'hoon-tahs)*
flexible duct	**el conducto flexible** *(ehl kohn-'dook-toh flehk-'see-bleh)*
flow switch	**el interruptor de flujo** *(ehl een-teh-rroop-'tohr deh 'floo-hoh)*
grill	**la rejilla** *(lah reh-'hee-yah)*
humidifier	**el humidificador** *(ehl oo-mee-dee-fee-kah-'dohr)*
ignitor	**el encendedor** *(ehl ehn-sehn-deh-'dohr)*
insulation	**el aislamiento** *(ehl ah-ees-lah-mee-'ehn-toh)*
lens	**el lente** *(ehl 'lehn-teh)*
lock	**la cerradura** *(lah seh-rrah-'doo-rah)*
mounting screw	**el tornillo de fijación** *(ehl tohr-'nee-yoh deh fee-hah-see-'ohn)*

pilot	**el piloto** *(ehl pee-'loh-'toh)*
pump	**la bomba** *(lah 'bohm-bah)*
purifier	**el purificador** *(ehl poo-ree-fee-kah-'dohr)*
regulator	**el regulador** *(ehl reh-goo-lah-'dohr)*
remote control	**el control remoto** *(ehl kohn-'trohl reh-'moh-toh)*
return	**el conducto de retorno** *(ehl kohn-'dook-toh deh reh-'tohr-noh)*
seal	**el sello** *(ehl 'seh-yoh)*
thermometer	**el termómetro** *(ehl tehr-'moh-meh-troh)*
thermostat	**el termostato** *(ehl tehr-mohs-'tah-toh)*
timer	**el reloj** *(ehl reh-'loh)*
transformer	**el transformador** *(ehl trahns-fohr-mah-'dohr)*

Try out this new terminology by using the plural form:

See (the)...	**Vea...** *('veh-ah)*
burners	**los quemadores** *(lohs keh-mah-'doh-rehs)*
coils	**las bobinas** *(lahs boh-'bee-nahs)*
condensers	**los condensadores** *(lohs kohn-dehn-sah-'doh-rehs)*
heating elements	**los elementos calefactores** *(lohs eh-leh-'mehn-tohs kah-leh-fahk-'toh-rehs)*
sensors	**los sensores** *(lohs sehn-'soh-rehs)*

 ## Working Words: OTHER MECHANICAL WORK

Work on (the)...	**Trabaje con...** *(trah-'bah-heh kohn)*

chimney	**la chimenea** *(lah chee-meh-'neh-ah)*
skylight	**el tragaluz** *(ehl trah-gah-'loos)*
vent tubes	**los tubos para ventilación** *(los 'too-bohs 'pah-rah vehn-tee-lah-see-'ohn)*
well	**el pozo** *(ehl 'poh-soh)*
cesspool	**el pozo negro** *(ehl 'poh-soh 'neh-groh)*
cooler	**el cuarto de refrigeración** *(ehl 'kwahr-toh deh reh-free-heh-rah-see-'ohn)*
furnace	**el horno** *(ehl 'ohr-noh)*
boiler	**la caldera** *(lah kahl-'deh-rah)*

These phrases are more complex:

soft water system	**el sistema para ablandar el agua** *(ehl sees-'teh-mah 'pah-rah ah-blahn-'dahr ehl 'ah-gwah)*
filtration system	**el sistema de filtración** *(ehl sees-'teh-mah deh feel-trah-see-'ohn)*
sewage system	**el sistema de alcantarillado** *(ehl sees-'teh-mah deh ahl-kahn-tah-ree-'yah-doh)*

Now, break your vocabulary into groups based on the specific job:

It's the pool _____.   **Es _____ para la piscina.** *(ehs 'pah-rah lah pee-'see-nah)*

drain	**el desagüe** *(ehl deh-'sah-gweh)*
filter	**el filtro** *(ehl 'feel troh)*
heater	**el calentador** *(ehl kah-lehn-tah-'dohr)*
light	**la luz** *(lah loos)*
pump	**la bomba** *(lah 'bohm-bah)*

Now focus on the installation:

Where's (the)...?   **¿Dónde está...?** *('dohn-deh ehs-'tah)*

gap	**el hueco** *(ehl 'hweh-koh)*
hole	**el hoyo** *(ehl 'oh-yoh)*
opening	**la abertura** *(lah ah-behr-'too-rah)*
slit	**la ranura** *(lah rah-'noo-rah)*
space	**el espacio** *(ehl ehs-'pah-see-oh)*

It's (made) of...   **Es de...** *(ehs deh)*

aluminum	**aluminio** *(ah-loo-'mee-nee-oh)*
brass	**latón** *(lah-'tohn)*
dry wall	**enyesado** *(ehn-yeh-'sah-doh)*
fiberglass	**fibra de vidrio** *('fee-brah deh 'vee-dree-oh)*
foam	**espuma** *(ehs-'poo-mah)*
glass	**vidrio** *('vee-dree-oh)*
iron	**hierro** *(ee-'eh-rroh)*
lead	**plomo** *('ploh-moh)*
plywood	**contrachapado** *(kohn-trah-chah-'pah-doh)*
rubber	**goma** *('goh-mah)*

| steel | **acero** *(ah-'seh-roh)* |
| wood | **madera** *(mah-'deh-rah)* |

We need (the)…	**Necesitamos…** *(neh-seh-see-'tah-mohs)*
acid	**el ácido** *(ehl 'ah-see-doh)*
battery	**la batería** *(lah bah-teh-'ree-ah)*
catalyst	**el catalizador** *(ehl kah-tah-lee-sah-'dohr)*
cell	**la célula** *(lah 'seh-loo-lah)*
chemical	**el producto químico** *(ehl proh-'dook-toh 'kee-mee-koh)*
chlorine	**el cloro** *(ehl 'kloh-roh)*
coal	**el carbón** *(ehl kahr-'bohn)*
compound	**el compuesto** *(ehl kohm-'pwehs-toh)*
diesel	**el diesel** *(ehl 'dee-sel)*
dye	**el tinte** *(ehl 'teen-teh)*
fluid	**el fluido** *(ehl floo-'ee-doh)*
fuel	**el combustible** *(ehl kohm-boos-'tee-bleh)*
gasoline	**la gasolina** *(lah gah-soh-'lee-nah)*
liquid	**el líquido** *(ehl 'lee-kee-doh)*
mixture	**la mezcla** *(lah 'mehs-klah)*
natural gas	**el gas natural** *(ehl gahs nah-too-'rahl)*
oil	**el aceite** *(ehl ah-'seh-ee-teh)*
propane	**el propano** *(ehl proh-'pah-noh)*
water	**el agua** *(ehl 'ah-gwah)*

What's (the)…?	**¿Cuál es…?** *(kwahl ehs)*
area	**la área** *(lah 'ah-reh-ah)*
circumference	**la circunferencia** *(lah seer-koon-feh-'rehn-see-ah)*
color	**el color** *(ehl koh-'lohr)*
diameter	**el diámetro** *(ehl dee-'ah-meh-troh)*
height	**la altura** *(lah ahl-'too-rah)*
length	**el largo** *(ehl 'lahr-goh)*
model	**el modelo** *(ehl moh-'deh-loh)*
percentage	**el porcentaje** *(ehl pohr-sehn-'tah-heh)*
size	**el tamaño** *(ehl tah-'mahn-yoh)*
temperature	**la temperatura** *(lah tehm-peh-rah-'too-rah)*
volume	**el volumen** *(ehl voh-'loo-mehn)*
width	**el ancho** *(ehl 'ahn-choh)*

How many…?	**¿Cuántos(as)…?** *('kwahn-tohs/ahs)*
degrees	**grados** *('grah-dohs)*
inches	**pulgadas** *(pool-'gah-dahs)*
ounces	**onzas** *('ohn-sahs)*

Look at (the)…	**Mire…** *('mee-reh)*
angle	**el ángulo** *(ehl 'ahn-goo-loh)*
distance	**la distancia** *(lah dees-'tahn-see-ah)*
slope	**la pendiente** *(lah pehn-dee-'ehn-teh)*
pattern	**el patrón** *(ehl pah-'trohn)*
position	**la posición** *(lah poh-see-see-'ohn)*
program	**el programa** *(ehl proh-'grah-mah)*

Pay attention to (the)…	**Preste atención a…** *('prehs-teh ah-tehn-see-'ohn ah)*
arrow	**la flecha** *(lah 'fleh-chah)*
cycle	**el ciclo** *(ehl 'seek-loh)*
dial	**la esfera** *(lah ehs-'feh-rah)*
line	**la linea** *(lah 'lee-neh-ah)*
signal	**la señal** *(lah seh-'nyahl)*
sound	**el sonido** *(ehl soh-'nee-doh)*
time	**el tiempo** *(ehl tee-'ehm-poh)*

Try Some

These are similar in Spanish and should be easy to translate:

chimney	_____
distance	_____
temperature	_____
diameter	_____
liquid	_____
program	_____

Working Words: MECHANICAL PROBLEMS

Mechanical work involves plenty of checking and testing. These one-liners will help:

Let's check it.	**Vamos a revisarla.** (*'vah-mohs ah reh-vee-'sahr-lah*)
Something is wrong.	**Algo está mal.** (*'ahl-goh ehs-'tah mahl*)
Start over.	**Empiece de nuevo.** (*ehm-pee-'eh-seh deh 'nweh-voh*)
We have to make sure.	**Tenemos que estar seguros.** (*teh-'neh-mohs keh ehs-'tahr seh-'goo-rohs*)
You need to fix it.	**Necesita repararlo.** (*neh-seh-'see-tah reh-pah-'rahr-loh*)

Do a _____ test.	**Haga una prueba de _____.** (*'ah-gah 'oo-nah proo-'eh-bah deh*)
continuity	**continuidad** (*kohn-tee-noo-ee-'dahd*)
diagnostic	**diagnóstico** (*dee-ahg-'nohs-tee-koh*)
pressure	**presión** (*preh-see-'ohn*)
safety	**seguridad** (*seh-goo-ree-'dahd*)
static	**estática** (*ehs-'tah-tee-kah*)
voltage	**voltaje** (*vohl-'tah-heh*)

Keep addressing your concerns:

Let's talk about (the)...	**Hablemos de...** (*ah-'bleh-mohs deh*)
advice	**el consejo** (*ehl kohn-'seh-hoh*)
danger	**el peligro** (*ehl peh-'lee-groh*)
precaution	**la precaución** (*lah preh-kah-oo-see-'ohn*)
prevention	**la prevención** (*lah preh-vehn-see-'ohn*)
suggestion	**la sugerencia** (*lah soo-heh-'rehn-see-ah*)
warning	**la advertencia** (*lah ahd-vehr-'tehn-see-ah*)

It's (the)...	**Es...** (*ehs*)
regulation	**el reglamento** (*ehl reh-glah-'mehn-toh*)
law	**la ley** (*lah 'leh-ee*)
code	**el código** (*ehl 'koh-dee-goh*)

Safety instructions:

Be careful with (the)...	**Tenga cuidado con...** *('tehn-gah kwee-'dah-doh kohn)*
ground wire	**el cable de tierra** *(ehl 'kah-bleh deh tee-'eh-rrah)*
heating elements	**los elementos calefactores** *(lohs eh-leh-'mehn-tohs kah-leh-fahk-'toh-rehs)*
power lines	**los cables del tendido eléctrico** *(lohs 'kah-blehs dehl tehn-'dee-doh eh-'lehk-tree-koh)*
service drop	**la toma de suministro eléctrico** *(lah 'toh-mah deh soo-mee-'nees-troh eh-'lehk-tree-koh)*
service entrance head	**la entrada principal de servicio** *(lah ehn-'trah-dah preen-see-'pahl deh sehr-'vee-see-oh)*
service mast	**el mástil de servicio eléctrico** *(ehl 'mahs-teel deh sehr-'vee-see-oh eh-'lehk-tree-koh)*
service panel	**el tablero de servicio** *(ehl tah-'bleh-roh deh sehr-'vee-see-oh)*

Keep going:

electric shock	**el choque eléctrico** *(ehl 'choh-keh eh-'lehk-tree-koh)*
explosion	**la explosión** *(lah ex-ploh-see-'ohn)*
heat	**el calor** *(ehl kah-'lohr)*
flame	**la llama** *(lah 'yah-mah)*
smoke	**el humo** *(ehl 'oo-moh)*
sparks	**las chispas** *(lahs 'chees-pahs)*
steam	**el vapor** *(ehl vah-'pohr)*

If water is a concern, use these descriptive words:

Is it...	**¿Es/Está...?** *(ehs/ehs-'tah)*

frozen	**congelado** *(kohn-heh-'lah-doh)*
moist	**húmedo** *('oo-meh-doh)*
soaked	**empapado** *(ehm-pah-'pah-doh)*
waterproof	**impermeable** *(eem-pehr-meh-'ah-bleh)*
watertight	**hermético** *(ehr-'meh-tee-koh)*
wet	**mojado** *(moh-'hah-doh)*

And if more problems arise, keep it short using words you already know:

There's trouble with (the)…	**Hay problemas con…** *('ah-ee proh-'bleh-mahs kohn)*
piece	**la pieza** *(lah pee-'eh-sah)*
connection	**la conexión** *(lah koh-nehk-see-'ohn)*
system	**el sistema** *(ehl sees-'teh-mah)*
support	**el apoyo** *(ehl ah-'poh-yoh)*
strength	**la resistencia** *(lah reh-sees-'tehn-see-ah)*
movement	**el movimiento** *(ehl moh-vee-mee-'ehn-toh)*
condition	**la condición** *(lah kohn-dee-see-'ohn)*
shape	**la forma** *(lah 'fohr-mah)*
age	**la edad** *(lah eh-'dahd)*
There are…	**Hay…** *('ah-ee)*
bubbles	**burbujas** *(boor-'boo-hahs)*
bumps	**bultos** *('bool-tohs)*
cracks	**grietas** *(gree-'eh-tahs)*
fumes	**escape** *(ehs-'kah-peh)*
holes	**huecos** *('hweh-kohs)*
knots	**nudos** *('noo-dohs)*
loops	**lazos** *('lah-sohs)*
pressure loss	**pérdida de presión** *('pehr-dee-dah deh preh-see-'ohn)*
puddles	**charcos** *('chahr-kohs)*
water leaks	**fugas** *('foo-gahs)*
Clean up (the)…	**Limpie…** *('leem-pee-eh)*

grease	**la grasa** *(lah 'grah-sah)*
waste	**la basura** *(lah bah-'soo-rah)*
dirt	**la suciedad** *(lah soo-see-eh-'dahd)*

And use (the)…	**Y use…** *(ee 'oo-seh)*
bucket	**el balde** *(ehl 'bahl-deh)*
mop	**el trapeador** *(ehl trah-peh-ah-'dohr)*
rag	**el trapo** *(ehl 'trah-poh)*
sponge	**la esponja** *(lah ehs-'pohn-hah)*
towel	**la toalla** *(lah toh-'ah-yah)*
It's…	**Está…** *(ehs-'tah)*
bent	**doblado** *(doh-'blah-doh)*
broken	**roto** *('roh-toh)*
burned	**quemado** *(keh-'mah-doh)*
contaminated	**contaminado** *(kohn-tah-mee-'nah-doh)*
corroded	**corroído** *(koh-rroh-'ee-doh)*
cracked	**agrietado** *(ah-gree-eh-'tah-doh)*
damaged	**dañado** *(dah-'nyah-doh)*
defective	**defectuoso** *(deh-fehk-too-'oh-soh)*
eroded	**erosionado** *(eh-roh-see-oh-'nah-doh)*
loose	**suelto** *('swehl-toh)*
old	**viejo** *(vee-'eh-hoh)*
scratched	**rascado** *(rahs-'kah-doh)*
stained	**manchado** *(mahn-'chah-doh)*
weak	**débil** *('deh-beel)*
worn	**gastado** *(gahs-'tah-doh)*
Call the _____ company.	**Llame la compañía de _____.** *('yah-meh lah kohm-pah-'nee-ah deh)*

cable	**cable** *('kah-bleh)*
electric	**electricidad** *(eh-lehk-tree-see-'dahd)*
gas	**gas** *(gahs)*
phone	**teléfono** *(teh-'leh-foh-noh)*
water	**agua** *('ah-gwah)*

It helps to find as many words as you can that look like English. In mechanical work, this terminology is everywhere:

conduction	**la conducción** *(lah kohn-dook-see-'ohn)*
operation	**la operación** *(lah oh-peh-rah-see-'ohn)*

lubrication	**la lubricación** *(lah loo-bree-kah-see-'ohn)*
contamination	**la contaminación** *(lah kohn-tah-mee-nah-see-'ohn)*
production	**la producción** *(lah proh-dook-see-'ohn)*
connection	**la conexión** *(lah koh-nehk-see-'ohn)*
purification	**la purificación** *(lah poo-ree-fee-kah-see-'ohn)*
concentration	**la concentración** *(lah kohn-sehn-trah-see-'ohn)*
filtration	**la filtración** *(lah feel-trah-see-'ohn)*
acclimatization	**la climatización** *(lah klee-mah-tee-sah-see-'ohn)*
refrigeration	**la refrigeración** *(lah reh-free-heh-rah-see-'ohn)*
calibration	**la calibración** *(lah kah-lee-brah-see-'ohn)*
dimension	**la dimensión** *(lah dee-mehn-see-'ohn)*
tension	**la tensión** *(lah tehn-see-'ohn)*
absorption	**la absorbción** *(lah ahb-sohr-see-'ohn)*
transmission	**la transmisión** *(lah trahns-mee-see-'ohn)*
precision	**la precisión** *(lah preh-see-see-'ohn)*
polarity	**la polaridad** *(lah poh-lah-ree-'dahd)*
intensity	**la intensidad** *(lah een-tehn-see-'dahd)*
security	**la seguridad** *(lah seh-goo-ree-'dahd)*

Try Some

Choose the best word to complete each sentence below:

Haga un prueba de…	**las chispas**
Tenga cuidado con…	**cable**
Está…	**la continuidad**
Limpie…	**congelado**
Llame la compañía de…	**la suciedad**

Translate these:

corriente eléctrica   <u>electric current</u>

alto voltaje   _____

el cable viejo   _____

la caja metálica   _____

☞ Working Words: DESCRIBING THE JOB

Say these words to describe everything around you:

It's...		**Es...** *(ehs)*
double	↓	**doble** *('doh-bleh)*
single	↑	**sencillo** *(sehn-'see-yoh)*
curved	↓	**curvo** *('koor-voh)*
straight	↑	**recto** *('rehk-toh)*
flat	↓	**plano** *('plah-noh)*
round	↑	**redondo** *(reh-'dohn-doh)*

Now use **Está** *(ehs-'tah)* instead of **Es** *(ehs)* to indicate more of a temporary condition:

It's...		**Está...** *(ehs-'tah)*
loose	↓	**flojo** *('floh-hoh)*
tight	↑	**apretado** *(ah-preh-'tah-doh)*
dry	↓	**seco** *('seh-koh)*
wet	↑	**mojado** *(moh-'hah-doh)*
hot	↓	**caliente** *(kah-lee-'ehn-teh)*
cold	↑	**frío** *('free-oh)*
live	↓	**vivo** *('vee-voh)*
dead	↑	**muerto** *('mwehr-toh)*
turned on	↓	**prendido** *(prehn-'dee-doh)*
turned off	↑	**apagado** *(ah-pah-'gah-doh)*

It looks...	**Se ve...** *(she veh)*
crossed	**cruzado** *(kroo-'sah-doh)*
in series	**en serie** *(ehn 'seh-ree-eh)*
interwoven	**entretejido** *(ehn-treh-teh-'hee-doh)*
lined up	**arreglado** *(ah-rreh-'glah-doh)*
parallel	**paralelo** *(pah-rah-'leh-loh)*

It's…	Es/Está… *(ehs/ehs-'tah)*
durable	**duradero** *(doo-rah-'deh-roh)*
fire resistant	**resistente contra el fuego** *(reh-sees-'tehn-teh 'kohn-trah ehl 'fweh-goh)*
grounded	**puesto a tierra** *('pwehs-toh ah tee-'eh-rrah)*
leakproof	**a prueba de goteras** *(ah proo-'eh-bah deh goh-'teh-rahs)*
rustproof	**inoxidable** *(ee-nohk-see-'dah-bleh)*
sealed	**sellado** *(seh-'yah-doh)*
shockproof	**a prueba de golpes** *(ah proo-'eh-bah deh 'gohl-pehs)*
treated	**tratado** *(trah-'tah-doh)*
underground	**subterráneo** *(soob-teh-'rrah-neh-oh)*
waterproof	**impermeable** *(eem-pehr-meh-'ah-bleh)*

Here's a selection that refers to lighting:

It's…	Es… *(ehs)*
decorative	**decorativo** *(deh-koh-rah-'tee-voh)*
incandescent	**incandescente** *(een-kahn-dehs-'sehn-teh)*
luminescent	**luminiscente** *(loo-mee-nees-'sehn-teh)*
neon	**de neón** *(deh neh-'ohn)*
reflective	**reflectivo** *(reh-flehk-'tee-voh)*
shiny	**brillante** *(bree-'yahn-teh)*

☞ Working Words: ON-SITE ACTIONS

Review these sets of opposites that relate to mechanical installation:

You need…		Necesita… *(neh-seh-'see-tah)*
to push	↓	**empujar** *(ehm-poo-'hahr)*
to pull	↑	**jalar** *(hah-'lahr)*
to tighten	↓	**apretar** *(ah-preh-'tahr)*
to loosen	↑	**aflojar** *(ah-floh-'hahr)*
to empty	↓	**vaciar** *(vah-see-'ahr)*
to fill	↑	**llenar** *(yeh-'nahr)*
to put inside	↓	**meter** *(meh-'tehr)*
to take out	↑	**sacar** *(sah-'kahr)*

| to lift | ↓ | **levantar** *(leh-vahn-'tahr)* |
| to lower | ↑ | **bajar** *(bah-'hahr)* |

| to open | ↓ | **abrir** *(ah-'breer)* |
| to close | ↑ | **cerrar** *(seh-'rrahr)* |

As you know, **des-** is added to some verbs in order to create an opposite:

| to plug in | ↓ | **enchufar** *(ehn-choo-'fahr)* |
| to unplug | ↑ | **desenchufar** *(dehs-ehn-choo-'fahr)* |

| to connect | ↓ | **conectar** *(koh-nehk-'tahr)* |
| to disconnect | ↑ | **desconectar** *(dehs-koh-nehk-'tahr)* |

| to assemble | ↓ | **armar** *(ahr-'mahr)* |
| to disassemble | ↑ | **desarmar** *(dehs-ahr-'mahr)* |

This selection of verbs refers to most mechanical installations. Take down the ones you'll be using right away:

It's necessary…	**Es necesario…** *(ehs neh-seh-'sah-ree-oh)*
to adjust	**ajustar** *(ah-hoos-'tahr)*
to align	**alinear** *(ah-lee-neh-'ahr)*
to apply	**aplicar** *(ah-plee-'kahr)*
to bond	**adherir** *(ah-deh-'reer)*
to bore	**calar** *(kah-'lahr)*
to carry	**llevar** *(yeh-vahr)*
to caulk	**calafatear** *(kah-lah-fah-teh-'ahr)*
to check	**revisar** *(reh-vee-'sahr)*
to circulate	**circular** *(seer-koo-'lahr)*
to connect	**conectar** *(koh-nehk-'tahr)*
to control	**controlar** *(kohn-troh-'lahr)*
to convert	**convertir** *(kohn-vehr-'teer)*
to cool	**enfriar** *(ehn-free-'ahr)*
to correct	**corregir** *(koh-rreh-'heer)*
to cover	**cubrir** *(koo-'breer)*
to cut	**cortar** *(kohr-'tahr)*
to distribute	**distribuir** *(dees-tree-boo-'eer)*
to divert	**desviar** *(dehs-vee-'ahr)*
to enlarge	**ampliar** *(ahm-plee-'ahr)*

to fill	**llenar** *(yeh-'nahr)*
to filter	**filtrar** *(feel-'trahr)*
to flip	**voltear** *(vohl-teh-'ahr)*
to glue	**encolar** *(ehn-koh-'lahr)*
to heat	**calentar** *(kah-lehn-'tahr)*
to install	**instalar** *(eens-tah-'lahr)*
to join	**unir** *(oo-'neer)*
to lubricate	**lubricar** *(loo-bree-'kahr)*
to measure	**medir** *(meh-'deer)*
to modify	**modificar** *(moh-dee-fee-'kahr)*
to mount	**montar** *(mohn-'tahr)*
to move	**mover** *(moh-'vehr)*
to operate	**operar** *(oh-peh-'rahr)*
to place	**colocar** *(koh-loh-'kahr)*
to program	**programar** *(proh-grah-'mahr)*
to protect	**proteger** *(proh-teh-'hehr)*
to put	**poner** *(poh-'nehr)*
to reach	**alcanzar** *(ahl-kahn-'sahr)*
to reduce	**reducir** *(reh-doo-'seer)*
to remove	**quitar** *(kee-'tahr)*
to repair	**reparar** *(reh-pah-'rahr)*
to replace	**sustituir** *(soos-tee-too-'eer)*
to roll up	**enrollar** *(ehn-roh-'yahr)*
to screw in	**atornillar** *(ah-tohr-nee-'yahr)*
to seal	**sellar** *(seh-'yahr)*
to splice	**empalmar** *(ehm-pahl-'mahr)*
to stretch	**estirar** *(ehs-tee-'rahr)*
to support	**apoyar** *(ah-poh-'yahr)*
to thread	**roscar** *(rohs-'kahr)*
to transmit	**transmitir** *(trahns-mee-'teer)*
to test	**probar** *(proh-'bahr)*
to turn off	**apagar** *(ah-pah-'gahr)*
to turn on	**encender** *(ehn-sehn-'dehr)*
to twist	**torcer** *(tohr-'sehr)*
to untangle	**desenredar** *(dehs-ehn-reh-'dahr)*
to upgrade	**subir de categoría** *(soo-'beer deh kah-teh-goh-'ree-ah)*
to use	**usar** *(oo-'sahr)*
to wrap	**envolver** *(ehn-vohl-'vehr)*

It needs...	**Necesita...** *(neh-seh-'see-tah)*
to return	**regresar** *(reh-greh-'sahr)*
to absorb	**absorber** *(ahb-sohr-'behr)*
to thaw	**descongelar** *(dehs-kohn-heh-'lahr)*
to ventilate	**ventilar** *(vehn-tee-'lahr)*
to start up	**arrancar** *(ah-rrahn-'kahr)*
to produce	**producir** *(proh-doo-'seer)*
to function	**funcionar** *(foon-see-oh-'nahr)*
to flow	**fluir** *(floo-'eer)*
It's going...	**Se va a...** *(she vah ah)*
to overflow	**rebosar** *(reh-boh-'sahr)*
to overheat	**recalentar** *(reh-kah-lehn-'tahr)*
to overload	**sobrecargar** *(soh-breh-kahr-'gahr)*
to drip	**gotear** *(goh-teh-'ahr)*
to stick	**pegar** *(peh-'gahr)*
to interrupt	**interrumpir** *(een-teh-rroom-'peer)*
to break	**romper** *(rohm-'pehr)*

Try Some

Can you recall the meanings of the verbs listed below? Notice how the sentences incorporate some of the verb tenses presented in the book thus far. Match each sentence with its appropriate ending:

No está goteando...	**...ahora**
Usaré los alicates...	**...ayer**
Estaba funcionando bien...	**...mañana**

Grammar Time

Spanish has two basic past tenses, the preterit and the imperfect. The preterit is a little more common, because it reports, narrates, or sums up activities that were completed in the past. We'll get to the imperfect tense a little later.

Let's take a look at a simple formula that shows how to create preterit forms with most verbs.

For regular **-ar** verbs, change the endings just like the example:

To Work	Trabajar *(trah-bah-'hahr)*
I worked	**trabajé** *(trah-bah-'heh)*
You (sing.); he, she worked	**trabajó** *(trah-bah-'hoh)*
We worked	**trabajamos** *(trah-bah-'hah-mohs)*
You (pl.); they worked	**trabajaron** *(trah-bah-'hah-rohn)*

In other words, drop the **-ar** from **trabajar** and add the endings as shown.

I worked yesterday.	**Trabajé ayer.** *(trah-bah-'heh ah-'yehr)*
Did they work?	**¿Trabajaron?** *(trah-bah-'hah-rohn)*
We didn't work.	**No trabajamos.** *(noh trah-bah-'hah-mohs)*

For regular verbs ending in **-er** and **-ir**, change the forms to look like these:

To Eat	comer *(koh-'mehr)*
I ate	**comí** *(koh-'mee)*
You (sing.); he, she ate	**comió** *(koh-mee-'oh)*
We ate	**comimos** *(koh-'mee-mohs)*
You (pl.); they ate	**comieron** *(koh-mee-'eh-rohn)*

They ate last night.	**Comieron anoche.** *(koh-mee-'eh-rohn ah-'noh-cheh)*
Did you eat?	**¿Comió usted?** *(koh-mee-'oh oos-'tehd)*
I didn't eat.	**No comí.** *(noh koh-'mee)*

Most **-ir** verbs are handled the same as the **-er** verbs. Notice the resemblance:

To Write	escribir *(ehs-kree-'beer)*
I wrote	**escribí** *(ehs-kree-'bee)*
You (sing.); he, she wrote	**escribió** *(ehs-kree-bee-'oh)*
We wrote	**escribimos** *(ehs-kree-'bee-mohs)*
You (pl.); they wrote	**escribieron** *(ehs-kree-bee-'eh-rohn)*

I wrote the list two weeks ago.	**Escribí la lista hace dos semanas.** *(ehs-kree-'bee lah 'lees-tah 'ah-seh dohs seh-'mah-nahs)*
He did not write the list.	**No escribió la lista.** *(noh ehs-kree-bee-'oh lah 'lees-tah)*
Did you guys write the list?	**¿Escribieron ustedes la lista?** *(ehs-kree-bee-'eh-rohn oos-'teh-dehs lah 'lees-tah)*

One-Liners

One technique to create one-liners is to attach a few words to a preposition:

with	**con** *(kohn)*	with the ladder	**con la escalera** *(kohn lah ehs-kah-'leh-rah)*
without	**sin** *(seen)*	without water	**sin el agua** *(seen ehl 'ah-gwah)*
to	**a** *(ah)*	to the kitchen	**a la cocina** *(ah lah koh-'see-nah)*
from, of	**de** *(deh)*	from the street	**de la calle** *(deh lah 'kah-yeh)*
in, on, at	**en** *(ehn)*	in the box	**en la caja** *(ehn lah 'kah-hah)*
for	**para** *('pah-rah)*	for the machine	**para la máquina** *('pah-rah lah 'mah-kee-nah)*
by, through	**por** *(pohr)*	through the pipes	**por los tubos** *(pohr lohs 'too-bohs)*

However, note that there are two contractions in the language:

of, from: **de** *(deh)* + the: **el** *(ehl)* = **del** *(dehl)*
It's from the other one.   **Es del otro.** *(ehs dehl 'oh-troh)*

to: **a** *(ah)* + the: **el** *(ehl)* = **al** *(ahl)*
It goes to the room.   **Va al cuarto.** *(vah ahl 'kwahr-toh)*

Grammar Time

Almost everyone struggles with the differences between **por** *(pohr)* and **para** *('pah-rah)* in Spanish. Generally speaking, **para** means *to, in order to,* and *for the purpose of,* whereas **por** means *by, through, because of* and *on account of.* Listen to how each are used in conversations, and you'll get a feel for them in no time.

Culture Issues

To avoid problems at the workplace, consider the following bilingual signs:

Open	**ABIERTO** *(ah-bee-'ehr-toh)*
Closed	**CERRADO** *(seh-'rrah-doh)*
Pull	**JALE** *('hah-leh)*
Push	**EMPUJE** *(ehm-'poo-heh)*

Danger	**PELIGRO** *(peh-'lee-groh)*
Out of Order	**DESCOMPUESTO** *(dehs-kohm-'pwehs-toh)*
Restrooms	**SANITARIOS** *(sah-nee-'tah-ree-ohs)*
No Smoking	**NO FUMAR** *(noh foo-'mahr)*

Authorized Personnel Only	**Sólo para personas autorizadas**
No Food Allowed	**No pasar con alimentos**
Emergency Exit	**Salida de emergencia**
Wet Floor	**Piso mojado**
High-Power Cables	**Cables de alto voltaje**
Do Not Block Entrance	**No obstruir la entrada**
Follow the Arrow	**Siga la flecha**
Use Other Door	**Favor de utilizar la otra puerta**
Employee Parking	**Estacionamiento para empleados**

Chapter Eight

Capítulo Ocho
(kah-'pee-too-loh 'oh-choh)

Exterior Work
El trabajo afuera
(ehl trah-'bah-hoh ah-'fweh-rah))

 Working Words: THE BUILDING'S EXTERIOR

Name the exterior parts of a typical home:

Go to (the)… **Vaya a…** *('vah-yah ah)*

front yard	**el patio enfrente** *(ehl 'pah-tee-oh ehn-'frehn-teh)*
backyard	**el patio trasero** *(ehl 'pah-tee-oh trah-'seh-roh)*
side yard	**el patio al lado** *(ehl 'pah-tee-oh ahl 'lah-doh)*
deck	**la terraza** *(lah teh-'rrah-sah)*
garden	**el jardín** *(ehl har-'deen)*
porch	**el pórtico** *(ehl 'pohr-tee-koh)*

Now name a few parts of the building itself. Follow the pattern as you give directions:

It's next to (the) _____. **Está al lado de** _____. *(ehs-'tah ahl 'lah-doh deh)*

entrance	**la entrada** *(lah ehn-'trah-dah)*
exit	**la salida** *(lah sah-'lee-dah)*
steps	**los escalones** *(lohs ehs-kah-'loh-nehs)*
garage	**el garaje** *(ehl gah-'rah-heh)*
carport	**la cochera** *(lah koh-'cheh-rah)*
walkway	**el camino** *(ehl kah-'mee-noh)*
stairs	**las escaleras** *(lahs ehs-kah-'leh-rahs)*
driveway	**la entrada para carros** *(lah ehn-'trah-dah 'pah-rah 'kah-rrohs)*
parking lot	**el estacionamento** *(ehl ehs-tah-see-oh-nah-mee-'ehn-toh)*

178

Focus on what you are going to be specifically working on:

We'll work on (the) ____.	**Trabajaremos con** ____. *(trah-bah-hah-'reh-mohs kohn)*
siding	**el revestimiento** *(ehl reh-vehs-tee-mee-'ehn-toh)*
stucco	**el estuco** *(ehl ehs-'too-koh)*
painting	**la pintura** *(lah peen-'too-rah)*
masonry	**la mampostería** *(lah mahm-pohs-teh-'ree-ah)*
carpentry	**la carpintería** *(lah kahr-peen-teh-'ree-ah)*
installation	**la instalación** *(lah eens-tah-lah-see-'ohn)*
finishing	**el acabado** *(ehl ah-kah-'bah-doh)*
framing	**el armazón** *(ehl ahr-mah-'sohn)*

We'll install (the) ____.	**Instalaremos** ____. *(eens-tah-lah-'reh-mohs)*
door	**la puerta** *(lah 'pwehr-tah)*
window	**la ventana** *(lah vehn-'tah-nah)*
flooring	**el piso** *(ehl 'pee-soh)*
wall	**la pared** *(lah pah-'rehd)*
roof	**el tejado** *(ehl teh-'hah-doh)*
gate	**el portón** *(ehl pohr-'tohn)*
fence	**la cerca** *(lah 'sehr-kah)*

Continue to name exterior features:

Go to (the)...	**Vaya a...** *('vah-yah ah)*
barbecue	**la parrilla** *(lah pah-'rree-yah)*
bench	**el banco** *(ehl 'bahn-koh)*
bridge	**el puente** *(ehl 'pwehn-teh)*
fire pit	**la fogata** *(lah foh-'gah-tah)*
flower box	**la plantera** *(lah plahn-'teh-rah)*
fountain	**la fuente** *(lah 'fwehn-teh)*
gazebo	**el quiosco** *(ehl kee-'ohs-koh)*
greenhouse	**el invernadero** *(ehl een-vehr-nah-'deh-roh)*
hot tub	**el jacuzzi** *(ehl yah-'koo-see)*
mailbox	**el buzón** *(ehl boo-'sohn)*
pool	**la piscina** *(lah pee-'see-nah)*
shed	**el cobertizo** *(ehl koh-behr-'tee-soh)*

It's easier if you practice new words in sets of threes:

Look at (the)...	Mire... *('mee-reh)*
curb	**el bordillo** *(ehl bohr-'dee-yoh)*
sidewalk	**la vereda** *(lah veh-'reh-dah)*
street	**la calle** *(lah 'kah-yeh)*
awning	**el toldo** *(ehl 'tohl-doh)*
balcony	**el balcón** *(ehl bahl-'kohn)*
doorway	**el portal** *(ehl pohr-'tahl)*
eaves	**el alero** *(ehl ah-'leh-roh)*
fascia	**la fachada** *(lah fah-'chah-dah)*
soffit	**la cubierta del alero** *(lah koo-bee-'ehr-tah dehl ah-'leh-roh)*
downspout	**la bajada de aguas** *(lah bah-'hah-dah deh 'ah-gwahs)*
drain	**el desagüe** *(ehl deh-'sah-gweh)*
gutter	**el canalón** *(ehl kah-nah-'lohn)*
block wall	**el muro de bloques** *(ehl 'moo-roh deh 'bloh-kehs)*
brick wall	**el muro de ladrillos** *(ehl 'moo-roh deh lah-'dree-yohs)*
stone wall	**el muro de piedra** *(ehl 'moo-roh deh pee-'eh-drah)*
arch	**el arco** *(ehl 'ahr-koh)*
column	**la columna** *(lah koh-'loom-nah)*
post	**el poste** *(ehl 'pohs-teh)*
chimney	**la chimenea** *(lah chee-meh-'neh-ah)*
light fixture	**el farol** *(ehl fah-'rohl)*
skylight	**el tragaluz** *(ehl trah-gah-'loos)*
barrier	**la barrera** *(lah bah-'rreh-rah)*
railing	**la baranda** *(lah bah-'rahn-dah)*
ramp	**la rampa** *(lah 'rahm-pah)*
tennis court	**la cancha de tenis** *(lah 'kahn-chah deh 'teh-nees)*
basketball court	**la cancha de baloncesto** *(lah 'kahn-chah deh bah-lohn-'sehs-toh)*
fishpond	**el estanque para peces** *(ehl ehs-'tahn-keh 'pah-rah 'peh-sehs)*

Exterior jobs include the same vocabulary as other projects:

It needs (the)...   **Necesita...** *(neh-seh-'see-tah)*

assembly	**el montaje** *(ehl mohn-'tah-heh)*
brace	**el soporte** *(ehl soh-'pohr-teh)*
coping	**el borde decorativo** *(ehl 'bohr-deh deh-koh-rah-'tee-voh)*
frame	**el marco** *(ehl 'mahr-koh)*
insulation	**el aislamiento** *(ehl ah-ees-lah-mee-'ehn-toh)*
joint	**la unión** *(lah oo-nee-'ohn)*
lathing	**el listón** *(ehl lees-'tohn)*
trim	**el adorno** *(ehl ah-'dohr-noh)*
wrapping	**el forro** *(ehl 'foh-rroh)*

Check (the)...   **Revise...** *(reh-'vee-seh)*

beams	**las vigas** *(lahs 'vee-gahs)*
cables	**los cables** *(lohs 'kah-blehs)*
faucets	**los grifos** *(lohs 'gree-fohs)*
footings	**las zapatas** *(lahs sah-'pah-tahs)*
outlets	**los enchufes** *(lohs ehn-'choo-fehs)*
pipes	**los tubos** *(lohs 'too-bohs)*
vents	**los conductos** *(lohs kohn-'dook-tohs)*
wires	**los alambres** *(lohs ah-'lahm-brehs)*

Now explain everything in detail:

It's made of ...   **Es hecho de...** *(ehs 'eh-choh deh)*

alloy	**la aleación** *(lah ah-leh-ah-see-'ohn)*
aluminum	**el aluminio** *(ehl ah-loo-'mee-nee-oh)*
brass	**el latón** *(ehl lah-'tohn)*
brick	**el ladrillo** *(ehl lah-'dree-yoh)*
cement	**el cemento** *(ehl seh-'mehn-toh)*
ceramic	**la cerámica** *(lah seh-'rah-mee-kah)*
clay	**la arcilla** *(lah ahr-'see-yah)*
composite	**el compuesto** *(ehl kohm-'pwehs-toh)*
drywall	**el enyesado** *(ehl ehn-yeh-'sah-doh)*
felt	**el fieltro** *(ehl fee-'ehl-troh)*
fiberglass	**la fibra de vidrio** *(lah 'fee-brah deh 'vee-dree-oh)*
glass	**el vidrio** *(ehl 'vee-dree-oh)*

iron	**el hierro** *(ehl ee-'eh-rroh)*
membrane	**la membrana** *(lah mehm-'brah-nah)*
mesh	**la malla** *(lah 'mah-yah)*
plastic	**el plástico** *(ehl 'plahs-tee-koh)*
plywood	**el contrachapado** *(ehl kohn-trah-chah-'pah-doh)*
rubber	**la goma** *(lah 'goh-mah)*
steel	**el acero** *(ehl ah-'seh-roh)*
stone	**la piedra** *(lah pee-'eh-drah)*
tin	**el estaño** *(ehl ehs-'tah-nyoh)*
vinyl	**el vinilo** *(ehl vee-'nee-loh)*
wood	**la madera** *(lah mah-'deh-rah)*

Just a Suggestion

Some Spanish words have a variety of meanings in English:

el enyesado *(ehl ehn-yeh-'sah-doh)* = drywall, sheetrock, plasterboard, gypsum board, etc.

Try Some

Name three outdoor features of a typical home in Spanish.

Name three outdoor construction projects in Spanish.

Name three different kinds of metal in Spanish.

Working Words: TOOLS AND MATERIALS

Most standard tools are needed for work on the exterior of a building:

Bring (the)…	**Traiga…** *('trah-ee-gah)*
air compressor	**el compresor de aire** *(ehl kohm-preh-'sohr deh 'ah-ee-reh)*
caulking gun	**la pistola de masilla** *(lah pees-'toh-lah deh mah-'see-yah)*
charger	**la cargadora** *(lah kahr-gah-'doh-rah)*
circular saw	**la sierra circular** *(lah see-'eh-rrah seer-koo-'lahr)*

cordless drill	**el taladro a pilas** *(ehl tah-'lah-droh ah 'pee-lahs)*
cutters	**la cizalla** *(lah see-'sah-yah)*
duct tape	**la cinta ploma** *(lah 'seen-tah 'ploh-mah)*
extension cord	**la extensión eléctrica** *(lah ex-tehn-see-'ohn eh-'lekh-tree-kah)*
file	**la lima** *(lah 'lee-mah)*
glue	**el pegamento/la cola** *(ehl peh-gah-'mehn-toh/lah 'koh-lah)*
hammer	**el martillo** *(ehl mahr-'tee-yoh)*
heating gun	**la pistola térmica** *(lah pees-'toh-lah 'tehr-mee-kah)*
level	**el nivel** *(ehl nee-'vehl)*
mallet	**el mazo** *(ehl 'mah-soh)*
masking tape	**la cinta pegajosa** *(lah 'seen-tah peh-gah-'hoh-sah)*
measuring tape	**la cinta métrica** *(lah 'seen-tah 'meh-tree-kah)*
miter saw	**la sierra de cortar en ángulos** *(lah see-'eh-rrah deh kohr-'tahr ehn 'ahn-goo-lohs)*
nail gun	**la pistola de clavos** *(lah pees-'toh-lah deh 'klah-vohs)*
pliers	**los alicates** *(los ah-lee-'kah-tehs)*
ratchet wrench	**la llave de trinquete** *(lah 'yah-veh deh treen-'keh-teh)*
rope	**la soga** *(lah 'soh-gah)*
sandpaper	**el papel de lija** *(ehl pah-'pehl deh 'lee-hah)*
scraper	**el raspador** *(ehl rahs-pah-'dohr)*
screwdriver	**el destornillador** *(ehl dehs-tohr-nee-yah-'dohr)*
stepladder	**la escalera baja** *(lah ehs-kah-'leh-rah 'bah-hah)*
utility knife	**la cuchilla** *(lah koo-'chee-yah)*
wrench	**la llave inglesa** *(lah 'yah-veh een-'gleh-sah)*

Now grab some of these smaller things:

Pick up (the)…	**Recoja…** *(reh-'koh-hah)*
adapter	**el adaptador** *(ehl ah-dahp-tah-'dohr)*
bit	**la broca** *(lah 'broh-kah)*
blade	**la hoja** *(lah 'oh-hah)*
bolt	**el perno** *(ehl 'pehr-noh)*
bracket	**el soporte** *(ehl soh-'pohr-teh)*
clamp	**la abrazadera** *(lah ah-brah-sah-'deh-rah)*
connector	**el acoplamiento** *(ehl ah-koh-plah-mee-'ehn-toh)*
fastener	**el sujetador** *(ehl soo-heh-tah-'dohr)*
insert	**el anclaje** *(ehl ahn-'klah-heh)*
joint	**la unión** *(leh oo-nee-'ohn)*
nail	**el clavo** *(ehl 'klah-voh)*

nut	**la tuerca** *(lah 'twehr-kah)*
pin	**la clavija** *(lah klah-'vee-hah)*
plate	**la placa** *(lah 'plah-kah)*
rod	**la barra** *(lah 'bah-rrah)*
screw	**el tornillo** *(ehl tohr-'nee-yoh)*
staple	**la grapa** *(lah 'grah-pah)*
strap	**la tira** *(lah 'tee-rah)*
washer	**la arandela** *(lah ah-rahn-'deh-lah)*

There are many different kinds of screws. Review your vocabulary:

They are _____ screws. **Son tornillos para _____.** *(sohn tohr-'nee-yohs 'pah-rah)*

decking	**terrazas** *(teh-'rrah-sahs)*
drywall	**enyesado** *(ehn-yeh-'sah-doh)*
fastening	**sujeción** *(soo-heh-see-'ohn)*
laminating	**laminado** *(lah-mee-'nah-doh)*
lathing	**listones** *(lees-'toh-nehs)*
masonry	**mampostería** *(mahm-pohs-teh-'ree-ah)*
roofing	**tejado** *(teh-'hah-doh)*
self-drilling	**autotaladrado** *(ah-oo-toh-tah-lah-'drah-doh)*

These heavier items may also be required:

cement mixer	**la mezcladora** *(lah mehs-klah-'doh-rah)*
crane	**la grúa** *(lah 'groo-ah)*
extension ladder	**la escalera de extensión** *(lah ehs-kah-'leh-rah deh ex-tehn-see-'ohn)*
forklift	**la carretilla elevadora** *(lah kah-rreh-'tee-yah eh-leh-vah-'doh-rah)*
scaffolding	**el andamio** *(ehl ahn-'dah-mee-oh)*
skid-steer loader	**la cargadora Bobcat** *(lah kahr-gah-'doh-rah 'bohb-kaht)*

Let's review specialized tools by listing them under different trades.

CARPENTRY

carpenter's hammer	**el martillo de carpintero** *(ehl mahr-'tee-yoh deh kahr-peen-'teh-roh)*
chalk	**la tiza** *(lah 'tee-sah)*
chisel	**el cincel** *(ehl seen-'sehl)*
flat pencil	**el lápiz plano** *(ehl 'lah-pees 'plah-noh)*

framing square	**la escuadra** *(lah ehs-'kwah-drah)*
hand saw	**el serrucho** *(ehl seh-'rroo-choh)*
plane	**el cepillo** *(ehl seh-'pee-yoh)*
plumb bob	**la plomada** *(lah ploh-'mah-dah)*
plumb line	**el hilo de plomada** *(ehl 'ee-loh deh ploh-'mah-dah)*
sander	**la lijadora** *(lah lee-hah-'doh-rah)*
stud finder	**el buscamontantes** *(ehl boos-kah-mohn-'tahn-tehs)*
vice	**la prensa** *(lah 'prehn-sah)*

MASONRY

brick-cutting saw	**la sierra para cortar ladrillos** *(lah see-'eh-rrah 'pah-rah kohr-'tahr lah-'dree-yohs)*
broom	**la escoba** *(lah ehs-'koh-bah)*
bull float	**la llana mecánica** *(lah 'yah-nah meh-'kah-nee-kah)*
edger	**la llana para bordes** *(lah 'yah-nah 'pah-rah 'bohr-dehs)*
finishing broom	**el cepillo de acabado** *(ehl seh-'pee-yoh deh ah-kah-'bah-doh)*
joint compound	**la pasta para uniones** *(lah 'pahs-tah 'pah-rah oo-nee-'oh-nehs)*
jointer	**el marcador de juntas** *(ehl mahr-kah-'dohr deh 'hoon-tahs)*
masonry hammer	**la maceta de albañil** *(lah mah-'seh-tah deh ahl-bah-'neel)*
pick	**el pico** *(ehl 'pee-koh)*
pump	**la bomba** *(lah 'bohm-bah)*
shovel	**la pala** *(lah 'pah-lah)*
stretcher	**el tensor** *(ehl tehn-'sohr)*
tie	**el sujetador** *(ehl soo-heh-tah-'dohr)*
tongs	**las tenazas** *(lahs teh-'nah-sahs)*
trowel	**la paleta** *(lah pah-'leh-tah)*
wheelbarrow	**la carretilla** *(lah kah-rreh-'tee-yah)*

Did you unload everything?

Give me (the)...	**Deme...** *('deh-meh)*
asphalt	**el asfalto** *(ehl ahs-'fahl-toh)*
block	**el bloque** *(ehl 'bloh-keh)*
brick	**el ladrillo** *(ehl lah-'dree-yoh)*
cement	**el cemento** *(ehl seh-'mehn-toh)*

chicken wire	**el alambre de gallinero** *(ehl ah-'lahm-breh deh gah-yee-'neh-roh)*
compound	**el compuesto** *(ehl kohm-'pwehs-toh)*
flashing	**el tapajuntas** *(ehl tah-pah-'hoon-tahs)*
grating	**la rejilla** *(lah reh-'hee-yah)*
lamination	**la lámina** *(lah 'lah-mee-nah)*
lumber	**la madera** *(lah mah-'deh-rah)*
pipe	**la tubería** *(lah too-beh-'ree-ah)*
plaster	**el yeso** *(ehl 'yeh-soh)*
rebar	**la varilla** *(lah vah-'ree-yah)*
sand	**la arena** *(lah ah-'reh-nah)*
sheet metal	**la chapa de metal** *(lah 'chah-pah deh meh-'tahl)*
tar paper	**el papel embreado** *(ehl pah-'pehl ehm-breh-'ah-doh)*
wire mesh	**la malla metálica** *(lah 'mah-yah meh-'tah-lee-kah)*

Now, specify exactly what you need:

I need (the)...	**Necesito...** *(neh-seh-'see-toh)*
slump stone	**el bloque de hormigón** *(ehl 'bloh-keh deh ohr-mee-'gohn)*
cinderblock	**el ladrillo grande de cemento** *(ehl lah-'dree-yoh 'grahn-deh deh seh-'mehn-toh)*
cultured stone	**la piedra prefabricada** *(lah pee-'eh-drah preh-fah-bree-'kah-dah)*

Combine these words with your materials:

bag	**el saco** *(ehl 'sah-koh)*
board	**la tabla** *(lah 'tah-blah)*
bucket	**el balde** *(ehl 'bahl-deh)*
bundle	**el bulto** *(ehl 'bool-toh)*
pallet	**la plataforma** *(lah plah-tah-'fohr-mah)*
panel	**el panel** *(ehl pah-'nehl)*
row	**la hilera** *(lah ee-'leh-rah)*
sheet	**la hoja** *(lah 'oh-hah)*
stack	**el montón** *(ehl mohn-'tohn)*
strip	**la tira** *(lah 'tee-rah)*

Just a Suggestion

Create specialized names for one specific item:

They are…	Son… *(sohn)*
cap blocks	**bloques de remate** *('bloh-kehs deh reh-'mah-teh)*
corner blocks	**bloques de esquina** *('bloh-kehs deh ehs-'kee-nah)*
decorative blocks	**bloques decorativos** *('bloh-kehs deh-koh-rah-'tee-vohs)*
planter blocks	**bloques para planteras** *('bloh-kehs 'pah-rah plahn-'teh-rahs)*
step blocks	**bloques para escalones** *('bloh-kehs 'pah-rah ehs-kah-'loh-nehs)*

Try Some

Translate:

la malla metálica _____

el sujetador _____

la llana mecánica _____

el bloque de hormigón _____

el buscamontantes _____

Working Words: DOOR AND WINDOW INSTALLATION

First mention any specialized item that will be needed for the job:

Give me (the)...	**Deme...** *('deh-meh)*
door hanger	**la colgadora de puertas** *(lah kohl-gah-'doh-rah deh 'pwehr-tahs)*
glass cutter	**el cortavidrios** *(ehl kohr-tah-'vee-dree-ohs)*
hinge templates	**las plantillas para bisagras** *(lahs plahn-'tee-yahs 'pah-rah bee-'sah-grahs)*
lock mortiser	**la embutidora de cerraduras** *(lah ehm-boo-tee-'doh-rah deh seh-rrah-'doo-rahs)*
lubricant	**el lubricante** *(ehl loo-bree-'kahn-teh)*
scraper	**el raspador** *(ehl rahs-pah-'dohr)*
sealant	**el sellador** *(ehl seh-yah-'dohr)*
utility knife	**la cuchilla** *(lah koo-'chee-yah)*

DOORS

With door installation, these words will be required first:

We have to install (a)...	**Debemos instalar...** *(deh-'beh-mohs eens-tah-'lahr)*
entry door	**la puerta de entrada** *(lah 'pwehr-tah deh ehn-'trah-dah)*
back door	**la puerta trasera/falsa** *(lah 'pwehr-tah trah-'seh-rah/ 'fahl-sah)*
double doors	**la doble puerta** *(lah 'doh-bleh 'pwehr-tah)*
Dutch door	**la puerta cortada** *(lah 'pwehr-tah kohr-'tah-dah)*
French door	**la puerta de dos hojas** *(lah 'pwehr-tah deh dohs 'oh-hahs)*
garage door	**la puerta del garaje** *(lah 'pwehr-tah dehl gah-'rah-heh)*
revolving door	**la puerta giratoria** *(lah 'pwehr-tah hee-rah-'toh-ree-ah)*
sliding door	**la puerta corrediza** *(lah 'pwehr-tah koh-rreh-'dee-sah)*
storm door	**la contrapuerta** *(lah kohn-trah-'pwehr-tah)*
swinging door	**la puerta giratoria** *(lah 'pwehr-tah hee-rah-'toh-ree-ah)*

They are _____ doors.	**Son puertas _____.** *(sohn 'pwehr-tahs)*
aluminum	**de aluminio** *(deh ah-loo-'mee-nee-oh)*
fiberglass	**de fibra de vidrio** *(deh 'fee-brah deh 'vee-dree-oh)*
hollow	**huecas** *('hweh-kahs)*

solid wood	**de madera maciza** *(deh mah-'deh-rah mah-'see-sah)*
steel	**de acero** *(deh ah-'seh-roh)*
vinyl	**de vinilo** *(deh vee-'nee-loh)*
wood-clad	**forradas en madera** *(foh-'rrah-dahs ehn mah-'deh-rah)*

It has (the)…	**Tiene…** *(tee-'eh-neh)*
grille	**el enrejado** *(ehl ehn-reh-'hah-doh)*
hardware	**el herraje** *(ehl eh-'rrah-heh)*
louvers	**las persianas** *(lah pehr-see-'ah-nahs)*
mail slot	**la placa del buzón** *(lah 'plah-kah dehl boo-'sohn)*
panels	**los paneles** *(lohs pah-'neh-lehs)*
transom	**el tragaluz** *(ehl trah-gah-'loos)*

Here's (the)…	**Aquí tiene…** *(ah-'kee tee-'eh-neh)*

casing	**el marco** *(ehl 'mahr-koh)*
deadbolt	**el pestillo** *(ehl pehs-'tee-yoh)*
hinge	**la bisagra** *(lah bee-'sah-grah)*
jamb	**la jamba** *(lah 'hahm-bah)*
molding	**la moldura** *(lah mohl-'doo-rah)*
pin	**el perno** *(ehl 'pehr-noh)*
pivot	**el pivote** *(ehl pee-'voh-teh)*
screen	**el mosquitero** *(ehl mohs-kee-'teh-roh)*
seal	**el sello** *(ehl 'seh-yoh)*
stop	**el tope** *(ehl 'toh-peh)*
threshold	**el umbral** *(ehl oom-'brahl)*
toe kick	**la tabla contragolpes** *(lah 'tah-blah kohn-trah-'gohl-pehs)*
weather strip	**el burlete** *(ehl boor-'leh-teh)*

Now work on the lock alone:

Use (the)…	**Use…** *('oo-seh)*
connecting screw	**el tornillo conector** *(ehl tohr-'nee-yoh koh-nehk-'tohr)*
cylinder	**el cilindro** *(ehl see-'leen-droh)*
key	**la llave** *(lah 'yah-veh)*
latch	**el cerrojo** *(ehl seh-'rroh-hoh)*
lock casing	**el cuerpo del pestillo** *(ehl 'kwehr-poh dehl pehs-'tee-yoh)*

lock nut	**la tuerca de seguridad** *(lah 'twehr-kah deh seh-goo-ree-'dahd)*
plate	**la placa-guía** *(lah 'plah-kah 'gee-ah)*
shaft	**el eje** *(ehl 'eh-heh)*

Even the garage door has specialized vocabulary:

Install (the)...	**Instale...** *(eens-'tah-leh)*
cables	**los cables** *(lohs 'kah-blehs)*
drums	**los tambores** *(lohs tahm-'boh-rehs)*
opener	**el abrepuerta automático** *(ahl ah-breh-'pwehr-tah ah-oo-toh-'mah-tee-koh)*
pulley	**la polea** *(lah poh-'leh-ah)*
rails	**los rieles** *(lohs ree-'eh-lehs)*
rollers	**los rodillos** *(lohs roh-'dee-yohs)*
sectional	**el seccional** *(ehl sehk-see-oh-'nahl)*
spring	**el resorte de torsión** *(ehl reh-'sohr-teh deh tohr-see-'ohn)*

Stay with short expressions that include related vocabulary:

Check (the)...	**Revise...** *(reh-'vee-seh)*
balance	**el equilibrio** *(ehl eh-kee-'lee-bree-oh)*
clearance	**la distancia de seguridad** *(lah dees-'tahn-see-ah deh seh-goo-ree-'dahd)*
slope	**el declive** *(ehl deh-'klee-veh)*

It's...	**Está...** *(ehs-'tah)*
level	**nivelado** *(nee-veh-'lah-doh)*
plumb	**justo en medio** *('hoos-toh ehn 'meh-dee-oh)*
square	**cuadrado** *(kwah-'drah-doh)*

Be careful with (the)...	**Tenga cuidado con...** *('tehn-gah kwee-'dah-doh kohn)*
lites	**los cristales** *(lohs krees-'tah-lehs)*
divided lites	**los cristales divididos** *(lohs krees-'tah-lehs dee-vee-'dee-dohs)*
sidelites	**los cristales laterales** *(lohs krees-'tah-lehs lah-teh-'rah-lehs)*

Where's (the)…?	¿Dónde está…? *('dohn-deh ehs-'tah)*

doorbell	el timbre *(ehl 'teem-breh)*
doorknob	la perilla *(lah peh-'ree-yah)*
door knocker	el picaporte *(ehl pee-kah-'pohr-teh)*

Just a Suggestion

Sometimes you'll need several words to describe a common door:

| left-hand in-swing | **la puerta de apertura interior hacia la izquierda** *(lah 'pwehr-tah deh ah-pehr-'too-rah een-teh-ree-'ohr 'ah-see-ah lah ees-kee-'ehr-dah)* |
| right-hand out-swing | **la puerta de apertura exterior hacia la derecha** *(lah 'pwehr-tah deh ah-pehr-'too-rah ex-teh-ree-'ohr 'ah-see-ah lah deh-'reh-chah)* |

WINDOWS

Install (the)…	Instale… *(eens-'tah-leh)*
awning window	la ventana-marquesina *(lah vehn-'tah-nah mahr-keh-'see-nah)*
bay window	la ventana salediza *(lah vehn-'tah-nah sah-leh-'dee-sah)*
bow window	la ventana curva *(lah vehn-'tah-nah 'koor-vah)*
casement window	la ventana a bisagra *(lah vehn-'tah-nah ah bee-'sah-grah)*
cellar window	el respirador *(ehl rehs-pee-rah-'dohr)*
double-pane window	la ventana con doble cristal *(lah vehn-'tah-nah kohn 'doh-bleh krees-'tahl)*
fixed window	la ventana fija *(lah vehn-'tah-nah 'fee-hah)*
hung window	la ventana guillotina *(lah vehn-'tah-nah gee-yoh-'tee-nah)*
sliding window	la ventana corrediza *(lah vehn-'tah-nah koh-rreh-'dee-sah)*
storm window	la guardaventana *(lah gwahr-dah-vehn-'tah-nah)*

Bring (the)…	**Traiga…** *('trah-ee-gah)*
arm	el **brazo** *(ehl 'brah-soh)*
balance	el **contrapeso** *(ehl kohn-trah-'peh-soh)*
breast	el **alfeízar** *(ehl ahl-'feh-ee-sahr)*
clip	el **sujetador** *(ehl soo-heh-tah-'dohr)*
cord	el **cordón** *(ehl kohr-'dohn)*
crank	la **manivela** *(lah mah-nee-'veh-lah)*
flashing	el **verteaguas** *(ehl vehr-teh-'ah-gwahs)*
guide	la **guía** *(lah 'gee-ah)*
handle	la **manija** *(lah mah-'nee-hah)*
head	la **cabecera** *(lah kah-beh-'seh-rah)*
hook	el **gancho** *(ehl 'gahn-choh)*
housing	la **cubierta** *(lah koo-bee-'ehr-tah)*
latch	el **trinquete** *(ehl treen-'keh-teh)*
lever	la **palanca** *(lah pah-'lahn-kah)*
lintel	el **dintel** *(ehl deen-'tehl)*
lock	la **cerradura** *(lah seh-rrah-'doo-rah)*
mounting screw	el **tornillo de montaje** *(ehl tohr-'nee-yoh deh mohn-'tah-heh)*
mullion	el **montante** *(ehl mohn-'tahn-teh)*
operator	el **operario** *(ehl oh-peh-'rah-ree-oh)*
pane glass	la **hoja de vidrio** *(lah 'oh-hah deh 'vee-dree-'oh)*
pulley	la **polea** *(lah poh-'leh-hah)*
reveal	la **jamba** *(lah 'hahm-bah)*
roller	el **rodillo** *(ehl roh-'dee-yoh)*
rubber stripping	la **tira de goma** *(lah 'tee-rah deh 'goh-mah)*
sash	el **bastidor de vidriera** *(ehl bahs-tee-'dohr deh veed-ree-'eh-rah)*
sill	el **antepecho** *(ehl ahn-teh-'peh-choh)*
spring	el **resorte** *(ehl reh-'sohr-teh)*
track	la **carrilera** *(lah kah-rree-'leh-rah)*
vinyl casing	el **marco de vinilo** *(ehl 'mahr-koh deh vee-'nee-loh)*
weather strip	el **burlete** *(ehl boor-'leh-teh)*

Keep talking about the window itself:

It's…	**Es/ Está…** *(ehs/ehs-'tah)*
double-pane	**de doble hoja** *(deh 'doh-bleh 'oh-hah)*
insulated	**aislada** *(ah-ees-'lah-dah)*

noise resistant	**resistente al ruído** *(reh-sees-'tehn-teh ahl roo-'ee-doh)*
sealed	**sellada** *(seh-'yah-dah)*
self-closing	**de autocierre** *(deh ah-oo-toh-see-'eh-rreh)*
steel-reinforced	**reforzada con acero** *(reh-fohr-'sah-dah kohn ah-'seh-roh)*
tinted	**sombreada** *(sohm-breh-'ah-dah)*
treated	**tratada** *(trah-'tah-dah)*
Unload (the)…	**Descargue…** *(dehs-'kahr-geh)*
accessory	**el accesorio** *(ehl ahk-seh-'soh-ree-oh)*
kit	**el conjunto** *(ehl kohn-'hoon-toh)*
package	**el paquete** *(ehl pah-'keh-teh)*
part	**la pieza** *(lah pee-'eh-sah)*
set	**el juego** *(ehl 'hweh-goh)*

Note how measurements and codes are used:

16-penny nail	**el clavo de dieciséis** *(ehl klah-voh deh dee-eh-see-'seh-ees)*
25-gauge steel	**el acero de calibre veinte y cinco** *(ehl ah-'seh-roh de kah-'lee-breh' veh-een-teh ee 'seen-koh)*
36-inch door	**la puerta de treinta y seis pulgadas** *(lah 'pwehr-tah deh 'treh-een-tah ee 'seh-ees pool-'gah-dahs)*
A-frame	**el marco en A** *(ehl 'mahr-koh ehn ah)*
R-20 insulation	**el aislamiento de veinte** *(ehl ah-ees-lah-mee-'ehn-toh deh 'veh-een-teh)*
V-groove	**la ranura en V** *(lah rah-'noo-rah ehn veh)*
Z-flashing	**el verteaguas en Z** *(ehl vehr-teh-'ah-gwahs ehn 'zeh-tah)*

Try Some

Delete the word that doesn't belong with the others:

el declive, el juego, el equipo
la llave, el pestillo, el timbre
la polea, la cubeta, el resorte

Working Words: STUCCO AND PAINT

The building is wrapped for stucco. Make sure you know these words:

It has (the)…	**Tiene…** *(tee-'eh-neh)*
chicken wire	**el alambre de gallinero** *(ehl ah-'lahm-breh deh gah-yee-'neh-roh)*
membrane	**la membrana** *(lah mehm-'brah-nah)*
tar paper	**el papel embreado** *(ehl pah-'pehl ehm-breh-'ah-doh)*
nails	**los clavos** *(lohs 'klah-vohs)*
hooks	**los ganchos** *(lohs 'gahn-chohs)*
screws	**los tornillos** *(lohs tohr-'nee-yohs)*
scratch coat	**la primera capa** *(lah pree-'meh-rah 'kah-pah)*
brown coat	**la segunda capa** *(lah seh-'goon-dah 'kah-pah)*
finish coat	**la capa final** *(lah 'kah-pah fee-'nahl)*
It needs (the)…	**Necesita…** *(neh-seh-'see-tah)*

additives	**los aditivos** *(lohs ah-dee-'tee-vohs)*
color	**el color** *(ehl koh-lohr)*
gravel	**la grava** *(lah 'grah-vah)*
lime	**el cal** *(lah kahl)*
mixture	**la mezcla** *(lah 'mehs-klah)*
mortar	**la argamasa** *(lah ahr-gah-'mah-sah)*
plaster	**el yeso** *(ehl 'yeh-soh)*
sand	**la arena** *(lah ah-'reh-nah)*
water	**el agua** *(ehl 'ah-gwah)*

They are…	**Son…** *(sohn)*
casing beads	**las molduras de contramarca** *(lahs mohl-'doo-rahs deh kohn-trah-'mahr-kah)*
control joints	**las juntas de control** *(lahs 'hoon-tahs deh kohn-'trohl)*
corner beads	**los bordones de esquina** *(lohs bohr-'doh-nehs deh ehs-'kee-nah)*
drip screeds	**las maestras de goteo** *(lahs mah-'ehs-trahs deh goh-'teh-oh)*

slip joints	**las juntas deslizantes** *(las 'hoon-tahs dehs-lee-'sahn-tehs)*
weep screeds	**las maestras inferiores** *(lahs mah-'ehs-trahs een-feh-ree-'oh-rehs)*

Check (the)...	**Revise...** *(reh-vee-seh)*
amount	**la cantidad** *(lah kahn-tee-'dahd)*
consistency	**la consistencia** *(lah kohn-sees-'tehn-see-ah)*
hydration	**la hidratación** *(lah ee-drah-tah-see-'ohn)*
surface	**la superficie** *(lah soo-pehr-'fee-see-eh)*
texture	**la textura** *(lah tehks-'too-rah)*
thickness	**el espesor** *(ehl ehs-peh-'sohr)*

Remove (the)...	**Quite...** *('kee-teh)*
blisters	**las ampollas** *(lahs ahm-'poh-yahs)*
chalking	**los álcalis** *(lohs 'ahl-kah-lees)*
chemical	**la sustancia química** *(lah soos-'tahn-see-ah 'kee-mee-kah)*
dirt	**la suciedad** *(lah soo-see-eh-'dahd)*
dust	**el polvo** *(ehl 'pohl-voh)*
mold	**el moho** *(ehl 'moh-hoh)*
oil	**el aceite** *(ehl ah-'seh-ee-teh)*
old paint	**la pintura vieja** *(lah peen-'too-rah vee-'eh-hah)*
rust	**el óxido** *(ehl 'ohk-see-doh)*
wax	**la cera** *(lah 'seh-rah)*

It's time for some painting, so begin with some common tools and materials:

Unload (the)...	**Descargue...** *(dehs-'kahr-geh)*
bucket	**el balde** *(ehl 'bahl-deh)*
caulking	**el sellador** *(ehl seh-yah-'dohr)*
compressor	**el compresor** *(ehl kohm-preh-'sohr)*
drop cloth	**la lona** *(lah 'loh-nah)*
exterior paint	**la pintura para el exterior** *(lah peen-'too-rah 'pah-rah ehl ex-teh-ree-'ohr)*
hose	**la manguera** *(lah mahn-'geh-rah)*
masking tape	**la cinta adhesiva** *(lah 'seen-tah ah-deh-'see-vah)*
paint brush	**la brocha para pintar** *(lah 'broh-chah 'pah-rah peen-'tahr)*
paint sprayer	**la pistola pintadora** *(lah pees-'toh-lah peen-tah-'doh-rah)*
pan	**el plato** *(ehl 'plah-toh)*

putty knife	**la espátula** *(lah ehs-'pah-too-lah)*
putty	**la masilla** *(lah mah-'see-yah)*
roller	**el rodillo** *(ehl roh-'dee-yoh)*
sander	**la lijadora** *(lah lee-hah-'doh-rah)*
sandpaper	**el papel de lija** *(ehl pah-'pehl deh 'lee-hah)*
scraper	**el raspador** *(ehl rahs-pah-'dohr)*
spackling	**el relleno/el mástique** *(ehl reh-'yeh-noh ehl mahs-'tee-keh)*
utility knife	**la cuchilla** *(lah koo-'chee-yah)*

All materials need to be identified:

I have (the)…	**Tengo…** *('tehn-goh)*
acrylic	**el acrílico** *(ehl ah-'kree-lee-koh)*
enamel	**el esmalte** *(ehl ehs-'mahl-teh)*
epoxy	**el epoxi/la epoxia** *(ehl eh-'poh-ksee/lah eh-'poh-ksee-ah)*
lacquer	**la laca** *(lah 'lah-kah)*
primer	**el imprimador** *(ehl eem-pree-mah-'dohr)*
stain	**el tinte** *(ehl 'teen-teh)*
varnish	**el barniz** *(ehl bahr-'nees)*

It needs (a)…	**Necesita…** *(neh-seh-'see-tah)*

another coat	**otra capa** *('oh-trah 'kah-pah)*
cleaning	**una limpiada** *('oo-nah leem-pee-'ah-dah)*
sanding	**una lijada** *('oo-nah lee-'hah-dah)*
stainblock	**un antimanchas** *(oon ahn-tee-'mahn-chahs)*
texture coat	**una capa de textura** *('oo-nah 'kah-pah deh tehks-'too-rah)*
washing	**una lavada** *('oo-nah lah-'vah-dah)*
waterproofing	**un impermeabilizante** *(oon eem-pehr-meh-ah-bee-lee-'sahn-teh)*

And don't forget these:

thinner	**el diluyente/el adelgazador** *(ehl dee-loo-'yehn-teh/ehl ah-dehl-gah-sah-'dohr)*
turpentine	**la trementina** *(lah treh-mehn-'tee-nah)*
mineral spirits	**el solvente** *(ehl sohl-'vehn-teh)*

Painters must know these basic colors, and may need the others that follow:

They want _____ paint. **Quieren la pintura** _____. *(kee-'eh-rehn lah peen-'too-rah)*

black	**negra** *('neh-grah)*
blue	**azul** *(ah-'sool)*
brown	**café** *(kah-'feh)*
green	**verde** *('vehr-deh)*
grey	**gris** *(grees)*
orange	**anaranjada** *(ah-nah-rahn-'hah-dah)*
purple	**morada** *(moh'rah-dah)*
red	**roja** *('roh-hah)*
white	**blanca** *('blahn-kah)*
yellow	**amarilla** *(ah-mah-'ree-yah)*

The color is... **El color es...** *(ehl koh-'lohr ehs)*

aquamarine	**verde mar** *('vehr-deh mahr)*
copper	**cobrizo** *(koh-'bree-soh)*
cream	**crema** *('kreh-mah)*
dark green	**verde oscuro** *('vehr-deh ohs-'koo-roh)*
golden	**dorado** *(doh-'rah-doh)*
light blue	**azul claro** *(ah-'sool klah-roh)*
navy blue	**azul marino** *(ah-'sool mah-'ree-noh)*
silver	**plateado** *(plah-teh-'ah-doh)*
sky blue	**celeste** *(seh-'lehs-teh)*
tan	**castaño claro** *(kahs-'tah-nyoh 'klah-roh)*

Many paint colors are similar to their equivalents in English:

emerald	**esmeralda** *(ehs-meh-'rahl-dah)*
lilac	**lila** *('lee-lah)*
olive	**oliva** *(oh-'lee-vah)*
rose	**rosado** *(roh-'sah-doh)*
scarlet	**escarlata** *(ehs-kahr-'lah-tah)*
turquoise	**turquesa** *(toor-'keh-sah)*
violet	**violeta** *(vee-oh-'leh-tah)*

Exterior painting requires care, so use all the words you know:

Look at (the)…	**Mire…** *('mee-reh)*
design	**el diseño** *(ehl dee-'seh-nyoh)*
pattern	**el patrón** *(ehl pah-'trohn)*
pigment	**el pigmento** *(ehl peeg-'mehn-toh)*
plan	**el plano** *(ehl 'plah-noh)*
shade	**el matiz** *(ehl mah-'tees)*
style	**el estilo** *(ehl ehs-'tee-loh)*
type	**el tipo** *(ehl 'tee-poh)*

Descriptive words heard around exterior paint are:

It looks…	**Se ve…** *(seh veh)*
bright	**brillante** *(bree-'yahn-teh)*
clean	**limpia** *('leem-pee-ah)*
decorative	**decorativa** *(deh-koh-rah-'tee-vah)*
dirty	**sucia** *('soo-see-ah)*
dry	**seca** *('seh-kah)*
fast drying	**rápida para secar** *('rah-pee-dah 'pah-rah seh-'kahr)*
flat	**mate** *('mah-teh)*
glossy	**lustrosa** *(loos-'troh-sah)*
opaque	**opaca** *(oh-'pah-kah)*
satin	**satinada** *(sah-tee-'nah-dah)*
semi-gloss	**semi-lustrosa** *(seh-mee-loos-'troh-sah)*
sticky	**pegajosa** *(peh-gah-'hoh-sah)*
synthetic	**sintética** *(seen-'teh-tee-kah)*
thick	**espesa** *(ehs-'peh-sah)*
thin	**aguada** *(ah-'gwah-dah)*
wet	**mojada** *(moh-'hah-dah)*

Try Some

Translate into English:

Quite el óxido.
Necesita más arena.
Traiga la pintura de color celeste.

Just a Suggestion

Painting jobs get messy, so use words that refer to cleaning:

Use (the)...	**Use...** *('oo-seh)*
mop	**el trapeador** *(ehl trah-peh-ah-'dohr)*
rag	**el trapo** *(ehl 'trah-poh)*
towel	**la toalla** *(lah toh-'ah-yah)*
sponge	**la esponja** *(lah ehs-'pohn-hah)*
bucket	**el balde** *(ehl 'bahl-deh)*

Working Words: OTHER EXTERIOR WORK

Remember the names for those working around you:

Speak with (the) ____. **Hable con** ____. *('ah-bleh kohn)*

plumber	**el plomero/el fontanero** *(ehl ploh-'meh-roh/ehl fohn-tah-'neh-roh)*
electrician	**el electricista** *(ehl eh-lehk-tree-'sees-tah)*
painter	**el pintor** *(ehl peen-'tohr)*
welder	**el soldador** *(ehl sohl-dah-'dohr)*
landscaper	**el jardinero** *(ehl har-dee-'neh-roh)*
carpenter	**el carpintero** *(ehl kahr-peen-'teh-roh)*
mason	**el albañil** *(ahl ahl-bah-'neel)*
worker	**el obrero** *(ehl oh-'breh-roh)*
bricklayer	**el albañil/el ladrillero** *(ehl ahl-bah-'neel/ehl lah-dree-'yeh-roh)*
drywaller	**el yesero** *(ehl yeh-'seh-roh)*
installer	**el instalador** *(ehl eens-tah-lah-'dohr)*
architect	**el arquitecto** *(ehl ahr-kee-'tehk-toh)*

SIDING

They want (the)…	**Quieren…** *(kee-'eh-rehn)*
fascia board	**la moldura del alero** *(lah mohl-'doo-rah dehl ah-'leh-roh)*
paneling	**los paneles** *(lohs pah-'neh-lehs)*
plank	**el tablón** *(ehl tah-'blohn)*
shake	**el listón** *(ehl lees-'tohn)*
sheathing	**el entablado** *(ehl ehn-tah-'blah-doh)*
sheeting	**la lámina** *(lah 'lah-mee-nah)*
shutter	**la contraventana** *(lah kohn-trah-vehn-'tah-nah)*
trim	**el adorno** *(ehl ah-'dohr-noh)*
veneer	**la chapa** *(lah 'chah-pah)*
wall tile	**el azulejo** *(ehl ah-soo-'leh-hoh)*

Use (the)…	**Use…** *('oo-seh)*
particle board	**la madera aglomerada** *(lah mah-'deh-rah ah-glo-meh-'rah-dah)*
fiberboard	**la madera de fibra** *(lah mah-'deh-rah deh 'fee-brah)*
vinyl board	**la tabla de vinilo** *(lah 'tah-blah deh vee-'nee-loh)*

It's…	**Es…** *(ehs)*
seamless	**sin costura** *(seen kohs-'too-rah)*
tapered	**ahusado** *(ah-oo-'sah-doh)*
wrapped	**forrado** *(foh-'rrah-doh)*

It's…	**Está…** *(ehs-'tah)*
overlapped	**superpuesto** *(soo-pehr-'pwehs-toh)*
straight	**recto** *('rehk-toh)*
aligned	**alineado** *(ah-lee-neh-'ah-doh)*

Look closer at the siding material:

I see (the)…	**Veo…** *('veh-oh)*
bevel	**el bisel** *(ehl bee-'sehl)*
tongue and groove	**la lengüeta y ranura** *(lah lehn-'gweh-tah ee rah-'noo-rah)*
channel	**el acanalado** *(ehl ah-kah-nah-'lah-doh)*

Just a Suggestion

Board is **la tabla** *(lah 'tah-blah)*, but this word generally changes when it becomes part of a specialized material:

ledger board	**el larguero** *(ehl lahr-'geh-roh)*
strand board	**el bambú** *(ehl bahm-'boo)*
mortar board	**el birrete** *(ehl bee-'rreh-teh)*
chip board	**el aglomerado** *(ehl ah-gloh-meh-'rah-doh)*
clap board	**la tablilla** *(lah tah-'blee-yah)*

FLOORING

Most outdoor flooring involves the following materials:

Let's use (the)…	**Usemos…** *(oo-'seh-mohs)*
bricks	**los ladrillos** *(lohs lah-'dree-yohs)*
cobblestones	**los adoquines** *(los ah-doh-'kee-nehs)*
concrete pads	**las losas de concreto** *(lah 'loh-sahs deh kohn-'kreh-toh)*
pavers	**los pavers** *(lohs 'peh-ee-vehrs)*
pebbles	**los guijarros** *(los gee-'hah-rrohs)*

Bring (the)…	**Traiga…** *('trah-ee-gah)*
cast stone	**la piedra moldeada** *(lah pee-'eh-drah mohl-deh-'ah-dah)*
flagstone	**la losa de piedra** *(lah 'loh-sah deh pee-'eh-drah)*
floor tile	**la baldosa** *(lah bahl-'doh-sah)*
granite	**el granito** *(ehl gra-'nee-toh)*
limestone	**la piedra caliza** *(lah pee-'eh-drah kah-'lee-sah)*
marble	**el mármol** *(ehl 'mahr-mohl)*
masonry tile	**el ladrillo cerámico** *(ehl lah-'dree-yoh seh-'rah-mee-koh)*
natural stone	**la piedra natural** *(lah pee-'eh-drah nah-too-'rahl)*
quartzite	**la cuarcita** *(lah kwahr-'see-tah)*
sandstone	**la piedra arenisca** *(lah pee-'eh-drah ah-reh-'nees-kah)*
slate	**la pizarra** *(lah pee-'sah-rrah)*
stepping-stone	**la piedra de escalón** *(lah pee-'eh-drah deh ehs-kah-'lohn)*
travertine	**la piedra travertina** *(lah pee-'eh-drah trah-vehr-'tee-nah)*

Here are some other kinds of outdoor flooring:

We have (the)...	**Tenemos...** *(teh-'neh-mohs)*
artificial grass	**el césped artificial** *(ehl 'sehs-pehd ahr-tee-fee-see-'ahl)*
carpet	**la alfombra** *(lah ahl-'fohm-brah)*
matting	**las esteras** *(lahs ehs-'teh-rahs)*
rubber tiles	**las tejas de goma** *(lahs 'teh-hahs deh 'goh-mah)*
wood decking	**el entarimado de madera** *(ehl ehn-tah-ree-'mah-doh deh mah-'deh-rah)*

Now learn the names of a few tools and materials needed for work with outdoor materials:

adhesive	**el adhesivo** *(ehl ah-deh-'see-voh)*
epoxy	**el epoxi/la epoxia** *(ehl eh-'pohk-see/lah eh-'pohk-see-ah)*
grout	**la lechada** *(lah leh-'chah-dah)*
masonry saw	**la sierra de mampostería** *(lah see-'eh-rrah deh mahm-pohs-teh-'ree-ah)*
notched trowel	**la llana dentada** *(lah 'yah-nah dehn-'tah-dah)*
rubber grout float	**la llana de goma** *(lah 'yah-nah deh 'goh-mah)*
rubber mallet	**el mazo de goma** *(ehl 'mah-soh deh 'goh-mah)*
spacers	**los espaciadores** *(lohs ehs-pah-see-ah-'doh-rehs)*

And describe what you see:

They are...	**Son/Están...** *(sohn/ehs-'tahn)*
clear	**claros** *('klah-rohs)*
colored	**coloreados** *(koh-loh-reh-'ah-dohs)*
dark	**oscuros** *(ohs-'koo-rohs)*
fixed	**fijos** *('fee-hohs)*
loose	**flojos** *('floh-hohs)*
polished	**pulidos** *(poo-'lee-dohs)*
porous	**porosos** *(poh-'roh-sohs)*

There is/are......	**Hay...** *('ah-ee)*
condensation	**condensación** *(kohn-dehn-sah-see-'ohn)*
corrosion	**corrosión** *(koh-rroh-see-'ohn)*
deterioration	**deterioro** *(deh-teh-ree-'oh-roh)*
discoloration	**descoloramiento** *(dehs-koh-loh-rah-mee-'ehn-toh)*
imperfections	**imperfecciones** *(eem-pehr-fehk-see-'oh-nehs)*
bubbles	**burbujas** *(boor-'boo-hahs)*
bumps	**bultos** *('bool-tohs)*
cracks	**grietas** *(gree-'eh-tahs)*
dents	**melladuras** *(meh-yah-'doo-rahs)*
holes	**hoyos** *('oh-yohs)*
knots	**nudos** *('noo-dohs)*

These words will help you with another outdoor concern:

It's...	**Es/Está...** *(ehs/ehs-'tah)*
frozen	**congelado** *(kohn-heh-'lah-doh)*
moist	**húmedo** *('oo-meh-doh)*
soaked	**empapado** *(ehm-pah-'pah-doh)*
waterproof	**impermeable** *(eem-pehr-meh-'ah-bleh)*
watertight	**hermético** *(ehr-'meh-tee-koh)*
wet	**mojado** *(moh-'hah-doh)*

Just a Suggestion

Words referring to chemicals are similar in both languages:

polyethylene	**polietileno** *(poh-lee-eh-tee-'leh-noh)*
polystyrene	**poliestireno** *(poh-lee-ehs-tee-'reh-noh)*
polymer	**polímero** *(poh-'lee-meh-roh)*
polyurethane	**poliuretano** *(poh-lee-oo-reh-'tah-noh)*
polychrome	**policromo** *(poh-lee-'kroh-moh)*

Try Some

Name three words that relate to the installation of siding in Spanish.

Name three professionals who work on the exterior of a home in Spanish.

Name three different kinds of exterior flooring in Spanish.

Working Words: DESCRIBING THE JOB

Start off with these pairs of opposites:

| cramped | ↓ | **estrecho** *(ehs-'treh-choh)* |
| spacious | ↑ | **amplio** *('ahm-plee-oh)* |

| loose | ↓ | **flojo** *('floh-hoh)* |
| tight | ↑ | **apretado** *(ah-preh-'tah-doh)* |

| hollow | ↓ | **hueco** *('hweh-koh)* |
| solid | ↑ | **macizo** *(mah-'see-soh)* |

| coarse | ↓ | **áspero** *('ahs-peh-roh)* |
| smooth | ↑ | **liso** *('lee-soh)* |

| exposed | ↓ | **expuesto** *(ex-poo-'ehs-toh)* |
| hidden | ↑ | **oculto** *(oh-'kool-toh)* |

Here are more words you should already know:

The _____ piece.	**La pieza _____.** *(lah pee-'eh-sah)*
corner	**de la esquina** *(deh lah ehs-'kee-nah)*
edge	**del borde** *(dehl 'bohr-deh)*
inside	**interior** *(een-teh-ree-'ohr)*
lower	**inferior** *(een-feh-ree-'ohr)*
outside	**exterior** *(ex-teh-ree-'ohr)*
side	**lateral** *(lah-teh-'rahl)*
surface	**de la superficie** *(deh lah soo-pehr-'fee-see-eh)*
upper	**superior** *(soo-peh-ree-'ohr)*

This time, give detail to the building itself:

The style is...	**El estilo es...** *(ehl ehs-'tee-loh ehs)*
classic	**clásico** *('klah-see-koh)*
coastal	**costeño** *(kohs-'teh-nyoh)*
colonial	**colonial** *(koh-loh-nee-'ahl)*
contemporary	**contemporaneo** *(kohn-tehm-poh-'rah-neh-oh)*
country	**campestre** *(kahm-'pehs-treh)*
French	**francés** *(frahn-'sehs)*
Italian	**italiano** *(ee-tah-lee-'ah-noh)*
Mediterranean	**mediterráneo** *(meh-dee-teh-'rrah-neh-oh)*
rustic	**rústico** *('roos-tee-koh)*
Spanish	**español** *(ehs-pahn-'yohl)*
traditional	**tradicional** *(trah-dee-see-oh-'nahl)*
Tudor	**tudor** *(too-'dohr)*
Victorian	**victoriano** *(veek-toh-ree-'ah-noh)*

It's...	**Es...** *(ehs)*
circular	**circular** *(seer-koo-'lahr)*
diagonal	**diagonal** *(dee-ah-goh-'nahl)*
half-circular	**medio-circular** *('meh-dee-oh seer-koo-'lahr)*
hexagonal	**hexagonal** *(ex-ah-goh-'nahl)*
horizontal	**horizontal** *(oh-ree-sohn-'tahl)*
octagonal	**octagonal** *(ohk-tah-goh-'nahl)*
quarter-circular	**cuarto-circular** *('kwahr-toh seer-koo-'lahr)*
square	**cuadrado** *(kwah-'drah-doh)*
triangular	**triangular** *(tree-ahn-goo-'lahr)*
vertical	**vertical** *(vehr-tee-'kahl)*

It will be...	**Será...** *(seh-'rah)*

custom-built	**hecho a la orden** *('eh-choh ah lah 'ohr-dehn)*
custom-designed	**diseñado a la orden** *(dee-seh-'nyah-doh ah lah 'ohr-dehn)*
custom-painted	**pintado a la orden** *(peen-'tah-doh ah lah 'ohr-dehn)*

And don't forget the characteristics of the materials:

It's...	Es/Está... *(ehs/ehs-'tah)*
sealed	**sellado** *(seh-'yah-doh)*
treated	**tratado** *(trah-'tah-doh)*
rustproof	**a prueba de corrosión** *(ah proo-'eh-bah deh koh-rroh-see-'ohn)*
durable	**duradero** *(doo-rah-'deh-roh)*
waterproof	**impermeable** *(eem-pehr-meh-'ah-bleh)*
leakproof	**estanco** *(ehs-'tahn-koh)*
lead-free	**sin plomo** *(seen 'ploh-moh)*
corrosion-resistant	**resistente a la corrosión** *(reh-sees-'tehn-teh ah lah koh-rroh-see-'ohn)*
stainless	**inoxidable** *(ee-nohk-see-'dah-bleh)*
galvanized	**galvanizado** *(gahl-vah-nee-'sah-doh)*
fire-resistant	**resistente al fuego** *(reh-sees-'tehn-teh ahl 'fweh-goh)*

Try Some

What is the opposite of the following Spanish words?

apretado _____

superior _____

doble _____

Working Words: ON-SITE ACTIONS

Learn these verbs and see if you can make sentences by adding articles and nouns, as shown:

You have…	**Tiene que** … *(tee-'eh-neh keh)*	
to adjust	**ajustar** *(ah-hoos-'tahr)*	<u>**Tiene que ajustar los rodillos.**</u>
to align	**alinear** *(ah-lee-neh-'ahr)*	_____
to apply	**aplicar** *(ah-plee-'kahr)*	_____
to bond	**adherir** *(ah-deh-'reer)*	_____
to bore	**calar** *(kah-'lahr)*	_____
to caulk	**calafatear** *(kah-lah-fah-teh-'ahr)*	_____
to check	**revisar** *(reh-vee-'sahr)*	_____
to clean	**limpiar** *(leem-pee-'ahr)*	_____
to connect	**conectar** *(koh-nehk-'tahr)*	_____
to correct	**corregir** *(koh-rreh-'heer)*	_____
to cover	**cubrir** *(koo-'breer)*	_____
to cut	**cortar** *(kohr-'tahr)*	_____
to distribute	**distribuir** *(dees-tree-boo-'eer)*	_____
to divert	**desviar** *(dehs-vee-'ahr)*	_____
to erect	**erigir** *(eh-ree-'heer)*	_____
to glue	**encolar** *(ehn-koh-'lahr)*	_____
to heat	**calentar** *(kah-lehn-'tahr)*	_____
to hold	**sostener** *(sohs-teh-'nehr)*	_____
to inlay	**embutir** *(ehm-boo-'teer)*	_____
to install	**instalar** *(eens-tah-'lahr)*	_____
to join	**juntar** *(hoon-'tahr)*	_____

to level	**nivelar** *(nee-veh-'lahr)*	_____
to loosen	**soltar** *(sohl-'tahr)*	_____
to lubricate	**lubricar** *(loo-bree-'kahr)*	_____
to measure	**medir** *(meh-'deer)*	_____
to modify	**modificar** *(moh-dee-fee-'kahr)*	_____
to mount	**montar** *(mohn-'tahr)*	_____
to operate	**operar** *(oh-peh-'rahr)*	_____
to paint	**pintar** *(peen-'tahr)*	_____
to pour	**verter** *(vehr-'tehr)*	_____
to pre-drill	**pretaladrar** *(preh-tah-lah-'drahr)*	_____
to prep	**preparar** *(preh-pah-'rahr)*	_____
to press	**apretar** *(ah-preh-'tahr)*	_____
to probe	**sondear** *(sohn-deh-'ahr)*	_____
to protect	**proteger** *(proh-teh-'hehr)*	_____
to put	**poner** *(poh-'nehr)*	_____
to reach	**alcanzar** *(ahl-kahn-'sahr)*	_____
to reduce	**reducir** *(reh-doo-'seer)*	_____
to refill	**rellenar** *(reh-yeh-'nahr)*	_____
to remove	**quitar** *(kee-'tahr)*	_____
to repair	**reparar** *(reh-pah-'rahr)*	_____
to replace	**sustituir** *(soos-tee-too-'eer)*	_____
to sand	**lijar** *(lee-'hahr)*	_____
to screw in	**atornillar** *(ah-tohr-nee-'yahr)*	_____
to seal	**sellar** *(seh-'yahr)*	_____
to separate	**separar** *(seh-pah-'rahr)*	_____
to set	**colocar** *(koh-loh-'kahr)*	_____

to smooth	**alisar** *(ah-lee-'sahr)*	_____
to soak	**remojar** *(reh-moh-'hahr)*	_____
to straighten	**enderezar** *(ehn-deh-reh-'sahr)*	_____
to stretch	**estirar** *(ehs-tee-'rahr)*	_____
to support	**sostener** *(sohs-teh-'nehr)*	_____
to touch up	**retocar** *(reh-toh-'kahr)*	_____
to wash	**lavar** *(lah-'vahr)*	_____
to wet	**mojar** *(moh-'hahr)*	_____
to wipe	**pasar un trapo** *(pah-'sahr oon 'trah-poh)*	_____
to wrap	**forrar** *(foh-'rrahr)*	_____

Note how, with one exception, **-se** is added at the end of the verb to indicate that the action is happening to itself:

It's going …	**Va a …** *(vah ah)*
to break	**romperse** *(rohm-'pehr-seh)*
to breathe	**respirar** *(rehs-pee-'rahr)*
to cure	**curarse** *(koo-'rahr-seh)*
to dry	**secarse** *(seh-'kahr-seh)*
to expand	**expandirse** *(ex-pahn-'deer-seh)*
to harden	**endurecerse** *(ehn-doo-reh-'sehr-seh)*
to peel	**pelarse** *(peh-'lahr-seh)*
to split	**partirse** *(pahr-'teer-seh)*
to stick	**pegarse** *(peh-'gahr-seh)*

Just a Suggestion

Several words can be formed from basic verbs. Notice the pattern:

to ventilate	**ventilar** *(vehn-tee-'lahr)*
ventilating	**ventilando** *(vehn-tee-'lahn-doh)*
ventilation	**la ventilación** *(lah vehn-tee-lah-see-'ohn)*
ventilated	**ventilado** *(vehn-tee-'lah-doh)*

Try Some

Follow the pattern as you create new words:

to form	**formar** *(fohr-'mahr)*	<u>formación</u>	<u>formado</u>
to penetrate	**penetrar** *(peh-neh-'trahr)*	_____	_____
to renovate	**renovar** *(reh-noh-'vahr)*	_____	_____
to install	**instalar** *(eens-tah-'lahr)*	_____	_____
to repair	**reparar** *(reh-pah-'rahr)*	_____	_____
to apply	**aplicar** *(ah-plee-'kahr)*	_____	_____
to classify	**clasificar** *(klah-see-fee-'kahr)*	_____	_____
to insulate	**aislar** *(ah-ees-'lahr)*	_____	_____

Grammar Time

Unlike the preterit, which expresses a completed action, the imperfect tense in Spanish expresses a continued, customary, or repeated action in the past. In other words, it's used to express what was happening or what used to happen before.

For regular verbs ending in **-ar**, change the endings as in this example:

To Work	**Trabajar** *(trah-bah-'hahr)*
I was working	**trabajaba** *(trah-bah-'hah-bah)*
You (sing.) were working; he, she was working	**trabajaba** *(trah-bah-'hah-bah)*
We were working	**trabajábamos** *(trah-bah-'hah-bah-mohs)*
You (pl.); they were working	**trabajaban** *(trah-bah-'hah-ban)*

Check out these translations. Note these actions were never really started and completed:

I used to work in Mexico.	**Trabajaba en México.** *(trah-bah-'hah-bah ehn 'meh-hee-koh)*

Were they working?	¿Trabajaban? *(trah-bah-'hah-bahn)*
We weren't working there.	No trabajábamos allí. *(noh trah-bah-'hah-bah-mohs ah-'yee)*

For regular verbs ending in **-er** and **-ir**, the endings are formed differently:

To Eat	Comer *(koh-'mehr)*
I was eating	**comía** *(koh-'mee-ah)*
You (sing.) were eating; he, she was eating	**comía** *(koh-'mee-ah)*
We were eating	**comíamos** *(koh-'mee-ah-mohs)*
You (pl.); they were eating	**comían** *(koh-'mee-ahn)*

Just a Suggestion

Practice by listening carefully to Spanish speakers. Knowing the difference between the preterit and imperfect can be important:

We were finishing.	**Terminábamos.** *(tehr-mee-'nah-bah-mohs)*
We finished.	**Terminamos.** *(tehr-mee-'nah-mohs)*

Try Some

Fill in the English. You don't need any help:

To Write	Escribir *(ehs-kree-'beer)*
I used to write.	**escribía**
You (sing.); he, she used to write	_____
We used to write	_____
You (pl.); they used to write	_____

One-Liners

Learn these common one-liners and how they are used. On each line the first is masculine and the second is feminine:

that one	**ese** *('eh-seh)* or **esa** *('eh-sah)*
these ones	**estos** *('ehs-tohs)* or **estas** *('ehs-tahs)*
this one	**este** *('ehs-teh)* or **esta** *('ehs-tah)*
those ones	**esos** *('eh-sohs)* or **esas** *('eh-sahs)*

When you don't care to be specific, use **esto** and **eso**:

What's this?	**¿Qué es esto?** *(keh ehs 'ehs-toh)*
What's that?	**¿Qué es eso?** *(keh ehs 'eh-soh)*

When the object of discussion is far away, try these:

That hammer is mine.	**Aquel martillo es mío.** *(ah-'kehl mahr-'tee-yoh ehs 'mee-oh)*
Those hammers are mine.	**Aquellos martillos son míos.** *(ah-'keh-yohs mahr-'tee-yohs sohn 'mee-ohs)*
That saw is mine.	**Aquella sierra es mía.** *(ah-'keh-yah see-'eh-rrah ehs 'mee-ah)*
Those saws are mine.	**Aquellas sierras son mías.** *(ah-'keh-yahs see-'eh-rrahs sohn 'mee-ahs)*

Culture Issues

No difference between them and us: Once a co-worker or employee establishes a friendly relationship, it's common for native Hispanics to use nicknames when referring to others. Most of the time, it is meant to show intimacy, and not disrespect.

Interior Work
El trabajo puertas adentro
(ehl trah-'bah-hoh 'pwehr-tahs ah-'dehn-troh)

 Working Words: THE BUILDING'S INTERIOR

First explain what you're going to be doing with the interior:

I'm working on (the)…   **Trabajo en…** *(trah-'bah-hoh ehn)*

carpentry	**la carpintería** *(lah kahr-peen-teh-'ree-ah)*
drywall	**el enyesado** *(ehl ehn-yeh-'sah-doh)*
finishing	**el acabado** *(ehl ah-kah-'bah-doh)*
flooring	**el solado** *(ehl soh-'lah-doh)*
insulation	**el aislamiento** *(ehl ah-ees-lah-mee-'ehn-toh)*
painting	**la pintura** *(lah peen-'too-rah)*
plumbing	**la fontanería** *(lah fohn-tah-neh-'ree-ah)*
wiring	**la instalación eléctrica** *(lah eens-tah-lah-see-'ohn eh-'lehk-tree-kah)*
lighting	**la iluminación** *(lah ee-loo-mee-nah-see-'ohn)*

It needs (the)…   **Necesita…** *(neh-seh-'see-tah)*

windows   **las ventanas** *(lahs vehn-'tah-nahs)*
doors   **las puertas** *(lahs 'pwehr-tahs)*
cabinets   **los gabinetes** *(lohs gah-bee-'neh-tehs)*

fixture   **el artefacto** *(ehl ahr-teh-'fahk-toh)*
appliance   **el electrodoméstico** *(ehl eh-lehk-troh-doh-'mehs-tee-koh)*
light   **la luz** *(lah loos)*

assembly	**el montaje** *(ehl mohn-'tah-heh)*
repair	**la reparación** *(lah reh-pah-rah-see-'ohn)*
installation	**la instalación** *(lah eens-tah-lah-see-'ohn)*

Now, name the interior features of a typical American home:

That is (the)…	**Eso es…** *('eh-soh ehs)*
attic	**el ático** *(ehl 'ah-tee-koh)*
balcony	**el balcón** *(ehl bahl-'kohn)*
basement	**el sótano** *(ehl 'soh-tah-noh)*
bathroom	**el baño** *(ehl 'bah-nyoh)*
bedroom	**el dormitorio** *(ehl dohr-mee-'toh-ree-oh)*
breakfast room	**el antecomedor** *(ehl ahn-teh-koh-meh-'dohr)*
den	**la sala de familia** *(lah 'sah-lah deh fah-'mee-lee-ah)*
dining room	**el comedor** *(ehl koh-meh-'dohr)*
dressing room	**el vestuario** *(ehl vehs-too-'ah-ree-oh)*
foyer	**el vestíbulo** *(ehl vehs-'tee-boo-loh)*
garage	**el garaje** *(ehl gah-'rah-heh)*
greenhouse	**el invernadero** *(ehl een-vehr-nah-'deh-roh)*
guest room	**el cuarto de visitas** *(ehl 'kwahr-toh deh vee-'see-tahs)*
hallway	**el pasillo** *(ehl pah-'see-yoh)*
kitchen	**la cocina** *(lah koh-'see-nah)*
laundry room	**la lavandería** *(lah lah-vahn-deh-'ree-ah)*
library	**la biblioteca** *(lah bee-blee-oh-'teh-kah)*
living room	**la sala** *(lah 'sah-lah)*
loft	**el desván** *(ehl dehs-'vahn)*
nursery	**el cuarto de los niños** *(ehl 'kwahr-toh deh lohs 'nee-'nyohs)*
office	**la oficina** *(lah oh-fee-'see-nah)*
playroom	**la sala de juegos** *(lah 'sah-lah deh 'hweh-gohs)*
storeroom	**el depósito** *(ehl deh-'poh-see-toh)*
studio	**el estudio** *(ehl ehs-'too-dee-oh)*
sunroom	**el solario** *(ehl soh-'lah-ree-oh)*
utility room	**la despensa** *(lah dehs-'pehn-sah)*

Let's go into detail.

Look at (the)…	**Mire…** *('mee-reh)*
ceiling	**el techo** *(ehl 'teh-choh)*
wall	**la pared** *(lah pah-'rehd)*
floor	**el piso** *(ehl 'pee-soh)*

closet	**el ropero** *(ehl roh-'peh-roh)*
counter	**el mostrador** *(ehl mohs-trah-'dohr)*
drawer	**el cajón** *(ehl kah-'hohn)*
steps	**los escalones** *(lohs ehs-kah-'loh-nehs)*
stairs	**las escaleras** *(lahs ehs-kah-'leh-rahs)*
railings	**las barandas** *(lahs bah-'rahn-dahs)*
bookshelf	**el librero** *(ehl lee-'breh-roh)*
fireplace	**el fogón** *(ehl foh-'gohn)*
bar	**el bar** *(ehl bahr)*
doorway	**el portal** *(ehl pohr-'tahl)*
column	**la columna** *(lah koh-'loom-nah)*
partition	**el tabique** *(ehl tah-'bee-keh)*

You'll find these in the bathroom:

shower	**la ducha** *(lah 'doo-chah)*
toilet	**el excusado** *(ehl ex-koo-'sah-doh)*
bathtub	**la tina de baño** *(lah 'tee-nah deh 'bah-nyoh)*
bathroom sink	**el lavabo** *(ehl lah-'vah-boh)*
mirror	**el espejo** *(ehl ehs-'peh-hoh)*
medicine chest	**el botiquín** *(ehl boh-tee-'keen)*
faucet	**el grifo** *(ehl 'gree-foh)*

Industrial buildings have their own names for interior features:

Go to (the)...	**Vaya a...** *('vah-yah ah)*
ground floor	**la planta baja** *(lah 'plahn-tah 'bah-hah)*
first floor	**el primer piso** *(ehl pree-'mehr 'pee-soh)*
second floor	**el segundo piso** *(ehl seh-'goon-doh 'pee-soh)*
entrance	**la entrada** *(lah ehn-'trah-dah)*
exit	**la salida** *(lah sah-'lee-dah)*
lobby	**el vestíbulo** *(ehl vehs-'tee-boo-loh)*
restroom	**el tocador/el baño/el retrete** *(ehl toh-kah-'dohr/ehl 'bahn-yoh/ehl reh-'treh-teh)*

elevator	**el ascensor** *(ehl ahs-sehn-'sohr)*
carport	**el cobertizo para carros** *(ehl koh-behr-'tee-soh 'pah-rah 'kah-rrohs)*

Be specific when you refer to an indoor project:

It needs (the)...	**Necesita...** *(neh-seh-'see-tah)*

baseboard	**el zócalo** *(ehl 'soh-kah-loh)*
counter top	**la cubierta del mostrador** *(lah koo-bee-'ehr-tah dehl mohs-trah-'dohr)*
mantle	**la repisa de la chimenea** *(lah reh-'pee-sah deh lah chee-meh-'neh-ah)*
molding	**la moldura** *(lah mohl-'doo-rah)*
paneling	**el panelado** *(ehl pah-neh-'lah-doh)*
shelf	**el estante** *(ehl ehs-'tahn-teh)*
soffit	**la cubierta del alero** *(lah koo-bee-'ehr-tah dehl ah-'leh-roh)*
trim	**el adorno** *(ehl ah-'dohr-noh)*
veneer	**la chapa** *(lah 'chah-pah)*
wall tile	**el azulejo** *(ehl ah-soo-'leh-hoh)*

☞ Working Words: TOOLS AND MATERIALS

Most of these tools are needed for work on the interior of a building:

Bring (the)...	**Traiga...** *('trah-ee-gah)*

air compressor	**el compresor de aire** *(ehl kohm-preh-'sohr deh 'ah-ee-reh)*
caulking gun	**la pistola de masilla** *(lah pees-'toh-lah deh mah-'see-yah)*
chisel	**el cincel** *(ehl seen-'sehl)*
circular saw	**la sierra circular** *(lah see-'eh-rrah seer-koo-'lahr)*
cordless drill	**el taladro portátil** *(ehl tah-'lah-droh pohr-'tah-teel)*
crowbar	**la pata de cabra** *(lah 'pah-tah deh 'kah-brah)*
dolly	**la plataforma con ruedas** *(lah plah-tah-'fohr-mah kohn 'rweh-dahs)*
duct tape	**la cinta ploma** *(lah 'seen-tah 'ploh-mah)*
extension cord	**la extension eléctrica** *(lah ex-tehn-see-'ohn eh-'lehk-tree-kah)*
file	**la lima** *(lah 'lee-mah)*
framing square	**la escuadra** *(lah ehs-'kwah-drah)*

glue	**la cola** *(lah 'koh-lah)*
hammer	**el martillo** *(ehl mahr-'tee-yoh)*
level	**el nivel** *(ehl nee-'vehl)*
masking tape	**la cinta adhesiva** *(lah 'seen-tah ah-deh-'see-vah)*
miter saw	**la sierra de cortar en ángulos** *(lah see-'eh-rrah deh kohr-'tahr ehn 'ahn-goo-lohs)*
nail gun	**la pistola de clavos** *(lah pees-'toh-lah deh 'klah-vohs)*
pliers	**los alicates** *(lohs ah-lee-'kah-tehs)*
plumb bob	**la plomada** *(lah ploh-'mah-dah)*
ratchet wrench	**la llave de trinquete** *(lah 'yah-veh deh treen-'keh-teh)*
sandpaper	**el papel de lija** *(ehl pah-'pehl deh 'lee-hah)*
scraper	**el raspador** *(ehl rahs-pah-'dohr)*
screwdriver	**el destornillador** *(ehl dehs-tohr-nee-yah-'dohr)*
shears	**las tijeras** *(lahs tee-'heh-rahs)*
stepladder	**la escalera baja** *(lah ehs-kah-'leh-rah 'bah-hah)*
stud finder	**el buscamontantes** *(ehl boos-kah-mohn-'tahn-tehs)*
tape measure	**la cinta métrica** *(lah 'seen-tah 'meh-tree-kah)*
utility knife	**la cuchilla** *(lah koo-'chee-yah)*
wet-dry vac	**la aspiradora mojada/seca** *(lah ahs-pee-rah-'doh-rah moh-'hah-dah/'seh-kah)*
wrench	**la llave inglesa** *(lah 'yah-veh een-'gleh-sah)*
I'm missing (the)…	**Me falta…** *(meh 'fahl-tah)*
nail	**el clavo** *(ehl 'klah-voh)*
staple	**la grapa** *(lah 'grah-pah)*
screw	**el tornillo** *(ehl tohr-'nee-yoh)*
fastener	**el sujetador** *(ehl soo-heh-tah-'dohr)*
nut	**la tuerca** *(lah 'twehr-kah)*
washer	**la arandela** *(lah ah-rahn-'deh-lah)*
bolt	**el perno** *(ehl 'pehr-noh)*
pin	**la clavija** *(lah klah-'vee-hah)*
bracket	**el soporte** *(ehl soh-'pohr-teh)*
clamp	**la abrazadera** *(lah ah-brah-sah-'deh-rah)*
plate	**la placa** *(lah 'plah-kah)*
joint	**el codo** *(ehl 'koh-doh)*
insert	**el anclaje** *(ehl ahn-'klah-heh)*
connector	**el conector/la conexión** *(ehl koh-nehk-'tohr/lah koh-nehk-see-'ohn)*

adapter	**el adaptador** *(ehl ah-dahp-tah-'dohr)*
flange	**el ala** *(ehl 'ah-lah)*
bolt	**el perno** *(ehl 'pehr-noh)*
bit	**la broca** *(lah 'broh-kah)*

| Use the... | **Use...** *('oo-seh)* |

glass	**el vidrio** *(ehl 'vee-dree-oh)*
lumber	**la madera** *(lah mah-'deh-rah)*
paint	**la pintura** *(lah peen-'too-rah)*
pipe	**la tubería** *(lah too-beh-'ree-ah)*
plaster	**el yeso** *(ehl 'yeh-soh)*
wire	**el alambre** *(ehl ah-'lahm-breh)*
cement	**el cemento** *(ehl seh-'mehn-toh)*

Try Some

Translate:	
I need the scraper.	**Necesito el raspador.**
I need the plaster.	_____
I need the stud-finder.	_____
I need the nut.	_____

Working Words: DRYWALL

Before hanging sheetrock, look at some drywalling tools and supplies:

C-clamp	**la prensa de tornillo** *(lah 'prehn-sah deh tohr-'nee-yoh)*
corner trowel	**la llana para esquinas** *(lah 'yah-nah 'pah-rah ehs-'kee-nahs)*
drywall hammer	**el martillo para tablarroca** *(ehl mahr-'tee-yoh 'pah-rah tah-blah-'roh-kah)*
drywall tape	**la cinta adhesiva** *(lah 'seen-tah ah-deh-'see-vah)*

electric screwdriver	**el destornillador eléctrico** *(ehl dehs-tohr-nee-yah-'dohr eh-'lehk-tree-koh)*
level	**el nivel** *(ehl nee-'vehl)*
mud mixer	**la mezcladora de masilla** *(lah mehs-klah-'doh-rah deh mah-'see-yah)*
pencil	**el lápiz** *(ehl 'lah-pees)*
plane	**el cepillo de mano** *(ehl seh-'pee-yoh deh 'mah-noh)*
power drill	**el taladro eléctrico** *(ehl tah-'lah-droh eh-'lehk-tree-koh)*
pump	**la bomba** *(lah 'bohm-bah)*
putty knife	**la espátula** *(lah ehs-'pah-too-lah)*
rasp	**la raspadora** *(lah rahs-pah-'doh-rah)*
router	**el acanalador** *(ehl ah-kah-nah-lah-'dohr)*
sponge	**la esponja** *(lah ehs-'pohn-hah)*
stapler	**la grapadora** *(lah grah-pah-'doh-rah)*
straightedge	**la regla metálica** *(lah 'reh-glah meh-'tah-lee-kah)*
tape measure	**la cinta métrica** *(lah 'seen-tah 'meh-tree-kah)*
taping knife	**la cuchilla para cinta adhesiva** *(lah koo-'chee-yah 'pah-rah 'seen-tah ah-deh-'see-vah)*
tin snips	**las tijeras para hojalata** *(lahs tee-'heh-rahs 'pah-rah oh-hah-'lah-tah)*
trowel hawk	**la llana enyesadora** *(lah 'yah-nah ehn-yeh-sah-'doh-rah)*
wallboard square	**la escuadra para paneles** *(lah ehs-'kwah-drah 'pah-rah pah-'neh-lehs)*

Learn the translation for these important items:

Do you have (the)…?	**¿Tiene usted…?** *(tee-'eh-neh oos-'tehd)*

drywall compound	**la masilla premezclada** *(lah mah-'see-yah preh-mehs-'klah-dah)*
drywall hammer	**el martillo para enyesado** *(ehl mahr-'tee-yoh 'pah-rah ehn-yeh-'sah-doh)*
drywall nails	**los clavos para enyesado** *(lohs 'klah-vohs 'pah-rah ehn-yeh-'sah-doh)*
drywall screws	**los tornillos para enyesado** *(lohs tohr-'nee-yohs 'pah-rah ehn-yeh-'sah-doh)*
drywall spackle	**el relleno/el mastique para resanar** *(ehl reh-'yeh-noh/ehl mahs-'tee-keh 'pah-rah reh-sah-'nahr)*

To learn the names for some tools, it's best to group them into smaller sets:

I brought (the)...　　**Traje...** *('trah-heh)*

plumb bob	**la plomada** *(lah ploh-'mah-dah)*
chalk	**la tiza** *(lah 'tee-sah)*
chalk line	**el cordón de tiza** *(ehl kohr-'dohn deh 'tee-sah)*
keyhole saw	**el serrucho de calar** *(ehl seh-'rroo-choh deh kah-'lahr)*
wallboard saw	**el serrucho corto** *(ehl seh-'rroo-choh 'kohr-toh)*
saber saw	**la sierra de vaivén** *(lah see-'eh-rrah deh vah-ee-'vehn)*
hand sander	**la lijadora de mano** *(lah lee-hah-'doh-rah deh 'mah-noh)*
sanding pole	**la lijadora de mango** *(lah lee-hah-'doh-rah deh 'mahn-goh)*
power sander	**la lijadora eléctrica** *(lah lee-hah-'doh-rah eh-'lehk-tree-kah)*

When drywall is involved, these other materials will be in demand:

Unload (the)...　　**Descargue...** *(dehs-'kahr-geh)*

backer board	**el respaldo** *(ehl rehs-'pahl-doh)*
control joint	**la junta de control** *(lah 'hoon-tah deh kohn-'trohl)*
corner bead	**el bordón de esquina** *(ehl bor-'dohn deh ehs-'kee-nah)*
flex strip	**la tira flexible** *(lah 'tee-rah flehk-'see-bleh)*
J bead	**el bordón en J** *(ehl bohr-'dohn ehn 'hoh-tah)*
L bead	**el bordón en L** *(ehl bohr-'dohn ehn 'eh-leh)*
mud	**el barro** *(ehl 'bah-rroh)*
panel	**el panel** *(ehl pah-'nehl)*
reveal	**la mocheta** *(lah moh-'cheh-tah)*
trim tab	**la aleta de contramarco** *(lah ah-'leh-tah deh kohn-trah-'mahr-koh)*
wall angle	**el ángulo de pared** *(ehl 'ahn-goo-loh deh pah-'rehd)*

Check (the)…	**Revise…** *(reh-'vee-seh)*
crack	**la grieta** *(lah gree-'eh-tah)*
hole	**el hoyo** *(ehl 'oh-yoh)*
joint	**la unión** *(lah oo-nee-'ohn)*
opening	**la abertura** *(lah ah-behr-'too-rah)*
seam	**la costura** *(lah kohs-'too-rah)*

It needs (the)…	**Necesita…** *(neh-seh-'see-tah)*
finish	**el acabado** *(ehl ah-kah-'bah-doh)*
coat	**la capa** *(lah 'kah-pah)*
texture	**la textura** *(lah tehks-'too-rah)*

Just a Suggestion

Double-check your measurements:

90° angle	**el ángulo de noventa grados** *(ehl 'ahn-goo-loh deh noh-'vehn-tah 'grah-dohs)*
one-inch bullnose	**la esquina boleada de una pulgada** *(lah ehs-'kee-nah boh-leh-'ah-dah deh 'oo-nah pool-'gah-dah)*
#10 screws	**los tornillos de número diez** *(los tohr-'nee-yohs deh 'noo-meh-roh dee-'ehs)*
¾-inch diameter	**un diámetro de tres cuartos de pulgada** *(oon dee-'ah-meh-troh deh trehs 'kwahr-tohs deh pool-'gah-dah)*
forty inches high	**de cuarenta pulgadas de alto** *(deh kwah-'rehn-tah pool-'gah-dahs deh 'ahl-toh)*

Try Some

Name three tools needed for drywall installation in Spanish.

Name three materials needed for drywall installation in Spanish.

👉 Working Words: CABINET INSTALLATION

Bring (the) ____ cabinets.	**Traiga los gabinetes** ____. *('trah-ee-gah lohs gah-bee-'neh-tehs)*
custom	**fabricados a la orden** *(fah-bree-'kah-dohs ah lah 'ohr-dehn)*
stock	**de almacenamiento** *(deh ahl-mah-seh-nah-mee-'ehn-toh)*
face-frame	**con marco visible** *(kohn 'mahr-koh vee-'see-bleh)*
frameless	**sin marco** *(seen 'mahr-koh)*
base	**de base** *(deh 'bah-seh)*
wall	**de pared** *(deh pah-'rehd)*
They're in (the)…	**Están en…** *(ehs-'tahn ehn)*

bathroom	**el baño** *(ehl 'bah-nyoh)*
bedroom	**el dormitorio** *(ehl dohr-mee-'toh-ree-oh)*
garage	**el garaje** *(ehl gah-'rah-heh)*
hallway	**el pasillo** *(ehl pah-'see-yoh)*
home office	**la oficina en casa** *(lah oh-fee-'see-nah ehn 'kah-sah)*
kitchen	**la cocina** *(lah koh-'see-nah)*
storage room	**el depósito** *(ehl deh-'poh-see-toh)*

The cabinets are part of the…	**Los gabinetes son parte de…** *(lohs gah-bee-'neh-tehs sohn 'pahr-teh deh)*

closet	**el ropero** *(ehl roh-'peh-roh)*
entertainment center	**el centro de entretenimiento** *(ehl 'sehn-troh deh ehn-treh-teh-nee-mee-'ehn-toh)*
wall unit	**la unidad de pared** *(lah oo-nee-'dahd deh pah-'rehd)*
window seat	**el asiento a pie de ventana** *(ehl ah-see-'ehn-toh ah pee-'eh deh vehn-'tah-nah)*
staircase	**las escaleras** *(lahs ehs-kah-'leh-rahs)*
desk	**el escritorio** *(ehl ehs-kree-'toh-ree-oh)*
bookshelf	**el librero** *(ehl lee-'breh-roh)*
filing cabinet	**el archivero** *(ehl ahr-chee-'veh-roh)*

It's time to name parts of the cabinet itself:

Here's (the)…	**Aquí tiene…** *(ah-'kee tee-'eh-neh)*
back plate	**la placa** *(lah 'plah-kah)*
bolt	**el perno** *(ehl 'pehr-noh)*
cabinet screw	**el tornillo de fijación** *(ehl tohr-'nee-yoh deh fee-hah-see-'ohn)*
catch	**la cerradura** *(lah seh-rrah-'doo-rah)*
door	**la puerta** *(lah 'pwehr-tah)*
drawer	**el cajón** *(ehl kah-'hohn)*
hinge	**la bisagra** *(lah bee-'sah-grah)*
knob	**el botón** *(ehl boh-'tohn)*
mounting screw	**el tornillo de montaje** *(ehl tohr-'nee-yoh deh mohn-'tah-heh)*
nut	**la tuerca** *(lah 'twehr-kah)*
divider	**el divisor** *(ehl dee-vee-'sohr)*
pull	**el tirador** *(ehl tee-rah-'dohr)*
shelf	**el estante** *(ehl ehs-'tahn-teh)*
slide	**la corredera** *(lah koh-rreh-'deh-rah)*
trim	**el adorno** *(ehl ah-'dohr-noh)*
washer	**la arandela** *(lah ah-rahn-'deh-lah)*
tray	**la bandeja** *(lah bahn-'deh-hah)*
clip	**la abrazadera** *(lah ah-brah-sah-'deh-rah)*
pegboard	**el tablero de clavijas** *(ehl tah-'bleh-roh deh klah-'vee-hahs)*
shelf pin	**la clavija para estantes** *(lah klah-'vee-hah 'pah-rah ehs-'tahn-tehs)*
bracket	**la ménsula** *(lah 'mehn-soo-lah)*

Now provide details about the materials you are working with:

It's made of…	**Es hecho de…** *(ehs 'eh-choh deh)*
brass	**latón** *(lah-'tohn)*
bronze	**bronce** *('brohn-seh)*
chrome	**cromo** *('kroh-moh)*
copper	**cobre** *('koh-breh)*
iron	**hierro** *(ee-'eh-rroh)*
nickel	**níquel** *('nee-kehl)*
pewter	**peltre** *('pehl-treh)*
veneer	**chapa** *('chah-pah)*
laminate	**lámina** *('lah-mee-nah)*
vinyl	**vinilo** *(vee-'nee-loh)*

The wood is...	**La madera es...** *(lah mah-'deh-rah ehs)*
cherry	**de cerezo** *(deh seh-'reh-soh)*
birch	**de abedul** *(deh ah-beh-'dool)*
spruce	**de abeto** *(deh ah-'beh-toh)*
cypress	**de ciprés** *(deh see-'prehs)*
cedar	**de cedro** *(deh 'seh-droh)*
oak	**de roble** *(deh 'roh-bleh)*
pine	**de pino** *(deh 'pee-noh)*
walnut	**de nogal** *(deh 'noh-gahl)*
maple	**de arce** *(deh 'ahr-seh)*
mahogany	**de caoba** *(deh kah-'oh-bah)*
plywood	**contrachapada** *(kohn-trah-chah-'pah-dah)*
elder	**de aliso** *(deh ah-'lee-soh)*

The style is...	**Es de estilo...** *(ehs deh ehs-'tee-loh)*
cathedral	**catedral** *(kah-teh-'drahl)*
contemporary	**contemporáneo** *(kohn-tehm-poh-'rah-neo-oh)*
mission	**misión** *(mee-see-'ohn)*
modern	**moderno** *(moh-'dehr-noh)*
Roman	**romano** *(roh-'mah-noh)*
traditional	**tradicional** *(trah-dee-see-oh-'nahl)*

Be sure to mention the cabinet hinge (**bisagra**—*bee-'sah-grah*):

It's ... type.	**Es de tipo...** *(ehs deh 'tee-poh)*
butterfly	**mariposa** *(mah-ree-'poh-sah)*
European	**europea** *(eh-oo-roh-'peh-ah)*
H-type	**de estilo H** *(deh ehs-'tee-loh 'ah-cheh)*
inset	**insertada** *(een-sehr-'tah-dah)*
offset	**con saliente** *(kohn sah-lee-'ehn-teh)*
overlay	**superpuesta** *(soo-pehr-'pwehs-tah)*
pin	**de perno** *(deh 'pehr-noh)*
T-type	**de tipo T** *(deh 'tee-poh teh)*
wraparound	**envolvente** *(ehn-vohl-'vehn-teh)*

It's ... finish.	**Es de acabado...** *(ehs deh ah-kah-'bah-doh)*
antique	**antiguo** *(ahn-'tee-gwoh)*
brushed	**mate** *('mah-teh)*

ceramic	**cerámico** *(seh-'rah-mee-koh)*
enameled	**esmaltado** *(ehs-mahl-'tah-doh)*
metallic	**metálico** *(meh-'tah-lee-koh)*
polished	**pulido** *(poo-'lee-doh)*
satin	**satinado** *(sah-tee-'nah-doh)*
shiny	**brillante** *(bree-'yahn-teh)*
silverplated	**plateado** *(plah-teh-'ah-doh)*

Try Some

Delete the word in each set that doesn't belong with the other two:

el pino, el adorno, el cedro
el hoyo, la abertura, el barro
cerámica, moderno, metálico
el antiguo, el escritorio, el librero
el látón, el cobre, el cajón

Working Words: INTERIOR DOOR INSTALLATION

The following tools and materials are used for hanging the interior door:

Use (the)…	**Use…** *('oo-seh)*
clamp	**la abrazadera** *(lah ah-brah-sah-'deh-rah)*
door hanger	**la colgadora de puertas** *(lah kohl-gah-'doh-rah deh 'pwehr-tahs)*
finishing nails	**los clavos sin cabeza** *(los 'klah-vohs seen kah-'beh-sah)*
lock mortiser	**la embutidora de cerraduras** *(lah ehm-boo-tee-'doh-rah deh seh-rrah-'doo-rahs)*
miter box	**la caja de ángulos** *(lah 'kah-hah deh 'ahn-goo-lohs)*
miter saw	**la sierra para cortar ángulos** *(lah see-'eh-rrah 'pah-rah kohr-'tahr 'ahn-goo-lohs)*
plane	**el cepillo** *(ehl seh-'pee-yoh)*
power sander	**la lijadora** *(lah lee-hah-'doh-rah)*
screws	**los tornillos** *(lohs tohr-'nee-yohs)*
shims	**las calzas** *(lahs 'kahl-sahs)*
vice	**la prensa** *(lah 'prehn-sah)*

Grab (the)...	**Agarre...** *(ah-'gah-rreh)*
casing	**el marco** *(ehl 'mahr-koh)*
deadbolt	**el pestillo** *(ehl pehs-'tee-yoh)*
door knob	**la perilla** *(lah peh-'ree-yah)*
hardware	**el herraje** *(ehl eh-'rrah-heh)*
hinge	**la bisagra** *(lah bee-'sah-grah)*
jamb	**la jamba** *(lah 'hahm-bah)*
molding	**la moldura** *(lah mohl-'doo-rah)*
pin	**el perno** *(ehl 'pehr-noh)*
pivot	**el pivote** *(ehl pee-'voh-teh)*
screen	**el mosquitero** *(ehl mohs-kee-'teh-roh)*
seal	**el sello** *(ehl 'seh-yoh)*
stop	**el tope** *(ehl 'toh-peh)*
threshold	**el umbral** *(ehl oom-'brahl)*
toe kick	**la tabla contragolpes** *(lah 'tah-blah kohn-trah-'gohl-pehs)*
weather stripping	**el burlete** *(ehl boor-'leh-teh)*

It needs (the)...	**Necesita...** *(neh-seh-'see-tah)*
connecting screw	**el tornillo conector** *(ehl tohr-'nee-yoh koh-nehk-'tohr)*
cylinder	**el cilindro** *(ehl see-'leen-droh)*
latch	**el cerrojo** *(ehl seh-'rroh-hoh)*
lock casing	**el cuerpo del pestillo** *(ehl 'kwehr-poh dehl pehs-'tee-yoh)*
lock nut	**la tuerca de seguridad** *(lah 'twehr-kah deh seh-goo-ree-'dahd)*
shaft	**el eje** *(ehl 'eh-heh)*
strike plate	**el cajetín** *(ehl kah-heh-'teen)*

Indicate what the job calls for:

Install (the)...	**Instale...** *(eens-'tah-leh)*
double doors	**la doble puerta** *(lah 'doh-bleh 'pwehr-tah)*
Dutch door	**la puerta cortada** *(lah 'pwehr-tah kohr-'tah-dah)*
folding door	**la puerta plegadiza** *(lah 'pwehr-tah pleh-gah-'dee-sah)*
French door	**la puerta de dos hojas** *(lah 'pwehr-tah deh dohs 'oh-hahs)*
multifold door	**la puerta de acordeón** *(lah 'pwehr-tah deh ah-kohr-deh-'ohn)*

pre-hung door	**la puerta prefabricada** *(lah 'pwehr-tah preh-fah-bree-'kah-dah)*
sliding door	**la puerta corrediza** *(lah 'pwehr-tah koh-rreh-'dee-sah)*
swinging door	**la puerta de vaivén** *(lah 'pwehr-tah deh vah-ee-'vehn)*
It's a/an…	**Es una…** *(ehs 'oo-nah)*
inswing door	**puerta que abre hacia adentro** *('pwehr-tah keh 'ah-breh ah-see-'ah ah-'dehn-troh)*
outswing door	**puerta que abre hacia afuera** *('pwehr-tah keh 'ah-breh 'ah-see-ah ah-'fweh-rah)*
left-hand door	**puerta de mano izquierda** *('pwehr-tah deh 'mah-noh ees-kee-'ehr-dah)*
right-hand door	**puerta de mano derecha** *('pwehr-tah deh 'mah-noh deh-'reh-chah)*
It has (the)…	**Tiene…** *(tee-'eh-neh)*
louvers	**las persianas** *(lahs pehr-see-'ah-nahs)*
panels	**los paneles** *(lohs pah-'neh-lehs)*
springs	**los resortes** *(lohs reh-'sohr-tehs)*
tracks	**los carriles** *(lohs kah-'rree-lehs)*
trim	**los adornos** *(lohs ah-'dohr-nohs)*
wheels	**las ruedecillas** *(lahs rweh-deh-'see-yahs)*
It's made of…	**Es de…** *(ehs deh)*

aluminum	**aluminio** *(ah-loo-'mee-nee-oh)*
fiberglass	**fibra de vidrio** *('fee-brah deh 'vee-dree-oh)*
glass	**vidrio** *('vee-dree-oh)*
hollow core	**hueca** *('hweh-kah)*
solid core	**maciza** *(mah-'see-sah)*
solid wood	**madera sólida** *(mah-'deh-rah 'soh-lee-dah)*
stainless steel	**acero inoxidable** *(ah-'seh-roh ee-nohk-see-'dah-bleh)*
vinyl	**vinilo** *(vee-'nee-loh)*
wood clad	**forro de madera** *('foh-rroh deh mah-'deh-rah)*

Now get to work on the installation:

Check (the)…	**Revise…** *(reh-'vee-seh)*

doorway	**el vano** *(ehl 'vah-noh)*
floor	**el piso** *(ehl 'pee-soh)*
frame	**el marco** *(ehl 'mahr-koh)*
sub-floor	**el subpiso** *(ehl soob-'pee-soh)*
wall	**la pared** *(lah pah-'rehd)*

Look at (the)…	**Mire…** *('mee-reh)*

balance	**el equilibrio** *(ehl eh-kee-'lee-bree-oh)*
chalk line	**la línea de marcar** *(lah 'lee-neh-ah deh mahr-'kahr)*
clearance	**la distancia de seguridad** *(lah dees-'tahn-see-ah deh seh-'goo-ree-dahd)*
corner	**la esquina** *(lah ehs-'kee-nah)*
dimensions	**las dimensiones** *(lahs dee-mehn-see-'oh-nehs)*
size	**el tamaño** *(ehl tah-'mah-nyoh)*
slope	**el declive** *(ehl deh-'klee-veh)*
style	**el estilo** *(ehl ehs-'tee-loh)*

Make sure it's…	**Asegúrese que esté…** *(ah-seh-'goo-reh-seh keh ehs-'teh)*

level	**nivelado** *(nee-veh-'lah-doh)*
plumb	**justo en medio** *('hoos-toh ehn 'meh-dee-oh)*
square	**escuadrado** *(ehs-kwah-'drah-doh)*

Try Some

Choose the correct ending to each sentence below:

La puerta de vinilo… …tiene carriles.
La puerta cerrediza… …necesita muchas bisagras.
La puerta de acordeón… …no es de madera sólida.

Working Words: APPLIANCES AND FIXTURES

Begin by reviewing the indoor work that still needs to be completed. Stick with those words you already know:

It needs (the)...   **Necesita...** *(neh-seh-'see-tah)*

cable	**el cable** *(ehl 'kah-bleh)*
pipe	**el tubo** *(ehl 'too-boh)*
wire	**el alambre** *(ehl ah-'lahm-breh)*

Finish with the...   **Termine con...** *(tehr-'mee-neh kohn)*

air conditioning	**el aire acondicionado** *(ehl 'ah-ee-reh ah-kohn-dee-see-oh-'nah-doh)*
electricity	**la electricidad** *(lah eh-lehk-tree-see-'dahd)*
heating	**la calefacción** *(lah kah-leh-fahk-see-'ohn)*
insulation	**el aislamiento** *(ehl ah-ees-lah-mee-'ehn-toh)*
lighting	**la iluminación** *(lah ee-loo-mee-nah-see-'ohn)*
plumbing	**la fontanería** *(lah fohn-tah-neh-'ree-ah)*

Check (the)...   **Revise...** *(reh-'vee-seh)*

digital cable	**el cable digital** *(ehl 'kah-bleh dee-hee-'tahl)*
fusebox	**la caja de fusibles** *(lah 'kah-hah deh foo-'see-blehs)*
gas meter	**el medidor de gas** *(ehl meh-dee-'dohr deh gahs)*
satellite dish	**el disco de satélite** *(ehl 'dees-koh deh sah-'teh-lee-teh)*
water valve	**la válvula de agua** *(lah 'vahl-voo-lah deh 'ah-gwah)*
bathtub	**la tina de baño** *(lah 'tee-nah deh 'bahn-yoh)*
boiler	**la caldera** *(lah kahl-'deh-rah)*
dryer	**la secadora** *(lah seh-kah-'doh-rah)*
furnace	**el horno** *(ehl 'ohr-noh)*
heater	**el calentador** *(ehl kah-lehn-tah-'dohr)*
shower	**la ducha** *(lah 'doo-chah)*
toilet	**el excusado** *(ehl ex-koo-'sah-doh)*
washer	**la lavadora** *(lah lah-vah-'doh-rah)*
water heater	**el calentador de agua** *(ehl kah-lehn-tah-'dohr deh 'ah-gwah)*

Keep going:

| Did you see...? | ¿Vió...? *(vee-'oh)* |

alarms	**las alarmas** *(lahs ah-'lahr-mahs)*
fans	**los ventiladores** *(lohs vehn-tee-lah-'doh-rehs)*
faucets	**los grifos** *(lohs 'gree-fohs)*
lights	**las luces** *(lahs 'loo-sehs)*
vents	**los conductos** *(lohs kohn-'dook-tohs)*

Now review some built-in appliances in the kitchen:

| Turn on (the)... | **Prenda...** *('prehn-dah)* |

cooktop	**el hornillo** *(ehl ohr-'nee-yoh)*
dishwasher	**el lavaplatos** *(ehl lah-vah-'plah-tohs)*
freezer	**el congelador** *(ehl kohn-heh-lah-'dohr)*
garbage disposal	**el triturador de basura** *(ehl tree-too-rah-'dohr deh bah-'soo-rah)*
microwave	**el horno de microonda** *(ehl 'ohr-noh deh mee-kroh-'ohn-dah)*
refrigerator	**el refrigerador** *(ehl reh-free-heh-rah-'dohr)*
stove	**la estufa** *(lah ehs-'too-fah)*
trash compactor	**la compactadora de basura** *(lah kohm-pahk-tah-'doh-rah deh bah-'soo-rah)*
wall oven	**el horno de pared** *(ehl 'ohr-noh deh pah-'rehd)*
warming drawer	**el calentador de comida** *(ehl kah-lehn-tah-'dohr deh koh-'mee-dah)*
water filter	**el filtro de agua** *(ehl 'feel-troh deh 'ah-gwah)*

Break up your interior work into three-word selections:

| Where's (the)... | ¿Dónde está...? *('dohn-deh ehs-'tah)* |

thermostat	**el termostato** *(ehl tehr-mohs-'tah-toh)*
electrical outlet	**el tomacorriente** *(ehl toh-mah-koh-rree-'ehn-teh)*
light switch	**el interruptor** *(ehl een-teh-rroop-'tohr)*

drain	**el desagüe/el drenaje** *(ehl deh-'sah-gweh/ehl dreh-'nah-heh)*
septic tank	**el foso séptico** *(ehl 'foh-soh 'sehp-tee-koh)*
water main	**la cañería matriz** *(lah kah-nyeh-'ree-ah mah-'trees)*

medicine cabinet	el botiquín *(ehl boh-tee-'keen)*
vanity unit	el lavabo empotrado *(ehl lah-'vah-boh ehm-poh-'trah-doh)*
utility cabinet	el gabinete de servicios *(ehl gah-bee-'neh-teh deh sehr-'vee-see-ohs)*
entertainment center	el centro de entretención *(ehl 'sehn-troh deh ehn-treh-tehn-see-'ohn)*
audio system	el sistema de audio *(ehl sees-'teh-mah deh 'ah-oo-dee-oh)*
home theater	el cine en hogar *(ehl 'see-neh ehn oh-'gahr)*

Home offices are often filled with built-in features:

It has (the)...	Tiene... *(tee-'eh-neh)*
antenna	la antena *(lah ahn-'teh-nah)*
camera	la cámara *(lah 'kah-mah-rah)*
clock	el reloj *(ehl reh-'loh)*
computer	la computadora *(lah kohm-poo-tah-'doh-rah)*
lamp	la lámpara *(lah 'lahm-pah-rah)*
monitor	el monitor *(ehl moh-nee-'tohr)*
player	el tocador *(ehl toh-kah-'dohr)*
printer	la impresora *(lah eem-preh-'soh-rah)*
receiver	el receptor *(ehl reh-sehp-'tohr)*
recorder	la grabadora *(lah grah-bah-'doh-rah)*
scanner	el escáner *(ehl ehs-'kah-nehr)*
screen	la pantalla *(lah pahn-'tah-yah)*
speaker	el parlante *(ehl pahr-'lahn-teh)*
telephone	el teléfono *(ehl teh-'leh-foh-noh)*
television	el televisor *(ehl teh-leh-vee-'sohr)*

To practice the names for these interior items, point them out in Spanish:

Try (the)...	Pruebe... *(proo-'eh-beh)*
undercabinet lighting	las luces bajo el gabinete *(lahs 'loo-sehs 'bah-hoh ehl gah-bee-'neh-teh)*
track lights	las luces en rieles *(lahs 'loo-sehs ehn ree-'eh-lehs)*
chandelier	el candelabro *(ehl kahn-deh-'lah-broh)*
ceiling fan	el ventilador de techo *(ehl vehn-tee-lah-'dohr deh 'teh-choh)*
dimmer switch	el potenciómetro *(ehl poh-tehn-see-'oh-meh-troh)*
control panel	el tablero de control *(ehl tah-'bleh-roh deh kohn-'trohl)*

smoke detector	**el detector de humo** *(ehl deh-tehk-'tohr deh 'oo-moh)*
sprinkler	**el aspesor** *(ehl ahs-pehr-'sohr)*
skylight	**el tragaluz** *(trah-gah-'loos)*

Install (the)…	**Instale…** *(eens-'tah-leh)*

curtains	**las cortinas** *(lahs kohr-'tee-nahs)*
draperies	**las colgaduras** *(lahs kohl-gah-'doo-rahs)*
blinds	**las persianas** *(lahs pehr-see-'ah-nahs)*

rolling shutters	**las persianas enrollables** *(lahs pehr-see-'ah-nahs ehn-rroh-'yah-blehs)*
folding shutters	**las contraventanas** *(lahs kohn-trah-vehn-'tah-nahs)*
plantation shutters	**las persianas de plantación** *(lahs pehr-see-'ah-nahs deh plahn-tah-see-'ohn)*

Provide more information about indoor lighting:

It's…	**Es…** *(ehs)*

flourescent	**flourescente** *(floo-oh-rehs-'sehn-teh)*
halogen	**halógena** *(ah-'loh-heh-nah)*
incandescent	**incandescente** *(een-kahn-dehs-'sehn-teh)*

Try Some

Which of the following statements are TRUE?

La tina de baño require una caja de fusibles. _____

El televisor está en el centro de entretención. _____

La luces en rieles pueden tener potenciómetros. _____

Working Words: PAINTING THE INTERIOR

Ask your helper to get the painting tools and materials:

Obtain (the)...	**Consiga...** *(kohn-'see-gah)*
steel wool	**la lana de acero** *(lah 'lah-nah deh ah-'seh-roh)*
rag	**el trapo** *(ehl 'trah-poh)*
bucket	**el balde** *(ehl 'bahl-deh)*
caulking	**el sellador** *(ehl seh-yah-'dohr)*
compressor	**el compresor** *(ehl kohm-preh-'sohr)*
drop cloth	**la lona** *(lah 'loh-nah)*
exterior paint	**la pintura para exterior** *(lah peen-'too-rah 'pah-rah ex-teh-ree-'ohr)*
hose	**la manguera** *(lah mahn-'geh-rah)*
masking tape	**la cinta adhesiva** *(lah 'seen-tah ah-deh-'see-vah)*
paint brush	**la brocha** *(lah 'broh-chah)*
paint sprayer	**la pistola pintadora** *(lah pees-'toh-lah peen-tah-'doh-rah)*
pan	**el plato** *(ehl 'plah-toh)*
putty knife	**la espátula** *(lah ehs-'pah-too-lah)*
putty	**la masilla** *(lah mah-'see-yah)*
roller	**el rodillo** *(ehl roh-'dee-yoh)*
sander	**la lijadora** *(lah lee-hah-'doh-rah*
sandpaper	**el papel de lija** *(ehl pah-'pehl deh 'lee-hah)*
scraper	**el raspador** *(ehl rahs-pah-'dohr)*
spackling	**el relleno/el mastique** *(ehl reh-'yeh-noh ehl mahs-'tee-keh)*
utility knife	**la cuchilla** *(lah koo-'chee-yah)*

Use (the)...	**Use...** *('oo-seh)*
enamel	**el esmalte** *(ehl ehs-'mahl-teh)*
finish	**el acabado** *(ehl ah-kah-'bah-doh)*
interior paint	**la pintura de interior** *(lah peen-'too-rah deh een-teh-ree-'ohr)*
lacquer	**la laca** *(lah 'lah-kah)*
oil-based paint	**la pintura al aceite** *(lah peen-'too-rah ahl ah-'seh-ee-teh)*
primer	**el imprimador** *(ehl eem-pree-mah-'dohr)*
sealer	**el sellador** *(ehl seh-yah-'dohr)*
stain	**el tinte** *(ehl 'teen-teh)*

thinner	**el disolvente** *(ehl dee-sohl-'vehn-teh)*
varnish	**el barniz** *(ehl bahr-'nees)*
water-based paint	**la pintura al agua** *(lah peen-'too-rah ahl 'ah-gwah)*

Give me (the)…	**Deme…** *('deh-meh)*

gallon	**el galón** *(ehl gah-'lohn)*
half gallon	**el medio galón** *(ehl 'meh-dee-oh gah-'lohn)*
quart	**el cuarto** *(ehl 'kwahr-toh)*

Check (the)…	**Revise…** *(reh-'vee-seh)*

amount	**la cantidad** *(lah kahn-tee-'dahd)*
color	**el color** *(ehl koh-'lohr)*
consistency	**la consistencia** *(lah kohn-sees-'tehn-see-ah)*
design	**el diseño** *(ehl dee-'seh-nyoh)*
pattern	**el patrón** *(ehl pah-'trohn)*
pigment	**el pigmento** *(ehl peeg-'mehn-toh)*
shade	**el matiz** *(ehl mah-'tees)*
sheen	**la luminosidad** *(lah loo-mee-noh-see-'dahd)*
style	**el estilo** *(ehl ehs-'tee-loh)*
surface	**la superficie** *(lah soo-pehr-'fee-see-eh)*

It needs…	**Necesita…** *(neh-seh-'see-tah)*

a cleaning	**una limpiada** *('oo-nah leem-pee-'ah-dah)*
a sanding	**una lijada** *('oo-nah lee-'hah-dah)*
a touch up	**un retoque** *(oon reh-'toh-keh)*
a washing	**una lavada** *('oo-nah lah-'vah-dah)*
another coat	**otra capa/mano** *('oh-trah 'kah-pah/'mah-noh)*
base coat	**la capa de base** *(lah 'kah-pah deh 'bah-seh)*
stain-block	**el antimanchas** *(ehl ahn-tee-'mahn-chahs)*
texture coat	**la capa de textura** *(lah 'kah-pah deh teks-'too-rah)*
waterproofing	**el impermeabilizante** *(ehl eem-pehr-meh-ah-bee-lee-'sahn-teh)*

The paint looks…	**La pintura se ve…** *(lah peen-'too-rah seh veh)*
bright	**brillante** *(bree-'yahn-teh)*
eggshell	**semi-mate** *('seh-mee-'mah-teh)*
fast drying	**rápida para secar** *('rah-pee-dah 'pah-rah seh-'kahr)*
flat	**mate** *('mah-teh)*
glossy	**lustrosa** *(loos-'troh-sah)*
opaque	**opaca** *(oh-'pah-kah)*
satin	**satinada** *(sah-tee-'nah-dah)*
semi-gloss	**semi-lustrosa** *(seh-mee-loos-'troh-sah)*

Be careful with (the)…	**Tenga cuidado con…** *('tehn-gah koo-ee-'dah-doh kohn)*
splashing	**las salpicaduras** *(lahs sahl-pee-kah-'doo-rahs)*
spillage	**el derrame** *(ehl deh-'rrah-meh)*
dripping	**el chorreo** *(ehl cho-'rreh-oh)*

Learn other colors of paint besides the basics:

Open the can of _____ .	**Abra la lata de color _____ .** *('ah-brah lah 'lah-tah deh koh-'lohr)*
copper	**cobrizo** *(koh-'bree-soh)*
cream	**crema** *('kreh-mah)*
golden	**dorado** *(doh-'rah-doh)*
navy blue	**azul marino** *(ah-'sool mah-'ree-noh)*
silver	**plateado** *(plah-teh-'ah-doh)*
sky blue	**celeste** *(seh-'lehs-teh)*

These words you probably know by now:

The paint is …		**La pintura está…** *(lah peen-'too-rah ehs-'tah)*
thick	↓	**espesa** *(ehs-'peh-sah)*
thin	↑	**aguada** *(ah-'gwah-dah)*
wet	↓	**mojada** *(moh-'hah-dah)*
dry	↑	**seca** *('seh-kah)*
dirty	↓	**sucia** *('soo-see-ah)*
clean	↑	**limpia** *('leem-pee-ah)*

Try Some

Name at least three procedures related to interior painting in Spanish.

Name three different colors of interior paint in Spanish.

Name three tools that are used on an interior paint job in Spanish.

Working Words: INDOOR FLOORING

Practice the names for indoor flooring material:

Unload (the)...	**Descargue...** *(dehs-'kahr-geh)*
brick	**el ladrillo** *(ehl lah-'dree-yoh)*
carpet	**la alfombra** *(lah ahl-'fohm-brah)*
cast stone	**la piedra moldeada** *(lah pee-'eh-drah mohl-deh-'ah-dah)*
ceramic tile	**la losa de cerámica** *(lah 'loh-sah deh seh-'rah-mee-kah)*
cultured stone	**la piedra prefabricada** *(lah pee-'eh-drah preh-fah-bree-'kah-dah)*
flagstone	**la losa de piedra** *(lah 'loh-sah deh pee-'eh-drah)*
floor tile	**la baldosa** *(lah bahl-'doh-sah)*
granite	**el granito** *(ehl grah-'nee-toh)*
hardwood	**la madera dura** *(lah mah-'deh-rah 'doo-rah)*
laminate	**el tablero laminado** *(ehl tah-'bleh-roh lah-mee-'nah-doh)*
limestone	**la piedra caliza** *(lah pee-'eh-drah kah-'lee-sah)*
linoleum	**el linóleo** *(ehl lee-'noh-leh-oh)*
marble	**el mármol** *(ehl 'mahr-mohl)*
mosaic	**el mosaico** *(ehl moh-'sah-ee-koh)*
parquet	**el parqué** *(ehl pahr-'keh)*
quartzite	**la cuarcita** *(lah kwahr-'see-tah)*
sandstone	**la piedra arenisca** *(lah pee-'eh-drah ah-reh-'nees-kah)*
slate	**la pizarra** *(lah pee-'sah-rrah)*
stone	**la piedra** *(lah pee-'eh-drah)*
throw rug	**el tapete** *(ehl tah-'peh-teh)*
travertine	**el travertino** *(ehl trah-vehr-'tee-noh)*

It's made of ...	**Está hecho de...** *(ehs-'tah 'eh-choh deh)*
mahogany	**caoba** *(kah-'oh-bah)*
oak	**roble** *('roh-bleh)*
cherry	**cerezo** *(seh-'reh-soh)*
beech	**haya** *('ah-yah)*
pine	**pino** *('pee-noh)*
poplar	**álamo** *('ah-lah-moh)*

List what you'll need to get the flooring material installed:

Give me (the)...	**Deme...** *('deh-meh)*
adhesive	**el adhesivo** *(ehl ah-deh-'see-voh)*
compound	**el compuesto** *(ehl kohm-'pwehs-toh)*
fastener	**el sujetador** *(ehl soo-heh-tah-'dohr)*
felt	**el fieltro** *(ehl fee-'ehl-troh)*
filler	**la masilla para el suelo** *(lah mah-'see-yah 'pah-rah ehl 'sweh-loh)*
glue	**la cola** *(lah 'koh-lah)*
grout	**la lechada** *(lah leh-'chah-dah)*
mastic	**el mastique** *(ehl mahs-'tee-keh)*
molding	**la moldura** *(lah mohl-'doo-rah)*
sealer	**el sellador** *(ehl seh-yah-'dohr)*
shim	**la calza** *(lah 'kahl-sah)*
solvent	**el disolvente** *(ehl dee-sohl-'vehn-teh)*
spacer	**el espaciador** *(ehl ehs-pah-see-ah-'dohr)*
tack strip	**la tira de tachuelas** *(lah 'tee-rah deh tah-choo-'eh-lahs)*
tape	**la cinta** *(lah 'seen-tah)*
underlayment	**la base del piso** *(lah 'bah-seh dehl 'pee-soh)*
moisture barrier	**la barrera contra humedad** *(lah bah-'rreh-rah 'kohn-trah oo-meh-'dahd)*

Use (the)...	**Use...** *('oo-seh)*
carpet roller	**el rodillo para alfombras** *(ehl roh-'dee-yoh 'pah-rah ahl-'fohm-brahs)*
carpet stretcher	**el estirador de alfombras** *(ehl ehs-tee-rah-'dohr deh ahl-'fohm-brahs)*
chisel	**el cincel** *(ehl seen-'sehl)*
coping saw	**la sierra de arco** *(lah see-'eh-rrah deh 'ahr-koh)*
finishing nails	**los clavos sin cabeza** *(lohs 'klah-vohs seen kah-'beh-sah)*

floor leveler	**el nivelador de piso** *(ehl nee-veh-lah-'dohr deh 'pee-soh)*
grinder	**la esmeriladora** *(lah ehs-meh-ree-lah-'doh-rah)*
masonry saw	**la sierra de mampostería** *(lah see-'eh-rrah deh mahm-pohs-teh-'ree-ah)*
notched trowel	**la llana dentada** *(lah 'yah-nah dehn-'tah-dah)*
pneumatic nailer	**la clavadora neumática** *(lah klah-vah-'doh-rah neh-oo-'mah-tee-kah)*
rubber grout float	**la llana de goma** *(lah 'yah-nah deh 'goh-mah)*
rubber mallet	**el mazo de goma** *(ehl 'mah-soh deh 'goh-mah)*
tile cutter	**el cortador de azulejos** *(ehl kohr-tah-'dohr deh ah-soo-'leh-hohs)*
tile nippers	**las pinzas cortazulejo** *(lahs 'peen-sahs kohr-tah-ah-soo-'leh-hoh)*

Prepare (the)…	**Prepare…** *(preh-'pah-reh)*

floor	**el piso** *(ehl 'pee-soh)*
ground	**el suelo** *(ehl 'sweh-loh)*
slab	**la losa** *(lah 'loh-sah)*
sub floor	**el subsuelo** *(ehl soob-'sweh-loh)*
surface	**la superficie** *(lah soo-pehr-'fee-see-eh)*

Measure (the)…	**Mida…** *('mee-dah)*
distance	**la distancia** *(lah dees-'tahn-see-ah)*
expansion gap	**la junta de dilatación** *(lah 'hoon-tah deh dee-lah-tah-see-'ohn)*
high spot	**el punto alto** *(ehl 'poon-toh 'ahl-toh)*
length	**el largo** *(ehl 'lahr-goh)*
line	**la línea** *(lah 'lee-neh-ah)*
low spot	**el punto bajo** *(ehl 'poon-toh 'bah-hoh)*
width	**el ancho** *(ehl 'ahn-choh)*

These words focus on carpet installation:

Check (the)…	**Revise…** *(reh-'vee-she)*
cork	**el corcho** *(ehl 'kohr-choh)*
foam	**la espuma** *(lah ehs-'poo-mah)*
liner	**el revestimiento** *(ehl reh-vehs-tee-mee-'ehn-toh)*

material	**la tela** *(lah 'teh-lah)*
padding	**el relleno** *(ehl reh-'yeh-noh)*
patch	**el parche** *(ehl 'pahr-cheh)*
seam	**la costura** *(lah kohs-'too-rah)*
thread	**el hilo** *(ehl 'ee-loh)*

Try Some

Translate these into English:

Use el cortador de azulejos.

Prepare la superficie.

Mira el punto alto.

Working Words: ON THE JOB

You should know everyone who is working on the interior:

Talk to (the)…   **Hable con…** *('ah-bleh kohn)*

plumber	**el plomero** *(ehl ploh-'meh-roh)*
electrician	**el electricista** *(ehl eh-lehk-tree-'sees-tah)*
painter	**el pintor** *(ehl peen-'tohr)*
carpenter	**el carpintero** *(ehl kahr-peen-'teh-roh)*
drywaller	**el yesero** *(ehl yeh-'seh-roh)*
installer	**el instalador** *(ehl eens-tah-lah-'dohr)*
cabinet maker	**el ebanista** *(ehl eh-bah-'nees-tah)*
locksmith	**el cerrajero** *(ehl seh-rrah-'heh-roh)*
designer	**el diseñador** *(ehl dee-seh-nyah-'dohr)*

Now have them check everything as you review:

Check (the)…   **Revise…** *(reh-'vee-seh)*

outlets	**los enchufes** *(lohs ehn-'choo-fehs)*
faucets	**los grifos** *(lohs 'gree-fohs)*
lights	**las luces** *(lahs 'loo-sehs)*
vents	**los conductos** *(lohs kohn-'dook-tohs)*

fixtures	**los artefactos** *(lohs ahr-teh-'fahk-tohs)*
appliances	**los electrodomésticos** *(lohs eh-lehk-troh-doh-'mehs-tee-kohs)*
cabinets	**los gabinetes** *(lohs gah-bee-'neh-tehs)*
doors	**las puertas** *(lahs 'pwehr-tahs)*
windows	**las ventanas** *(lahs vehn-'tah-nahs)*
floors	**los pisos** *(lohs 'pee-sohs)*
It has (a) _____ countertop.	**Tiene el mostrador de _____.** *(tee-'eh-neh ehl mohs-trah-'dohr deh)*
ceramic tile	**azulejos** *(ah-soo-'leh-hohs)*
Corian®	**corian** *('koh-ree-ahn)*
Formica®	**formica** *(fohr-'mee-kah)*
granite	**granito** *(grah-'nee-toh)*
laminate	**lámina** *('lah-mee-nah)*
marble	**mármol** *('mahr-mohl)*
natural stone	**piedra natural** *(pee-'eh-drah nah-too-'rahl)*
stainless steel	**acero inoxidable** *(ah-'seh-roh ee-nohk-see-'dah-bleh)*

Are you breaking your vocabulary into usable sets?

Tell me the _____.	**Dígame _____.** *('dee-gah-meh)*
percentage	**el porcentaje** *(ehl pohr-sehn-'tah-heh)*
square footage	**los pies cuadrados** *(lohs pee-'ehs kwah-'drah-dohs)*
sum	**la suma** *(lah 'soo-mah)*
Where are the…?	**¿Dónde están…?** *('dohn-deh ehs-'tahn)*

rolls	**los rollos** *(lohs 'roh-yohs)*
sheets	**las hojas** *(lahs 'oh-hahs)*
stacks	**las pilas** *(lahs 'pee-lahs)*

Make (the)…	**Haga…** *('ah-gah)*

grooves	**las ranuras** *(lahs rah-'noo-rahs)*
holes	**los hoyos** *(lohs 'oh-yohs)*
mortise slots	**las mortajas** *(lahs mohr-'tah-hahs)*

Solve (the)...	**Solucione...** *(soh-loo-see-'oh-neh)*
rattle	**el traqueteo** *(ehl trah-keh-'teh-oh)*
rumble	**el estruendo** *(ehl ehs-troo-'ehn-doh)*
squeak	**el chirrido** *(ehl chee-'rree-doh)*

Try Some

Fill in the blank with a word that makes sense:

Tiene el mostrador de _____.

Es el instalador de _____.

Repare _____.

Learn a few words with opposite meanings:

Give me (the) _____ piece.	**Deme la pieza** _____. *('deh-meh lah pee-'eh-sah)*

front	↓	**frontal** *(frohn-'tahl)*
back	↑	**trasera** *(trah-'seh-rah)*

outside	↓	**exterior** *(ex-teh-ree-'ohr)*
inside	↑	**interior** *(een-teh-ree-'ohr)*

lower	↓	**inferior** *(een-feh-ree-'ohr)*
upper	↑	**superior** *(soo-peh-ree-'ohr)*

Use the following to describe worthless material:

It looks...	**Se ve...** *(seh veh)*
bowed	**combado** *(kohm-'bah-doh)*
chipped	**mellado** *(meh-'yah-doh)*
curved	**curvado** *(koor-'vah-doh)*
damaged	**dañado** *(dah-'nyah-doh)*
ripped	**roto** *('roh-toh)*
stained	**manchado** *(mahn-'chah-doh)*
tarnished	**deslucido** *(dehs-loo-'see-doh)*

The following may describe your tools and materials:

The tool is...	**La herramienta es...** *(lah eh-rrah-mee-'ehn-tah ehs)*
adjustable	**ajustable** *(ah-hoos-'tah-bleh)*
lightweight	**ligera** *(lee-'heh-rah)*
pneumatic	**neumática** *(neh-oo-'mah-tee-kah)*
pressurized	**presurizada** *(preh-soo-ree-'sah-dah)*

This is...	**Esto es/Esto está...** *('ehs-toh ehs/'ehs-toh ehs-'tah)*
asbestos-free	**sin asbesto** *(seen ahs-'behs-toh)*
sealed	**sellado** *(seh-'yah-doh)*
treated	**tratado** *(trah-'tah-doh)*
durable	**duradero** *(doo-rah-'deh-roh)*
waterproof	**impermeable** *(eem-pehr-meh-'ah-bleh)*
leak-proof	**estanco** *(ehs-'tahn-koh)*
lead free	**sin plomo** *(seen 'ploh-moh)*
anti-corrosive	**resistente a la corrosión** *(reh-sees-'tehn-the ah lah koh-rroh-see-'ohn)*
stainless	**inoxidable** *(ee-nohk-see-'dah-bleh)*
galvanized	**galvanizado** *(gahl-vah-nee-'sah-doh)*
fire-resistant	**resistente al fuego** *(reh-sees-'tehn-teh ahl 'fweh-goh)*

To discuss the interior style:

The style is...	**El estilo es...** *(ehl ehs-'tee-loh ehs)*
colonial	**colonial** *(koh-loh-nee-'ahl)*
contemporary	**contemporáneo** *(kohn-tehm-poh-'rah-neh-oh)*
country	**campestre** *(kahm-'pehs-treh)*
French	**francés** *(frahn-'sehs)*
high tech	**de alta tecnología** *(deh 'ahl-tah tehk-noh-loh-'hee-ah)*
Italian	**italiano** *(ee-tah-lee-'ah-noh)*
Mediterranean	**mediterráneo** *(meh-dee-teh-'rrah-neh-oh)*
modern	**moderno** *(moh-'dehr-noh)*
Southwestern	**suroeste** *(soor-oh-'ehs-teh)*
traditional	**tradicional** *(trah-dee-see-oh-'nahl)*
Victorian	**victoriano** *(veek-toh-ree-'ah-noh)*

All of these focus on the ceiling:

It needs (the)...	**Necesita...** *(neh-seh-'see-tah)*
acoustic ceiling	**el techo acústico** *(ehl 'teh-choh ah-'koos-tee-koh)*
beamed ceiling	**el techo vigado** *(ehl 'teh-choh vee-'gah-doh)*
conventional ceiling	**el techo tradicional** *(ehl 'teh-choh trah-dee-see-oh-'nahl)*
false ceiling	**el techo falso** *(ehl 'teh-choh 'fahl-soh)*
suspended ceiling	**el techo suspendido** *(ehl 'teh-choh soos-pehn-'dee-doh)*
textured ceiling	**el techo texturizado** *(ehl 'teh-choh tehks-too-ree-'sah-doh)*
vaulted ceiling	**el techo abovedado** *(ehl 'teh-choh ah-boh-veh-'dah-doh)*

 ## Working Words: ON-SITE ACTIONS

Look at the following verbs. Now you will be able to add tools and materials to them and create full sentences:

We're going...	**Vamos a...** *('vah-mohs ah)*
to add	**añadir** *(ah-'nyah-deer)*
to adjust	**ajustar** *(ah-hoos-'tahr)*
to align	**alinear** *(ah-lee-neh-'ahr)*
to apply	**aplicar** *(ah-plee-'kahr)*
to bond	**adherir** *(ahd-eh-'reer)*
to bore	**calar** *(kah-'lahr)*
to caulk	**calafatear** *(kah-lah-fah-teh-'ahr)*
to center	**centrar** *(sehn-'trahr)*
to check	**revisar** *(reh-vee-'sahr)*
to clean	**limpiar** *(leem-pee-'ahr)*
to coat	**cubrir** *(koo-'breer)*
to connect	**conectar** *(koh-nehk-'tahr)*
to correct	**corregir** *(koh-rreh-'heer)*
to cover	**cubrir** *(koo-'breer)*
to cross	**atravesar** *(ah-trah-veh-'sahr)*
to cut	**cortar** *(kohr-'tahr)*
to deliver	**repartir** *(reh-pahr-'teer)*
to distribute	**distribuir** *(dees-tree-boo-'eer)*
to expand	**ampliar/expandir** *(ahm-plee-'ahr/ex-pahn-'deer)*
to fasten	**fijar** *(fee-'hahr)*

to fill	**llenar** *(yeh-'nahr)*
to form	**formar** *(fohr-'mahr)*
to glue	**pegar** *(peh-'gahr)*
to hide	**esconder** *(ehs-kohn-'dehr)*
to hold	**sostener** *(sohs-teh-'nehr)*
to install	**instalar** *(eens-tah-'lahr)*
to insulate	**aislar** *(ah-ees-'lahr)*
to join	**juntar** *(hoon-'tahr)*
to level	**nivelar** *(nee-veh-'lahr)*
to lift	**levantar** *(leh-vahn-'tahr)*
to loosen	**soltar** *(sohl-'tahr)*
to measure	**medir** *(meh-'deer)*
to modify	**modificar** *(moh-dee-fee-'kahr)*
to mount	**montar** *(mohn-'tahr)*
to nail	**clavar** *(klah-'vahr)*
to operate	**operar** *(oh-peh-'rahr)*
to paint	**pintar** *(peen-'tahr)*
to patch	**parchar** *(pahr-'chahr)*
to perforate	**perforar** *(pehr-foh-'rahr)*
to place	**colocar** *(koh-loh-'kahr)*
to polish	**pulir** *(poo-'leer)*
to pour	**verter** *(vehr-'tehr)*
to pre-drill	**pretaladrar** *(preh-tah-lah-'drahr)*
to prep	**preparar** *(preh-pah-'rahr)*
to press	**presionar** *(preh-see-oh-'nahr)*
to protect	**proteger** *(proh-teh-'hehr)*
to putty	**enmasillar** *(ehn-mah-see-'yahr)*
to reduce	**reducir** *(reh-doo-'seer)*
to repair	**reparar** *(reh-pah-'rahr)*
to replace	**sustituir** *(soos-tee-too-'eer)*
to sand	**lijar** *(lee-'hahr)*
to scrape	**raspar** *(rahs-'pahr)*
to screw in	**atornillar** *(ah-tohr-nee-'yahr)*
to seal	**sellar** *(seh-'yahr)*
to smooth	**alisar** *(ah-lee-'sahr)*
to stagger	**alternar** *(ahl-tehr-'nahr)*
to straighten	**enderezar** *(ehn-deh-reh-'sahr)*
to stretch	**estirar** *(ehs-tee-'rahr)*

to take down	**retirar** *(reh-tee-'rahr)*
to tighten	**apretar** *(ah-preh-'tahr)*
to touch up	**retocar** *(reh-toh-'kahr)*
to trace	**trazar** *(trah-'sahr)*
to unroll	**desenrollar** *(deh-sehn-rroh-'yahr)*
to ventilate	**ventilar** *(vehn-tee-'lahr)*
to wallpaper	**empapelar** *(ehm-pah-peh-'lahr)*

These specialized actions may require a bit more practice:

You need...	**Necesita...** *(neh-seh-'see-tah)*
to mask off	**poner cinta** *(poh-'nehr 'seen-tah)*
to mud	**poner yeso** *(poh-'nehr 'yeh-soh)*
to pull wire	**jalar alambre** *(hah-'lahr ah-'lahm-breh)*
to shim	**colocar la calza** *(koh-loh-'kahr lah 'kahl-sah)*
to snap the line	**marcar con linea de tiza** *(mahr-'kahr kohn 'lee-neh-ah deh 'tee-sah)*
to spray paint	**pintar a presión** *(peen-'tahr ah preh-see-'ohn)*
to wipe	**pasar un trapo** *(pah-'sahr oon 'trah-poh)*

Just a Suggestion

Don't omit those verbs that express a problem or concern:

It's going...	**Va a...** *(vah ah)*
to splash	**salpicar** *(sahl-pee-'kahr)*
to drip	**derramar** *(deh-rrah-'mahr)*
to stain	**manchar** *(mahn-'chahr)*
to slide	**resbalarse** *(rehs-bah-'lahr-seh)*
to swell	**hincharse** *(een-'chahr-seh)*
to split	**partirse** *(pahr-'teer-seh)*

Grammar Time

Here's still another way to talk about the past in Spanish. It is a two-part form with a fancy name—the present perfect, and it expresses action that already has been done:

Have you started?   **¿Ha comenzado?** *(ah koh-mehn-'sah-doh)*
I've finished.   **He terminado.** *(eh tehr-mee-'nah-doh)*

- In most cases, the present perfect is formed by changing the endings of **-ar** verbs to **-ado** and the **-er** or **-ir** verbs to **-ido**:

  To drive: **manejar** *(mah-neh-'hahr)* → Driven: **manejado** *(mah-neh-'hah-doh)*
  To eat: **comer** *(koh-'mehr)* → Eaten: **comido** *(koh-'mee-doh)*

- You already learned the verb *to have*: **Tener** *(teh-'nehr)*. Now is the time for you to learn that Spanish has two *to have* verbs: **Tener** and **haber** *(ah-'behr)*. **Haber** is often used as an auxiliary with past participles to form the present perfect.

To have	**Haber** *(ah-'behr)*
I have	**he** *(eh)*
You (sing.) have; he, she has	**ha** *(ah)*
We have	**hemos** *('eh-mohs)*
You (pl.); they have	**han** *(ahn)*

- It takes the verb **haber** and the **-ado** ending to put the present perfect together:

  trabajar *(trah-bah-'hahr—to work):* **(haber) + trabajado**
  Yo he trabajado. *(yoh eh trah-bah-'hah-doh)* I have worked.

  terminar *(tehr-mee-'nahr—to finish:* **(haber) + terminado**
  Hemos terminado. *('eh-mohs tehr-mee-'nah-doh)* We have finished.

  comer *(koh-'mehr—to eat):* **(haber) + comido**
  Pablo ha comido. *('pah-bloh ah koh-'mee-doh)* Pablo has eaten.

  salir *(sah-'leer—to leave):* **(haber) + salido**
  ¿Han salido? *(ahn sah-'lee-doh)* Have they left?

- A few irregular past participles break all the rules, so you'll have to memorize them:

ver *(vehr—to see)* → **visto** *('vees-toh—seen)*
He visto el dueño. *(eh 'vees-toh ehl 'dweh-nyoh)* I've seen the owner.

poner *(poh-'nehr—to put)* → **puesto** *('pwehs-toh—put)*
He puesto todo aquí. *(eh 'pwehs-toh 'toh-doh ah-'kee)* I've put everything here.

hacer *(ah'sehr—to do, to make)* → **hecho** *('eh-choh—done, made)*
He hecho el trabajo. *(eh 'eh-choh ehl trah-'bah-hoh)* I've done the job.

abrir *(ah-'breer—to open)* → **abierto** *(ah-bee-'ehr-toh—opened)*
He abierto la puerta. *(eh ah-bee-'ehr-toh lah 'pwehr-tah)* I've opened the door.

romper *(rohm-'pehr—to break)* → **roto** *('roh-toh—broken)*
He roto la pieza. *(eh 'roh-toh lah pee-'eh-sah)* I've broken the piece.

Try Some

These phrases are for you to translate:

Hemos comenzado. _____

No he terminado. _____

¿Han comido? _____

You're Done!
¡Ya terminó!
(yah tehr-mee-'noh)

You've just completed *Spanish for the Construction Trade*. We hope that much of what you have read has already been put into practice, and you are excited about learning more. Everything in this guidebook has been designed to get you started, so now, fellow Spanish-speaker, the rest is up to you.

The following material comprises two quick-reference sections dealing with subjects that must be attended to as soon as they present themselves: Employment and Emergencies. Finally, the English-Spanish Glossary provides a useful list of vocabulary that you may consult at any moment.

¡Adiós, amigo, y muy buena suerte!

Bill Harvey

Employment

The Employment Form
El formulario de empleo
(ehl fohr-moo-'lah-ree-oh deh ehm-'pleh-oh)

Please fill out this form.
Favor de llenar este formulario.
(fah-'vohr deh yeh-'nahr 'ehs-teh fohr-moo-'lah-ree-oh)

What is your...?	**¿Cuál es su...?** *(kwahl ehs soo)*
address	**dirección** *(dee-rehk-see-'ohn)*
age	**edad** *(eh-'dahd)*
area code	**código de área** *('koh-dee-goh deh áh-reh-ah)*
date of birth	**fecha de *nacimiento*** *('feh-chah deh nah-see-mee-'ehn-toh)*
first name	**primer nombre** *(pree-'mehr 'nohm-breh)*
full name	**nombre completo** *('nohm-breh kohm-'pleh-toh)*
last name	**apellido** *(ah-peh-'yee-doh)*
license number	**número de licencia** *('noo-meh-roh deh lee-'sehn-see-ah)*
marital status	**estado civil** *(ehs-'tah-doh see-'veel)*
nationality	**nacionalidad** *(nah-see-oh-nah-lee-'dahd)*
place of birth	**lugar de nacimiento** *(loo-'gahr deh nah-see-mee-'ehn-toh)*
relationship	**relación** *(reh-lah-see-'ohn)*
social security number	**número de seguro *social*** *('noo-meh-roh deh seh-'goo-roh soh-see-'ahl)*
telephone number	**número de teléfono** *('noo-meh-roh deh teh-'leh-foh-noh)*
cell number	**número de teléfono celular** *('noo-meh-roh deh teh-'leh-foh-noh seh-loo-'lahr)*
e-mail address	**correo electrónico** *(koh-'rreh-oh eh-lehk-'troh-nee-koh)*
zip code	**zona postal** *('soh-nah pohs-'tahl)*
last place of employment	**último lugar de *empleo*** *('ool-tee-mohloo-'gahr deh ehm-'pleh-oh)*

A Few More Questions
Unas preguntas más
('oo-nahs preh-'goon-tahs mahs)

What's your...?	**¿Cuál es su...?** *(kwahl ehs soo)*
skill	**habilidad** *(ah-bee-lee-'dahd)*
field	**campo de trabajo** *('kahm-poh deh trah-'bah-hoh)*
title	**título** *('tee-too-loh)*
specialty	**especialidad** *(ehs-peh-see-ah-lee-'dahd)*
level	**nivel** *(nee-'vehl)*
pay	**pago** *('pah-goh)*
salary	**salario** *(sah-'lah-ree-oh)*
fee	**precio** *('preh-see-oh)*

Who's your ...?	**¿Quién es su ...?** *(kee-'ehn ehs soo)*
closest relative	**pariente mas cercano** *(pah-ree-'ehn-teh mahs sehr-'kah-noh)*
friend	**amigo** *(ah-'mee-goh)*
neighbor	**vecino** *(veh-'see-noh)*
spouse	**esposo/a** *(ehs-'poh-soh/ehs-'poh-sah)*
family physician	**médico familiar** *('meh-dee-koh fah-mee-lee-'ahr)*
reference	**referencia** *(reh-feh-'rehn-see-ah)*
previous employer	**empresario previo** *(ehm-preh-'sah-ree-oh 'preh-vee-oh)*

Do You Have It?
¿Lo tiene? *(loh tee-'eh-neh)*

Tener *(teh-'nehr—to have)* is a powerful verb in Spanish. As you speak, listen for the answers, **sí** *(see)* or **no** *(noh)* to this question:

Do you have ...?	**¿Tiene...?** *(tee-'eh-neh)*
an appointment	**una cita** *('oo-nah 'see-tah)*
application	**la solicitud** *(lah soh-lee-see-'tood)*
card	**la tarjeta** *(lah tahr-'heh-tah)*
certificate	**el certificado** *(ehl sehr-tee-fee-'kah-doh)*
contract	**el contrato** *(ehl kohn-'trah-toh)*
equipment	**el equipo** *(ehl eh-'kee-poh)*
experience	**la experiencia** *(lah ex-peh-ree-'ehn-see-ah)*
form	**el formulario** *(ehl fohr-moo-'lah-ree-oh)*

I.D.	**la identificación** *(lah ee-dehn-tee-fee-kah-see-'ohn)*
insurance	**el seguro** *(ehl seh-'goo-roh)*
license	**la licencia** *(lah lee-'sehn-see-ah)*
record	**el récor** *(ehl 'reh-kohr)*
résumé	**el currículum** *(ehl koo-'rree-koo-loom)*
schedule	**el horario** *(ehl oh-'rah-ree-oh)*
tools	**las herramientas** *(lahs eh-rrah-mee-'ehn-tahs)*
transportation	**el transporte** *(ehl trahns-'pohr-teh)*
uniform	**el uniforme** *(ehl oo-nee-'fohr-meh)*

Citizenship
La ciudadanía
(lah see-oo-dah-dah-'nee-ah)

Are you a U.S. citizen?	**¿Es ciudadano de Estados Unidos?** *(ehs see-oo-dah-'dah-noh deh ehs-'tah-dohs oo-'nee-dohs)*
Do you have a green card?	**¿Tiene tarjeta de residente?** *(tee-'eh-neh tahr-'heh-tah deh reh-see-'dehn-teh)*
Are you a Canadian citizen?	**¿Es ciudadano de Canadá?** *(ehs see-oo-dah-'dah-noh deh kah-nah-'dah)*
What's your resident number?	**¿Cuál es su número de residente?** *(kwahl ehs soo 'noo-meh-roh deh reh-see-'dehn-teh)*
Do you have a work permit?	**¿Tiene permiso de trabajo?** *(tee-'eh-neh pehr-'mee-soh deh trah-'bah-hoh)*

Emergency

In Case of Emergency!
¡En caso de emergencia!
(ehn 'kah-soh deh eh-mehr-'hehn-see-ah)

To check if someone's feeling OK, use these expressions:

Do you need help?	**¿Necesita ayuda?** *(neh-seh-'see-tah ah-'yoo-dah)*
What's the matter?	**¿Qué pasó?** *(keh pah-'soh)*
Where does it hurt?	**¿Dónde le duele?** *('dohn-deh leh 'dweh-leh)*
Calm down.	**Cálmese.** *('kahl-meh-seh)*
Lie down.	**Acuéstese.** *(ah-'kwehs-teh-seh)*
Don't worry.	**No se preocupe.** *(noh seh preh-oh-'koo-peh)*
Are you…?	**¿Está…?** *(ehs-'tah)*
hurt	**herido** *(eh-'ree-doh)*
sick	**enfermo** *(ehn-'fehr-moh)*
dizzy	**mareado** *(mah-reh-'ah-doh)*
exhausted	**agotado** *(ah-goh-'tah-doh)*
sore	**dolorido** *(doh-loh-'ree-doh)*
feeling ill	**sintiéndose mal** *(seen-tee-'ehn-doh-seh mahl)*
He's got (a)…	**Tiene un/una…** *(tee-'eh-neh oon/'oo-nah)*
broken bone	**hueso quebrado** *('hweh-soh keh-'brah-doh)*
bruise	**contusión** *(kohn-too-see-'ohn)*
burn	**quemadura** *(keh-mah-'doo-rah)*
cold	**resfriado** *(rehs-free-'ah-doh)*
cut	**cortadura** *(kohr-tah-'doo-rah)*
fever	**fiebre** *(fee-'eh-breh)*
flu	**influenza** *(een-floo-'ehn-sah)*
sprain	**torcedura** *(tohr-seh-'doo-rah)*

The word *pain* is **dolor** *(doh-'lohr)*. Check out the pattern:

I have (a)...	**Tengo...** *('tehn-goh)*
headache	**dolor de cabeza** *(doh-'lohr deh kah-'beh-sah)*
sore throat	**dolor de garganta** *(doh-'lohr deh gahr-'gahn-tah)*
stomach ache	**dolor de estómago** *(doh-'lohr deh ehs-'toh-mah-goh)*

To be on the safe side, get acquainted with these expressions:

He/She is bleeding.	**Está sangrando.** *(ehs-'tah sahn-'grahn-doh)*
He/She is vomiting.	**Está vomitando.** *(ehs-'tah voh-mee-'tahn-doh)*
He/She is unconscious.	**Está inconsciente.** *(ehs-'tah een-kohn-see-'ehn-teh)*

Tell me about (the) ...	**Hábleme sobre...** *('ah-bleh-meh 'soh-breh)*
accident	**el accidente** *(ehl ahk-see-'dehn-teh)*
bad fall	**la mala caída** *(lah 'mah-lah kah-'ee-dah)*
fatigue	**la fatiga** *(lah fah-'tee-gah)*
seizure	**el ataque** *(ehl ah-'tah-keh)*
sunstroke	**la insolación** *(lah een-soh-lah-see-'ohn)*
electric shock	**el choque eléctrico** *(ehl 'choh-keh eh-'lehk-tree-koh)*

You never know what can happen, so keep on pronouncing:

He's suffering from...	**Sufre de...** *('soo-freh deh)*
dehydration	**deshidratación** *(dehs-ee-drah-tah-see-'ohn)*
shock	**postración nerviosa** *(pohs-trah-see-'ohn nehr-vee-'oh-sah)*
frostbite	**congelamiento** *(kohn-heh-lah-mee-'ehn-toh)*
heat stroke	**postración por calor** *(pohs-trah-see-'ohn pohr kah-'lohr)*
poisoning	**envenenamiento** *(ehn-veh-neh-nah-mee-'ehn-toh)*
insect bite	**picadura de insecto** *(pee-kah-'doo-rah deh een-'sehk-toh)*

Bring (the)...	**Traiga...** *('trah-ee-gah)*
aspirin	**la aspirina** *(lah ahs-pee-'ree-nah)*
Band-Aid®	**la curita** *(lah koo-'ree-tah)*
bandage	**el vendaje** *(ehl vehn-'dah-heh)*
crutches	**las muletas** *(lahs moo-'leh-tahs)*

disinfectant	**el desinfectante** *(ehl deh-seen fehk-'tahn-teh)*
medicine	**la medicina** *(lah meh-dee-'see-nah)*
first-aid kit	**el botiquín de primeros auxilios** *(ehl boh-tee-'keen deh pree-'meh-rohs ah-oo-'ksee-lee-ohs)*
extinguisher	**el extintor** *(ehl ex-teen-'tohr)*
He needs...	**Necesita...** *(neh-seh-'see-tah)*
CPR	**respiración artificial** *(rehs-pee-rah-see-'ohn ahr-tee-fee-see-'ahl)*
medical attention	**ayuda médica** *(ah-'yoo-dah 'meh-dee-kah)*
an interpreter	**un intérprete** *(oon een-'tehr-preh-teh)*

Stay with command words and phrases. Memorize a few at a time:

Call (the) ...	**Llame a ...** *('yah-meh ah)*
911	**nueve-uno-uno** *(noo-'eh-veh'oo-noh 'oo-noh)*
ambulance	**la ambulancia** *(lah ahm-boo-'lahn-see-ah)*
clinic	**la clínica** *(lah 'klee-nee-kah)*
doctor	**el doctor** *(ehl dohk-'tohr)*
office	**la oficina** *(lah oh-fee-'see-nah)*
hospital	**el hospital** *(ehl ohs-pee-'tahl)*
neighbor	**el vecino** *(ehl veh-'see-noh)*
operator	**la operadora** *(lah oh-peh-rah-'doh-rah)*
paramedic	**el paramédico** *(ehl pah-rah-'meh-dee-koh)*
police	**la policía** *(lah poh-lee-'see-ah)*
relative	**el pariente** *(ehl pah-ree-ehn-teh)*
tow truck	**la grúa** *(lah 'groo-ah)*
home	**la casa** *(lah 'kah-sah)*
fire department	**el departamento de bomberos** *(ehl deh-pahr-tah-'mehn-toh deh bohm-'beh-rohs)*

a lot	**mucho** *('moo-choh)*
a/an	**un, una** *(oon/'oo-nah)*
above	**encima** *(ehn-'see-mah)*
ABS pipe	**la tubería negra** *(lah too-beh-'ree-ah 'neh-grah)*
ABS stabilizers	**los soportes ABS** *(lohs soh-'pohr-tehs ah beh 'eh-seh)*
absorption	**la absorción** *(lah ahb-sohr-see-'ohn)*
accessory	**el accesorio** *(ehl ahk-seh-'soh-ree-oh)*
accident	**el accidente** *(ehl ahk-see-'dehn-teh)*
acetylene	**el acetileno** *(ehl ah-seh-tee-'leh-noh)*
acid	**el ácido** *(ehl 'ah-see-doh)*
acoustic	**acústico** *(ah-'koos-tee-koh)*
across	**a través** *(ah trah-'vehs)*
acrylic	**el acrílico** *(ehl ah-'kree-lee-koh)*
adapter	**el adaptador** *(ehl ah-dahp-tah-'dohr)*
add-on	**la adición** *(lah ah-dee-see-'ohn)*
adhesive	**el adhesivo** *(ehl ah-deh-'see-voh)*
adjustable	**ajustable** *(ah-hoos-'tah-bleh)*
adobe	**el adobe** *(ehl ah-'doh-beh)*
A-frame	**el armazón en A** *(ehl ahr-mah-'sohn ehn ah)*
after	**después** *(dehs-'pwehs)*
age	**la edad** *(lah eh-'dahd)*
air	**el aire** *(ehl 'ah-ee-reh)*
air compressor	**el compresor de aire** *(ehl kohm-preh-'sohr deh 'ah-ee-reh)*
air conditioner	**el acondicionador de aire** *(ehl ah-kohn-dee-see-oh-nah-'dohr deh 'ah-ee-reh)*
air conditioning	**el aire acondicionado** *(ehl 'ah-ee-reh ah-kohn-dee-see-oh-'nah-doh)*
air filter	**el filtro de aire** *(ehl 'feel-troh deh 'ah-ee-reh)*
air intake vent	**el respiradero** *(ehl rehs-pee-rah-'deh-roh)*
air vent	**el conducto de aire** *(ehl kohn-'dook-toh deh 'ah-ee-reh)*
airless	**sin presión** *(seen preh-see-'ohn)*
alarm	**la alarma** *(lah ah-'lahr-mah)*
aligned	**alineado** *(ah-lee-neh-'ah-doh)*
alkaline	**alcalino** *(ahl-kah-'lee-noh)*
all	**todo** *('toh-doh)*
alley	**el callejón** *(ehl kah-yeh-'hohn)*
alloy	**la aleación** *(lah ah-leh-ah-see-'ohn)*
almost	**casi** *('kah-see)*
alone	**solo** *('soh-loh)*
along	**a lo largo** *(ah loh 'lahr-goh)*
already	**ya** *(yah)*

also	**también** *(tahm-bee-'ehn)*
alternating	**alternante** *(ahl-tehr-'nahn-teh)*
aluminum	**aluminio** *(ah-loo-'mee-nee-oh)*
always	**siempre** *(see-'ehm-preh)*
ambulance	**la ambulancia** *(lah ahm-boo-'lahn-see-ah)*
amount	**la cantidad** *(lah kahn-tee-'dahd)*
amp	**el amperio** *(ehl ahm-'peh-ree-oh)*
amperage	**el amperaje** *(ehl ahm-peh-'rah-heh)*
anchor	**el anclaje** *(ehl ahn-'klah-heh)*
and	**y** *(ee)*
angle	**el ángulo** *(ehl 'ahn-goo-loh)*
angle beam	**la viga angular** *(lah 'vee-gah ahn-goo-'lahr)*
angle valve	**la válvula angular** *(lah 'vahl-voo-lah ahn-goo-'lahr)*
angry	**enojado** *(eh-noh-'hah-doh)*
ankle	**el tobillo** *(ehl toh-'bee-yoh)*
antenna	**la antena** *(lah ahn-'teh-nah)*
anti-corrosive	**resistente a la corrosión** *(res-sees-'tehn-teh ah lah koh-rroh-see-'ohn)*
antique	**de estilo antiguo** *(deh ehs-'tee-loh ahn-'tee-gwoh)*
anyone	**cualquiera** *(kwahl-kee-'eh-rah)*
anything	**cualquier cosa** *(kwahl-kee-'ehr 'koh-sah)*
anywhere	**en cualquier sitio** *(ehn kwahl-kee-'ehr 'see-tee-oh)*
apartment	**el apartamento** *(ehl ah-pahr-tah-'mehn-toh)*
appliance	**el electrodoméstico** *(ehl eh-lehk-troh-doh-'mehs-tee-koh)*
application	**la solicitud** *(lah soh-lee-see-'tood)*
apprentice	**el aprendiz** *(ehl ah-prehn-'dees)*
apron	**el mandil** *(ehl mahn-'deel)*
arc	**el arco** *(ehl 'ahr-koh)*
arcing	**el arqueo** *(ehl ahr-'keh-oh)*
architect	**el arquitecto** *(ehl ahr-kee-'tehk-toh)*
area	**la área** *(lah 'ah-reh-ah)*
around	**alrededor** *(ahl-reh-deh-'dohr)*
artificial	**artificial** *(ahr-tee-fee-see-'ahl)*
asbestos-free	**sin asbesto** *(seen ahs-'behs-toh)*
asphalt	**el asfalto** *(ehl ahs-'fahl-toh)*
assembly	**el montaje** *(ehl mohn-'tah-heh)*
at	**en** *(ehn)*
attachment	**la conexión** *(lah koh-nehk-see-'ohn)*
attic	**el ático** *(ehl 'ah-tee-koh)*
audio system	**el audio** *(ehl 'ah-oo-dee-oh)*
auger	**el barrenador mecánico** *(ehl bah-rreh-nah-'dohr meh-'kah-nee-koh)*
automatic	**automático** *(ah-oo-toh-'mah-tee-koh)*
awning	**el toldo** *(ehl 'tohl-doh)*

awning window	**la marquesina** *(lah mahr-keh-'see-nah)*
ax	**el hacha** *(ehl 'ah-chah)*
back	**atrás** *(ah-'trahs)*
back door	**la puerta falsa** *(lah 'pwehr-tah 'fahl-sah)*
back pay	**el sueldo atrasado** *(ehl 'swehl-doh ah-trah-'sah-doh)*
back plate	**la placa** *(lah 'plah-kah)*
backhoe	**la retroexcavadora** *(lah reh-troh-ex-kah-vah-'doh-rah)*
backing	**el respaldo** *(ehl rehs-'pahl-doh)*
backwards	**hacia atrás** *('ah-see-ah ah-'trahs)*
backyard	**el patio trasero** *(ehl 'pah-tee-oh trah-'seh-roh)*
bad	**malo** *('mah-loh)*
bag	**la bolsa** *(lah 'bohl-sah)*
balance	**el equilibrio** *(ehl eh-kee-'lee-bree-oh)*
balance (window)	**el contrapeso** *(ehl kohn-trah-'peh-soh)*
balanced	**balanceado** *(bah-lahn-seh-'ah-doh)*
balcony	**el balcón** *(ehl bahl-'kohn)*
ball	**la bola** *(lah 'boh-lah)*
ball valve	**la válvula de bola** *(lah 'vahl-voo-lah deh 'boh-lah)*
band saw	**la sierra de cinta** *(lah see-'eh-rrah deh 'seen-tah)*
bank	**el banco** *(ehl 'bahn-koh)*
bar bender	**la dobladora** *(lah doh-blah-'doh-rah)*
bar (metal)	**la barra** *(lah 'bah-rrah)*
barbed	**con púas** *(kohn 'poo-ahs)*
barbeque	**la parrilla** *(lah pah-'rree-yah)*
barrel	**el barril** *(ehl bah-'rreel)*
barrier	**la barrera** *(lah bah-'rreh-rah)*
base	**la base** *(lah 'bah-seh)*
baseboard	**el zócalo** *(ehl 'soh-kah-loh)*
basement	**el sótano** *(ehl 'soh-tah-noh)*
basin	**la cuenca** *(lah 'kwehn-kah)*
basket	**la canasta** *(lah kah-'nahs-tah)*
bathroom	**el baño** *(ehl 'bah-nyoh)*
bathroom sink	**el lavabo** *(ehl lah-'vah-boh)*
bathtub	**la tina de baño** *(lah 'tee-nah deh 'bah-nyoh)*
battery	**la batería/la pila** *(lah bah-teh-'ree-ah/lah 'pee-lah)*
bay (framing)	**el bache** *(ehl 'bah-cheh)*
bay window	**la ventana saliente** *(lah vehn-'tah-nah sah-lee-'ehn-teh)*
beach	**la playa** *(lah 'plah-yah)*
beam	**la viga** *(lah 'vee-gah)*
bearing wall	**el muro de carga** *(ehl 'moo-roh deh 'kahr-gah)*
bearing	**el cojinete** *(ehl koh-hee-'neh-teh)*
bedrock	**el lecho de roca** *(ehl 'leh-choh deh 'roh-kah)*

bedroom	**el dormitorio/la recámara** *(ehl dohr-mee-'toh-ree-oh/lah reh-'kah-mah-rah)*
before	**antes** *('ahn-tehs)*
beginning	**el principio** *(ehl preen-'see-pee-oh)*
behind	**detrás** *(deh-'trahs)*
below	**abajo** *(ah-'bah-hoh)*
belt	**el cinturón** *(ehl seen-too-'rohn)*
belt (tool)	**la banda** *(lah 'bahn-dah)*
bench	**la banca** *(lah 'bahn-kah)*
bend	**el recodo** *(ehl reh-'koh-doh)*
bent	**doblado** *(doh-'blah-doh)*
better	**mejor** *(meh-'hohr)*
between	**entre** *('ehn-treh)*
bevel	**el bisel** *(ehl bee-'sehl)*
big	**grande** *('grahn-deh)*
bird bath	**la bañera de pájaros** *(lah bah-'nyeh-rah deh 'pah-hah-rohs)*
bit (drill)	**la broca** *(lah 'broh-kah)*
bitumen	**el bitumen** *(ehl bee-'too-mehn)*
black	**negro** *('neh-groh)*
black paper	**el papel negro** *(ehl pah-'pehl 'neh-groh)*
blade (saw)	**la hoja** *(lah 'oh-hah)*
blinds	**las persianas** *(lahs pehr-see-'ah-nahs)*
blisters	**las ampollas** *(lahs ahm-'poh-yahs)*
block	**el bloque** *(ehl 'bloh-keh)*
block wall	**el muro de bloque** *(ehl 'moo-roh deh 'bloh-keh)*
blocking	**el bloqueo** *(ehl bloh-'keh-oh)*
blower	**la sopladora** *(lah soh-plah-'doh-rah)*
blue	**azul** *(ah-'sool)*
blueprint	**el cianotipo** *(ehl see-ah-noh-'tee-poh)*
board (mech.)	**el tablero** *(ehl tah-'bleh-roh)*
board (wood)	**la tabla** *(lah 'tah-blah)*
Bobcat	**el bobcat** *(ehl 'bohb-kaht)*
boiler	**la caldera** *(lah kahl-'deh-rah)*
bolt	**el perno** *(ehl 'pehr-noh)*
bone	**el hueso** *(ehl hoo-'eh-soh)*
bookshelf	**el librero** *(ehl lee-'breh-roh)*
boom (crane)	**el aguilón** *(ehl ah-gee-'lohn)*
boots	**las botas** *(lahs 'boh-tahs)*
bored	**aburrido** *(ah-boo-'rree-doh)*
boss	**el jefe** *(ehl 'heh-feh)*
both	**ambos** *('ahm-bohs)*
bottle	**la botella** *(lah boh-'teh-yah)*
bottom	**el fondo** *(ehl 'fohn-doh)*

boundary	**el límite** *(ehl 'lee-mee-teh)*
bow window	**la ventana curva** *(lah vehn-'tah-nah 'koor-vah)*
bowed	**combado** *(kohm-'bah-doh)*
box	**la caja** *(lah 'kah-hah)*
box nail	**el clavo para madera** *(ehl 'klah-voh 'pah-rah mah-'deh-rah)*
box-ended wrench	**la llave fija** *(lah 'yah-veh 'fee-hah)*
brace (framing)	**la abrazadera/la riostra** *(lah ah-brah-sah-'deh-rah/lah ree-'ohs-trah)*
braced	**arriostrada** *(ah-rree-ohs-'trah-dah)*
bracket (framing)	**el soporte** *(ehl soh-'pohr-teh)*
bracket (mech.)	**la ménsula** *(lah 'mehn-soo-lah)*
brass	**el latón** *(ehl lah-'tohn)*
break	**la rotura** *(lah roh-'too-rah)*
breakfast	**el desayuno** *(ehl deh-sah-'yoo-noh)*
breakfast room	**el antecomedor** *(ehl ahn-teh-koh-meh-'dohr)*
brick	**el ladrillo** *(ehl lah-'dree-yoh)*
brick-cutting saw	**la sierra para ladrillos** *(lah see-'eh-rrah 'pah-rah lah-'dree-yohs)*
brick wall	**el muro de ladrillo** *(ehl 'moo-roh deh lah-'dree-yoh)*
bridge	**el puente** *(ehl 'pwehn-teh)*
bridging	**el puntal** *(ehl poon-'tahl)*
bright	**brillante** *(bree-'yahn-teh)*
broken	**roto/quebrado/descompuesto** *('roh-toh/keh-'brah-doh/dehs-kohm-'pwehs-toh)*
bronze	**el bronce** *(ehl 'brohn-seh)*
broom	**la escoba** *(lah ehs-'koh-bah)*
brown	**café** *(kah-'feh)*
brown coat	**la segunda capa/mano** *(lah seh-'goon-dah 'kah-pah/'mah-noh)*
bruise	**la contusión** *(lah kohn-too-see-'ohn)*
brush	**el cepillo** *(ehl seh-'pee-yoh)*
brush (paint)	**la brocha** *(lah 'broh-chah)*
brushed (color)	**mate** *('mah-teh)*
bubbles	**las burbujas** *(lahs boor-'boo-hahs)*
bucket	**el balde/la cubeta** *(ehl 'bahl-deh/lah koo-'beh-tah)*
bucket (mech.)	**el cucharón** *(ehl koo-chah-'rohn)*
builder	**el constructor** *(ehl kohns-trook-'tohr)*
building	**el edificio** *(ehl eh-dee-'fee-see-oh)*
bulb	**el foco/la bombilla** *(ehl 'foh-koh/lah bohm-'bee-yah)*
bull float	**la llana mecánica** *(lah 'yah-nah meh-'kah-nee-kah)*
bull-nosed	**la esquina boleada** *(lah ehs-'kee-nah boh-leh-'ah-dah)*
bulldozer	**el tractor oruga/el buldózer** *(ehl trahk-'tohr oh-roo-gah/ehl bool-'doh-sehr)*
bumps	**los bultos** *(lohs 'bool-tohs)*
bundle	**el lío** *(ehl 'lee-oh)*
bungalow	**el búngalo** *(ehl 'boon-gah-loh)*

burlap	**la lona** *(lah 'loh-nah)*
burn	**la quemadura** *(lah keh-mah-'doo-rah)*
burned	**quemado** *(keh-'mah-doh)*
burners	**los quemadores** *(lohs keh-mah-'doh-rehs)*
bush	**el arbusto** *(ehl ahr-'boos-toh)*
bush hammer	**el martillo para texturizar** *(ehl mahr-'tee-yoh 'pah-rah tehks-too-ree-'sahr)*
but	**pero** *('peh-roh)*
butted	**bien pegado/a tope** *(bee-'ehn peh-'gah-doh/ah 'toh-peh)*
butterfly valve	**la válvula de mariposa** *(lah 'vahl-voo-lah deh mah-ree-'poh-sah)*
button	**el botón** *(ehl boh-'tohn)*
buttress	**el contrafuerte** *(ehl kohn-trah-'fwehr-teh)*
by	**por** *(pohr)*
bypass switch	**el interruptor de derivación** *(ehl een-teh-rroop-'tohr deh deh-ree-vah-see-'ohn)*
cabin	**la cabaña** *(lah kah-'bah-nyah)*
cab (mech.)	**la cabina** *(lah kah-'bee-nah)*
cabinet-maker	**el ebanista** *(ehl eh-bah-'nees-tah)*
cabinet	**el gabinete** *(ehl gah-bee-'neh-teh)*
cable	**el cable** *(ehl 'kah-bleh)*
caisson	**el cajón** *(ehl kah-'hohn)*
calendar	**el calendario** *(ehl kah-lehn-'dah-ree-oh)*
camera	**la cámara** *(lah 'kah-mah-rah)*
can	**la lata** *(lah 'lah-tah)*
canal	**el canal** *(ehl kah-'nahl)*
cap	**la corona** *(lah koh-'roh-nah)*
cap (clothing)	**la gorra** *(lah 'goh-rrah)*
capacitors	**los capacitores** *(lohs kah-pah-see-'toh-rehs)*
capacity	**la capacidad** *(lah kah-pah-see-'dahd)*
capped	**coronado** *(koh-roh-'nah-doh)*
card	**la tarjeta** *(lah tahr-'heh-tah)*
cardboard	**el cartón** *(ehl kahr-'tohn)*
carpenter	**el carpintero** *(ehl kahr-peen-'teh-roh)*
carpentry	**la carpintería** *(lah kahr-peen-teh-'ree-ah)*
carpet	**la alfombra** *(lah ahl-'fohm-brah)*
carpet roller	**el rodillo para alfombras** *(ehl roh-'dee-yoh 'pah-rah ahl-'fohm-brahs)*
carpet stretcher	**el estirador de alfombras** *(ehl ehs-tee-rah-'dohr deh ahl-'fohm-brahs)*
carport	**la cochera** *(lah koh-'cheh-rah)*
cartridge	**el cartucho** *(ehl kahr-'too-choh)*
case	**la caja** *(lah 'kah-hah)*
casement window	**la ventana a bisagra** *(lah vehn-'tah-nah ah bee-'sah-grah)*
casing	**el marco** *(ehl 'mahr-koh)*

casing beads	**las molduras de contramarca** *(lahs mohl-'doo-rahs deh kohn-trah-'mahr-kah)*
casing nail	**el clavo de cabeza perdida** *(ehl 'klah-voh deh kah-'beh-sah pehr-'dee-dah)*
cast stone	**la piedra moldeada** *(lah pee-'eh-drah mohl-deh-'ah-dah)*
catalyst	**el catalizador** *(ehl kah-tah-lee-sah-'dohr)*
catch (window)	**la cerradura** *(lah seh-rrah-'doo-rah)*
caulking	**el sellador/la masilla** *(ehl seh-yah-'dohr/lah mah-'see-yah)*
caulking gun	**la pistola de masilla/el sellador** *(lah pees-'toh-lah deh mah-'see-yah/ehl seh-yah-'dohr)*
C-clamp (framing)	**la prensa de tornillo** *(lah 'prehn-sah deh tohr-'nee-yoh)*
C-clamp (mech.)	**la abrazadera tipo C** *(lah ah-brah-sah-'deh-rah 'tee-poh seh)*
ceiling	**el techo** *(ehl 'teh-choh)*
ceiling fan	**el ventilador de techo** *(ehl vehn-tee-lah-'dohr deh 'teh-choh)*
cell	**la célula** *(lah 'seh-loo-lah)*
cellar window	**el respirador** *(ehl rehs-pee-rah-'dohr)*
cement	**el cemento** *(ehl seh-'mehn-toh)*
cement block	**el bloque de hormigón** *(ehl 'bloh-keh deh ohr-mee-'gohn)*
cement mixer	**la mezcladora de cemento** *(lah mehs-klah-'doh-rah deh seh-'mehn-toh)*
cement saw	**la sierra para cortar cemento** *(lah see-'eh-rrah 'pah-rah kohr-'tahr seh-'mehn-toh)*
cement truck	**el camión hormigonero** *(ehl kah-mee-'ohn ohr-mee-goh-'neh-roh)*
cent	**el centavo** *(ehl sehn-'tah-voh)*
center	**el centro** *(ehl 'sehn-troh)*
centralized	**centralizado** *(sehn-trah-lee-'sah-doh)*
ceramic	**la cerámica** *(lah seh-'rah-mee-kah)*
ceramic tile	**el azulejo/la losa de cerámica** *(ehl ah-soo-'leh-hoh/lah 'loh-sah deh seh-'rah-mee-kah)*
ceramic tile (roofing)	**el ladrillo cerámico** *(ehl lah-'dree-yoh seh-'rah-mee-koh)*
certificate	**el certificado** *(ehl sehr-tee-fee-'kah-doh)*
certification	**la certificación** *(lah sehr-tee-fee-kah-see-'ohn)*
cesspool	**el pozo negro** *(ehl 'poh-soh 'neh-groh)*
chain	**la cadena** *(lah kah-'deh-nah)*
chain wrench	**la llave de cadena** *(lah 'yah-veh deh kah-'deh-nah)*
chainsaw	**la motosierra** *(lah moh-toh-see-'eh-rrah)*
chalk	**la tiza** *(lah 'tee-sah)*
chalk box	**la cajita de tiza** *(lah kah-'hee-tah deh 'tee-sah)*
chalk line	**el cordón/la cuerda/la línea de tiza** *(ehl kohr-'dohn/lah 'kwehr-dah/ lah 'lee-neh-ah deh 'tee-sah)*
chalk powder	**el polvo de tiza** *(ehl 'pohl-voh deh 'tee-sah)*
chandelier	**la lámpara de araña** *(lah 'lahm-pah-rah deh ah-'rah-nyah)*
changes	**los cambios** *(lohs 'kahm-bee-ohs)*

channel	**el canal** *(ehl kah-'nahl)*
channel-lock pliers	**los alicates ajustables** *(lohs ah-lee-'kah-tehs ah-hoos-'tah-blehs)*
charger	**la cargadora** *(lah kahr-gah-'doh-rah)*
chassis	**el bastidor** *(ehl bahs-tee-'dohr)*
check valve	**la válvula de antirretorno** *(lah 'vahl-voo-lah deh ahn-tee-reh-'tohr-noh)*
chemical	**el producto químico** *(ehl proh-'dook-toh 'kee-mee-koh)*
cherry wood	**la madera de cerezo** *(lah mah-'deh-rah deh seh-'reh-soh)*
chicken wire	**el alambre de gallinero/el mallazo** *(ehl ah-'lahm-breh deh gah-yee-'neh-roh/ehl mah-'yah-soh)*
chimney	**la chimenea** *(lah chee-meh-'neh-ah)*
chimney flue	**el conducto de humo en la chimenea** *(ehl kohn-'dook-toh deh 'oo-moh ehn lah chee-meh-'neh-ah)*
chipboard	**el aglomerado** *(ehl ah-gloh-meh-'rah-doh)*
chipped	**mellado** *(meh-'yah-doh)*
chipper	**la melladora** *(lah meh-yah-'doh-rah)*
chips (stone)	**la gravilla** *(lah grah-'vee-yah)*
chisel	**el cincel** *(ehl seen-'sehl)*
chlorine	**el cloro** *(ehl 'kloh-roh)*
chrome	**el cromo** *(ehl 'kroh-moh)*
cinderblock	**el ladrillo grande de cemento** *(ehl lah-'dree-yoh 'grahn-deh deh seh-'mehn-toh)*
circuit board	**el tablero de circuitos** *(ehl tah-'bleh-roh deh seer-koo-'ee-tohs)*
circuit breaker	**el cortacircuitos** *(ehl kohr-tah seer-koo-'ee-tohs)*
circuit tester	**el probador de circuitos** *(ehl proh-bah-'dohr deh seer-koo-'ee-tohs)*
circular saw	**la sierra circular** *(lah see-'eh-rrah seer-koo-'lahr)*
circumference	**la circunferencia** *(lah seer-koon-feh-'rehn-see-ah)*
clamp	**la abrazadera/la prensa de sujetar** *(lah ah-brah-sah-'deh-rah/lah 'prehn-sah deh soo-heh-'tahr)*
clapboard	**la tablilla** *(lah tah-'blee-yah)*
clay	**la greda/la arcilla** *(lah 'greh-dah/la ahr-'see-yah)*
clean	**limpio** *('leem-pee-oh)*
clean-out	**el registro** *(ehl reh-'hees-troh)*
clean-out stop	**el tapón de limpieza** *(ehl tah-'pohn deh leem-pee-'eh-sah)*
clear (color)	**claro** *('klah-roh)*
clear (weather)	**despejado** *(dehs-peh-'hah-doh)*
clearance	**la distancia de seguridad** *(lah dees-'tahn-see-ah deh seh-goo-ree-'dahd)*
clerk	**el dependiente** *(ehl deh-pehn-dee-'ehn-teh)*
client	**el cliente** *(ehl klee-'ehn-teh)*
clip (elec.)	**la clavija** *(lah klah-'vee-hah)*
clip (framing)	**la sujetadora** *(lah soo-heh-tah-'doh-rah)*
clip (plumbing)	**la abrazadera** *(lah ah-brah-sah-'deh-rah)*

clock	**el reloj** *(ehl reh-'loh)*
clog	**la obstrucción** *(lah ohbs-trook-see-'ohn)*
closed	**cerrado** *(seh-'rrah-doh)*
closed circuit	**el sistema de circuito cerrado** *(ehl sees-'teh-mah deh seer-koo-'ee-toh seh-'rrah-doh)*
closet	**el ropero** *(ehl roh-'peh-roh)*
cloth	**la tela** *(lah 'teh-lah)*
clothing	**la ropa** *(lah 'roh-pah)*
cloudy	**nublado** *(noo-'blah-doh)*
clutch	**el embrague** *(ehl ehm-'brah-geh)*
CO_2	**el anhídrido carbónico** *(ehl ah-'nee-dree-doh kahr-'boh-nee-koh)*
coarse	**áspero** *('ahs-peh-roh)*
coastal	**costeño** *(kohs-'teh-nyoh)*
coat	**la capa/la mano** *(lah 'kah-pah/lah 'mah-noh)*
coated	**bañado** *(bah-'nyah-doh)*
coating	**la capa** *(lah 'kah-pah)*
cobblestones	**los adoquines** *(lohs ah-doh-'kee-nehs)*
code	**el código** *(ehl 'koh-dee-goh)*
coffee	**el café** *(ehl kah-'feh)*
coil	**el rollo** *(ehl 'roh-yoh)*
coil (elec.)	**la bobina** *(lah boh-'bee-nah)*
cold	**frío** *('free-oh)*
cold (illness)	**el resfriado** *(ehl rehs-free-'ah-doh)*
collar tie	**la vigueta de amarre** *(lah vee-'geh-tah deh ah-'mah-rreh)*
color	**el color** *(ehl koh-'lohr)*
column	**la columna** *(lah koh-'loom-nah)*
combination wrench	**la llave combinada** *(lah 'yah-veh kohm-bee-'nah-dah)*
combustible	**combustible** *(kohm-boos-'tee-bleh)*
compactor	**la compactadora** *(lah kohm-pahk-tah-'doh-rah)*
complete	**completo** *(kohm-'pleh-toh)*
completely	**completamente** *(kohm-pleh-tah-'mehn-teh)*
complex	**el complejo** *(ehl kohm-'pleh-hoh)*
component	**el componente** *(ehl kohm-poh-'nehn-teh)*
compound	**el compuesto** *(ehl kohm-'pwehs-toh)*
compressor	**el compresor** *(ehl kohm-preh-'sohr)*
computer	**la computadora** *(lah kohm-poo-tah-'doh-rah)*
concrete	**el concreto** *(ehl kohn-'kreh-toh)*
condensers	**los condensadores** *(lohs kohn-dehn-sah-'doh-rehs)*
condition	**la condición** *(lah kohn-dee-see-'ohn)*
condominium	**el condominio** *(ehl kohn-doh-'mee-nee-oh)*
conduit	**el conducto** *(ehl kohn-'dook-toh)*
connecting screw	**el tornillo conector** *(ehl tohr-'nee-yoh koh-nehk-'tohr)*

connection	**la conexión/el acoplamiento** *(lah koh-nehk-see-'ohn/ehl ah-koh-plah-mee-'ehn-toh)*
connection box	**la caja de empalmes** *(lah 'kah-hah deh ehm-'pahl-mehs)*
connector	**el conector/la conexión** *(ehl koh-nehk-'tohr/lah koh-nehk-see-'ohn)*
contact	**el contacto** *(ehl kohn-'tahk-toh)*
contact plate	**la placa de contacto** *(lah 'plah-kah deh kohn-'tahk-toh)*
contaminated	**contaminado** *(kohn-tah-mee-'nah-doh)*
continuous	**contínuo** *(kohn-'tee-nwoh)*
contract	**el contrato** *(ehl kohn-'trah-toh)*
contractor	**el contratista** *(ehl kohn-trah-'tees-tah)*
control	**el control** *(ehl kohn-'trohl)*
control box	**la caja de control** *(lah 'kah-hah deh kohn-'trohl)*
control joint	**la junta de control** *(lah 'hoon-tah deh kohn-'trohl)*
control panel	**el tablero de control** *(ehl tah-'bleh-roh deh kohn-'trohl)*
conveyor	**la cinta transportadora** *(lah 'seen-tah trahns-pohr-tah-'doh-rah)*
cooktop	**el hornillo** *(ehl ohr-'nee-yoh)*
cool	**fresco** *('frehs-koh)*
coping	**el borde decorativo** *(ehl 'bohr-deh deh-koh-rah-'tee-voh)*
coping saw	**la sierra de arco** *(lah see-'eh-rrah deh 'ahr-koh)*
copper	**el cobre** *(ehl 'koh-breh)*
corbel	**el saledizo** *(ehl sah-leh-'dee-soh)*
cord	**el cordón** *(ehl kohr-'dohn)*
cordless	**inalámbrico** *(ee-nah-'lahm-bree-koh)*
cordless drill	**el taladro portátil** *(ehl tah-'lah-droh pohr-'tah-teel)*
Corian	**la corian** *(lah 'koh-ree-ahn)*
cork	**el corcho** *(ehl 'kohr-choh)*
corner	**la esquina** *(lah ehs-'kee-nah)*
cornice	**la cornisa** *(lah kohr-'nee-sah)*
corrosion	**la corrosión** *(lah koh-rroh-see-'ohn)*
corrugated steel	**el acero corrugado** *(ehl ah-'seh-roh koh-rroo-'gah-doh)*
couch	**el sofá** *(ehl soh-'fah)*
counter	**el mostrador** *(ehl mohs-trah-'dohr)*
counterclockwise	**contra las agujas del reloj** *('kohn-trah lahs ah-'goo-hahs dehl reh-'loh)*
countertop	**la cubierta del mostrador** *(lah koo-bee-'ehr-tah dehl mohs-trah-'dohr)*
coupler	**el acoplador** *(ehl ah-koh-plah-'dohr)*
coupling (framing)	**el enganche** *(ehl ehn-'gahn-cheh)*
coupling (mech.)	**el acoplamiento/el cople** *(ehl ah-koh-plah-mee-'ehn-toh/ehl 'koh-pleh)*
course	**la hilera** *(lah ee-'leh-rah)*
courtyard	**el patio** *(ehl 'pah-tee-oh)*
covering	**la cubierta** *(lah koo-bee-'ehr-tah)*
cracked	**agrietado** *(ah-gree-eh-'tah-doh)*
cracks	**las grietas** *(lahs gree-'eh-tahs)*

crane	**la grúa** *(lah 'groo-ah)*
crane truck	**el camión grúa** *(ehl kah-mee-'ohn 'groo-ah)*
crank	**la manivela** *(lah mah-nee-'veh-lah)*
crate	**la jaba/la caja para transporte** *(lah 'hah-bah/lah 'kah-hah 'pah-rah trahns-'pohr-teh)*
crawl space	**el espacio angosto** *(ehl ehs-'pah-see-oh ahn-'gohs-toh)*
cripple (framing)	**el refuerzo** *(ehl reh-foo-'ehr-soh)*
crooked	**torcido** *(tohr-'see-doh)*
crossbar	**el travesaño** *(ehl trah-veh-'sah-nyoh)*
crossbeam	**el travesaño** *(ehl trah-veh-'sah-nyoh)*
crossed	**cruzado** *(kroo-'sah-doh)*
crowbar	**la pata de cabra** *(lah 'pah-tah deh 'kah-brah)*
crusher	**la aplastadora** *(lah ah-plahs-tah-'doh-rah)*
cubic	**cúbico** *('koo-bee-koh)*
cultured stone	**la piedra prefabricada** *(lah pee-'eh-drah preh-fah-bree-'kah-dah)*
cup	**la taza** *(lah 'tah-sah)*
curb	**el bordillo** *(ehl bohr-'dee-yoh)*
current	**la corriente** *(lah coh-rree-'ehn-teh)*
curtains	**las cortinas** *(lahs kohr-'tee-nahs)*
curved	**curvo** *('koor-voh)*
custom	**personalizado** *(pehr-soh-nah-lee-'sah-doh)*
custom-built	**hecho a la orden** *('eh-choh ah lah 'ohr-dehn)*
custom-designed	**diseñado a la orden** *(dee-seh-'nyah-doh ah lah 'ohr-dehn)*
custom-painted	**pintado a la orden** *(peen-'tah-doh ah lah 'ohr-dehn)*
cut (wood)	**la cortada** *(lah kohr-'tah-dah)*
cut yard	**la área para cortar** *(lah 'ah-reh-ah 'pah-rah kohr-'tahr)*
cutters	**las cortadoras/la cizalla** *(lahs kohr-tah-'doh-rahs/lah see-'sah-yah)*
cutting	**el corte** *(ehl 'kohr-teh)*
cutting board	**la tabla para cortar** *(lah 'tah-blah 'pah-rah kohr-'tahr)*
cycle	**el ciclo** *(ehl 'seek-loh)*
cylinder	**el cilindro** *(ehl see-'leen-droh)*
damage	**el daño** *(ehl 'dah-nyoh)*
damaged	**dañado** *(dah-'nyah-doh)*
danger	**el peligro** *(ehl peh-'lee-groh)*
dangerous	**peligroso** *(peh-lee-'groh-soh)*
darby	**la paleta de madera** *(lah pah-'leh-tah deh mah-'deh-rah)*
dark	**oscuro** *(ohs-'koo-roh)*
dead	**muerto** *(moo-'ehr-toh)*
deadbolt	**el pestillo** *(ehl pehs-'tee-yoh)*
debris	**los escombros** *(lohs ehs-'kohm-brohs)*
deck	**la terraza** *(lah teh-'rrah-sah)*
deck (wood)	**el entarimado** *(ehl ehn-tah-ree-'mah-doh)*

decking screws	**los tornillos de terraza** *(lohs tohr-'nee-yohs deh teh-'rrah-sah)*
decolorization	**el descoloramiento** *(ehl dehs-koh-loh-rah-mee-'ehn-toh)*
decorated	**decorado** *(deh-koh-'rah-doh)*
decorative	**decorativo** *(deh-koh-rah-'tee-voh)*
deep	**profundo** *(proh-'foon-doh)*
defective	**defectuoso** *(deh-fehk-too-'oh-soh)*
defroster	**el descongelador** *(ehl dehs-kohn-heh-lah-'dohr)*
degrees	**grados** *('grah-dohs)*
den	**la sala de familia** *(lah 'sah-lah deh fah-'mee-lee-ah)*
density	**la densidad** *(lah dehn-see-'dahd)*
dented	**abollado** *(ah-boh-'yah-doh)*
depth	**la profundidad** *(lah proh-foon-dee-'dahd)*
design	**el diseño** *(ehl dee-'seh-nyoh)*
designer	**el diseñador** *(ehl dee-seh-nyah-'dohr)*
desk	**el escritorio** *(ehl ehs-kree-'toh-ree-oh)*
detector	**el detector** *(ehl deh-tehk-'tohr)*
device	**el dispositivo** *(ehl dees-poh-see-'tee-voh)*
diagnostic	**diagnóstico** *(dee-ahg-'nohs-tee-koh)*
diagonal	**diagonal** *(dee-ah-goh-'nahl)*
dial	**el dial** *(ehl dee-'ahl)*
diameter	**el diámetro** *(ehl dee-'ah-meh-troh)*
diesel	**el diésel** *(ehl dee-'eh-sehl)*
difference	**la diferencia** *(lah dee-feh-'rehn-see-ah)*
different	**diferente** *(dee-feh-'rehn-teh)*
difficult	**difícil** *(dee-'fee-seel)*
digital cable	**el cable digital** *(ehl 'kah-bleh dee-hee-'tahl)*
dimensions	**las dimensiones** *(lahs dee-'mehn-see-'oh-nehs)*
dimmer switch	**el interruptor con regulador/el potenciómetro** *(ehl een-teh-rroop-'tohr kohn reh-goo-lah-'dohr/ehl poh-tehn-see-'oh-meh-troh)*
dining room	**el comedor** *(ehl koh-meh-'dohr)*
diodes	**los diodos** *(lohs dee-'oh-dohs)*
dirt	**la tierra/la suciedad** *(lah tee-'eh-rrah/lah soo-see-eh-'dahd)*
dirty	**sucio** *('soo-see-oh)*
dishwasher	**el lavaplatos** *(ehl lah-vah-'plah-tohs)*
distance	**la distancia** *(lah dees-'tahn-see-ah)*
distribution board	**el tablero auxiliar** *(ehl tah-'bleh-roh ah-oo-ksee-lee-'ahr)*
distribution pipe	**la tubería de derivación** *(lah too-beh-'ree-ah deh deh-ree-vah-see-'ohn)*
divider	**el divisor** *(ehl dee-vee-'sohr)*
doctor	**el doctor** *(ehl dohk-'tohr)*
dollar	**el dólar** *(ehl 'doh-lahr)*
dolly	**la plataforma con ruedas** *(lah plah-tah-'fohr-mah kohn 'rweh-dahs)*
door	**la puerta** *(lah 'pwehr-tah)*
door hanger	**la colgadora de puertas** *(lah kohl-gah-'doh-rah deh 'pwehr-tahs)*

doorbell	**el timbre** *(ehl 'teem-breh)*
doorknob	**la perilla** *(lah peh-'ree-yah)*
doorway	**el portal** *(ehl pohr-'tahl)*
dormer	**la buhardilla** *(lah boo-hahr-'dee-yah)*
double	**el doble** *(ehl 'doh-bleh)*
double doors	**la doble puerta** *(lah 'doh-bleh 'pwehr-tah)*
double-pane window	**la ventana con doble cristal** *(lah vehn-'tah-nah kohn 'doh-bleh krees-'tahl)*
dowel	**la espiga** *(lah ehs-'pee-gah)*
down	**abajo** *(ah-'bah-hoh)*
downhill	**cuesta abajo** *('kwehs-tah ah-'bah-hoh)*
downspout	**la bajada/el bajante de aguas** *(lah bah-'hah-dah/ehl bah-'hahn-teh deh 'ah-gwahs)*
dozen	**la docena** *(lah doh-'seh-nah)*
drain	**el desagüe/el drenaje** *(ehl deh-'sah-gweh/ehl dreh-'nah-heh)*
drain plug	**el tapón del drenaje** *(ehl tah-'pohn deh dreh-'nah-heh)*
drain waste vent	**la chimenea de ventilación** *(lah chee-meh-'neh-ah deh vehn-tee-lah-see-'ohn)*
drainage	**el drenaje** *(ehl dreh-'nah-heh)*
drainage tank	**el tanque de drenaje** *(ehl 'tahn-keh deh dreh-'nah-heh)*
drainpipe	**el desagüe** *(ehl deh-'sah-gweh)*
draperies	**las colgaduras** *(lahs kohl-gah-'doo-rahs)*
drawer	**el cajón** *(ehl kah-'hohn)*
drawing	**el dibujo** *(ehl dee-'boo-hoh)*
dressing room	**el cuarto de vestir** *(ehl 'kwahr-toh deh vehs-'teer)*
drill	**el taladro** *(ehl tah-'lah-droh)*
driller	**la perforadora/la taladradora** *(lah pehr-foh-rah-'doh-rah/lah tah-lah-drah-'doh-rah)*
drink	**la bebida** *(lah beh-'bee-dah)*
drinking water	**el agua potable** *(ehl 'ah-gwah poh-'tah-bleh)*
drip edge	**el borde de goteo** *(ehl 'bohr-deh deh goh-'teh-oh)*
drip screeds	**las maestras de goteo** *(lahs mah-'ehs-trahs deh goh-'teh-oh)*
drippings	**el goteo/el escurrimiento** *(ehl goh-'teh-oh/ehl ehs-koo-rree-mee-'ehn-toh)*
drive (comp.)	**la disquetera** *(lah dees-keh-'teh-rah)*
driveway	**el camino de entrada para carros** *(ehl kah-'mee-noh deh ehn-'trah-dah 'pah-rah 'kah-rrohs)*
drizzle	**la llovizna** *(lah yoh-'vees-nah)*
drop cloth	**la lona** *(lah 'loh-nah)*
drop light	**el foco de extensión** *(ehl 'foh-koh deh ex-tehn-see-'ohn)*
drum (mech.)	**el rulo** *(ehl 'roo-loh)*
dry	**seco** *('seh-koh)*
dry rot	**la podredumbre seca** *(lah poh-dreh-'doom-breh 'seh-kah)*

dryer	**la secadora** *(lah seh-kah-'doh-rah)*
drywall	**el enyesado** *(ehl ehn-yeh-'sah-doh)*
drywall compound	**la masilla premezclada** *(lah mah-'see-yah preh-mehs-'klah-dah)*
drywall hammer	**el martillo para enyesado** *(ehl mahr-'tee-yoh 'pah-rah ehn-yeh-'sah-doh)*
drywall nails	**los clavos para enyesado** *(lohs 'klah-vohs 'pah-rah ehn-yeh-'sah-doh)*
drywall screws	**los tornillos para enyesado** *(lohs tohr-'nee-yohs 'pah-rah ehn-yeh-'sah-doh)*
drywall spackle	**el relleno/el mastique para el enyesado** *(ehl reh-'yeh-noh/ ehl mahs-'tee-keh 'pah-rah ehl ehn-yeh-'sah-doh)*
drywall tape	**la cinta adhesiva para enyesado** *(lah 'seen-tah ah-deh-'see-vah 'pah-rah ehn-yeh-'sah-doh)*
drywaller	**el yesero** *(ehl yeh-'seh-roh)*
duct	**el conducto** *(ehl kohn-'dook-toh)*
duct tape	**la cinta adhesiva** *(lah 'seen-tah ah-deh-'see-vah)*
dull	**romo** *('roh-moh)*
dump truck	**el camión volquete** *(ehl kah-mee-'ohn vohl-'keh-teh)*
dumpster	**el basurero grande** *(ehl bah-soo-'reh-roh 'grahn-deh)*
durable	**duradero** *(doo-rah-'deh-roh)*
during	**durante** *(doo-'rahn-teh)*
dust	**el polvo** *(ehl 'pohl-voh)*
dustpan	**la pala de recoger basura** *(lah 'pah-lah deh reh-koh-'hehr bah-'soo-rah)*
Dutch door	**la puerta cortada** *(lah 'pwehr-tah kohr-'tah-dah)*
dye	**el tinte** *(ehl 'teen-teh)*
earplugs	**los tapones del oído** *(lohs tah-'poh-nehs dehl oh-'ee-doh)*
early	**temprano** *(tehm-'prah-noh)*
east	**el este** *(ehl 'ehs-teh)*
easy	**fácil** *('fah-seel)*
eaves	**el alero** *(ehl ah-'leh-roh)*
edge	**el borde** *(ehl 'bohr-deh)*
edge trim	**el reborde** *(ehl reh-'bohr-deh)*
edger (gardening)	**la caladora** *(lah kah-lah-'doh-rah)*
edger (masonry)	**la llana para bordes** *(lah 'yah-nah 'pah-rah 'bohr-dehs)*
eggshell (paint)	**semi-mate** *(seh-mee-'mah-teh)*
eighth	**octavo** *(ohk-'tah-voh)*
either	**cualquiera** *(kwahl-kee-'eh-rah)*
elbow	**el codo** *(ehl 'koh-doh)*
elbow pipe	**el codo de cuarenta y cinco grados** *(ehl 'koh-doh deh kwah-'rehn-tah ee 'seen-koh 'grah-dohs)*
electric	**eléctrico** *(eh-'lehk-tree-koh)*
electric cord	**el cable de extensión** *(ehl 'kah-bleh deh ex-tehn-see-'ohn)*

electric drill	**el taladro eléctrico** *(ehl tah-'lah-droh eh-'lehk-tree-koh)*
electric shock	**el choque eléctrico** *(ehl 'choh-keh eh-'lehk-tree-koh)*
electrical outlet	**el enchufe** *(ehl ehn-'choo-feh)*
electrical wiring	**la instalación eléctrica** *(lah eens-tah-lah-see-'ohn eh-'lehk-tree-kah)*
electrician	**el electricista** *(ehl eh-lehk-tree-'sees-tah)*
electrician's tape	**la cinta aislante** *(lah 'seen-tah ah-ees-'lahn-teh)*
electricity	**la electricidad** *(lah eh-lehk-tree-see-'dahd)*
electrode	**el electrodo** *(ehl eh-lehk-'troh-doh)*
electrode holder	**el portaelectrodos** *(ehl pohr-tah-eh-lehk-'troh-dohs)*
electromagnetic	**electromagnético** *(eh-lehk-troh-mahg-'neh-tee-koh)*
electronic	**electrónico** *(eh-lehk-'troh-nee-koh)*
elevation	**la altura** *(lah ahl-'too-rah)*
elevator	**el ascensor** *(ehl ah-sehn-'sohr)*
eleventh	**undécimo** *(oon-'deh-see-moh)*
embedded	**incrustado** *(een-kroos-'tah-doh)*
emery cloth	**la tela de esmeril** *(lah 'teh-lah deh ehs-meh-'reel)*
employee	**el empleado** *(ehl ehm-pleh-'ah-doh)*
employer	**el empresario** *(ehl ehm-preh-'sah-ree-oh)*
empty	**vacío** *(vah-'see-oh)*
EMT pipe	**la tubería de EMT** *(lah too-beh-'ree-ah deh eh 'eh-meh teh)*
enamel	**el esmalte** *(ehl ehs-'mahl-teh)*
end	**el fin** *(ehl feen)*
end pipe	**el tubo de acabado** *(ehl 'too-boh deh ah-kah-'bah-doh)*
energy	**la energía** *(lah eh-nehr-'hee-ah)*
engine	**el motor** *(ehl moh-'tohr)*
engineer	**el ingeniero** *(ehl een-heh-nee-'eh-roh)*
enough	**bastante** *(bahs-'tahn-teh)*
entertainment center	**el centro de entretención** *(ehl 'sehn-troh deh ehn-treh-tehn-see-'ohn)*
entrance	**la entrada** *(lah ehn-'trah-dah)*
entry door	**la puerta de entrada** *(lah 'pwehr-tah deh ehn-'trah-dah)*
environmental	**ambiental** *(ahm-bee-ehn-'tahl)*
epoxy	**la epoxi/la epoxia** *(lah eh-'poh-ksee/lah eh-'poh-ksee-ah)*
equipment	**el equipo** *(ehl eh-'kee-poh)*
erosion	**la erosión** *(lah eh-roh-see-'ohn)*
errand	**el encargo** *(ehl ehn-'kahr-goh)*
European	**europeo** *(eh-oo-roh-'peh-oh)*
even	**nivelado** *(nee-veh-'lah-doh)*
even (equal)	**igual** *(ee-'gwahl)*
everybody	**todos** *('toh-dohs)*
everything	**todo** *('toh-doh)*
everywhere	**por todas partes** *(pohr 'toh-dahs 'pahr-tehs)*
exact	**preciso** *(preh-'see-soh)*

exhaust pipe	**el tubo de escape** *(ehl 'too-boh deh ehs-'kah-peh)*
exhausted	**agotado** *(ah-goh-'tah-doh)*
exit	**la salida** *(lah sah-'lee-dah)*
expansion bolt	**el perno de expansión** *(ehl 'pehr-noh deh ex-pahn-see-'ohn)*
expansive	**expansivo** *(ex-pahn-'see-voh)*
expensive	**caro** *('kah-roh)*
experience	**la experiencia** *(lah ex-peh-ree-'ehn-see-ah)*
explosion	**la explosión** *(lah ex-ploh-see-'ohn)*
explosive	**explosivo** *(ex-ploh-'see-voh)*
exposed	**expuesto** *(ex-'pwehs-toh)*
extension	**la extensión** *(lah ex-tehn-see-'ohn)*
extension clamp	**la abrazadera de extensión** *(lah ah-brah-sah-'deh-rah deh ex-tehn-see-'ohn)*
extension cord	**la extension eléctrica/ el cordón eléctrico** *(lah ex-tehn-see-'ohn eh-'lehk-tree-kah/ehl kohr-'dohn eh-'lehk-tree-koh)*
extension ladder	**la escalera de extensión** *(lah ehs-kah-'leh-rah deh ex-tehn-see-'ohn)*
exterior paint	**la pintura para exteriores** *(lah peen-'too-rah 'pah-rah ex-teh-ree-'oh-rehs)*
fabric	**la tela** *(lah 'teh-lah)*
fabricated	**fabricado** *(fah-bree-'kah-doh)*
factory	**la fábrica** *(lah 'fah-bree-kah)*
fall equipment	**la protección contra caídas** *(lah proh-tehk-see-'ohn 'kohn-trah kah-'ee-dahs)*
fall (season)	**el otoño** *(ehl oh-'toh-nyoh)*
family	**la familia** *(lah fah-'mee-lee-ah)*
fan	**el ventilador** *(ehl vehn-tee-lah-'dohr)*
far	**lejos** *('leh-hohs)*
farm	**la granja** *(lah 'grahn-hah)*
fascia	**la fachada** *(lah fah-'chah-dah)*
fascia board	**la moldura de la fachada** *(lah mohl-'doo-rah deh lah fah-'chah-dah)*
fase	**la fase** *(lah 'fah-seh)*
fast	**rápido** *('rah-pee-doh)*
fastener	**el sujetador** *(ehl soo-heh-tah-'dohr)*
faucet	**el grifo** *(ehl 'gree-foh)*
felt	**el fieltro** *(ehl fee-'ehl-troh)*
female	**la hembra** *(lah 'ehm-brah)*
fence	**la cerca** *(lah 'sehr-kah)*
fertilizer	**el fertilizante** *(ehl fehr-tee-lee-'sahn-teh)*
fever	**la fiebre** *(lah fee-'eh-breh)*
fiber	**la fibra** *(lah 'fee-brah)*
fiberboard	**la tabla de fibra** *(lah 'tah-blah deh 'fee-brah)*
fiberglass	**la fibra de vidrio** *(lah 'fee-brah deh 'vee-dree-oh)*

field	el campo *(ehl 'kahm-poh)*
fifth	quinto *('keen-toh)*
filament	el filamento *(ehl fee-lah-'mehn-toh)*
file	la lima *(lah 'lee-mah)*
filing cabinet	el archivero *(ehl ahr-chee-'veh-roh)*
filled	rellenado *(reh-yeh-'nah-doh)*
filler	la masilla para rellenar *(lah mah-'see-yah 'pah-rah reh-yeh-'nahr)*
filter	el filtro *(ehl 'feel-troh)*
filtered	filtrado *(feel-'trah-doh)*
filtration system	el sistema de filtración *(ehl sees-'teh-mah deh feel-trah-see-'ohn)*
fine	bien *(bee-'ehn)*
finish	el acabado *(ehl ah-kah-'bah-doh)*
finishing coat	la capa/la mano final *(lah 'kah-pah/lah 'mah-noh fee-'nahl)*
finishing nail	el clavo sin cabeza *(ehl 'klah-voh seen kah-'beh-sah)*
finishing trowel	la llana para acabado *(lah 'yah-nah 'pah-rah ah-kah-'bah-doh)*
fire	el incendio *(ehl een-'sehn-dee-oh)*
fire block	el cortafuego *(ehl kohr-tah-'fweh-goh)*
fire department	el departamento de bomberos *(ehl deh-pahr-tah-'mehn-toh deh bohm-'beh-rohs)*
fire-resistant	resistente contra el fuego *(reh-sees-'tehn-teh 'kohn-trah ehl 'fweh-goh)*
firefighter	el bombero *(ehl bohm-'beh-roh)*
fireplace	el fogón *(ehl foh-'gohn)*
fireproof	incombustible *(een-kohm-boos-'tee-bleh)*
fire-rated	resistente al fuego *(reh-sees-'tehn-teh ahl 'fweh-goh)*
first	primero *(pree-'meh-roh)*
fishpond	el estanque para peces *(ehl ehs-'tahn-keh 'pah-rah 'peh-sehs)*
fitting	el acoplamiento/la conexión *(ehl ah-koh-plah-mee-'ehn-toh/lah koh-nehk-see-'ohn)*
fixed	fijo *('fee-hoh)*
fixture	el artefacto *(ehl ahr-teh-'fahk-toh)*
flagpole	el asta de bandera *(ehl 'ahs-tah deh bahn-'deh-rah)*
flagstone	la losa de piedra *(lah 'loh-sah deh pee-'eh-drah)*
flame	la llama *(lah 'yah-mah)*
flammable	inflamable *(een-flah-'mah-bleh)*
flange	el ala *(ehl 'ah-lah)*
flashing	el tapajuntas/el verteaguas *(ehl tah-pah-'hoon-tahs/ehl vehr-teh-'ah-gwahs)*
flashlight	la linterna *(lah leen-'tehr-nah)*
flat	plano/llano *('plah-noh/yah-noh)*
flat (paint)	mate *('mah-teh)*
flatbed truck	el camión plataforma *(ehl kah-mee-'ohn plah-tah-'fohr-mah)*
flex strip	la tira flexible *(lah 'tee-rah flehk-'see-bleh)*

flexible copper	**el cobre flexible** *(ehl 'koh-breh flehk-'see-bleh)*
flexible duct	**el conducto flexible** *(ehl kohn-'dook-toh flehk-'see-bleh)*
float (plumbing)	**el flotador** *(ehl floh-tah-'dohr)*
floating	**flotante** *(floh-'tahn-teh)*
floor	**el piso** *(ehl 'pee-soh)*
floor drain	**el desagüe del piso** *(ehl deh-'sah-gweh dehl 'pee-soh)*
floor joist	**la vigueta del piso** *(lah vee-'geh-tah dehl 'pee-soh)*
floor leveler	**el nivelador de piso** *(ehl nee-veh-lah-'dohr deh 'pee-soh)*
floor tile	**la baldosa/la loseta** *(lah bahl-'doh-sah/lah loh-'seh-tah)*
flooring	**el solado/la instalación del piso** *(ehl soh-'lah-doh/lah eens-tah-lah-see-'ohn dehl 'pee-soh)*
fluorescent	**fluorescente** *(floo-oh-reh-'sehn-teh)*
flow	**el flujo** *(ehl 'floo-hoh)*
flow switch	**el interruptor de flujo** *(ehl een-teh-rroop-'tohr deh 'floo-hoh)*
fluid	**el fluido** *(ehl floo-'ee-doh)*
flush	**a tope/a ras de** *(ah 'toh-peh/ah rahs deh)*
foam	**la espuma** *(lah ehs-'poo-mah)*
fog	**la neblina** *(lah neh-'blee-nah)*
folding	**plegable** *(pleh-'gah-bleh)*
food	**la comida** *(lah koh-'mee-dah)*
foot	**el pie** *(ehl pee-'eh)*
footing	**la zapata/el cimiento** *(lah sah-'pah-tah/ehl see-mee-'ehn-toh)*
for	**para/por** *('pah-rah/pohr)*
force	**la fuerza** *(lah 'fwehr-sah)*
foreman	**el capataz** *(ehl kah-pah-'tahs)*
forest	**el bosque** *(ehl 'bohs-keh)*
forged	**fundido** *(foon-'dee-doh)*
forklift	**la carretilla elevadora/el montacargas** *(lah kah-rreh-'tee-yah eh-leh-vah-'doh-rah/ehl mohn-tah-'kahr-gahs)*
form	**el formulario** *(ehl fohr-moo-'lah-ree-oh)*
form (masonry)	**el molde** *(ehl 'mohl-deh)*
Formica	**la formica** *(lah fohr-'mee-kah)*
forward	**adelante** *(ah-deh-'lahn-teh)*
foundation	**los cimientos** *(lohs see-mee-'ehn-tohs)*
fountain	**la fuente** *(lah 'fwehn-teh)*
fourth	**cuarto** *('kwahr-toh)*
foyer	**el vestíbulo** *(ehl vehs-'tee-boo-loh)*
frame	**el marco** *(ehl 'mahr-koh)*
framed	**enmarcado** *(ehn-mahr-'kah-doh)*
frameless	**sin marco** *(seen 'mahr-koh)*
framework	**el entramado** *(ehl ehn-trah-'mah-doh)*
framing	**el armazón** *(ehl ahr-mah-'sohn)*
framing square	**la escuadra** *(lah ehs-'kwah-drah)*

freezer	**el congelador** *(ehl kohn-heh-lah-'dohr)*
French	**francés** *(frahn-'sehs)*
French door	**la puerta de dos hojas** *(lah 'pwehr-tah deh dohs 'oh-hahs)*
frequency	**la frecuencia** *(lah freh-'kwehn-see-ah)*
friction	**la fricción/el roce** *(lah freek-see-'ohn/ehl 'roh-seh)*
from	**de** *(deh)*
front yard	**el patio delantero** *(ehl 'pah-tee-oh deh-lahn-'teh-roh)*
frost	**la escarcha** *(lah ehs-'kahr-chah)*
frozen	**congelado** *(kohn-heh-'lah-doh)*
fuel	**el combustible** *(ehl kohm-boos-'tee-bleh)*
full	**lleno** *('yeh-noh)*
fumes	**los gases de escape** *(lohs 'gah-sehs deh ehs-'kah-peh)*
function	**la función** *(lah foon-see-'ohn)*
furnace	**el horno** *(ehl 'ohr-noh)*
furniture	**los muebles** *(lohs moo-'eh-blehs)*
furrow	**el surco** *(ehl 'soor-koh)*
fuse	**el fusible** *(ehl foo-'see-bleh)*
fuse box	**la caja de fusibles** *(lah 'kah-hah deh foo-'see-blehs)*
gable	**el aguilón** *(ehl ah-gee-'lohn)*
gallon	**el galón** *(ehl gah-'lohn)*
galvanized	**galvanizado** *(gahl-vah-nee-'sah-doh)*
gambrel	**el techo a la holandesa** *(ehl 'teh-choh ah lah oh-lahn-'deh-sah)*
gap	**el boquete** *(ehl boh-'keh-teh)*
garage	**el garaje** *(ehl gah-'rah-heh)*
garage door	**la puerta del garaje** *(lah 'pwehr-tah dehl gah-'rah-heh)*
garage door opener	**el abridor de garajes** *(ehl ah-bree-'dohr deh gah-'rah-hehs)*
garbage disposal	**el desechador** *(ehl deh-seh-chah-'dohr)*
garden	**el jardín** *(ehl hahr-'deen)*
gas	**el gas** *(ehl gahs)*
gas fireplace	**el fogón de gas** *(ehl foh-'gohn deh gahs)*
gas line	**la línea de gas** *(lah 'lee-neh-ah deh gahs)*
gas meter	**el medidor de gas** *(ehl meh-dee-'dohr deh gahs)*
gas station	**la gasolinera** *(lah gah-soh-lee-'neh-rah)*
gasket	**el empaque** *(ehl ehm-'pah-keh)*
gasoline	**la gasolina** *(lah gah-soh-'lee-nah)*
gate	**el portón** *(ehl pohr-'tohn)*
gauge	**el indicador** *(ehl een-dee-kah-'dohr)*
gazebo	**el quiosco/la pérgola** *(ehl kee-'ohs-koh/lah 'pehr-goh-lah)*
gear	**el engranaje** *(ehl ehn-grah-'nah-heh)*
general contractor	**el contratista principal** *(ehl kohn-trah-'tees-tah preen-see-'pahl)*
girder	**la viga** *(lah 'vee-gah)*
glass	**el vidrio** *(ehl 'vee-dree-oh)*

glass cutter	el **cortavidrios** *(ehl kohr-tah-'vee-dree-ohs)*
glass (drinking)	el **vaso** *(ehl 'vah-soh)*
glossy	**lustroso** *(loos-'troh-soh)*
gloves	los **guantes** *(lohs 'gwahn-tehs)*
glue	el **pegamento/la cola** *(ehl peh-gah-'mehn-toh/lah 'koh-lah)*
Glue-lam beams	las **vigas Glue-lam** *(lahs 'vee-gahs gloo-lahm)*
golden	**dorado** *(doh-'rah-doh)*
good	**bueno** *('bweh-noh)*
grab bars	las **barras de apoyo** *(lahs 'bah-rrahs deh ah-'poh-yoh)*
grade	la **calificación/el grado** *(lah kah-lee-fee-kah-see-'ohn/ehl 'grah-doh)*
graded	**clasificado** *(klah-see-fee-'kah-doh)*
grader	la **niveladora** *(lah nee-veh-lah-'doh-rah)*
grading	la **nivelación** *(lah nee-veh-lah-see-'ohn)*
granite	el **granito** *(ehl grah-'nee-toh)*
graphite	el **grafito** *(ehl grah-'fee-toh)*
grass	el **pasto** *(ehl 'pahs-toh)*
grating	el **enrejado/la rejilla** *(ehl ehn-reh-'hah-doh/lah reh-'hee-yah)*
gravel	la **grava** *(lah 'grah-vah)*
gray	**gris** *(grees)*
grease	la **grasa** *(lah 'grah-sah)*
green	**verde** *('vehr-deh)*
greenhouse	el **invernadero** *(ehl een-vehr-nah-'deh-roh)*
grill	la **reja** *(lah 'reh-hah)*
grinder	la **esmeriladora/la moledora** *(lah ehs-meh-ree-lah-'doh-rah/lah moh-leh-'doh-rah)*
groove	la **ranura** *(lah rah-'noo-rah)*
groover	la **ranuradora** *(lah rah-noo-rah-'doh-rah)*
ground	el **suelo** *(ehl 'sweh-loh)*
ground floor	el **primer piso** *(ehl pree-'mehr 'pee-soh)*
ground wire	el **cable de tierra** *(ehl 'kah-bleh deh tee-'eh-rrah)*
grounded	**puesto a tierra** *('pwehs-toh ah tee-'eh-rrah)*
group	el **grupo** *(ehl 'groo-poh)*
grout	la **lechada** *(lah leh-'chah-dah)*
guardrails	las **barandas** *(lahs bah-'rahn-dahs)*
guest room	el **cuarto de visitas** *(ehl 'kwahr-toh deh vee-'see-tahs)*
guide	la/el **guía** *(lah/ehl 'gee-ah)*
gutter	el **canalón** *(ehl kah-nah-'lohn)*
gypsum	el **yeso** *(ehl 'yeh-soh)*
gypsum board	el **enyesado** *(ehl ehn-yeh-'sah-doh)*
hacksaw	el **serrucho para cortar metal/la sierra de arco** *(ehl seh-'rroo-choh 'pah-rah kohr-'tahr meh-'tahl/lah see-'eh-rrah deh 'ahr-koh)*
hail	el **granizo** *(ehl grah-'nee-soh)*

half	**la mitad** *(lah mee-'tahd)*
half gallon	**el medio galón** *(ehl 'meh-dee-oh gah-'lohn)*
half round	**la media caña** *(lah 'meh-dee-ah 'kah-nyah)*
half-circular	**medio circular** *('meh-dee-oh seer-koo-'lahr)*
hallway	**el pasillo** *(ehl pah-'see-yoh)*
halogen	**halógeno** *(ah-'loh-heh-noh)*
hammer	**el martillo** *(ehl mahr-'tee-yoh)*
hammock	**la hamaca** *(lah ah-'mah-kah)*
hand sander	**la lijadora de mano** *(lah lee-hah-'doh-rah deh 'mah-noh)*
handful	**el puñado** *(ehl poo-'nyah-doh)*
handle	**la manija/la perilla/el mango** *(lah mah-'nee-hah/lah peh-'ree-yah/ehl 'mahn-goh)*
handsaw	**el serrucho** *(ehl seh-'rroo-choh)*
hanger	**el gancho** *(ehl 'gahn-choh)*
hanger rod	**la barra colgante** *(lah 'bah-rrah kohl-'gahn-teh)*
happy	**feliz** *(feh-'lees)*
hard	**duro** *('doo-roh)*
hard drive	**el disco duro** *(ehl 'dees-koh 'doo-roh)*
hard hat	**el casco duro** *(ehl 'kahs-koh 'doo-roh)*
hardware	**el herraje** *(ehl eh-'rrah-heh)*
hardwood	**la madera dura** *(lah mah-'deh-rah 'doo-rah)*
Hardy walls	**los muros Hardy** *(lohs 'moo-rohs 'har-dee)*
harness	**el correaje** *(ehl koh-rreh-'ah-heh)*
hawk (masonry)	**el esparavel** *(ehl ehs-pah-rah-'vehl)*
head	**la cabeza** *(lah kah-'beh-sah)*
head (framing)	**la cabecera** *(lah kah-beh-'seh-rah)*
headache	**el dolor de cabeza** *(ehl doh-'lohr deh kah-'beh-sah)*
heat	**el calor** *(ehl kah-'lohr)*
heater	**el calentador/la calentadora** *(ehl kah-lehn-tah-'dohr/lah kah-lehn-tah-'doh-rah)*
heating	**la calefacción** *(lah kah-leh-fahk-see-'ohn)*
heating elements	**los elementos calefactores** *(lohs eh-leh-'mehn-tohs kah-leh-fahk-'toh-rehs)*
heating gun	**la pistola térmica** *(lah pees-'toh-lah 'tehr-mee-kah)*
heating system	**el sistema de calefacción** *(ehl sees-'teh-mah deh kah-leh-fahk-see-'ohn)*
heavy	**pesado** *(peh-'sah-doh)*
hedge	**el seto** *(ehl 'seh-toh)*
hedge trimmer	**la podadora** *(lah poh-dah-'doh-rah)*
height	**la altura** *(lah ahl-'too-rah)*
helmet	**el casco protector** *(ehl 'kahs-koh proh-tehk-'tohr)*
helper	**el ayudante** *(ehl ah-yoo-'dahn-teh)*
here	**aquí** *(ah-'kee)*

hexagonal	**hexagonal** *(ex-ah-goh-'nahl)*
hidden	**escondido/oculto** *(ehs-kohn-'dee-doh/oh-'kool-toh)*
high	**alto** *('ahl-toh)*
high-rise	**el edificio de muchos pisos** *(ehl eh-dee-'fee-see-oh deh 'moo-chohs 'pee-sohs)*
high tech	**de alta tecnología** *(deh 'ahl-tah tehk-noh-loh-'hee-ah)*
hill	**el cerro** *(ehl 'seh-rroh)*
hinge	**la bisagra** *(lah bee-'sah-grah)*
hinge templates	**las plantillas para bisagras** *(lahs plahn-'tee-yahs 'pah-rah bee-'sah-grahs)*
hip post	**el poste de la lima** *(ehl 'pohs-teh deh lah 'lee-mah)*
hip (roofing)	**la limatesa** *(lah lee-mah-'teh-sah)*
hipped	**de varias aguas** *(deh 'vah-ree-ahs 'ah-gwahs)*
hoe	**el azadón** *(ehl ah-sah-'dohn)*
hoist	**el montacargas** *(ehl mohn-tah-'kahr-gahs)*
hold-down	**el soporte** *(ehl soh-'pohr-teh)*
hole	**el hueco/el hoyo/la abertura** *(ehl 'hweh-koh/ehl 'oh-yoh/lah ah-behr-'too-rah)*
hollow	**hueco** *('hweh-koh)*
home	**la casa/el hogar** *(lah 'kah-sah/ehl oh-'gahr)*
home office	**la oficina en casa** *(lah oh-fee-'see-nah ehn 'kah-sah)*
home theater	**el cine doméstico** *(ehl 'see-neh doh-'mehs-tee-koh)*
hook	**el gancho** *(ehl 'gahn-choh)*
hoop	**el zuncho** *(ehl 'soon-choh)*
horizontal	**horizontal** *(oh-ree-sohn-'tahl)*
hose	**la manguera** *(lah mahn-'geh-rah)*
hospital	**el hospital** *(ehl ohs-pee-'tahl)*
hot	**caliente** *(kah-lee-'ehn-teh)*
hot tub	**el jacuzzi** *(ehl chah-'koo-see)*
hot-water heater	**el calentador para el agua** *(ehl kah-lehn-tah-'dohr 'pah-rah ehl 'ah-gwah)*
hot-water pipe	**el tubo para agua caliente** *(ehl 'too-boh 'pah-rah 'ah-gwah kah-lee-'ehn-teh)*
house	**la casa** *(lah 'kah-sah)*
housing (mech.)	**la cubierta** *(lah koo-bee-'ehr-tah)*
H-style (framing)	**de estilo H** *(deh ehs-'tee-loh 'ah-cheh)*
humidifier	**el humedecedor** *(ehl oo-meh-deh-seh-'dohr)*
hung window	**la ventana de guillotina** *(lah vehn-'tah-nah deh gee-yoh-'tee-nah)*
hurricane	**el huracán** *(ehl oo-rah-'kahn)*
hurt	**herido** *(eh-'ree-doh)*
hydrant	**la boca de agua** *(lah 'boh-kah deh 'ah-gwah)*
hydration	**la hidratación** *(lah ee-drah-tah-see-'ohn)*
hydraulic	**hidráulico** *(ee-'drah-oo-lee-koh)*

I.D.	**la identificación** *(lah ee-dehn-tee-fee-kah-see-'ohn)*
I-beam	**la viga en I** *(lah 'vee-gah ehn ee)*
ice	**el hielo** *(ehl ee-'eh-loh)*
ignitor	**el encendedor** *(ehl ehn-sehn-deh-'dohr)*
ill	**enfermo** *(ehn-'fehr-moh)*
illustration	**la ilustración** *(lah ee-loos-trah-see-'ohn)*
impact wrench	**la llave eléctrica** *(lah 'yah-veh eh-'lehk-tree-kah)*
in	**en** *(ehn)*
in front	**enfrente** *(ehn-'frehn-teh)*
in order	**arreglado/ordenado** *(ah-rreh-'glah-doh/ohr-deh-'nah-doh)*
in series	**en serie** *(ehn 'seh-ree-eh)*
in the middle	**en medio** *(ehn 'meh-dee-oh)*
incandescent	**incandescente** *(een-kahn-deh-'sehn-teh)*
inch	**la pulgada** *(lah pool-'gah-dah)*
inexpensive	**barato** *(bah-'rah-toh)*
inlaid	**incrustado** *(enn-kroos-'tah-doh)*
insecticide	**el insecticida** *(ehl een-sehk-tee-'see-dah)*
insert	**el anclaje** *(ehl ahn-'klah-heh)*
inset	**insertada** *(een-sehr-'tah-dah)*
inside	**adentro** *(ah-'dehn-troh)*
inside out	**al revés** *(ahl reh-'vehs)*
inspection	**la inspección** *(lah eens-pehk-see-'ohn)*
inspector	**el inspector** *(ehl eens-pehk-'tohr)*
installation	**la instalación** *(lah eens-tah-lah-see-'ohn)*
installed	**instalado** *(eens-tah-'lah-doh)*
installer	**el instalador** *(ehl eens-tah-lah-'dohr)*
instant	**inmediato** *(een-meh-dee-'ah-toh)*
insulated	**aislada** *(ah-ees-'lah-dah)*
insulation	**el aislamiento** *(ehl ah-ees-lah-mee-'ehn-toh)*
insulators	**los aisladores** *(lohs ah-ees-lah-'doh-rehs)*
insurance	**el seguro** *(ehl seh-'goo-roh)*
integrated circuits	**los circuitos integrados** *(lohs seer-koo-'ee-tohs een-teh-'grah-dohs)*
intensity	**la intensidad** *(lah een-tehn-see-'dahd)*
interchangeable	**intercambiable** *(een-tehr-kahm-bee-'ah-bleh)*
intercom system	**el sistema de intercomunicación** *(ehl sees-'teh-mah deh een-tehr-koh-moo-nee-kah-see-'ohn)*
interior paint	**la pintura para interiores** *(lah peen-'too-rah 'pah-rah een-teh-ree-'oh-rehs)*
interpreter	**el intérprete** *(ehl een-'tehr-preh-teh)*
interview	**la entrevista** *(lah ehn-treh-'vees-tah)*
interwoven	**entretejidos** *(ehn-treh-teh-'hee-dohs)*
inverted	**invertido** *(een-vehr-'tee-doh)*
invoice	**la factura** *(lah fahk-'too-rah)*

iron	**el hierro** *(ehl ee-'eh-rroh)*
irrigation	**la irrigación** *(lah ee-rree-gah-see-'ohn)*
island workspace	**la isla de trabajo para la cocina** *(lah 'ees-lah deh trah-'bah-hoh 'pah-rah lah koh-'see-nah)*
J bead	**el bordón de J** *(ehl bohr-'dohn deh 'hoh-tah)*
J bolts	**los pernos en J** *(lohs 'pehr-nohs ehn 'hoh-tah)*
jack	**el cabrio corto** *(ehl 'kah-bree-oh 'kohr-toh)*
jack (roofing)	**la rejilla** *(lah reh-'hee-yah)*
jacket	**la chaqueta** *(lah chah-'keh-tah)*
jackhammer	**el martillo neumático** *(ehl mahr-'tee-yoh neh-oo-'mah-tee-koh)*
Jacuzzi	**el jacuzzi** *(ehl chah-'koo-see)*
jamb	**la jamba** *(lah 'hahm-bah)*
jar	**la jarra** *(lah 'hah-rrah)*
jigsaw	**la sierra de vaivén** *(lah see-'eh-rrah deh vah-ee-'vehn)*
job	**el trabajo** *(ehl trah-'bah-hoh)*
joint	**la unión/la junta** *(lah oo-nee-'ohn/lah 'hoon-tah)*
joint compound	**la pasta para las uniones** *(lah 'pahs-tah 'pah-rah lahs oo-nee-'oh-nehs)*
joint (plumbing)	**el codo** *(ehl 'koh-doh)*
jointer	**el marcador de juntas** *(ehl mahr-kah-'dohr deh 'hoon-tahs)*
joist	**la vigueta** *(lah vee-'geh-tah)*
journeyman	**el rutinero/el alquiladizo** *(ehl roo-tee-'neh-roh/ehl ahl-kee-lah-'dee-soh)*
key	**la llave** *(lah 'yah-veh)*
keyboard	**el teclado** *(ehl tehk-'lah-doh)*
keyhole saw	**el serrucho de calar** *(ehl seh-'rroo-choh deh kah-'lahr)*
kit	**el conjunto** *(ehl kohn-'hoon-toh)*
kitchen	**la cocina** *(lah koh-'see-nah)*
kitchen cabinets	**los gabinetes para la cocina** *(lohs gah-bee-'neh-tehs 'pah-rah lah koh-'see-nah)*
kitchen sink	**el fregadero** *(ehl freh-gah-'deh-roh)*
kneepads	**las rodilleras** *(lahs roh-dee-'yeh-rahs)*
knife	**la navaja** *(lah nah-'vah-hah)*
knob	**el botón** *(ehl boh-'tohn)*
knots	**los nudos** *(lohs 'noo-dohs)*
L-bead	**el bordón de L** *(ehl bohr-'dohn deh 'eh-leh)*
laborer	**el obrero** *(ehl oh-'breh-roh)*
lacquer	**la laca** *(lah 'lah-kah)*
ladder	**la escalera** *(lah ehs-kah-'leh-rah)*
lag bolt	**el tirafondo** *(ehl tee-rah-'fohn-doh)*

lake	**el lago** *(ehl 'lah-goh)*
laminate	**la lámina** *(lah 'lah-mee-nah)*
laminated	**laminado** *(lah-mee-'nah-doh)*
lamp	**la lámpara** *(lah 'lahm-pah-rah)*
lampshade	**la pantalla** *(lah pahn-'tah-yah)*
land	**el terreno** *(ehl teh-'rreh-noh)*
landfill	**el terreno suelto** *(ehl teh-'rreh-noh 'swehl-toh)*
landing (stairs)	**el descanso** *(ehl dehs-'kahn-soh)*
landscaper	**el diseñador de jardines** *(ehl dee-seh-nyah-'dohr deh har-'dee-nehs)*
landscaping	**el diseño de jardines** *(ehl dee-'seh-nyoh deh har-'dee-nehs)*
large	**grande** *('grahn-deh)*
large board	**el tablón** *(ehl tah-'blohn)*
laser	**el láser** *(ehl 'lah-sehr)*
latch	**el cerrojo** *(ehl seh-'rroh-hoh)*
late	**tarde** *('tahr-deh)*
later	**luego** *('lweh-goh)*
latex	**el látex** *(ehl 'lah-tehks)*
lathing	**el listón** *(ehl lees-'tohn)*
laundry room	**la lavandería** *(lah lah-vahn-deh-'ree-ah)*
law	**la ley** *(lah 'leh-ee)*
lawn	**el césped** *(ehl 'sehs-pehd)*
lawnmower	**la cortadora de césped** *(lah kohr-tah-'doh-rah deh 'sehs-pehd)*
lawyer	**el abogado** *(ehl ah-boh-'gah-doh)*
layout	**el diseño/el trazado** *(ehl dee-'seh-nyoh/ehl trah-'sah-doh)*
lazy Susan	**la bandeja giratoria** *(lah bahn-'deh-hah hee-rah-'toh-ree-ah)*
lead	**el plomo** *(ehl 'ploh-moh)*
lead-free	**sin plomo** *(seen 'ploh-moh)*
lead line	**el cable de conexión** *(ehl 'kah-bleh deh koh-nehk-see-'ohn)*
lead man	**el líder** *(ehl 'lee-dehr)*
leak	**la gotera/la fuga** *(lah goh-'teh-rah/lah 'foo-gah)*
leak (gas)	**el escape** *(ehl ehs-'kah-peh)*
leakproof	**estanco** *(ehs-'tahn-koh)*
leather	**el cuero** *(ehl 'kweh-roh)*
leaves	**las hojas** *(lahs 'oh-hahs)*
ledger board	**el larguero** *(ehl lahr-'geh-roh)*
left	**la izquierda** *(lah ees-kee-'ehr-dah)*
length	**el largo** *(ehl 'lahr-goh)*
lens	**el lente** *(ehl 'lehn-teh)*
level (floor)	**llano** *('yah-noh)*
level (height)	**nivelado** *(nee-veh-'lah-doh)*
level (tool)	**el nivel** *(ehl nee-'vehl)*
lever	**la palanca** *(lah pah-'lahn-kah)*

license	**la licencia** *(lah lee-'sehn-see-ah)*
lid	**la tapa** *(lah 'tah-pah)*
light (color)	**ligero** *(lee-'heh-roh)*
light (elect.)	**la luz** *(lah loos)*
light (weight)	**ligero/liviano** *(lee-'heh-roh/lee-vee-'ah-noh)*
light post (fixture)	**el farol** *(ehl fah-'rohl)*
light switch	**el interruptor** *(ehl een-teh-rroop-'tohr)*
lighting	**la iluminación** *(lah ee-loo-mee-nah-see-'ohn)*
lime	**la cal** *(lah kahl)*
limestone	**la piedra caliza** *(lah pee-'eh-drah kah-'lee-sah)*
line	**la línea** *(lah 'lee-neh-ah)*
linear feet	**los pies lineales** *(lohs pee-'ehs lee-neh-'ah-lehs)*
lined up	**arreglados/en fila** *(ah-rreh-'glah-dohs/ehn 'fee-lah)*
liner	**el revestimiento/el encofrado** *(ehl reh-vehs-tee-mee-'ehn-toh/ehl ehn-koh-'frah-doh)*
lining	**el forro** *(ehl 'foh-rroh)*
linoleum	**el linóleo** *(ehl lee-'noh-leh-oh)*
lintel	**el dintel** *(ehl deen-'tehl)*
liquid	**el líquido** *(ehl 'lee-kee-doh)*
live (elec.)	**activa** *(ahk-'tee-vah)*
living room	**la sala** *(lah 'sah-lah)*
load	**la carga** *(lah 'kahr-gah)*
loader	**la cargadora** *(lah kahr-gah-'doh-rah)*
lock	**la cerradura** *(lah seh-rrah-'doo-rah)*
lock casing	**la caja del pestillo** *(lah 'kah-hah dehl pehs-'tee-yoh)*
lock mortiser	**la embutidora de cerraduras** *(lah ehm-boo-tee-'doh-rah deh seh-rrah-'doo-rahs)*
lock nut	**la tuerca de seguridad** *(lah 'twehr-kah deh seh-goo-ree-'dahd)*
locksmith	**el cerrajero** *(ehl seh-rrah-'heh-roh)*
loft	**el desván** *(ehl dehs-'vahn)*
long	**largo** *('lahr-goh)*
long beam	**el larguero** *(ehl lahr-'geh-roh)*
loop	**el lazo** *(ehl 'lah-soh)*
loose	**flojo/suelto** *('floh-hoh/'swehl-toh)*
lot	**el lote** *(ehl 'loh-teh)*
loud	**ruidoso** *(roo-ee-'doh-soh)*
louvers	**las persianas** *(lahs pehr-see-'ah-nahs)*
low	**bajo** *('bah-hoh)*
lubricant	**el lubricante** *(ehl loo-bree-'kahn-teh)*
lumber	**la madera** *(lah mah-'deh-rah)*
luminescent	**luminiscente** *(loo-mee-nee-'sehn-teh)*
lunch	**el almuerzo** *(ehl ahl-'mwehr-soh)*

machine operator	**el maquinista** *(ehl mah-kee-'nees-tah)*
machinery	**la maquinaria** *(lah mah-kee-'nah-ree-ah)*
magnesium	**el magnesio** *(ehl mahg-'neh-see-oh)*
magnet	**el imán** *(ehl ee-'mahn)*
magnetic	**magnético** *(mahg-'neh-tee-koh)*
mahogany	**la caoba** *(lah kah-'oh-bah)*
mail slot	**la placa del buzón** *(lah 'plah-kah dehl boo-'sohn)*
mailbox	**el buzón** *(ehl boo-'sohn)*
main beam	**la viga maestra** *(lah 'vee-gah mah-'ehs-trah)*
main line	**la línea principal** *(lah 'lee-neh-ah preen-see-'pahl)*
main power switch	**el interruptor principal** *(ehl een-teh-rroop-'tohr preen-see-'pahl)*
make (brand)	**la marca** *(lah 'mahr-kah)*
male	**el macho** *(ehl 'mah-choh)*
malfunction	**el mal funcionamiento** *(ehl mahl foon-see-oh-nah-mee-'ehn-toh)*
mallet	**el mazo** *(ehl 'mah-soh)*
manager	**el gerente** *(ehl heh-'rehn-teh)*
manhole	**la boca del alcantarillado** *(lah 'boh-kah dehl ahl-kahn-tah-ree-'yah-doh)*
mansard	**la mansarda** *(lah mahn-'sahr-dah)*
mantelpiece	**la repisa de la chimenea** *(lah reh-'pee-sah deh lah chee-meh-'neh-ah)*
marble	**el mármol** *(ehl 'mahr-mohl)*
mark	**la marca** *(lah 'mahr-kah)*
marker	**el marcador** *(ehl mahr-kah-'dohr)*
mask	**la máscara** *(lah 'mahs-kah-rah)*
masking tape	**la cinta adhesiva** *(lah 'seen-tah ah-deh-'see-vah)*
mason	**el albañil** *(ehl ahl-bah-'neel)*
mason's trowel	**la llana de madera** *(lah 'yah-nah deh mah-'deh-rah)*
masonry	**la mampostería** *(lah mahm-pohs-teh-'ree-ah)*
masonary nails	**los clavos de mampostería** *(lohs 'klah-vohs deh mahm-pohs-teh-'ree-ah)*
masonry saw	**la sierra de mampostería** *(lah see-'eh-rrah deh mahm-pohs-teh-'ree-ah)*
masonry tile	**el ladrillo cerámico** *(ehl lah-'dree-yoh seh-'rah-mee-koh)*
mastic	**el mastique** *(ehl mahs-'tee-keh)*
mat	**el tapete** *(ehl tah-'peh-teh)*
material (cloth)	**la tela** *(lah 'teh-lah)*
matting	**la superficie mate** *(lah soo-pehr-'fee-see-eh 'mah-teh)*
MDF	**la madera sintética** *(lah mah-'deh-rah seen-'teh-tee-kah)*
measurement	**la medida** *(lah meh-'dee-dah)*
measuring tape	**la cinta métrica** *(lah 'seen-tah 'meh-tree-kah)*
mechanic	**el mecánico** *(ehl meh-'kah-nee-koh)*
medicine cabinet	**el botiquín** *(ehl boh-tee-'keen)*
medium	**mediano** *(meh-dee-'ah-noh)*

membrane	**la membrana** *(lah mehm-'brah-nah)*
mesh	**la malla** *(lah 'mah-yah)*
metal	**el metal** *(ehl meh-'tahl)*
metallic	**metálico** *(meh-'tah-lee-koh)*
meter	**el medidor** *(ehl meh-dee-'dohr)*
metric	**métrico** *('meh-tree-koh)*
microphone	**el micrófono** *(ehl mee-'kroh-foh-noh)*
microprocessors	**los microprocesadores** *(lohs mee-kroh-proh-seh-sah-'doh-rehs)*
microwave	**el horno de microonda** *(ehl 'ohr-noh deh mee-kroh-'ohn-dah)*
middle	**el centro/el medio** *(ehl 'sehn-troh/ehl 'meh-dee-oh)*
mile	**la milla** *(lah 'mee-yah)*
mineral spirit	**el solvente** *(ehl sohl-'vehn-teh)*
mirror	**el espejo** *(ehl ehs-'peh-hoh)*
missing	**perdido** *(pehr-'dee-doh)*
miter box	**la caja de ángulos** *(lah 'kah-hah deh 'ahn-goo-lohs)*
miter saw	**la sierra de cortar en ángulos** *(lah see-'eh-rrah deh kohr-'tahr ehn 'ahn-goo-lohs)*
mixer	**la mezcladora** *(lah mehs-klah-'doh-rah)*
mixture	**la mezcla** *(lah 'mehs-klah)*
model	**el modelo** *(ehl moh-'deh-loh)*
moist	**húmedo** *('oo-meh-doh)*
moisture	**la humedad** *(lah oo-meh-'dahd)*
moisture barrier	**la barrera contra humedad** *(lah bah-'rreh-rah 'kohn-trah oo-meh-'dahd)*
mold	**el moho** *(ehl 'moh-hoh)*
mold (masonry)	**el molde** *(ehl 'mohl-deh)*
molding	**el encofrado/la moldura** *(ehl ehn-koh-'frah-doh/lah mohl-'doo-rah)*
monitor	**el monitor** *(ehl moh-nee-'tohr)*
mop	**el trapeador** *(ehl trah-peh-ah-'dohr)*
mortar	**la argamasa** *(lah ahr-gah-'mah-sah)*
mortise (carp.)	**la mortaja** *(lah mohr-'tah-hah)*
mortise and tenon	**la caja y espiga** *(lah 'kah-hah ee ehs-'pee-gah)*
mortise gauge	**el gramil para mortajas** *(ehl grah-'meel 'pah-rah mohr-'tah-hahs)*
mortise lock	**la cerradura embutida** *(lah seh-rrah-'doo-rah ehm-boo-'tee-dah)*
mortising chisel	**el formón** *(ehl fohr-'mohn)*
mosaic	**el mosaico** *(ehl moh-'sah-ee-koh)*
most	**la mayor parte** *(lah mah-'yohr 'pahr-teh)*
motor	**el motor** *(ehl moh-'tohr)*
mountain	**la montaña** *(lah mohn-'tah-nyah)*
mounting	**el montaje** *(ehl mohn-'tah-heh)*
mounting screw	**el tornillo de fijación** *(ehl tohr-'nee-yoh deh fee-hah-see-'ohn)*
movement	**el movimiento** *(ehl moh-vee-mee-'ehn-toh)*
mud	**el barro/ el lodo** *(ehl 'bah-rroh/ehl 'loh-doh)*

mulch	**el esteriécol con paja** *(ehl ehs-tee-'ehr-kohl kohn 'pah-hah)*
mullion	**el montante** *(ehl mohn-'tahn-teh)*
multifold door	**la puerta de acordeón** *(lah 'pwehr-tah deh ah-kohr-deh-'ohn)*
nail	**el clavo** *(ehl 'klah-voh)*
nail gun	**la clavadora neumática** *(lah klah-vah-'doh-rah neh-oo-'mah-tee-kah)*
nail puller	**el sacaclavos** *(ehl sah-kah-'klah-vohs)*
nailer	**la clavadora** *(lah klah-vah-'doh-rah)*
narrow	**estrecho** *(ehs-'treh-choh)*
natural gas	**el gas natural** *(ehl gahs nah-too-'rahl)*
natural stone	**la piedra natural** *(lah pee-'eh-drah nah-too-'rahl)*
near	**cerca** *('sehr-kah)*
neck	**el cuello** *(ehl 'kweh-yoh)*
needle	**la aguja** *(lah ah-'goo-hah)*
needle-nose pliers	**los alicates de punta** *(lohs ah-lee-'kah-tehs deh 'poon-tah)*
negative	**negativo** *(neh-gah-'tee-voh)*
neither	**ninguno** *(neen-'goo-noh)*
neon	**neón** *(neh-'ohn)*
never	**nunca** *('noon-kah)*
new	**nuevo** *('nweh-voh)*
next to	**al lado de** *(ahl 'lah-doh deh)*
nickel	**el níquel** *(ehl 'nee-kehl)*
ninth	**noveno** *(noh-'veh-noh)*
nipple	**el niple** *(ehl 'nee-pleh)*
no one	**nadie** *('nah-dee-eh)*
noise	**ruido** *(roo-'ee-doh)*
noise-resistant	**insonorizado** *(een-soh-noh-ree-'sah-doh)*
none	**ninguno** *(neen-'goo-noh)*
north	**el norte** *(ehl nohr-teh)*
not bad	**así-así** *(ah-'see ah-'see)*
not well	**mal** *(mahl)*
notched	**dentado** *(dehn-'tah-doh)*
nothing	**nada** *('nah-dah)*
nowhere	**en ningún sitio** *(ehn neen-'goon 'see-tee-oh)*
nozzle	**la boquilla/el pitón** *(lah boh-'kee-yah/ehl pee-'tohn)*
number	**el número** *(ehl 'noo-meh-roh)*
nursery	**el cuarto de los niños** *(ehl 'kwahr-toh deh lohs 'nee-nyohs)*
nursery (gardening)	**el vivero** *(ehl vee-'veh-roh)*
nut	**la tuerca** *(lah 'twehr-kah)*
octagonal	**octagonal** *(ohk-tah-goh-'nahl)*
of	**de** *(deh)*
office	**la oficina** *(lah oh-fee-'see-nah)*

offset	**con saliente** *(kohn sah-lee-'ehn-teh)*
oil	**el aceite** *(ehl ah-'seh-ee-teh)*
oil-based paint	**la pintura al aceite** *(lah peen-'too-rah ahl ah-'seh-ee-teh)*
OK	**regular** *(reh-goo-'lahr)*
old	**viejo** *(vee-'eh-hoh)*
on	**en** *(ehn)*
on grade	**a nivel** *(ah nee-'vehl)*
only	**solamente** *('soh-lah-'mehn-teh)*
opaque	**opaco** *(oh-'pah-koh)*
open	**abierto** *(ah-bee-'ehr-toh)*
opener	**el abrepuerta automático** *(ehl ah-breh-'pwehr-tah ah-oo-toh-'mah-tee-koh)*
opening	**la abertura** *(lah ah-behr-'too-rah)*
operator	**el operario/el operador** *(ehl oh-peh-'rah-ree-oh/ehl oh-peh-rah-'dohr)*
optic	**óptico** *('ohp-tee-koh)*
or	**o** *(oh)*
orange (color)	**anaranjado** *(ah-nah-rahn-'hah-doh)*
order	**la orden** *(lah 'ohr-dehn)*
OSB board	**la tabla OSB** *(lah 'tah-blah oh 'eh-seh beh)*
ounce	**la onza** *(lah 'ohn-sah)*
outdoor lighting	**la iluminación al aire libre** *(lah ee-loo-mee-nah-see-'ohn ahl 'ah-ee-reh 'lee-breh)*
outlet	**el tomacorriente/el enchufe** *(ehl toh-mah-koh-rree-'ehn-teh/ehl ehn-'choo-feh)*
outside	**afuera** *(ah-foo-'eh-rah)*
oven	**el horno** *(ehl 'ohr-noh)*
over	**sobre** *('soh-breh)*
over there	**allá** *(ah-'yah)*
overflow	**el rebosadero** *(ehl reh-boh-sah-'deh-roh)*
overhang	**el voladizo** *(ehl voh-lah-'dee-soh)*
overlapping	**sobrepuesto** *(soh-breh-'pwehs-toh)*
owner	**el dueño** *(ehl 'dweh-nyoh)*
oxygen	**el oxígeno** *(ehl ohk-'see-heh-noh)*
package	**el paquete** *(ehl pah-'keh-teh)*
packet	**la bolsita** *(lah bohl-'see-tah)*
pad	**la losa/la plataforma** *(lah 'loh-sah/lah plah-tah-'fohr-mah)*
padding	**el relleno** *(ehl reh-'yeh-noh)*
paint	**la pintura** *(lah peen-'too-rah)*
paint brush	**la brocha de pintar** *(lah 'broh-chah deh peen-'tahr)*
paint sprayer	**la pistola pintadora/la pintadora neumática** *(lah pees-'toh-lah peen-tah-'doh-rah/lah peen-tah-'doh-rah neh-oo-'mah-tee-kah)*
painted	**pintado** *(peen-'tah-doh)*

painter	**el pintor** *(ehl peen-'tohr)*
pallet	**la plataforma** *(lah plah-tah-'fohr-mah)*
pan	**el plato** *(ehl 'plah-toh)*
pane glass	**la hoja de vidrio** *(lah 'oh-hah deh 'vee-dree-oh)*
panel	**el panel** *(ehl pah-'nehl)*
paneling	**el empanelado** *(ehl ehm-pah-neh-'lah-doh)*
pantry cupboard	**el armario de la despensa** *(ehl ahr-'mah-ree-oh deh lah dehs-'pehn-sah)*
paperwork	**el papeleo** *(ehl pah-peh-'leh-oh)*
parallel	**paralelo** *(pah-rah-'leh-loh)*
paramedic	**el paramédico** *(ehl pah-rah-'meh-dee-koh)*
park	**el parque** *(ehl 'pahr-keh)*
parking lot	**el estacionamiento** *(ehl ehs-tah-see-oh-nah-mee-'ehn-toh)*
parquet	**el parqué** *(ehl pahr-'keh)*
part	**la parte/la pieza** *(lah 'pahr-teh/lah pee-'eh-sah)*
partial	**parcial** *(pahr-see-'ahl)*
particle board	**la madera aglomerada** *(lah mah-'deh-rah ah-gloh-meh-'rah-dah)*
partition	**el tabique** *(ehl tah-'bee-keh)*
paste	**la pasta** *(lah 'pahs-tah)*
patch	**el parche/el remiendo** *(ehl 'pahr-cheh/ehl reh-mee-'ehn-doh)*
path	**el sendero** *(ehl sehn-'deh-roh)*
patio	**el patio** *(ehl 'pah-tee-oh)*
pattern	**el patrón** *(ehl pah-'trohn)*
pavement	**el pavimento** *(ehl pah-vee-'mehn-toh)*
pay	**el pago** *(ehl 'pah-goh)*
pebbles	**los guijarros** *(lohs gee-'hah-rrohs)*
pedestal	**el pedestal** *(ehl peh-dehs-'tahl)*
peg	**la clavija** *(lah klah-'vee-hah)*
pegboard	**el tablero de clavijas** *(ehl tah-'bleh-roh deh klah-'vee-hahs)*
pencil	**el lápiz** *(ehl 'lah-pees)*
percentage	**el porcentaje** *(ehl pohr-sehn-'tah-heh)*
perforated	**perforado** *(pehr-foh-'rah-doh)*
permanent	**permanente** *(pehr-mah-'nehn-teh)*
pewter	**el peltre** *(ehl 'pehl-treh)*
Phillips head	**el destornillador en cruz** *(ehl dehs-tohr-nee-yah-'dohr ehn kroos)*
phone lines	**las líneas del teléfono** *(lahs 'lee-neh-ahs dehl teh-'leh-foh-noh)*
photo	**la foto** *(lah 'foh-toh)*
pick	**el pico** *(ehl 'pee-koh)*
pick-up truck	**la camioneta** *(lah kah-mee-oh-'neh-tah)*
picture	**el cuadro/la pintura** *(ehl 'kwah-droh/lah peen-'too-rah)*
piece	**el pedazo** *(ehl peh-'dah-soh)*
piece (mech.)	**la pieza** *(lah pee-'eh-sah)*
pigment	**el pigmento** *(ehl peeg-'mehn-toh)*

pilaster	**la pilastra** *(lah pee-'lahs-trah)*
pile	**el montón/la pila** *(ehl mohn-'tohn/lah 'pee-lah)*
pile driver	**el vibrador hidráulico** *(ehl vee-brah-'dohr ee-'drah-oo-lee-koh)*
pillar	**el pilar** *(ehl pee-'lahr)*
pilon	**la columna** *(lah koh-'loom-nah)*
pin (mech.)	**la clavija** *(lah klah-'vee-hah)*
pincers	**las tenazas** *(lahs teh-'nah-sahs)*
pink	**rosado** *(roh-'sah-doh)*
pint	**la pinta** *(lah 'peen-tah)*
pipe	**el tubo/la cañería** *(ehl 'too-boh/lah kah-nyeh-'ree-ah)*
pipe cutters	**el cortatubos** *(ehl kohr-tah-'too-bohs)*
pipe vise	**el prensatubos** *(ehl prehn-sah-'too-bohs)*
pipe wrench	**la llave para tubos** *(lah 'yah-veh 'pah-rah 'too-bohs)*
piston	**el émbolo** *(ehl 'ehm-boh-loh)*
pit	**el foso/el pozo** *(ehl 'foh-soh/ehl 'poh-soh)*
pitched	**inclinado** *(een-klee-'nah-doh)*
pivot	**el pivote** *(ehl pee-'voh-teh)*
place	**el lugar** *(ehl loo-'gahr)*
plan	**el plano** *(ehl 'plah-noh)*
plane (carpentry)	**el cepillo de mano** *(ehl seh-'pee-yoh deh 'mah-noh)*
plank	**el tablón** *(ehl tah-'blohn)*
plant	**la planta** *(lah 'plahn-tah)*
plantation shutters	**las persianas de plantación** *(lahs pehr-see-'ah-nahs deh plahn-tah-see-'ohn)*
plaster	**el yeso** *(ehl 'yeh-soh)*
plasterboard	**el enyesado** *(ehl ehn-yeh-'sah-doh)*
plastic	**el plástico** *(ehl 'plahs-tee-koh)*
plates (framing)	**las placas** *(lahs 'plah-kahs)*
playroom	**la sala de juegos** *(lah 'sah-lah deh 'hweh-gohs)*
plenty	**bastante** *(bahs-'tahn-teh)*
pliers	**los alicates** *(lohs ah-lee-'kah-tehs)*
plot	**la parcela** *(lah pahr-'seh-lah)*
plug (elec.)	**el enchufe** *(ehl ehn-'choo-feh)*
plug (plumbing)	**la espiga** *(lah ehs-'pee-gah)*
plumb	**vertical/recto** *(vehr-tee-'kahl/rehk-toh)*
plumb bob	**la plomada** *(lah ploh-'mah-dah)*
plumb line	**el hilo de la plomada** *(ehl 'ee-loh deh lah ploh-'mah-dah)*
plumber	**el fontanero/el plomero/el gásfiter** *(ehl fohn-tah-'neh-roh/ehl ploh-'meh-roh/ehl 'gahs-fee-tehr)*
plumber's tape	**la cinta aislante** *(lah 'seen-tah ah-ees-'lahn-teh)*
plumbing	**la fontanería/la cañería/la plomería** *(lah fohn-tah-neh-'ree-ah/lah kah-nyeh-'ree-ah/lah ploh-meh-'ree-ah)*

plywood	**el contrachapado/el aglomerado** *(ehl kohn-trah-chah-'pah-doh/ehl ah-gloh-meh-'rah-doh)*
pneumatic	**neumático** *(neh-oo-'mah-tee-koh)*
pneumatic nailer	**la clavadora neumática** *(lah klah-vah-'doh-rah neh-oo-'mah-tee-kah)*
pointed	**puntiagudo/afilado** *(poon-tee-ah-'goo-doh/ah-fee-'lah-doh)*
polarity	**la polaridad** *(lah poh-lah-ree-'dahd)*
police force	**la policía** *(lah poh-lee-'see-ah)*
police officer	**el policía** *(ehl poh-lee-'see-ah)*
police station	**la estación de policía** *(lah ehs-tah-see-'ohn deh poh-lee-'see-ah)*
polished	**pulido** *(poo-'lee-doh)*
pollution	**la contaminación** *(lah kohn-tah-mee-nah-see-'ohn)*
polymer	**el polímero** *(ehl poh-'lee-meh-roh)*
polystyrene	**el poliestireno** *(ehl poh-lee-ehs-tee-'reh-noh)*
polyurethane	**el poliuretano** *(ehl poh-lee-oo-reh-'tah-noh)*
pond	**la charca** *(lah 'chahr-kah)*
pool	**la piscina/la aberca** *(lah pee-'see-nah/lah ahl-'behr-kah)*
poor	**pobre** *('poh-breh)*
porcelain	**la porcelana** *(lah pohr-seh-'lah-nah)*
porch	**el pórtico/el portal** *(ehl 'pohr-tee-koh/ehl pohr-'tahl)*
porous	**poroso** *(poh-'roh-soh)*
portable	**portátil** *(pohr-'tah-teel)*
Porta-potty	**el retrete portátil** *(ehl reh-'treh-teh pohr-'tah-teel)*
position	**la posición** *(lah poh-see-see-'ohn)*
positive	**positivo** *(poh-see-'tee-voh)*
post	**el poste** *(ehl 'pohs-teh)*
post digger	**la excavadora para postes** *(lah ex-kah-vah-'doh-rah 'pah-rah 'pohs-tehs)*
post office	**el correo** *(ehl koh-'rreh-oh)*
pottery	**la alfarería** *(lah ahl-fah-reh-'ree-ah)*
pound	**la libra** *(lah 'lee-brah)*
powder	**el polvo** *(ehl 'pohl-voh)*
power	**el poder** *(ehl poh-'dehr)*
power drill	**el taladro eléctrico** *(ehl tah-'lah-droh eh-'lehk-tree-koh)*
power (elec.)	**la potencia** *(lah poh-'tehn-see-ah)*
power lines	**los cables del tendido eléctrico** *(lohs 'kah-blehs dehl tehn-'dee-doh eh-'lehk-tree-koh)*
power shovel	**la pala motorizada** *(lah 'pah-lah moh-toh-ree-'sah-dah)*
precast	**premoldado/prevaciado/preformado** *(preh-mohl-'dah-doh/preh-vah-see-'ah-doh/preh-fohr-'mah-doh)*
precaution	**la precaución** *(lah preh-kah-oo-see-'ohn)*
precut	**precortado** *(preh-kohr-'tah-doh)*
prefabricated	**prefabricado** *(preh-fah-bree-'kah-doh)*
pre-hung door	**la puerta prefabricada** *(lah 'pwehr-tah preh-fah-bree-'kah-dah)*

pressed wood	**la madera prensada** *(lah mah-'deh-rah prehn-'sah-dah)*
pressure	**la presión** *(lah preh-see-'ohn)*
pressurized	**presurizado** *(preh-soo-ree-'sah-doh)*
pretty	**bonito** *(boh-'nee-toh)*
prevention	**la prevención** *(lah preh-vehn-see-'ohn)*
printer	**el impresor/la impresora** *(ehl eem-preh-'sohr/lah eem-preh-'soh-rah)*
probe	**la sonda** *(lah 'sohn-dah)*
processors	**los procesadores** *(lohs proh-seh-sah-'doh-rehs)*
program	**el programa** *(ehl proh-'grah-mah)*
programmed	**programado** *(proh-grah-'mah-doh)*
project	**el proyecto** *(ehl proh-'yehk-toh)*
project manager	**el gerente del trabajo** *(ehl heh-'rehn-teh dehl trah-'bah-hoh)*
propane	**el propano** *(ehl proh-'pah-noh)*
property	**la propiedad** *(lah proh-pee-eh-'dahd)*
protected	**protegido** *(proh-teh-'hee-doh)*
pruners	**el cortador de ramas** *(ehl kohr-tah-'dohr deh 'rah-mahs)*
pry bar	**la pata de cabra** *(lah 'pah-tah deh 'kah-brah)*
PSL beam	**la viga PSL** *(lah 'vee-gah peh 'eh-seh 'eh-leh)*
P-trap	**el sifón tipo P** *(ehl see-'fohn 'tee-poh peh)*
puddles	**los charcos** *(lohs 'chahr-kohs)*
pull	**el tirador** *(ehl tee-rah-'dohr)*
pulley	**la polea** *(lah poh-'leh-ah)*
pullout trash container	**el bote de basura extraíble** *(ehl 'boh-teh deh bah-'soo-rah ex-trah-'ee-bleh)*
pump	**la bomba** *(lah 'bohm-bah)*
purifier	**el purificador** *(ehl poo-ree-fee-kah-'dohr)*
purple	**morado** *(moh-'rah-doh)*
purpose	**el propósito** *(ehl proh-'poh-see-toh)*
putty	**la masilla** *(lah mah-'see-yah)*
putty knife	**la espátula** *(lah ehs-'pah-too-lah)*
PVC pipe	**la tubería de plástico/el PVC** *(lah too-beh-'ree-ah deh 'plahs-tee-koh/ehl peh veh seh)*
pyramidal	**piramidal** *(pee-rah-mee-'dahl)*
quality	**la calidad** *(lah kah-lee-'dahd)*
quart	**el cuarto** *(ehl 'kwahr-toh)*
quartzite	**la cuarcita** *(lah 'kwahr-see-tah)*
quickly	**rápidamente** *(rah-pee-dah-'mehn-teh)*
R-20 insulation	**el aislamiento de R-veinte** *(ehl ah-ees-lah-mee-'ehn-toh deh 'eh-rreh 'veh-een-teh)*
radiator	**el radiador** *(ehl rah-dee-ah-'dohr)*
rafter	**el cabrio** *(ehl 'kah-bree-oh)*

rag	**el trapo** *(ehl 'trah-poh)*
railing (fence)	**la reja** *(lah 'reh-hah)*
railings	**las barandas** *(lahs bah-'rahn-dahs)*
rails (mech.)	**los rieles** *(lohs ree-'eh-lehs)*
rain	**la lluvia** *(lah 'yoo-vee-ah)*
raincoat	**el impermeable** *(ehl eem-pehr-meh-'ah-bleh)*
rake	**el rastrillo** *(ehl rahs-'tree-yoh)*
rake (framing)	**el borde inclinado** *(ehl 'bohr-deh een-klee-'nah-doh)*
rake board	**la moldura del techo** *(lah mohl-'doo-rah dehl 'teh-choh)*
rake wall	**el muro de tope inclinado** *(ehl 'moo-roh deh 'toh-peh een-klee-'nah-doh)*
ramp	**la rampa** *(lah 'rahm-pah)*
rasp	**la raspadora** *(lah rahs-pah-'doh-rah)*
ratchet	**el trinquete** *(ehl treen-'keh-teh)*
ratchet wrench	**la llave de trinquete** *(lah 'yah-veh deh treen-'keh-teh)*
ratio	**la relación** *(lah reh-lah-see-'ohn)*
rattle	**el traqueteo** *(ehl trah-keh-'teh-oh)*
raw timber	**la madera cruda/la madera brava** *(lah mah-'deh-rah 'kroo-dah/lah mah-'deh-rah 'brah-vah)*
rebar	**la varilla** *(lah vah-'ree-yah)*
receiver	**el receptor** *(ehl reh-sehp-'tohr)*
recess (door, window)	**el alféizar** *(ehl ahl-'feh-ee-sahr)*
reciprocating saw	**la sierra alternativa** *(lah see-'eh-rrah ahl-tehr-nah-'tee-vah)*
reconstruction	**la reconstrucción** *(lah reh-kohns-trook-see-'ohn)*
record	**el registro/el récord** *(ehl reh-'hees-troh/ehl 'reh-kohrd)*
recorder	**la grabadora** *(lah grah-bah-'doh-rah)*
red	**rojo** *('roh-hoh)*
refinished	**el reacabado** *(ehl reh-ah-kah-'bah-doh)*
reflective	**reflexivo** *(reh-flehk-'see-voh)*
reflectors	**los reflectores** *(lohs reh-flehk-'toh-rehs)*
refrigerator	**el refrigerador** *(ehl reh-free-heh-rah-'dohr)*
registers	**los registros** *(lohs reh-'hees-trohs)*
regulation	**el reglamento** *(ehl reh-glah-'mehn-toh)*
regulator	**el regulador** *(ehl reh-goo-lah-'dohr)*
reinforced	**reforzado** *(reh-fohr-'sah-doh)*
reinforced concrete	**el hormigón armado** *(ehl ohr-mee-'gohn ahr-'mah-doh)*
reinforcement	**el refuerzo** *(ehl reh-'fwehr-soh)*
remote control	**el control remoto** *(ehl kohn-'trohl reh-'moh-toh)*
repair	**la reparación** *(lah reh-pah-rah-see-'ohn)*
requirement	**el requisito** *(ehl reh-kee-'see-toh)*
re-roofing	**el reemplazo del tejado** *(ehl reh-ehm-'plah-soh dehl teh-'hah-doh)*
reset button	**el botón de reinicio** *(ehl boh-'tohn deh reh-ee-'nee-see-oh)*
resin	**la resina** *(lah reh-'see-nah)*

resistance	**la resistencia** *(lah reh-sees-'tehn-see-ah)*
resistors	**los resistores** *(lohs reh-sees-'toh-rehs)*
respirator	**el respirador** *(ehl rehs-pee-rah-'dohr)*
rest	**el resto** *(ehl 'rehs-toh)*
restoration	**la restauración** *(lah rehs-tah-oo-rah-see-'ohn)*
résumé	**el currículum** *(ehl koo-'rree-koo-loom)*
retaining wall	**el muro de apoyo** *(ehl 'moo-roh deh ah-'poh-yoh)*
return pipe	**el tubo de retorno** *(ehl 'too-boh deh reh-'tohr-noh)*
reveal	**la mocheta** *(lah moh-'cheh-tah)*
revolving door	**la puerta giratoria** *(lah 'pwehr-tah hee-rah-'toh-ree-ah)*
rich	**rico** *('ree-koh)*
ridge	**el caballete** *(ehl kah-bah-'yeh-teh)*
ridge board	**la tabla del caballete** *(lah 'tah-blah dehl kah-bah-'yeh-teh)*
right	**correcto** *(koh-'rrehk-toh)*
right (direction)	**la derecha** *(lah deh-'reh-chah)*
right now	**ahora mismo** *(ah-'oh-rah 'mees-moh)*
rim	**el borde** *(ehl 'bohr-deh)*
ring	**el anillo** *(ehl ah-'nee-yoh)*
riser pipe	**el tubo vertical** *(ehl 'too-boh vehr-tee-'kahl)*
river	**el río** *(ehl 'ree-oh)*
rivet	**el remache** *(ehl reh-'mah-cheh)*
rock	**la piedra** *(lah pee-'eh-drah)*
rod	**la varilla/la barra** *(lah vah-'ree-yah/lah 'bah-rrah)*
rolled	**enrollado** *(ehn-roh-'yah-doh)*
roller (grading)	**la aplanadora** *(lah ah-plah-nah-'doh-rah)*
roller (paint)	**el rodillo** *(ehl roh-'dee-yoh)*
rollers (mech.)	**los rodillos** *(lohs roh-'dee-yohs)*
rolling shutters	**las persianas enrollables** *(lahs pehr-see-'ah-nahs ehn-rroh-'yah-blehs)*
rooftop	**la azotea** *(lah ah-soh-'teh-ah)*
roof	**el tejado/el techo** *(ehl teh-'hah-doh/ehl 'teh-choh)*
roofing	**la techumbre/la instalación del tejado** *(lah teh-'choom-breh/lah eens-tah-lah-see-'ohn dehl teh-'hah-doh)*
room	**el cuarto** *(ehl 'kwahr-toh)*
roots	**los raíces** *(lahs rah-'ee-sehs)*
rope	**la soga/la cuerda** *(lah 'soh-gah/lah 'kwehr-dah)*
rotary switch	**el interruptor giratorio** *(ehl een-teh-rroop-'tohr hee-rah-'toh-ree-oh)*
rotor	**el rotor** *(ehl roh-'tohr)*
rototiller	**la aflojadora de tierra** *(lah ah-floh-hah-'doh-rah deh tee-'eh-rrah)*
rotten	**podrido** *(poh-'dree-doh)*
rough	**áspero** *('ahs-peh-roh)*
rough-in	**de mano gruesa** *(deh 'mah-noh groo-'eh-sah)*
round	**redondo** *(reh-'dohn-doh)*
round timber	**la madera en troncos** *(lah mah-'deh-rah ehn 'trohn-kohs)*

router	**el acanalador/ la ranuradora** *(ehl ah-kah-nah-lah-'dohr/lah rah-noo-rah-'doh-rah)*
row	**la hilera** *(lah ee-'leh-rah)*
rubber	**la goma** *(lah 'goh-mah)*
rubber mallet	**el mazo de goma** *(ehl 'mah-soh deh 'goh-mah)*
rubber stripping	**la tira de goma** *(lah 'tee-rah deh 'goh-mah)*
rubble	**la rocalia** *(lah roh-'kah-lee-ah)*
ruined	**destruido** *(dehs-troo-'ee-doh)*
rumble	**el estruendo** *(ehl ehs-troo-'ehn-doh)*
rust	**el óxido** *(ehl 'ohk-see-doh)*
rustic	**rústico** *('roos-tee-koh)*
rustproof	**inoxidable** *(ee-nohk-see-'dah-bleh)*
rusty	**oxidado** *(ohk-see-'dah-doh)*
saber saw	**la sierra de vaivén** *(lah see-'eh-rrah deh vah-ee-'vehn)*
sack	**el saco** *(ehl 'sah-koh)*
sad	**triste** *('trees-teh)*
saddle (framing)	**el asiento** *(ehl ah-see-'ehn-toh)*
safety	**la seguridad** *(lah seh-goo-ree-'dahd)*
safety glasses	**los lentes de seguridad** *(lohs 'lehn-tehs deh seh-goo-ree-'dahd)*
safety line	**la cuerda de seguridad** *(lah 'kwehr-dah deh seh-goo-ree-'dahd)*
safety valve	**la válvula de seguridad** *(lah 'vahl-voo-lah deh seh-goo-ree-'dahd)*
salary	**el salario** *(ehl sah-'lah-ree-oh)*
salesman	**el vendedor** *(ehl vehn-deh-'dohr)*
salt	**la sal** *(lah sahl)*
same	**mismo/igual** *('mees-moh/ee-'gwahl)*
sand	**la arena** *(lah ah-'reh-nah)*
sandbag	**el saco de arena** *(ehl 'sah-koh deh ah-'reh-nah)*
sander	**la lijadora** *(lah lee-hah-'doh-rah)*
sanding	**la lijada** *(lah lee-'hah-dah)*
sanding pole	**la lijadora de mango** *(lah lee-hah-'doh-rah deh 'mahn-goh)*
sandstone	**la piedra arenisca** *(lah pee-'eh-drah ah-reh-'nees-kah)*
sash (window)	**la vidriera** *(lah vee-dree-'eh-rah)*
satellite dish	**el disco de satélite** *(ehl 'dees-koh deh sah-'teh-lee-teh)*
satin (paint)	**satinado** *(sah-tee-'nah-doh)*
saw	**la sierra** *(lah see-'eh-rrah)*
saw (hand)	**el serrucho** *(ehl seh-'rroo-choh)*
sawdust	**el aserrín** *(ehl ah-seh-'rreen)*
sawhorses	**los caballetes** *(lohs kah-bah-'yeh-tehs)*
sawzall	**la sierra alternativa** *(lah see-'eh-rrah ahl-tehr-nah-'tee-vah)*
scaffolding	**el andamio** *(ehl ahn-'dah-mee-oh)*
schedule	**el horario** *(ehl oh-'rah-ree-oh)*
schematic	**esquemático** *(ehs-keh-'mah-tee-koh)*

school	**la escuela** *(lah ehs-'kweh-lah)*
scrap	**los desperdicios/el desecho** *(lohs dehs-pehr-'dee-see-ohs/ehl deh-'seh-choh)*
scraper	**el raspador** *(ehl rahs-pah-'dohr)*
scratch coat	**la primera capa/mano** *(lah pree-'meh-rah 'kah-pah/'mah-noh)*
scratched	**rayado** *(rah-'yah-doh)*
scratches	**las rayaduras** *(lahs rah-yah-'doo-rahs)*
screen	**el mosquitero** *(ehl mohs-kee-'teh-roh)*
screen (mech.)	**la pantalla** *(lah pahn-'tah-yah)*
screw	**el tornillo** *(ehl tohr-'nee-yoh)*
screw gun	**la pistola de tornillos/la atornilladora neumática** *(lah pees-'toh-lah deh tohr-'nee-yohs/lah ah-tohr-nee-yah-'doh-rah neh-oo-'mah-tee-kah)*
screwdriver	**el destornillador** *(ehl dehs-tohr-nee-yah-'dohr)*
screw joint	**la junta roscada** *(lah 'hoon-tah rohs-'kah-dah)*
scroll saw	**la sierra caladora** *(lah see-'eh-rrah kah-lah-'doh-rah)*
SDS screws	**los tornillos SDS** *(lohs tohr-'nee-yohs 'eh-seh deh 'eh-seh)*
sea	**el mar** *(ehl mahr)*
sea level	**el nivel del mar** *(ah nee-'vehl dehl mahr)*
seal	**el sello** *(ehl 'seh-yoh)*
sealed	**sellado** *(seh-'yah-doh)*
sealer	**el sellador** *(ehl seh-yah-'dohr)*
seam	**la costura** *(lah kohs-'too-rah)*
seamless	**sin costura** *(seen kohs-'too-rah)*
seat	**el asiento** *(ehl ah-see-'ehn-toh)*
seat wrench	**la llave del grifo** *(lah 'yah-veh dehl 'gree-foh)*
second	**segundo** *(seh-'goon-doh)*
second floor	**el segundo piso/la segunda planta** *(ehl seh-'goon-doh 'pee-soh/lah seh-'goon-dah 'plahn-tah)*
secretary	**el secretario** *(ehl seh-kreh-'tah-ree-oh)*
section	**la sección** *(lah sehk-see-'ohn)*
secure	**seguro** *(seh-'goo-roh)*
sediment	**el sedimento** *(ehl seh-dee-'mehn-toh)*
seeds	**las semillas** *(lahs seh-'mee-yahs)*
self-closing	**de autocierre** *(deh ah-oo-toh-see-'eh-rreh)*
semiconductors	**los semiconductores** *(lohs seh-mee-kohn-dook-'toh-rehs)*
semifinished	**semiacabado** *(seh-mee-ah-kah-'bah-doh)*
semi-gloss	**semilustroso** *(seh-mee-loos-'troh-soh)*
sensors	**los sensores** *(lohs sehn-'soh-rehs)*
separation	**la separación** *(lah seh-pah-rah-see-'ohn)*
septic system	**el sistema séptico** *(ehl sees-'teh-mah 'sehp-tee-koh)*
septic tank	**la fosa séptica** *(lah 'foh-sah 'sehp-tee-kah)*
service	**el servicio** *(ehl sehr-'vee-see-oh)*

service drop	**la toma de suministro eléctrico** *(lah 'toh-mah deh soo-mee-'nees-troh eh-'lehk-tree-koh)*
service panel	**el tablero de servicio** *(ehl tah-'bleh-roh deh sehr-'vee-see-oh)*
set	**el juego** *(ehl 'hweh-goh)*
seventh	**séptimo** *('sehp-tee-moh)*
sewage	**las aguas de alcantarilla** *(lahs 'ah-gwahs deh ahl-kahn-tah-'ree-yah)*
sewage system	**el alcantarillado** *(ehl ahl-kahn-tah-ree-'yah-doh)*
sewer	**la alcantarilla** *(lah ahl-kahn-tah-'ree-yah)*
sewerage	**el alcantarillado** *(ehl ahl-kahn-tah-ree-'yah-doh)*
shack	**el cobertizo/la chabola** *(ehl koh-behr-'tee-soh/lah chah-'boh-lah)*
shade (paint)	**el matiz** *(ehl mah-'tees)*
shadow	**la sombra** *(lah 'sohm-brah)*
shaft	**el eje/el astil** *(ehl 'eh-heh/ehl ahs-'teel)*
shake	**el listón** *(ehl lees-'tohn)*
shallow	**bajo** *('bah-hoh)*
shape	**la forma** *(lah 'fohr-mah)*
shaped	**formado** *(fohr-'mah-doh)*
sharp	**afilado** *(ah-fee-'lah-doh)*
shear wall	**el muro sismorresistente** *(ehl 'moo-roh sees-moh-rreh-sees-'tehn-teh)*
shears	**las tijeras** *(lahs tee-'heh-rahs)*
sheathing	**el entablado/el revestimiento** *(ehl ehn-tah-'blah-doh/ehl reh-vehs-tee-mee-'ehn-toh)*
shed	**el cobertizo** *(ehl koh-behr-'tee-soh)*
sheen	**la luminosidad** *(lah loo-mee-noh-see-'dahd)*
sheer panel	**la cabria** *(lah 'kah-bree-ah)*
sheet	**la hoja** *(lah 'oh-hah)*
sheet (framing)	**la plancha** *(lah 'plahn-chah)*
sheet metal	**la plancha de metal** *(lah 'plahn-chah deh meh-'tahl)*
sheeting	**la lámina** *(lah 'lah-mee-nah)*
sheetrock	**el enyesado** *(ehl ehn-yeh-'sah-doh)*
shelf	**el estante** *(ehl ehs-'tahn-teh)*
shelf pin	**la clavija para estantes** *(lah klah-'vee-hah 'pah-rah ehs-'tahn-tehs)*
shim	**la calza** *(lah 'kahl-sah)*
shin guard	**la espinillera** *(lah ehs-pee-nee-'yeh-rah)*
shingle	**la teja de asfalto** *(lah 'teh-hah deh ahs-'fahl-toh)*
shiny	**luminoso/brillante** *(loo-mee-'noh-soh/bree-'yahn-teh)*
shockproof	**antigolpes** *(ahn-tee-'gohl-pehs)*
shopping center	**el centro comercial** *(ehl 'sehn-troh koh-mehr-see-'ahl)*
shoring	**el apuntalamiento** *(ehl ah-poon-tah-lah-mee-'ehn-toh)*
short (in height)	**bajo** *('bah-hoh)*
short (in length)	**corto** *('kohr-toh)*
shovel	**la pala** *(lah 'pah-lah)*
shower	**la ducha** *(lah 'doo-chah)*

shutoff switch	**el interruptor principal** *(ehl een-teh-rroop-'tohr preen-see-'pahl)*
shutoff valve	**la válvula de cierre** *(lah 'vahl-voo-lah deh see-'eh-rreh)*
shutter	**la contraventana/el postigo** *(lah kohn-trah-vehn-'tah-nah/ehl pohs-'tee-goh)*
sick	**enfermo** *(ehn-'fehr-moh)*
side	**el costado/el lado** *(ehl kohs-'tah-doh/ehl 'lah-doh)*
side by side	**al lado** *(ahl 'lah-doh)*
side yard	**el patio del lado** *(ehl 'pah-tee-oh dehl 'lah-doh)*
sidewalk	**la vereda/la acera** *(lah veh-'reh-dah/lah ah-'seh-rah)*
siding	**el revestimiento** *(ehl reh-vehs-tee-mee-'ehn-toh)*
signal	**la señal** *(lah seh-'nyahl)*
silicone	**la silicona** *(lah see-lee-'koh-nah)*
sill	**el antepecho** *(ehl ahn-teh-'peh-choh)*
sill plate	**la placa de solera** *(lah 'plah-kah deh soh-'leh-rah)*
silver	**la plata** *(lah 'plah-tah)*
silverplated	**plateado** *(plah-teh-'ah-doh)*
similar	**similar** *('see-mee-lahr)*
Simpson strong wall	**el muro Simpson** *(ehl 'moo-roh 'seem-psohn)*
since	**desde** *('dehs-deh)*
single	**único/solo** *('oo-nee-koh/'soh-loh)*
sink	**el lavabo/el fregadero** *(ehl lah-'vah-boh/ehl fre-gah-'deh-roh)*
site	**el sitio** *(ehl 'see-tee-oh)*
sixth	**sexto** *('sehks-toh)*
size	**el tamaño** *(ehl tah-'mah-nyoh)*
skid-steer loader	**la cargadora Bobcat** *(lah kahr-gah-'doh-rah 'bohb-kaht)*
skill	**la habilidad** *(lah ah-bee-lee-'dahd)*
skill saw	**la sierra circular** *(lah see-'eh-rrah seer-koo-'lahr)*
skin	**la piel** *(lah pee-'ehl)*
sky	**el cielo** *(ehl see-'eh-loh)*
skylight	**el tragaluz** *(ehl trah-gah-'loos)*
skyscraper	**el rascacielos** *(ehl rahs-kah-see-'eh-lohs)*
slab	**la losa** *(lah 'loh-sah)*
slate	**la pizarra** *(lah pee-'sah-rrah)*
sledge	**la almádena** *(lah ahl-'mah-deh-nah)*
slide (window)	**la corredera** *(lah koh-rreh-'deh-rah)*
sliding door	**la puerta corrediza** *(lah 'pwehr-tah koh-rreh-'dee-sah)*
sliding window	**la ventana corrediza** *(lah vehn-'tah-nah koh-rreh-'dee-sah)*
slip joints	**las juntas deslizantes** *(lahs 'hoon-tahs dehs-lee-'sahn-tehs)*
slit	**la muesca** *(lah 'mwehs-kah)*
slope	**la cuesta/el declive** *(lah 'kwehs-tah/ehl deh-'klee-veh)*
sloped	**inclinado** *(een-klee-'nah-doh)*
slot	**la ranura** *(lah rah-'noo-rah)*
slow	**lento** *('lehn-toh)*

slowly	**lentamente** *(lehn-tah-'mehn-teh)*
slump stone	**el bloque de hormigón** *(ehl 'bloh-keh deh ohr-mee-'gohn)*
small	**chico/pequeño** *('chee-koh/peh-'keh-nyoh)*
smell	**el olor** *(ehl oh-'lohr)*
smoke	**el humo** *(ehl 'oo-moh)*
smoke detector	**el detector de humo** *(ehl deh-tehk-'tohr deh 'oo-moh)*
smooth	**liso/suave** *('lee-soh/'swah-veh)*
snack	**la merienda** *(lah meh-ree-'ehn-dah)*
snow	**la nieve** *(lah nee-'eh-veh)*
soaked	**empapado** *(ehm-pah-'pah-doh)*
socket wrench	**la llave de cubo** *(lah 'yah-veh deh 'koo-boh)*
sod	**el césped/el tepe** *(ehl 'sehs-pehd/ehl 'teh-peh)*
soffit	**el sofito/la cubierta del alero** *(ehl soh-'fee-toh/lah koo-bee-'ehr-tah deh ah-'leh-roh)*
soft	**blando** *('blahn-doh)*
soft drink	**el refresco** *(ehl reh-'frehs-koh)*
soft water system	**el sistema para suavizar el agua** *(ehl sees-'teh-mah 'pah-rah soo-ah-vee-'sahr ehl 'ah-gwah)*
soft wood	**la madera blanda** *(lah mah-'deh-rah 'blahn-dah)*
soil	**la tierra** *(lah tee-'eh-rrah)*
solar panels	**los paneles solares** *(lohs pah-'neh-lehs soh-'lah-rehs)*
soldering iron	**la pistola de soldar** *(lah pees-'toh-lah deh sohl-'dahr)*
soldering wire	**el alambre de soldadura** *(ehl ah-'lahm-breh deh sohl-dah-'doo-rah)*
sole plate	**la placa de solera** *(lah 'plah-kah deh soh-'leh-rah)*
solid	**sólido/macizo** *('soh-lee-doh/mah-'see-soh)*
solid wood	**la madera sólida** *(lah mah-'deh-rah 'soh-lee-dah)*
solvent	**el disolvente** *(ehl dee-sohl-'vehn-teh)*
some	**algunos** *(ahl-'goo-nohs)*
someone	**alguien** *('ahl-gee-ehn)*
something	**algo** *('ahl-goh)*
sometimes	**a veces** *(ah 'veh-sehs)*
somewhere	**en algún sitio** *(ehn ahl-'goon 'see-tee-oh)*
soon	**pronto** *('prohn-toh)*
sore	**dolorido** *(doh-loh-'ree-doh)*
sound	**el sonido** *(ehl soh-'nee-doh)*
south	**el sur** *(ehl soor)*
spa	**el balneario** *(ehl bahl-neh-'ah-ree-oh)*
space	**el espacio** *(ehl ehs-'pah-see-oh)*
spacers	**los espaciadores** *(lohs ehs-pah-see-ah-'doh-rehs)*
spacious	**amplio** *('ahm-plee-oh)*
spackling	**el relleno/el mastique** *(ehl reh-'yeh-noh/ehl mahs-'tee-keh)*
Spanish	**el español** *(ehl ehs-pahn-'yohl)*
spark	**la chispa** *(lah 'chees-pah)*

speaker	**el parlante/el altavoz** *(ehl pahr-'lahn-teh/ehl ahl-tah-'vohs)*
specifications	**las especificaciones** *(lahs ehs-peh-see-fee-kah-see-'oh-nehs)*
speed	**la velocidad** *(lah veh-loh-see-'dahd)*
spigot	**la llave de paso** *(lah 'yah-veh deh 'pah-soh)*
spillage	**el derrame** *(ehl deh-'rrah-meh)*
spiral	**la espiral** *(lah ehs-pee-'rahl)*
splashing	**las salpicaduras** *(lahs sahl-pee-kah-'doo-rahs)*
splayed	**achaflanada** *(ah-chah-flah-'nah-dah)*
splice plate	**la placa de empalme** *(lah 'plah-kah deh ehm-'pahl-meh)*
split	**rajado** *(rah-'hah-doh)*
split ring clamp	**la abrazadera de anillo separado** *(lah ah-brah-sah-'deh-rah deh ah-'nee-yoh seh-pah-'rah-doh)*
sponge	**la esponja** *(lah ehs-'pohn-hah)*
spool	**el carrete** *(ehl kah-'rreh-teh)*
spot	**el punto** *(ehl 'poon-toh)*
sprayer	**el rociador** *(ehl roh-see-ah-'dohr)*
spreader	**la esparcidora** *(lah ehs-pahr-see-'doh-rah)*
spring	**el resorte** *(ehl reh-'sohr-teh)*
spring (season)	**la primavera** *(lah pree-mah-'veh-rah)*
sprinklers	**los aspersores/los rociadores** *(lohs ahs-pehr-'soh-rehs/lohs roh-see-ah-'doh-rehs)*
square	**cuadrado** *(kwah-'drah-doh)*
square (tool)	**la escuadra** *(lah ehs-'kwah-drah)*
square beams	**las vigas cuadradas** *(lahs 'vee-gahs kwah-'drah-dahs)*
square feet	**los pies cuadrados** *(lohs pee-'ehs kwah-'drah-dohs)*
square inches	**las pulgadas cuadradas** *(lahs pool-'gah-dahs kwah-'drah-dahs)*
squared	**escuadrado** *(ehs-kwah-'drah-doh)*
squeak	**el chirrido** *(ehl chee-'rree-doh)*
ST straps	**las cubrejuntas ST** *(lahs koo-breh-'hoon-tahs 'eh-seh teh)*
stable	**estable** *(ehs-'tah-bleh)*
stack	**el montón/la pila** *(ehl mohn-'tohn/lah 'pee-lah)*
stain	**la mancha** *(lah 'mahn-chah)*
stain (painting)	**el tinte** *(ehl 'teen-teh)*
stainblock	**el antimanchas** *(ehl ahn-tee-'mahn-chahs)*
stained	**manchado** *(mahn-'chah-doh)*
stainless	**inoxidable** *(ee-nohk-see-'dah-bleh)*
stainless steel	**el acero inoxidable** *(ehl ah-'seh-roh ee-nohk-see-'dah-bleh)*
stair landing	**el descanso de las escaleras** *(ehl dehs-'kahn-soh deh lahs ehs-kah-'leh-rahs)*
stairs	**las escaleras** *(lahs ehs-kah-'leh-rahs)*
stairwell	**la caja de las escaleras** *(lah 'kah-hah deh lahs ehs-kah-'leh-rahs)*
stake	**la estaca** *(lah ehs-'tah-kah)*
standard	**estándar** *(ehs-'tahn-dahr)*

staple	**la grapa** *(lah 'grah-pah)*
staple gun	**la pistola de grapas/la engrapadora neumática** *(lah pees-'toh-lah deh 'grah-pahs/lah ehn-grah-pah-'doh-rah neh-oo-'mah-tee-kah)*
stapler	**la grapadora** *(lah grah-pah-'doh-rah)*
static	**estático** *(ehs-'tah-tee-koh)*
statue	**la estatua** *(lah ehs-'tah-twah)*
steam	**el vapor** *(ehl vah-'pohr)*
steel	**el acero** *(ehl ah-'seh-roh)*
steel mesh	**la malla de acero** *(lah 'mah-yah deh ah-'seh-roh)*
steel plate	**la plancha de acero** *(lah 'plahn-chah deh ah-'seh-roh)*
steel wool	**la lana de acero** *(lah 'lah-nah deh ah-'seh-roh)*
steep	**empinado** *(ehm-pee-'nah-doh)*
steering wheel	**el volante** *(ehl voh-'lahn-teh)*
stepladder	**la escalera baja** *(lah ehs-kah-'leh-rah 'bah-hah)*
stepping stone	**la piedra de escalón** *(lah pee-'eh-drah deh ehs-kah-'lohn)*
steps	**los escalones** *(lohs ehs-kah-'loh-nehs)*
sticky	**pegajoso** *(peh-gah-'hoh-soh)*
stirrup	**el estribo** *(ehl ehs-'tree-boh)*
stone	**la piedra** *(lah pee-'eh-drah)*
stone wall	**el muro de piedras** *(ehl 'moo-roh deh pee-'eh-drahs)*
stonemason	**el albañil** *(ehl ahl-bah-'neel)*
stoop	**el umbral** *(ehl oom-'brahl)*
stop (door)	**el tope** *(ehl 'toh-peh)*
stop sign	**la señal de parada** *(lah seh-'nyahl deh pah-'rah-dah)*
storage room	**el depósito** *(ehl deh-'poh-see-toh)*
store	**la tienda** *(lah tee-'ehn-dah)*
storm	**la tormenta** *(lah tohr-'mehn-tah)*
storm door	**la contrapuerta** *(lah kohn-trah-'pwehr-tah)*
storm drain	**la tubería de desagüe** *(lah too-beh-'ree-ah deh deh-'sah-gweh)*
storm window	**la guardaventana** *(lah gwahr-dah-vehn-'tah-nah)*
stove	**la estufa** *(lah ehs-'too-fah)*
straight	**recto** *('rehk-toh)*
straight ahead	**adelante** *(ah-deh-'lahn-teh)*
straightedge	**la regla metálica** *(lah 'reh-glah meh-'tah-lee-kah)*
strap	**la tira** *(lah 'tee-rah)*
strap (framing)	**la cubrejunta** *(lah koo-breh-'hoon-tah)*
strap wrench	**la llave de cincho** *(lah 'yah-veh deh 'seen-choh)*
stream	**el arroyo** *(ehl ah-'rroh-yoh)*
street	**la calle** *(lah 'kah-yeh)*
strength	**la fuerza/la resistencia** *(lah 'fwehr-sah/lah reh-sees-'tehn-see-ah)*
stretcher	**el tensor** *(ehl tehn-'sohr)*
strike plate	**el cajetín** *(ehl kah-heh-'teen)*
string	**la cuerda/el hilo** *(lah 'kwehr-dah/ehl 'ee-loh)*

strip	**la tira** *(lah 'tee-rah)*
strong	**fuerte** *('fwehr-teh)*
strong wall	**el muro fuerte** *(ehl 'moo-roh 'fwehr-teh)*
structural	**estructural** *(ehs-trook-too-'rahl)*
structural steel	**el acero estructural** *(ehl ah-'seh-roh ehs-trook-too-'rahl)*
structure	**la estructura** *(lah ehs-trook-'too-rah)*
strut	**el puntal** *(ehl poon-'tahl)*
stucco	**el estuco** *(ehl ehs-'too-koh)*
stud	**el montante** *(ehl mohn-'tahn-teh)*
stud finder	**el buscamontantes** *(ehl boos-kah-mohn-'tahn-tehs)*
studio	**el estudio** *(ehl ehs-'too-dee-oh)*
style	**el estilo** *(ehl ehs-'tee-loh)*
subcontractor	**el subcontratista** *(ehl soob-kohn-trah-'tees-tah)*
sub-floor	**el subpiso** *(ehl soob-'pee-soh)*
sub-roof	**el subtecho** *(ehl soob-'teh-choh)*
subway	**el metro** *(ehl 'meh-troh)*
suggestion	**la sugerencia** *(lah soo-heh-'rehn-see-ah)*
sulphate	**el sulfato** *(ehl sool-'fah-toh)*
sulphate-resistant	**resistente al sulfato** *(reh-sees-'tehn-teh ahl sool-'fah-toh)*
sum	**la suma** *(lah 'soo-mah)*
summer	**el verano** *(ehl veh-'rah-noh)*
sun	**el sol** *(ehl sohl)*
sunroom	**el solario** *(ehl soh-'lah-ree-oh)*
sunscreen	**la protección para el sol** *(lah proh-tehk-see-'ohn 'pah-rah ehl sohl)*
supermarket	**el supermercado** *(ehl soo-pehr-mehr-'kah-doh)*
supervisor	**el supervisor** *(ehl soo-pehr-vee-'sohr)*
supply	**el suministro** *(ehl soo-mee-'nees-troh)*
support	**el soporte/el apoyo** *(ehl soh-'pohr-teh/ehl ah-'poh-yoh)*
surface	**la superficie** *(lah soo-pehr-'fee-see-eh)*
surveyor	**el agrimensor** *(ehl ah-gree-mehn-'sohr)*
suspension	**la suspensión** *(lah soos-pehn-see-'ohn)*
switch	**el interruptor** *(ehl een-teh-rroop-'tohr)*
switch plate	**la placa de interruptor** *(lah 'plah-kah deh een-teh-rroop-'tohr)*
swivel	**giratorio** *(hee-rah-'toh-ree-oh)*
swollen	**hinchado** *(een-'chah-doh)*
symmetrical	**simétrico** *(see-'meh-tree-koh)*
synthetic	**sintético** *(seen-'teh-tee-koh)*
system	**el sistema** *(ehl sees-'teh-mah)*
tab	**la aleta** *(lah ah-'leh-tah)*
tab (roofing)	**la teja expuesta** *(lah 'teh-hah ex-'pwehs-tah)*
table saw	**la sierra de banco** *(lah see-'eh-rrah deh 'bahn-koh)*
tack	**la tachuela** *(lah tah-choo-'eh-lah)*

tack strip	**la tira de tachuelas** *(lah 'tee-rah deh tah-choo-'eh-lahs)*
tall	**alto** *('ahl-toh)*
tamper	**el pisón** *(ehl pee-'sohn)*
tan	**café claro** *(kah-'feh 'klah-roh)*
tank	**el tanque/el cilindro** *(ehl 'tahn-keh/ehl see-'leen-droh)*
tape	**la cinta** *(lah 'seen-tah)*
tape measure	**la cinta métrica** *(lah 'seen-tah 'meh-tree-kah)*
tapered	**ahusado** *(ah-oo-'sah-doh)*
tapestry	**el tapiz** *(ehl tah-'pees)*
tar	**la brea** *(lah 'breh-ah)*
tarnished	**deslustrado** *(dehs-loos-'trah-doh)*
task	**la tarea** *(lah tah-'reh-ah)*
T-beam	**la viga en T** *(lah 'vee-gah ehn teh)*
teacher	**el maestro** *(ehl mah-'ehs-troh)*
teak	**la teca** *(lah 'teh-kah)*
technician	**el técnico** *(ehl 'tehk-nee-koh)*
Teflon	**el teflón** *(ehl teh-'flohn)*
telephone	**el teléfono** *(ehl teh-'leh-foh-noh)*
telephone pole	**el poste de teléfono** *(ehl 'pohs-teh deh teh-'leh-foh-noh)*
television	**el televisor** *(ehl teh-leh-vee-'sohr)*
television cables	**los cables de televisión** *(lohs 'kah-blehs deh teh-leh-vee-see-'ohn)*
temperature	**la temperatura** *(lah tehm-peh-rah-'too-rah)*
template	**la plancha** *(lah 'plahn-chah)*
temporary	**provisional** *(proh-vee-see-oh-'nahl)*
tension	**la tensión** *(lah tehn-see-'ohn)*
tenth	**décimo** *('deh-see-moh)*
termites	**las termitas** *(lahs tehr-'mee-tahs)*
texture	**la textura** *(lah tehks-'too-rah)*
texture coat	**la capa de textura** *(lah 'kah-pah deh tehks-'too-rah)*
textured	**texturizado** *(tehks-too-ree-'sah-doh)*
the	**el/la/los/las** *(ehl/lah/lohs/lahs)*
then	**entonces** *(ehn-'tohn-sehs)*
there	**allí** *(ah-'yee)*
thermometer	**el termómetro** *(ehl tehr-'moh-meh-troh)*
thermostat	**el termostato** *(ehl tehr-mohs-'tah-toh)*
thick (liquid)	**espeso** *(ehs-'peh-soh)*
thick (solid)	**grueso** *(groo-'eh-soh)*
thickness	**el espesor** *(ehl ehs-peh-'sohr)*
thin	**delgado** *(dehl-'gah-doh)*
thing	**la cosa** *(lah 'koh-sah)*
thinner	**el diluyente** *(ehl dee-loo-'yehn-teh)*
third	**tercero** *(tehr-'seh-roh)*
thread (cloth)	**el hilo** *(ehl 'ee-loh)*

thread (screw)	**la rosca** *(lah 'rohs-kah)*
threaded	**roscado** *(rohs-'kah-doh)*
three-way plug	**el enchufe de tres puntas** *(ehl ehn-'choo-feh deh trehs 'poon-tahs)*
threshold	**el umbral** *(ehl oom-'brahl)*
through	**por** *(pohr)*
throw rug	**el tapete** *(ehl tah-'peh-teh)*
tie (framing)	**la traviesa** *(lah trah-vee-'eh-sah)*
tie (general)	**el amarre** *(ehl ah-'mah-rreh)*
tie (mech.)	**el sujetador** *(ehl soo-heh-tah-'dohr)*
tight	**apretado** *(ah-preh-'tah-doh)*
tile (floor)	**la loseta/la baldosa** *(lah loh-'seh-tah/lah bahl-'doh-sah)*
tile (roof)	**la teja de arcilla** *(lah 'teh-hah deh ahr-'see-yah)*
tile (wall)	**el azulejo** *(ehl ah-soo-'leh-hoh)*
tile cutter	**la cortabaldosas** *(lah kohr-tah-bahl-'doh-sahs)*
tile nippers	**las pinzas cortazulejo** *(lahs 'peen-sahs kohr-tah-soo-'leh-hoh)*
time (clock)	**la hora** *(lah 'oh-rah)*
time (weather)	**el tiempo** *(ehl tee-'ehm-poh)*
timer	**el contador** *(ehl kohn-tah-'dohr)*
times	**veces** *('veh-sehs)*
tin	**el estaño** *(ehl ehs-'tah-nyoh)*
tin snips	**las tijeras para hojalata** *(lahs tee-'heh-rahs 'pah-rah oh-hah-'lah-tah)*
tinted	**sombreado** *(sohm-breh-'ah-doh)*
tip	**la punta** *(lah 'poon-tah)*
tired	**cansado** *(kahn-'sah-doh)*
title	**el título** *(ehl 'tee-too-loh)*
to	**a** *(ah)*
today	**hoy** *('oh-ee)*
toe kick	**la tabla contragolpes** *(lah 'tah-blah kohn-trah-'gohl-pehs)*
together	**junto** *('hoon-toh)*
toilet	**el excusado** *(ehl ex-koo-'sah-doh)*
tomorrow	**mañana** *(mah-'nyah-nah)*
ton	**la tonelada** *(lah toh-neh-'lah-dah)*
tongs (large)	**las tenazas** *(lahs teh-'nah-sahs)*
tongs (small)	**las pinzas** *(lahs 'peen-sahs)*
tongue and groove	**la lengüeta y ranura** *(lah lehn-'gweh-tah ee rah-'noo-rah)*
too	**también** *(tahm-bee-'ehn)*
too much	**demasiado** *(deh-mah-see-'ah-doh)*
tools	**las herramientas** *(lahs eh-rrah-mee-'ehn-tahs)*
tooth	**el diente** *(ehl dee-'ehn-teh)*
top	**la cima/la tapa** *(lah 'see-mah/lah 'tah-pah)*
top plate	**la placa superior** *(lah 'plah-kah soo-peh-ree-'ohr)*
torch (light)	**la antorcha** *(lah ahn-'tohr-chah)*
torch (welding)	**el soplete** *(ehl soh-'pleh-teh)*

torque	**el esfuerzo de torsión** *(ehl ehs-'fwehr-soh deh tohr-see-'ohn)*
tow hook	**el gancho de remolque** *(ehl 'gahn-choh deh reh-'mohl-keh)*
tow line	**la cuerda de remolque** *(lah 'kwehr-dah deh reh-'mohl-keh)*
toward	**hacia** *('ah-see-ah)*
towel	**la toalla** *(lah toh-'ah-yah)*
tower	**la torre** *(lah 'toh-rreh)*
towing	**el remolque** *(ehl reh-'mohl-keh)*
town house	**la casa urbana** *(lah 'kah-sah oor-'bah-nah)*
T-pipe	**el tubo en T** *(ehl 'too-boh ehn teh)*
tracks (door)	**los carriles** *(lohs kah-'rree-lehs)*
track lights	**las luces en rieles** *(lahs 'loo-sehs ehn ree-'eh-lehs)*
tractor	**el tractor** *(ehl trahk-'tohr)*
trailer	**el remolque** *(ehl reh-'mohl-keh)*
training	**el entrenamiento** *(ehl ehn-treh-nah-mee-'ehn-toh)*
transformer	**el transformador** *(ehl trahns-fohr-mah-'dohr)*
transistor	**el transistor** *(eh trahn-sees-'tohr)*
transit	**el tránsito** *(ehl 'trahn-see-toh)*
transom	**el travesaño/la durmiente** *(ehl trah-veh-'sah-nyoh/lah door-mee-'ehn-teh)*
transportation	**el transporte** *(ehl trahns-'pohr-teh)*
trap (plumbing)	**el sifón** *(ehl see-'fohn)*
trash	**la basura** *(lah bah-'soo-rah)*
trash bag	**la bolsa para basura** *(lah 'bohl-sah 'pah-rah bah-'soo-rah)*
trash can	**el bote de basura** *(ehl 'boh-teh deh bah-'soo-rah)*
trash compactor	**la compactadora de basura** *(lah kohm-pahk-tah-'doh-rah deh bah-'soo-rah)*
travertine	**la travertina** *(lah trah-vehr-'tee-nah)*
tray	**la bandeja** *(lah bahn-'deh-hah)*
treated	**tratado** *(trah-'tah-doh)*
tree	**el árbol** *(ehl 'ahr-bohl)*
tree tie	**el amarre para el árbol** *(ehl ah-'mah-rreh 'pah-rah ehl 'ahr-bohl)*
trellis	**el enrejado** *(ehl ehn-reh-'hah-doh)*
trench	**la zanja** *(lah 'sahn-hah)*
trencher	**la excavadora** *(lah ex-kah-vah-'doh-rah)*
triangular	**triangular** *(tree-ahn-goo-'lahr)*
trim	**el adorno** *(ehl ah-'dohr-noh)*
trimmer	**la recortadora/la cepilladora** *(lah reh-kohr-tah-'doh-rah/lah seh-pee-yah-'doh-rah)*
tripler	**el triple** *(ehl 'tree-pleh)*
trowel	**la paleta** *(lah pah-'leh-tah)*
trowel hawk	**la llana enyesadora** *(lah 'yah-nah ehn-yeh-sah-'doh-rah)*
truck	**el camión** *(ehl kah-mee-'ohn)*
truck driver	**el camionero** *(ehl kah-mee-oh-'neh-roh)*

truckbed	**la plataforma de carga** *(lah plah-tah-'fohr-mah deh 'kahr-gah)*
truckload	**la camionada** *(lah kah-mee-oh-'nah-dah)*
truss	**la armadura** *(lah ahr-mah-'doo-rah)*
T-shirt	**la camiseta** *(lah kah-mee-'seh-tah)*
T-style	**de estilo T** *(deh ehs-'tee-loh teh)*
tub	**la tina** *(lah 'tee-nah)*
tube	**el tubo** *(ehl 'too-boh)*
tube bender	**la dobladora de tubos** *(lah doh-blah-'doh-rah deh 'too-bohs)*
tube wrench	**la llave tubular** *(lah 'yah-veh too-boo-'lahr)*
Tudor	**tudor** *(too-'dohr)*
tunnel	**el túnel** *(ehl 'too-nehl)*
turned off	**apagado** *(ah-pah-'gah-doh)*
turned on	**prendido** *(prehn-'dee-doh)*
turpentine	**la trementina** *(lah treh-mehn-'tee-nah)*
twisted	**torcido** *(tohr-'see-doh)*
type	**el tipo** *(ehl 'tee-poh)*
UBC caps	**las coronas UBC** *(lahs koh-'roh-nahs oo beh seh)*
ugly	**feo** *('feh-oh)*
under	**debajo** *(deh-'bah-hoh)*
undercabinet lighting	**la iluminación bajo el gabinete** *(lah ee-loo-mee-nah-see-'ohn 'bah-hoh ehl gah-bee-'neh-teh)*
underground	**subterráneo** *(soob-teh-'rrah-neh-oh)*
underlayment	**el base del piso** *(lah 'bah-seh dehl 'pee-soh)*
uneven	**desigual** *(deh-see-'gwahl)*
uniform	**uniforme** *(oo-nee-'fohr-meh)*
uniform (clothing)	**el uniforme** *(ehl oo-nee-'fohr-meh)*
union	**la unión** *(lah oo-nee-'ohn)*
unit	**la unidad** *(lah oo-nee-'dahd)*
until	**hasta** *('ahs-tah)*
up	**arriba** *(ah-'ree-bah)*
uphill	**cuesta arriba** *('kwehs-tah ah-'ree-bah)*
upside down	**boca abajo** *('boh-kah ah-'bah-hoh)*
urinal	**el orinal** *(ehl oh-ree-'nahl)*
use	**el uso** *(ehl 'oo-soh)*
utility cabinet	**el gabinete de servicios** *(ehl gah-bee-'neh-teh deh sehr-'vee-see-ohs)*
utility knife	**la cuchilla/la navaja** *(lah koo-'chee-yah/lah nah-'vah-hah)*
utility room	**la despensa** *(lah dehs-'pehn-sah)*
vacuum cleaner	**la aspiradora** *(lah ahs-pee-rah-'doh-rah)*
valley	**el valle** *(ehl 'vah-yeh)*
valley (roof)	**la lima hoya** *(lah 'lee-mah 'oh-yah)*
valve	**la válvula** *(lah 'vahl-voo-lah)*

vanity unit	**el lavabo empotrado** *(ehl lah-'vah-boh ehm-poh-'trah-doh)*
variation	**la variación** *(lah vah-ree-ah-see-'ohn)*
varnish	**el barniz** *(ehl bahr-'nees)*
veneer	**la chapa** *(lah 'chah-pah)*
vent	**el conducto** *(ehl kohn-'dook-toh)*
vent tube	**el tubo para ventilación** *(ehl 'too-boh 'pah-rah vehn-tee-lah-see-'ohn)*
ventilation	**la ventilación** *(lah vehn-tee-lah-see-'ohn)*
vertical	**vertical** *(vehr-tee-'kahl)*
vest	**el chaleco** *(ehl chah-'leh-koh)*
V-groove	**la ranura en V** *(lah rah-'noo-rah ehn veh)*
vibration	**la vibración** *(lah vee-brah-see'ohn)*
Victorian	**victoriano** *(veek-toh-ree-'ah-noh)*
vinyl	**el vinilo** *(ehl vee-'nee-loh)*
vinyl board	**la tabla de vinilo** *(lah 'tah-blah deh vee-'nee-loh)*
vise	**la prensa de tornillo** *(lah 'prehn-sah deh tohr-'nee-yoh)*
Vise-grip pliers	**los alicates de presión** *(lohs ah-lee-'kah-tehs deh preh-see-'ohn)*
visor	**la visera** *(lah vee-'seh-rah)*
volt	**el voltio** *(ehl 'vohl-tee-oh)*
voltage	**el voltaje** *(ehl vohl-'tah-heh)*
volume	**el volumen** *(ehl voh-'loo-mehn)*
walk-in closet	**el ropero empotrado** *(ehl roh-'peh-roh ehm-poh-'trah-doh)*
walkway	**el sendero/el camino** *(ehl sehn-'deh-roh/ehl kah-'mee-noh)*
wall	**la pared/el muro** *(lah pah-'rehd/ehl 'moo-roh)*
wall oven	**el horno de pared** *(ehl 'ohr-noh deh pah-'rehd)*
wall safe	**la caja fuerte de pared** *(lah 'kah-hah 'fwehr-teh deh pah-'rehd)*
wall tile	**el azulejo** *(ehl ah-soo-'leh-hoh)*
wall unit	**el mueble de pared** *(ehl 'mweh-bleh deh pah-'rehd)*
wallboard saw	**el serrucho corto** *(ehl seh-'rroo-choh 'kohr-toh)*
wallboard square	**la escuadra para paneles** *(lah ehs-'kwah-drah 'pah-rah pah-'neh-lehs)*
warehouse	**el almacén** *(ehl ahl-mah-'sehn)*
warm	**tibio** *('tee-bee-oh)*
warming drawer	**el cajón calentador** *(ehl kah-'hohn kah-lehn-tah-'dohr)*
warning	**la advertencia** *(lah ahd-vehr-'tehn-see-ah)*
warped	**combado** *(kohm-'bah-doh)*
washer (tool)	**la arandela** *(lah ah-rahn-'deh-lah)*
washing	**el lavado** *(ehl lah-'vah-doh)*
washing machine	**la lavadora** *(lah lah-vah-'doh-rah)*
waste valve	**la válvula de desagüe** *(lah 'vahl-voo-lah deh deh-'sah-gweh)*
waste water	**las aguas residuales** *(lahs 'ah-gwahs reh-see-'dwah-lehs)*
wastepipe	**el desagüe** *(ehl deh-'sah-gweh)*
water	**el agua** *(ehl 'ah-gwah)*

water-based paint	**la pintura al agua** *(lah peen-'too-rah ahl 'ah-gwah)*
water filter	**el filtro de agua** *(ehl 'feel-troh deh 'ah-gwah)*
water heater	**el calentador del agua** *(ehl kah-lehn-tah-'dohr deh 'ah-gwah)*
water leak	**la fuga de agua** *(lah 'foo-gah deh 'ah-gwah)*
water main	**la cañería matriz** *(lah kah-nyeh-'ree-ah mah-'trees)*
water meter	**el medidor de agua** *(ehl meh-dee-'dohr deh 'ah-gwah)*
water pipe	**la tubería de agua** *(lah too-beh-'ree-ah deh 'ah-gwah)*
water table	**el nivel de agua** *(ehl nee-'vehl deh 'ah-gwah)*
water tank truck	**el camión cisterna** *(ehl kah-mee-'ohn sees-'tehr-nah)*
water valve	**la válvula de agua** *(lah 'vahl-voo-lah deh 'ah-gwah)*
waterfall	**la catarata** *(lah kah-tah-'rah-tah)*
waterproof	**impermeable** *(eem-pehr-meh-'ah-bleh)*
waterproofing	**la impermeabilización** *(lah eem-pehr-meh-ah-bee-lee-sah-see-'ohn)*
watertight	**estanco** *(ehs-'tahn-koh)*
watt	**el vatio** *(ehl 'vah-tee-oh)*
watt-hour meter	**el medidor de vatios por hora** *(ehl meh-dee-'dohr deh 'vah-tee-ohs pohr 'oh-rah)*
wattage	**la potencia en vatios** *(lah poh-'tehn-see-ah ehn 'vah-tee-ohs)*
wax	**la cera** *(lah 'seh-rah)*
weather strip	**el burlete** *(ehl boor-'leh-teh)*
weathervane	**la veleta** *(lah veh-'leh-tah)*
wedge	**la cuña** *(lah 'koo-nyah)*
weed	**la mala yerba** *(lah 'mah-lah 'yehr-bah)*
weedwacker	**el desyerbador** *(ehl dehs-yehr-bah-'dohr)*
weep hole	**el hueco para drenaje** *(ehl 'hweh-koh 'pah-rah dreh-'nah-heh)*
weight	**el peso** *(ehl 'peh-soh)*
welded	**soldado** *(sohl-'dah-doh)*
welder	**el soldador** *(ehl sohl-dah-'dohr)*
welding	**la soldadura** *(lah sohl-dah-'doo-rah)*
west	**el oeste** *(ehl oh-'ehs-teh)*
wet	**mojado** *(moh-'hah-doh)*
wet-dry vac	**la aspiradora de agua** *(lah ahs-pee-rah-'doh-rah deh 'ah-gwah)*
wheel	**la rueda** *(lah 'rweh-dah)*
wheelbarrow	**la carretilla** *(lah kah-rreh-'tee-yah)*
while	**mientras** *(mee-'ehn-trahs)*
white	**blanco** *('blahn-koh)*
wide	**ancho** *('ahn-choh)*
width	**la anchura/el ancho** *(lah ahn-'choo-rah/ehl 'ahn-choh)*
winch	**el torno** *(ehl 'tohr-noh)*
wind	**el viento** *(ehl vee-'ehn-toh)*
window	**la ventana** *(lah vehn-'tah-nah)*
window sash	**el bastidor de vidriera** *(ehl bahs-tee-'dohr deh veed-ree-'eh-rah)*

window frame	**el marco para la ventana** *(ehl 'mahr-koh 'pah-rah lah vehn-'tah-nah)*
window seat	**el asiento a pie de ventana** *(ehl ah-see-'ehn-toh ah pee-'eh deh vehn-'tah-nah)*
winter	**el invierno** *(ehl een-vee-'ehr-noh)*
wire	**el alambre** *(ehl ah-'lahm-breh)*
wire brush	**el cepillo de alambre** *(ehl seh-'pee-yoh deh ah-'lahm-breh)*
wire cutters	**los alicates cortacable** *(lohs ah-lee-'kah-tehs kohr-tah-'kah-bleh)*
wire mesh	**la malla metálica/ la malla de alambre** *(lah 'mah-yah meh-'tah-lee-kah/lah 'mah-yah deh ah-'lahm-breh)*
wire strippers	**los alicates para terminales** *(lohs ah-lee-'kah-tehs 'pah-rah tehr-mee-'nah-lehs)*
wiring	**la instalación eléctrica** *(lah eens-tah-lah-see-'ohn eh-'lehk-tree-kah)*
with	**con** *(kohn)*
without	**sin** *(seen)*
wood	**la madera** *(lah mah-'deh-rah)*
wood block	**el adoquín de madera** *(ehl ah-doh-'keen deh mah-'deh-rah)*
wood composite	**la madera compuesta** *(lah mah-'deh-rah kohm-'pwehs-tah)*
woodclad	**de forro de madera** *(deh 'foh-rroh deh mah-'deh-rah)*
wooden floor	**el entablado** *(ehl ehn-tah-'blah-doh)*
work	**el trabajo** *(ehl trah-'bah-hoh)*
workbench	**el banco de trabajo** *(ehl 'bahn-koh deh trah-'bah-hoh)*
worn	**gastado** *(gahs-'tah-doh)*
worried	**preocupado** *(preh-oh-koo-'pah-doh)*
worse	**peor** *(peh-'ohr)*
wrapped	**forrado** *(foh-'rrah-doh)*
wrapping	**el forro** *(ehl 'foh-rroh)*
wrecking ball	**la bola de demolición** *(lah 'boh-lah deh deh-moh-lee-see-'ohn)*
wrench	**la llave inglesa** *(lah 'yah-veh een-'gleh-sah)*
yard	**la yarda** *(lah 'yahr-dah)*
yellow	**amarillo** *(ah-mah-'ree-yoh)*
yesterday	**ayer** *(ah-'yehr)*
young	**joven** *('hoh-vehn)*
Z-flashing	**el verteaguas en Z** *(ehl vehr-teh-'ah-gwahs ehn 'zeh-tah)*
zinc	**el cinc** *(ehl seenk)*
zone	**la zona** *(lah 'soh-nah)*

VERBS

to absorb	**absorber** *(ahb-sohr-'behr)*
to add	**añadir/agregar** *(ah-nyah-'deer/ah-greh-'gahr)*
to add (math)	**sumar** *(soo-'mahr)*
to adjust	**ajustar** *(ah-hoos-'tahr)*
to align	**alinear** *(ah-lee-neh-'ahr)*
to allow	**permitir/dejar** *(pehr-mee-'teer/deh-'hahr)*
to alter	**modificar/alterar** *(moh-dee-fee-'kahr/ahl-teh-'rahr)*
to amplify	**amplificar** *(ahm-plee-fee-'kahr)*
to answer	**contestar** *(kohn-tehs-'tahr)*
to apply	**aplicar** *(ah-plee-'kahr)*
to arrive	**llegar** *(yeh-'gahr)*
to ask	**preguntar** *(preh-goon-'tahr)*
to ask for	**pedir** *(peh-'deer)*
to assemble	**armar/ensamblar** *(ahr-'mahr/ehn-sahm-'blahr)*
to attach	**conectar** *(koh-nehk-'tahr)*
to avoid	**evitar** *(eh-vee-'tahr)*
to begin	**empezar/comenzar** *(ehm-peh-'sahr/koh-mehn-'sahr)*
to bend	**doblar** *(doh-'blahr)*
to block	**bloquear** *(bloh-keh-'ahr)*
to bond	**adherir** *(ah-deh-'reer)*
to bore	**calar/taladrar** *(kah-'lahr/tah-lah-'drahr)*
to break	**romper/quebrar** *(rohm-'pehr/keh-'brahr)*
to breathe	**respirar** *(rehs-pee-'rahr)*
to bring	**traer** *(trah-'ehr)*
to build	**construir** *(kohns-troo-'eer)*
to bury	**enterrar** *(ehn-teh-'rrahr)*
to buy	**comprar** *(kohm-'prahr)*
to bypass	**evitar** *(eh-vee-'tahr)*
to calculate	**calcular** *(kahl-koo-'lahr)*
to call	**llamar** *(yah-'mahr)*
to carry	**llevar/cargar** *(yeh-'vahr/kahr-'gahr)*
to caulk	**calafatear** *(kah-lah-fah-teh-'ahr)*
to center	**centrar** *(sehn-'trahr)*
to change	**cambiar** *(kahm-bee-'ahr)*
to channel	**canalizar** *(kah-nah-lee-'sahr)*
to check	**revisar/averiguar** *(reh-vee-'sahr/ah-veh-ree-'gwahr)*
to chop	**tajar** *(tah-'hahr)*
to circulate	**circular** *(seer-koo-'lahr)*
to clean	**limpiar** *(leem-pee-'ahr)*

to climb	**subir** *(soo-'beer)*
to close	**cerrar** *(seh-'rrahr)*
to coat	**poner capa/cubrir** *(poh-'nehr 'kah-pah/koo-'breer)*
to combine	**combinar** *(kohm-bee-'nahr)*
to come	**venir** *(veh-'neer)*
to compact	**compactar** *(kohm-pahk-'tahr)*
to connect	**conectar** *(koh-nehk-'tahr)*
to control	**controlar** *(kohn-troh-'lahr)*
to convert	**convertir** *(kohn-vehr-'teer)*
to cool	**enfriar** *(ehn-free-'ahr)*
to correct	**corregir** *(koh-rreh-'heer)*
to cover	**cubrir/tapar** *(koo-'breer/tah-'pahr)*
to crack	**agrietarse** *(ahg-ree-eh-'tahr-seh)*
to cross	**atravesar/cruzar** *(ah-trah-veh-'sahr/kroo-'sahr)*
to crown	**coronar** *(koh-roh-'nahr)*
to crush	**aplastar** *(ah-plahs-'tahr)*
to cure	**curar** *(koo-'rahr)*
to cut	**cortar** *(kohr-'tahr)*
to deliver	**repartir** *(reh-pahr-'teer)*
to design	**diseñar** *(dee-'seh-'nyahr)*
to dig	**cavar** *(kah-'vahr)*
to disassemble	**desarmar** *(dehs-ahr-'mahr)*
to disconnect	**desconectar** *(dehs-koh-nehk-'tahr)*
to distribute	**distribuir** *(dees-tree-boo-'eer)*
to divert	**desviar** *(dehs-vee-'ahr)*
to divide	**dividir** *(dee-vee-'deer)*
to do	**hacer** *(ah-'sehr)*
to draw	**dibujar** *(dee-boo-'hahr)*
to drink	**beber/tomar** *(beh-'behr/toh-'mahr)*
to drip	**gotear/escurrir** *(goh-teh-'ahr/ehs-koo-'rreer)*
to drive	**manejar** *(mah-neh-'hahr)*
to dry	**secar** *(seh-'kahr)*
to dump	**descargar** *(dehs-kahr-'gahr)*
to eat	**comer** *(koh-'mehr)*
to edge	**cortar el borde del césped** *(kohr-'tahr ehl 'bohr-deh dehl 'sehs-pehd)*
to empty	**vaciar** *(vah-see-'ahr)*
to enclose	**encerrar** *(ehn-seh-'rrahr)*
to end	**terminar** *(tehr-mee-'nahr)*
to erect	**erigir** *(eh-ree-'heer)*

to examine	**examinar** *(ex-ah-mee-'nahr)*
to expand	**ampliar** *(ahm-plee-'ahr)*
to fade	**descolorar** *(dehs-koh-loh-'rahr)*
to fall	**caer** *(kah-'ehr)*
to fasten	**fijar** *(fee-'hahr)*
to fill	**llenar** *(yeh-'nahr)*
to filter	**filtrar** *(feel-'trahr)*
to finish	**acabar/terminar** *(ah-kah-'bahr/tehr-mee-'nahr)*
to flip	**voltear** *(vohl-teh-'ahr)*
to float	**flotar** *(floh-'tahr)*
to float (flooring)	**elevar** *(eh-leh-'vahr)*
to flow	**fluir** *(floo-'eer)*
to form	**formar** *(fohr-'mahr)*
to frame	**armar con armazón** *(ahr-'mahr kohn ahr-mah-'sohn)*
to function	**funcionar** *(foon-see-oh-'nahr)*
to give	**dar** *(dahr)*
to glue	**encolar** *(ehn-koh-'lahr)*
to go	**ir** *(eer)*
to grade	**nivelar** *(nee-veh-'lahr)*
to grind	**moler** *(moh-'lehr)*
to guess	**adivinar** *(ah-dee-vee-'nahr)*
to harden	**endurecer** *(ehn-doo-reh-'sehr)*
to haul	**transportar** *(trahns-pohr-'tahr)*
to heat	**calentar** *(kah-lehn-'tahr)*
to help	**ayudar** *(ah-yoo-'dahr)*
to hide	**esconder** *(ehs-kohn-'dehr)*
to hold	**sostener** *(sohs-teh-'nehr)*
to hook	**enganchar** *(ehn-gahn-'chahr)*
to hot-mop	**poner brea** *(poh-'nehr 'breh-ah)*
to indicate	**indicar** *(een-dee-'kahr)*
to inlay	**embutir** *(ehm-boo-'teer)*
to insert	**meter** *(meh-'tehr)*
to insist	**insistir** *(een-sees-'teer)*
to inspect	**inspeccionar** *(eens-pehk-see-oh-'nahr)*
to install	**instalar** *(eens-tah-'lahr)*
to insulate	**aislar** *(ah-ees-'lahr)*
to interlace	**entrelazar** *(ehn-treh-lah-'sahr)*
to interrupt	**interrumpir** *(een-teh-rroom-'peer)*

to join	**juntar/unir** *(hoon-'tahr/oo-'neer)*
to last	**durar** *(doo-'rahr)*
to lay foundation	**cimentar** *(see-mehn-'tahr)*
to lean	**recostar/inclinar** *(reh-kohs-'tahr/een-klee-'nahr)*
to learn	**aprender** *(ah-prehn-'dehr)*
to leave	**salir/dejar** *(sah-'leer/deh-'hahr)*
to level	**nivelar** *(nee-veh-'lahr)*
to lift	**levantar** *(leh-vahn-'tahr)*
to line up	**alinear** *(ah-lee-neh-'ahr)*
to listen	**escuchar** *(ehs-koo-'chahr)*
to live	**vivir** *(vee-'veer)*
to load	**cargar** *(kahr-'gahr)*
to look	**mirar** *(mee-'rahr)*
to loosen	**soltar** *(sohl-'tahr)*
to lower	**bajar** *(bah-'hahr)*
to lubricate	**lubricar** *(loo-bree-'kahr)*
to make	**hacer** *(ah-'sehr)*
to mark	**marcar** *(mahr-'kahr)*
to mask	**poner cinta** *(poh-nehr 'seen-tah)*
to match	**armonizar** *(ahr-moh-nee-'sahr)*
to measure	**medir** *(meh-'deer)*
to mix	**mezclar** *(mehs-'klahr)*
to modify	**modificar** *(moh-dee-fee-'kahr)*
to mount	**montar** *(mohn-'tahr)*
to move	**mover** *(moh-'vehr)*
to move (residence)	**mudarse** *(moo-'dahr-seh)*
to mow	**cortar el césped** *(kohr-'tahr ehl 'sehs-pehd)*
to mud	**enyesar** *(ehn-yeh-'sahr)*
to nail	**clavar** *(klah-'vahr)*
to notch	**mellar** *(meh-'yahr)*
to open	**abrir** *(ah-'breer)*
to operate	**operar** *(oh-peh-'rahr)*
to organize	**organizar** *(ohr-gah-nee-'sahr)*
to overflow	**rebosar** *(reh-boh-'sahr)*
to overhang	**sobresalir** *(soh-breh-sah-'leer)*
to overheat	**recalentar** *(reh-kah-lehn-'tahr)*
to overlap	**sobreponer** *(soh-breh-poh-'nehr)*
to overload	**sobrecargar** *(soh-breh-kahr-'gahr)*

to paint	**pintar** *(peen-'tahr)*
to patch	**remendar** *(reh-mehn-'dahr)*
to pay	**pagar** *(pah-'gahr)*
to peel	**pelarse** *(peh-'lahr-seh)*
to penetrate	**penetrar** *(peh-neh-'trahr)*
to perforate	**perforar** *(pehr-foh-'rahr)*
to permit	**permitir** *(pehr-mee-'teer)*
to place	**colocar** *(koh-loh-'kahr)*
to plan	**planear** *(plah-neh-'ahr)*
to plant	**plantar** *(plahn-'tahr)*
to plate	**poner placa** *(poh-'nehr 'plah-kah)*
to plug in	**enchufar** *(ehn-choo-'fahr)*
to plumb	**aplomar** *(ah-ploh-'mahr)*
to polish	**pulir** *(poo-'leer)*
to position	**situar** *(see-too-'ahr)*
to pound	**golpear** *(gohl-peh-'ahr)*
to pour	**verter/echar** *(vehr-'tehr/eh-'chahr)*
to predrill	**pretaladrar** *(preh-tah-lah-'drahr)*
to prep	**preparar** *(preh-pah-'rahr)*
to press	**oprimir/apretar** *(oh-pree-'meer/ah-preh-'tahr)*
to pressure-wash	**lavar a presión** *(lah-'vahr ah preh-see-'ohn)*
to probe	**sondear** *(sohn-deh-'ahr)*
to produce	**producir** *(proh-doo-'seer)*
to program	**programar** *(proh-grah-'mahr)*
to prohibit	**prohibir** *(proh-ee-'beer)*
to protect	**proteger** *(proh-teh-'hehr)*
to pry	**levantar con palanca** *(leh-vahn-'tahr kohn pah-'lahn-kah)*
to pull wire	**jalar alambre** *(hah-'lahr ah-'lahm-breh)*
to pump	**bombear** *(bohm-beh-'ahr)*
to put	**poner** *(poh-'nehr)*
to put in	**meter** *(meh-'tehr)*
to putty	**enmasillar** *(ehn-mah-see-'yahr)*
to rabbet	**rebajar/ranurar** *(reh-bah-'hahr/rah-noo-'rahr)*
to raise	**levantar** *(leh-vahn-'tahr)*
to reach	**alcanzar** *(ahl-kahn-'sahr)*
to read	**leer** *(leh-'ehr)*
to receive	**recibir** *(reh-see-'beer)*
to recommend	**recomendar** *(reh-koh-mehn-'dahr)*
to redo	**volver a hacer** *(vohl-'vehr ah ah-'sehr)*
to reduce	**reducir** *(reh-doo-'seer)*
to refer	**referir** *(reh-feh-'reer)*
to refill	**rellenar** *(reh-yeh-'nahr)*

to reinforce	**reforzar** *(reh-fohr-'sahr)*
to remove	**sacar/quitar** *(sah-'kahr/kee-'tahr)*
to repair	**reparar** *(reh-pah-'rahr)*
to replace	**sustituir** *(soos-tee-too-'eer)*
to rest	**descansar** *(dehs-kahn-'sahr)*
to return	**regresar/volver** *(reh-greh-'sahr/vohl-'vehr)*
to roll up	**enrollar** *(ehn-roh-'yahr)*
to ruin	**arruinar** *(ah-rroo-ee-'nahr)*
to run	**correr** *(koh-'rrehr)*
to sag	**hundirse** *(oon-'deer-seh)*
to sand	**lijar** *(lee-'hahr)*
to say	**decir** *(deh-'seer)*
to score	**marcar** *(mahr-'kahr)*
to scrape	**raspar** *(rahs-'pahr)*
to screed	**enrasar** *(ehn-rah-'sahr)*
to screw in	**atornillar** *(ah-tohr-nee-'yahr)*
to seal	**sellar** *(seh-'yahr)*
to see	**ver** *(vehr)*
to seed	**semillar** *(seh-mee-'yahr)*
to sell	**vender** *(vehn-'dehr)*
to separate	**separar** *(seh-pah-'rahr)*
to set up	**eregir** *(eh-reh-'heer)*
to set	**colocar** *(koh-loh-'kahr)*
to settle	**depositarse** *(deh-poh-see-'tahr-seh)*
to shape	**formar** *(fohr-'mahr)*
to sharpen	**afilar** *(ah-fee-'lahr)*
to shift	**moverse** *(moh-'vehr-seh)*
to shim	**colocar calza** *(koh-loh-'kahr 'kahl-sah)*
to shore up	**apuntalar** *(ah-poon-tah-'lahr)*
to sight	**fijarse** *(fee-'hahr-seh)*
to sink	**hundir** *(oon-'deer)*
to sleep	**dormir** *(dohr-'meer)*
to slip	**resbalar** *(rehs-bah-'lahr)*
to smooth out	**alisar** *(ah-lee-'sahr)*
to snap the line	**marcar con línea de tiza** *(mahr-'kahr kohn 'lee-neh-ah deh 'tee-sah)*
to soak	**empapar/remojar** *(ehm-pah-'pahr/reh-moh-'hahr)*
to sort	**clasificar** *(klah-see-fee-'kahr)*
to speak	**hablar** *(ah-'blahr)*
to spill	**derramar** *(deh-rrah-'mahr)*
to spin	**girar** *(hee-'rahr)*
to splatter	**salpicar** *(sahl-pee-'kahr)*
to splice	**empalmar** *(ehm-pahl-'mahr)*

to split	**agrietarse/partirse** *(ah-gree-eh-'tahr-seh pahr-'teer-seh)*
to spray	**rociar** *(roh-see-'ahr)*
to spray (paint)	**pintar a presión** *(peen-'tahr ah preh-see-'ohn)*
to spread	**repartir** *(reh-pahr-'teer)*
to spread	**esparcir** *(ehs-pahr-'seer)*
to sprinkle	**rociar** *(roh-see-'ahr)*
to squirt	**chorrear** *(choh-rreh-'ahr)*
to stabilize	**estabilizar** *(ehs-tah-bee-lee-'sahr)*
to stack	**apilar** *(ah-pee-'lahr)*
to stagger	**alternar** *(ahl-tehr-'nahr)*
to stain	**manchar** *(mahn-'chahr)*
to stamp (crush)	**triturar** *(tree-too-'rahr)*
to stamp (cut out)	**troquelar** *(troh-keh-'lahr)*
to stamp (pound)	**hollar** *(oh-'yahr)*
to staple	**engrapar** *(ehn-grah-'pahr)*
to start up	**arrancar** *(ah-rrahn-'kahr)*
to step	**pisar** *(pee-'sahr)*
to stick	**pegarse/pegar** *(peh-'gahr-seh/peh-'gahr)*
to stop	**parar/terminar/acabar** *(pah-'rahr/tehr-mee-'nahr/ah-kah-'bahr)*
to straighten	**enderezar** *(ehn-deh-reh-'sahr)*
to stretch	**estirar** *(ehs-tee-'rahr)*
to support	**apoyar/soportar** *(ah-poh-'yahr/soh-pohr-'tahr)*
to surround	**rodear** *(roh-deh-'ahr)*
to survey	**medir** *(meh-'deer)*
to swell	**hincharse** *(een-'chahr-seh)*
to tack	**fijar con tachuelas** *(fee-'hahr kohn tah-choo-'eh-lahs)*
to take	**tomar/llevar** *(toh-'mahr/yeh-'vahr)*
to take down	**retirar** *(reh-'tee-rahr)*
to take out	**sacar/quitar** *(sah-'kahr/kee-'tahr)*
to tape	**encintar** *(ehn-seen-'tahr)*
to test	**probar** *(proh-'bahr)*
to thaw	**descongelar** *(dehs-kohn-heh-'lahr)*
to thread	**roscar** *(rohs-'kahr)*
to throw away	**tirar/botar** *(tee-'rahr/boh-'tahr)*
to tie	**amarrar/atar** *(ah-mah-'rrahr/ah-'tahr)*
to tie in	**conectar** *(koh-nehk-'tahr)*
to tighten	**apretar** *(ah-preh-'tahr)*
to toenail	**clavar en ángulo** *(klah-'vahr ehn 'ahn-goo-loh)*
to touch up	**retocar** *(reh-toh-'kahr)*
to trace	**trazar** *(trah-'sahr)*
to transmit	**transmitir** *(trahns-mee-'teer)*
to trench	**zanjar/atrincherar** *(sahn-'hahr/ah-treen-cheh-'rahr)*